In *British Fiction and the Production of Social Order*, Miranda Burgess examines what Romantic-period writers called "romance": a hybrid genre defined by its role in the negotiation of conflicts between political economy and moral philosophy. Reading a broad range of fictional and nonfictional works published between 1740 and 1830, Burgess places authors such as Richardson, Scott, Austen, and Wollstonecraft in a new economic, social, and cultural context. She explores the ways in which some romances illustrated and produced among their readers particular forms of gendered virtue and feeling, even as the same genre, in the hands of other writers, provided tools for resisting such forms. Burgess argues that the romance held a key role in remaking the national order of a Britain dependent on ideologies of human nature for justification of its social, economic, and political systems.

MIRANDA BURGESS is Assistant Professor of English at the University of British Columbia. Her work in the area of eighteenth-century and Romantic British and Irish studies has been published in *MLQ: A Journal of Literary History*, and *Novel: A Forum on Fiction*.

CAMBRIDGE STUDIES IN ROMANTICISM 43

BRITISH FICTION AND THE PRODUCTION OF SOCIAL ORDER, 1740–1830

CAMBRIDGE STUDIES IN ROMANTICISM

This series aims to foster the best new work in one of the most challenging fields within English literary studies. From the early 1780s to the early 1830s a formidable array of talented men and women took to literary composition, not just in poetry, which some of them famously transformed, but in many modes of writing. The expansion of publishing created new opportunities for writers, and the political stakes of what they wrote were raised again by what Wordsworth called those "great national events" that were "almost daily taking place": the French Revolution, the Napoleonic and American wars, urbanization, industrialization, religious revival, an expanded empire abroad, and the reform movement at home. This was an enormous ambition, even when it pretended otherwise. The relations between science, philosophy, religion, and literature were reworked in texts such as *Frankenstein* and *Biographia Literaria*; gender relations in *A Vindication of the Rights of Woman* and *Don Juan*; journalism by Cobbett and Hazlitt; poetic form, content, and style by the Lake School and the Cockney School. Outside Shakespeare studies, probably no body of writing has produced such a wealth of response or done so much to shape the responses of modern criticism. This indeed is the period that saw the emergence of those notions of "literature" and of literary history, especially national literary history, on which modern scholarship in English has been founded.

The categories produced by Romanticism have also been challenged by recent historicist arguments. The task of the series is to engage both with a challenging corpus of Romantic writings and with the changing field of criticism they have helped to shape. As with other literary series published by Cambridge, this one will represent the work of both younger and more established scholars, on either side of the Atlantic and elsewhere.

For a complete list of titles published see end of book

BRITISH FICTION AND THE PRODUCTION OF SOCIAL ORDER, 1740–1830

MIRANDA J. BURGESS

University of British Columbia

CAMBRIDGE
UNIVERSITY PRESS

PUBLISHED BY THE PRESS SYNDICATE OF THE UNIVERSITY OF CAMBRIDGE
The Pitt Building, Trumpington Street, Cambridge, United Kingdom

CAMBRIDGE UNIVERSITY PRESS
The Edinburgh Building, Cambridge CB2 2RU, UK   www.cup.cam.ac.uk
40 West 20th Street, New York, NY 10011-4211, USA   www.cup.org
10 Stamford Road, Oakleigh, Melbourne 3166, Australia
Ruiz de Alarcón 13, 28014 Madrid, Spain

© Miranda J. Burgess 2000

First published 2000

Printed in the United Kingdom at the University Press, Cambridge

Typeset in 11/12.5pt Baskerville [VN]

A catalogue record for this book is available from the British Library

Library of Congress cataloguing in publication data
Burgess, Miranda J.
British fiction and the production of social order, 1740–1830/Miranda J. Burgess.
p.   cm. – (Cambridge studies in Romanticism; 43)
Includes bibliographical references
ISBN 0 521 11773 296 (hardback)
1. English fiction – 18th century – History and criticism.   2. Literature and society
– Great Britain – History – 18th century.   3. Literature and society – Great Britain
– History – 19th century.   4. English fiction – 19th century – History and criticism.
5. Politics and literature – Great Britain – History.   6. Books and reading –
Great Britain – History.   7. Romanticism – Great Britain.
8. Social ethics in literature.   I. Title.   II. Series.
PR858.S62 B87 2000
823.609355 – dc21   90-086370
ISBN 0 521 773296 hardback

For my parents

Contents

Figure

Acknowledgements

In writing about books and the ways in which they can help to produce constellations of readers, it seems especially appropriate to begin by acknowledging the contributions of the friends and colleagues who have made up my own reading and writing communities. I am indebted to Jon Klancher and Michael Prince, who respectively supervised and read the dissertation with which this book began, and from whose questions, criticisms, and example I have benefited immeasurably. Other teachers and colleagues also read the manuscript. I am grateful to Ian Duncan and to the first, unknown reader for Cambridge University Press for incisive readings and invaluable suggestions for revision, to James Chandler for advice about final revision, and to Virginia Jackson, Charles Rzepka, and James Siemon. I wish to thank Josie Dixon of Cambridge University Press for guidance and encouragement at all stages in bringing this book to press. My colleagues at the University of British Columbia and the University of New Brunswick have been congenial and learned interlocutors; I am particularly grateful to Nicholas Hudson for his erudition and advice and to Mary Brodkorb for many stimulating conversations. The undergraduates who have taken my eighteenth-century and Romantic-period courses will recognize their energy and questions in the shape of this book.

Research for this book was supported by a research grant and a doctoral fellowship from the Social Sciences and Humanities Research Council of Canada, a grant from the University of New Brunswick, and doctoral and dissertation fellowships from Boston University. An earlier version of parts of chapter two was originally published in *Novel: A Forum on Fiction*, copyright 1995, by Brown University, and is reprinted with the permission of the copyright owner. Portions of chapter four appeared in earlier form in *Lessons of Romanticism: A Critical Companion*, edited by Thomas Pfau and Robert F. Gleckner, copyright 1998, by Duke University Press.

Abbreviations

C	Richardson, *Clarissa; Or the History of a Young Lady*
DL	*Diary and Letters of Frances Burney*
ED	Frances Burney, *Early Diary 1768–1778*
ELH	*English Literary History*
LCS	The London Corresponding Society
MLQ	*Modern Language Quarterly*
n.d.	no date
NLH	*New Literary History*
n.p.	no page number
n.s.	new series
P1	Richardson, *Pamela*
P2	[Richardson], *Pamela: Or, Virtue Rewarded. The Third and Fourth Volumes*
PMLA	*Publications of the Modern Language Association of America*
RM	Wollstonecraft, *Vindication of the Rights of Men*
RW	Wollstonecraft, *Vindication of the Rights of Woman*
ST	Hume, "Of the Standard of Taste", in *Essays, Moral, Political, and Literary*
T	Hume, *Treatise of Human Nature*
T1	Locke, *First Treatise*, in *Two Treatises of Government*
T2	Locke, *Essay Concerning the True Original, Extent and End of Civil Government*, in *Two Treatises of Government*
TMS	Adam Smith, *The Theory of the Moral Sentiments*

Introduction
Romantic economies

This book investigates the evolution of British romance between 1740 and 1830. It defines romance as a genre uniquely but diversely imbricated with political economy. It argues that the genre alternately competes with, supplements, and works with its readers to displace the contemporary philosophical and social debates of political economy, yet remains thoroughly invested in the questions political economy addresses. I argue for the recognition of generic struggle and change as powerful agents in the social order, and later in the nationhood, of Britain. Genre, political economy, social and national change and cohesion provide the analytic framework for a literary history extending from Samuel Richardson's romances – his best British remedies for a "World . . . debauched by pernicious Novels"[1] and the influence of France – to the ironic counter-romances of Frances Sheridan, Frances Burney, and Mary Wollstonecraft, politically polarized but united in contesting the gendered injustice of a social order produced in large part by the genre of romance; and to the self-conscious embrace of romance as Jane Austen and Walter Scott grant the genre a new, specifically national, respectability and stability. If this framework risks abstraction, it is because it is a work in translation, bringing to bear a late-twentieth-century critical vocabulary on the formal definition and social role of romance, two major preoccupations of the eighteenth-century and Romantic fiction and criticism this book discusses. The most appropriate place to begin, therefore, is with the introduction to an earlier work on the history and theory of fiction: a Romantic literary history that names with great precision the central questions with which the present book is engaged, but which also places them in the context of their contemporary significance.

Anna Laetitia Barbauld's essay "On the Origin and Progress of Novel-Writing" establishes a literary history for European fiction, extending from classical antiquity through medieval courts into the nineteenth-century present. It prefaces her pioneering edition of *The British Novelists* (1810), which instituted a canon of "standard" British fiction. Its conclusion is explicitly modern. Enacting the interval in which the past and future of British fiction come into unsettling collision, Barbauld admits the continued pressure of a still-unanswered national political question and makes a plea for Britain's future:

> It was said by Fletcher of Saltoun, "Let me make the ballads of a nation, and I care not who makes the laws." Might it not be said with as much propriety, Let me make the novels of a country, and let who will make the systems?[2]

An important work by a relatively minor writer, the essay occupies me here for two reasons. It identifies a narrative genre that is defined by its unsettled engagement with the changing contemporary forms of political economy and British social order; and it rejects the genre label "romance" in a manner germane to the historical moment it self-consciously captures in positioning "the novel" (in both senses of the word) between the Britain of the future and the past. What the essay's climactic conclusion poses is an avowedly contemporary problem that remains in the forefront of critical debate on British fiction even into the present. But Barbauld's question had also been, as we will see, a self-consciously pivotal, indeed defining, concern of romance as a genre since the middle of the eighteenth century. My purpose here, broadly speaking, is to propose an answer to Barbauld's question about the relation between the "novels" and "systems" of Britain and to historicize the terms in which the question is asked. To do so will be to begin defining the categories and assumptions of my own literary history while starting to unfold the history itself.

Writing amid the uncertainties of the Peninsular Wars, Barbauld trusts to the stability of literary historical and national retrospect in the same measure as she seeks to bestow this stability on Britain's precarious future prospects. On the one hand, to the extent that the "propriety" of conceiving fiction as an ordering force within "a country" remains the subject of an unanswered question, the future relations between fiction and nation necessarily remain uncertain. Thus the univocal assent of British readers is the means by which this national role of fiction must be institutionalized, and the orderliness of prose fiction may be legitimated by consensus for, Barbauld notes, fiction is "a species of books which every body reads" (59). On the other hand, the reader's answer depends to a large degree on the evidence of national and literary history. The query is predicated on the accepted existence of "Britain" as "a country," one that avowedly incorporates and unifies not just England, but Scotland and Ireland as well. Equally, the reader's answer to the question of Britain's future depends on Barbauld's proof that works of fiction and their readers have collectively produced the Britain now extant. Only thus can Britain's fiction, now and in years to come, effectively supersede competitor "systems," and only thus can the answer to Barbauld's nationalist plea be "yes."

The answers I propose, however, are necessarily equivocal, and not only because of the long perspective lent by hindsight. Contemporary responses to the question of British fiction's future were equally uncertain. In part, they were ambivalent because the continuing histories of the country and the "species of books" alike had lost little of the particularity and indeterminacy that had characterized them throughout the second half of the eighteenth century, remaining fractious and refusing a coherent teleological form even as the "modern" works of Barbauld and her younger contemporaries Austen and Scott passed into the literary past. But contemporary responses to the problem of social order were fundamentally divided as well as historically uncertain, not least because the propriety of modelling Britain's national order continued to be called into question from divergent perspectives expressed in certain works of fiction. Pairing the tasks of "making a novel" and "making a country" meant rendering culturally respectable those works of past and present fiction that productively engaged the form and dynamics of social order, and sidelining those that did not. These tasks were complicated by Barbauld's use of the term "novel" to designate this group of works – as we will see, a genre more usually and more properly identified as "romance" – and by the internal tensions of romance itself.

It should be clear by this point that to examine the evolving relations between Romantic-period Britain, its fiction, and its philosophies and methods of producing a national social order in the face of disorderly modernity, this book must also trace the historical mutations of the "species of fiction," especially through the rival categories of "novel" and "romance" within it. These changes cannot be outlined without addressing their relation to the intersecting ideas of "propriety" and "system," and the constitution of the united, ideal Britain they came to produce and to regulate. Beginning with the schematic terms of this introduction, to be extended and complicated in the chapters that follow, I aim to explain how the idea of a united Britain emerged from transformations that took place within the genre of romance as diverse

romances echoed and revised the developing logic of contemporary
theories of social order, conceived first in theological, then in political
economic, and later in national terms. It is equally this book's business
to show how these transformations threatened the Britain they helped to
produce.

THE GENRE OF ROMANCE AND THE SPECIES OF FICTION

The notion of a distinct and autonomous "species" of prose fiction was of
mid-eighteenth-century provenance. To the writers who used it, the
implications of the category were both broadly comprehensible and
highly specific. As a metaphor for a literary genre, "species" derived
from natural history, a subject with complex investments in theology,
moral philosophy, and political economy, but one that even middle-class
young women were permitted by the rules of propriety to study.[3] Unlike
the stable Aristotelian framework of genres to which the sixteenth- and
seventeenth-century poetics of Sidney and Dryden were subscribed, the
notion of "species" was fraught with development and change. Used in
literary history, it sat athwart Enlightenment notions of progress in
national history and development in nature as processes unfolding in
discrete, recoverable stages. Such taxonomic natural histories of fiction
allowed for the subgrouping of individuals within the species as distinct
but related kinds – sometimes, in disregard of taxonomic accuracy, also
identified as "species" – marked by surviving traces of earlier stages of
the larger species or differing from the standard in some shared subset of
traits.[4] These two conceptions of the generic subgroup characterize the
contemporary confrontations between rival accounts of romance within
the larger and more unified conception of prose fiction as a species, a
major preoccupation of eighteenth-century literary criticism as well as of
recent criticism of eighteenth-century literature.

   The conflict of romance and novel has often been understood within
Enlightenment intellectual frameworks, that is to say developmentally
or teleologically. Eighteenth-century and Romantic literary historians
such as Clara Reeve, Richard Hurd, and Scott postulated that "the
novel" developed as the result of the confrontation between seventeenth-century French courtly romances and discerning readers hungry
for verisimilitude as well as for moral instruction, though not always
with happy moral consequences. Twentieth-century criticism has made
similar formal claims, often with comparable ethical conclusions. It was
for many years the consensus in Anglo-American criticism, shaped by

Ian Watt and his revisers, including some literary historians who dissent from large aspects of his argument, that the novel "rose" (Watt), "emerged" (J. Paul Hunter), or reached "'institutional' stability" (Michael McKeon) as the dominant form of fiction in Britain by 1740.[5] In these readings, the novel is usually, though not invariably, shown to arrive at maturity by breaking loose from its Œdipal struggles with the fallen romances it is said to incorporate, to transform dialectically, and finally to supersede.[6] (The novel histories of Lennard Davis, Nancy Armstrong, and Hunter are important exceptions, sidelining romance ancestry in favour of newspapers, conduct books, and chapbooks.)[7]

Implicit, and sometimes explicit, in these literary histories is a fixed association of romance with aristocracy, folk tradition, and conservatism, inherited from Northrop Frye's classic conception of the genre as a displaced but highly stable wish-fulfilling myth, as well as from eighteenth-century historical critics such as Hurd and Reeve, equally invested in notions of tradition and development, who assimilated the "roman" of modern Europe to the chivalric histories of medieval knights.[8] Romance itself appears, in extreme forms of this argument – exemplified by Tobias Smollett's categorical denial in 1748 that novels have anything to do with "Romance," which "owes its origin to ignorance, vanity and superstition" – as an effete antique survivor, easily finished off by the novel, a genre named to emphasize its contrasting hearty modernity.[9] But the relations between romance and novel can also be seen in less organically developmental and more conflicted and contingent terms. It is in such terms of difference rather than development that Watt's consensus about the conquest and near-demise of romance has been challenged in the last decade by a lengthening series of books that refashion the genre as crucial to the shaping of nationhood in the Romantic period. As James Chandler, Ian Duncan, Ina Ferris, Katie Trumpener, and Nicola Watson variously argue, romance does not "persist," as McKeon has put it, in reactionary anti-novels or in ghostly or nostalgic traces within novels, not knowing it is dead. Rather, it lives and grows within the species of fiction, declaring itself distinct from the novel but also emerging at discrete moments within novels, providing the present with the images and influence of a lost, beloved, but invented past. Trumpener and Watson in particular emphasize the political roominess of this role: in the romance works they discuss, the oppositional potential latent in nostalgia and nationalism is occasionally fulfilled. Producing various pasts for itself and the Britain it represents, Romantic romance takes on new and energetic kinds of life.[10]

In calling for a broadened and diversified cultural role for romance in early-nineteenth-century Britain, this book is indebted to these recent reconsiderations of the genre. Nevertheless, it differs from them in two respects. One is a relatively minor matter of historical emphasis. My understanding of romance as it evolved during the Romantic period is founded on a continuing process of intertextual conversation and mutation rather than shaped by a model in which submersion or repression is followed by a surfacing or return. Consequently, my discussion departs from recent literary histories of the ties between romance and nationhood by addressing the writing of romance in the mid-eighteenth as well as in the early nineteenth century, and by discussing the relations of romance not just to nationalist discourse but to the more general theorizing of social order that preoccupied eighteenth-century political economy. A larger philosophical difference lies in my approach to genre theory and therefore in my historical method. I treat romance not as a stably definable Romantic mode, but rather as a hybrid or conglomerate genre. Its sustained internal dynamics and changing angles of confrontation with political economic intertexts, and the resulting dialectic of recognition and transformation in its relation to its readers, make it uniquely capable of conveying more than one approach to tradition and more than one conception of nationhood. The question of intertexts and romance's diverse ways of coding them is one to which I return in subsequent sections of this introduction. For the present I want briefly to outline some theoretical and historical implications of my treatment of generic change, which also seem to me necessary consequences of the eighteenth-century conception of genres as "species" of texts.

Among Anglo-American literary theorists writing in the late twentieth century, Ralph Cohen has pioneered the historical study of generic fluidity. Outlining the large, overlapping variety of genre definitions that can be arrayed to explain particular groups of texts at any given moment in literary history, he rebuts the Aristotelian and archetypalist notions of genre, as well as post-structuralist attacks on genre theory as an outmoded essentialism, without reducing generic identities either to short-lived products of chance perception or to each reader's personal choice among infinite possibilities.[11] Cohen's account of generic identities as contingent historical and institutional products has been further historicized by Clifford Siskin, who argues the force of generic fluidity and aggregation as a motor of eighteenth- and early-nineteenth-century cultural formation and social change.[12] Read from the perspective of such theories and histories that pair generic confrontation and change with social transformation, eighteenth-century romance looks less like Smollett's stable mode than like a historically inflected composite genre, the moving point of intersection for a shifting array of intertexts. None of this is to suggest, as Laurie Langbauer proposes, that romance became by the mid-eighteenth century little more than an unfixed term of abuse hurled by critics at whatever narratives depart from "masculine," serious, artistic, and novelistic convention.[13] Rather, as a genre cross-cut by the narrative conventions and obsessions of political economy as they evolve and are transformed throughout the late eighteenth and early nineteenth centuries, romance provides a mutually recognized field for thinkers about and debaters of social and national order whose backgrounds, assumptions, and principles seem otherwise irreconcilably diverse. The genre is never so formless or so borderless that writers do not know, in employing or encountering "romance" and the associated terminology it often shared with political philosophy – "chivalry," "sentiment," "romantic," "gothic" – that a genre is their referent and meeting-place.

Yet even viewed from within this conception of romance as a generic common ground where ethical and historical debates on political economy could be enacted and encouraged, it is evident that the distinctness, the fluidity, and the national investments of the genre within the larger species of fiction are more than the preoccupation of late-twentieth-century literary theorists engrossed in dialectics. A glance at Ioan Williams's *Novel and Romance, 1700–1800*, a compilation of précis that address the genre in its battles with the novel, reveals the multifarious and complex generic definitions that contemporaries advanced.[14] To illustrate this generic fluidity more concretely, therefore, we should return to Barbauld's question at the end of "Origin and Progress of Novel-Writing," and to the eighteenth-century romances and the debates on their connection with social order and competition with novels that together form its context. Barbauld's conclusion reprises representative arguments made by William Godwin, Maria Edgeworth, Reeve, and Wollstonecraft about romance between 1785 and 1801. It was, I will argue, the continuing political discord between such contemporary writers and critics, within and about the romance genre, that provoked Barbauld to rename what her predecessors called romance and thus to reframe what they assumed was the mutually enabling bond between romance and British social order as a question awaiting her reader's answer.

In a 1797 essay "On History and Romance," Godwin proposed "romance" as a means "to understand" what he called, in political economic terms, "the machine of society." He assumed, as a rationalist and perfectibilist, that for his readers to understand how social order worked was for them "to direct it to its best purposes." Thus romance provided Godwin with an allegorical antidote to the lassitude-inducing "generalities of historical abstraction," the shapeless facts that characterize "national history" as well as the political economy he himself had written and restlessly revised in *Political Justice*, which could offer little insight into the specific principles of British society's ideal or actual functioning. Where political economy and history were without effect, romance was to spur British nationals to "fruitful . . . activity."[15] The argument provides a reader's guide to Godwin's radical gothic romance *Things as they Are; or the Adventures of Caleb Williams*, in which practical demonstration and functional critique of the British class and legal systems are woven together with his hero's experiences and responses. In a preface to her national political fiction *Castle Rackrent* (1801), Edgeworth similarly asserted that every nation's history is "so decked out by the fine fancy of the professed historian" that the synecdochic romance of "secret memoirs" (a subset of romance I discuss in chapter 1, and which was associated in particular with the Jacobite feminist writers Aphra Behn, Delarivière Manley, Eliza Haywood, and, later, Sophia Lee) provides the only keys to the principles of human nature and so to social and national improvement.[16]

Edgeworth and Godwin implicitly accept Reeve's developmental definition of *The Progress of Romance* (1785), which was to influence developmental histories of European fiction from Barbauld through Watt by drawing the "progress" of fiction "through the land of romance" to its teleological endpoint in modern Britain.[17] Reeve argues that contemporary Britain is divided between "modern Romances," in which "fictitious stories" and "true history" are "so blended together, that a common reader could not distinguish them," and "novels," in which "such things, as pass every day before our eyes" masquerade as factual narrative (1: 64–5, 111). The difference between the genres, as McKeon will similarly argue, rests on a distinction between history and verisimilitude – but Reeve defines the characteristic historicity of romance as the enactment of national problems and events in avowedly representative, private narrative form.[18] Although she calls novels "a public evil," producing "false expectations" of society and false pictures of legitimate domestic and social authority, she notes their "striking resemblance" to romance, which "prejudice only" denies (I: 24, II: 7). The genres blur together as Reeve cites the reviewers' conviction that Frances Sheridan's 1761 "modern novel", *Sidney Bidulph*, had represented "true history": the second genre borrows the identity of the first (II: 24). "Novels" emerge as a brief digression in literary history, a sport of nature produced by the progressive evolution of romance – unlikely to multiply too much, and already dying out. Meanwhile "romance" itself, as Reeve's title implies, continues to "progress."

For Barbauld, however, as the final question of "Origin and Progress of Novel-Writing" implies, the role of romance in social order – indeed, the social role of fiction – was less certain than Reeve had hoped and Edgeworth and Godwin insisted. Questioning the stability and national effects of the genre, even as her title echoes Reeve's, Barbauld replaces "romance" with "novel-writing," defining "*the Novel*," which has "within half a century" become the dominant form among "works of fiction," as "the lighter species of this kind of writing" (34). By limiting the scope of romance to the presumably "heavier" narratives of medieval and seventeenth-century Britain, she moves the genre into the past – although, like Reeve, she also blurs its edges, referring to Reeve's recent works of fiction as "romances" and to Aphra Behn's seventeenth-century secret histories as "Novels" (24, 35).

Barbauld may well have been made uneasy by the vicissitudes of romance as it was framed by such writers as Sheridan and Burney in their disagreements with Richardson, which registered dissent from the political economic assumptions his romances of female suffering and reward sustained. As I show in the second chapter of this book, these conservative women ironized Richardson's genre in ways that enacted the corruption, lawlessness, and female suffering they feared in societies shaped, and gendered, by romance writers seduced by liberal political economy. More troublingly, romance passed into the hands of radicals, including the pugnacious Wollstonecraft. Her *Wrongs of Woman; or, Maria* (posthumously published in 1798) insisted in Godwinian terms that its heroine's experiences are those "of woman" rather than "of an individual," but at the same time explicitly parodied gothic romance as a pallid failure to capture those depths of real female social, economic, and legal oppression that she, like Burney, saw as products of romance. Wollstonecraft attacked the pseudo-organic basis on which romance-writers cooperated with political economists to erect the avowedly natural socioeconomic order of modern Britain. In her fictions, and in the generic parodies she embedded in her political treatises, Wollstonecraft wrote radical romance while attacking the genre in all its forms, from the "romantic enthusiasm" of French revolutionaries who literally elevated women to pedestals while denying them *les droits de l'homme et du citoyen*, to the "romantic sentiment" of popular fictions that taught female readers to "look for happiness" only in the impossible utopia of (heterosexual) "love."

When the British press united to repel Wollstonecraft's sallies, painting them contradictorily as "romantic" excess and "cool, calculating, intellectual wickedness," it was above all the romance of *Wrongs* that made romance disreputable: as early as 1801 Edgeworth used another label for the genre she, in identical terms to Godwin's, recommended.[19] Austen, as I show in chapter 4, was to direct the romance burlesque of *Northanger Abbey* and *Persuasion* against Wollstonecraft's counter-romances, upholding a British social order actively and explicitly produced by the romance-reading and -writing of women within millions of individual British homes. But it was not until she and Scott began publishing their romances that the genre of romance was relegitimated.

THE VALUE OF SYSTEMS: POLITICAL PHILOSOPHY AND POLITICAL ECONOMY

Defined in large part by its enactment and narrative reshaping of the dynamics of social order, romance is the eighteenth-century genre most likely to go head-to-head with questions of social organization. As the practical debates on romance between Burney and Richardson, Wollstonecraft and Austen suggest, the genre could be used to convey a variety of positions oppositional to or supportive of contemporary social organizations from the domestic to the political; it could, with equal effectiveness, enact conservative or radical social critique in its gendered generic terms. Romance did not, however, characteristically address a society unmediated by philosophies of human nature, ethics, and political order. Whether because its writers envisioned contemporary British society as an inadequate product of political economy or because they sought to forestall the practical effects of the political economic innovation they feared and protested, the objects as well as the acts of romance social criticism exist well within the "republic of letters" or its prosaic counterpart, the "reading market."[20] As Godwin and Edgeworth argued, romance was more adequate to social reform than were the discourses it supplemented, and so it presented itself as a superior successor to the politics and history that were its objects of critique.

Romance, as Barbauld also saw it, provided a supplement to the faulty connection between "Britain" and its "systems" by offering them an alternative meeting-place.

To delineate this alternative requires some account of the evolution of "system" in eighteenth-century and Romantic thought, a discussion for which David Kaufmann provides the background. Like Carol Kay, Catherine Gallagher, Claudia Johnson, and James Thompson, Kaufmann addresses the homologous but overlapping bodies of theory and law that regulated distinct aspects of eighteenth- and early-nineteenth-century social dynamics.[21] Arguing that postmodern conceptions of "system" offer an apt model for relations among these discourses, he provides a new way of balancing the paradoxical relations among genres at once parallel, discrete, and profoundly mutually implicated. Borrowing an analogy from Niklas Luhmann's theory of "social systems," Kaufmann posits that each distinct discourse or theory that orders a society – each "system" – runs on similar principles, moves in similar ways, and exists independently of the others. Yet no system can identify its own inability to describe the workings of the whole society adequately, an intrinsic weakness that must be revealed and remedied by the supplemental actions of rival systems.[22] For Kaufmann, this theory corrects and updates Theodor Adorno's account of the cultural-critical function of a relatively autonomous literary art by placing letters within a Habermasian public sphere where competing systems, including writing and the book trade, encounter one another.[23] In practice, this mapping of interlocking discourses across eighteenth-century British society resembles the sociological practice of Pierre Bourdieu.[24] It makes "novels" and "classical economics" parallel systems dedicated to ensuring the order and justice of the society in and for which both function – each in its separate sphere, yet each also demonstrating that no system or sphere can operate in isolation if the needs of the whole social subject and the whole society are to be effectively addressed.[25] For Kaufmann as for Barbauld, Godwin, and Edgeworth, fiction defines the privacy in which, characteristically, it is read, but it is also written, published, and bought in public. Its dynamically doubled character makes it at once a stabilizing influence on and alternative to political and economic theory.

Theoretically elegant, Kaufmann's argument also rigorously outlines the cultural roles of competing eighteenth-century discourses of fiction and political economy. The terms of his analysis, however, bear further historical scrutiny, especially given the resemblance he does not address between Luhmann's relatively neutral account of systems and Barbauld's critical dismissal of them. First, it is clear that for Barbauld, and implicitly for Godwin and Edgeworth, the writing and reading of fiction emphatically do not constitute a system. Systems, Barbauld remarks, are best left to those "who will" trouble themselves with them, while fiction becomes a matter for the general and practical concern of the public, beginning with the authoritative editor and her readers. Secondly and more crucially, the contemporary idea of "system" itself needs investigation, for the treatment of systems among the eighteenth-century *literati* had evolved dramatically while producing the apparatus that Barbauld and her colleagues rejected. The resulting changes in contemporary accounts of the utility and virtue of political philosophy are a major thread in my argument about the evolution of romance: providing more than context, they mingle with and help to account for the diversity and evolution of romance itself.

The questions before us now are these: how did "system" evolve away from Alexander Pope's explication of human society as one in a series of concentric circles – the "great chain . . . upheld by God" in which "worlds on worlds compose one universe" and "system into system runs" as "Man" unknowingly "Touches some wheel, or verges to some goal"?[26] How did Pope's didactically devotional joy give way to Edmund Burke's impassioned attack on the "cold hearts and muddy understandings" of those who argue the virtue of "private speculations" and uphold the "mechanic philosophy" of political economy, and to S. T. Coleridge's denunciation of an "idolatrous reliance on false philosophy" that leads "planners and constitution-makers" to postulate that "states and governments" function "as machines, every movement of which might be foreseen and taken into previous calculation"?[27] In short, how did conservative thinkers trade their search for God in a theoretical perfection they aligned with organic social orders for an opposition to systematic thought that was, as Seamus Deane reiterates, a revolt against theory?[28]

My account of these changing responses to political economy, which I, like Kaufmann, discuss as the major eighteenth-century British social "system" of which Barbauld and others speak, centres on the transformation of political economy itself. Further, I tie the changes in political economy to the problem of its consonance with British history, an issue to which I return in the final section of this introduction. The transformation begins, I argue, with a shift, at once doctrinal and strategic, driven by historiographical conflicts and the conflicts of real history, away from the broadly accepted hands-on role of "Providence" in political society toward a more detached role for first causes in political economy. God, that is, ceases to be represented as an intrusive force in the British polity, the immediate cause of inequity and suffering as well as of rectitude and reward, but instead is shown to have established the principles on which that society runs. Above all, a divine intelligence is credited with creating a set of emotional laws and invariable behavioural norms intrinsic to "human nature." Gender differences, and resulting "natural" differences in authority, form the paradigmatic instance of the second cause. Among the theocentric accounts of political organization this new thinking superseded, I place not only Robert Filmer's insistence that worldly kings are lineal descendants and heirs of the biblical Adam, the first-created patriarch and king whose God-given subjects were his wife and children, but also John Locke's Genesis-story of a created masculine authority operating in the putatively natural, pre-political realm of the household, to which he tenaciously adheres even as he rejects the view that such authority is kingship.[29]

The first three chapters of this book trace this turn away from Filmer and Locke toward a new social thinking centred on "human nature" and thus on observable modern history. Very explicitly, I should note, the transformation is not a rejection of all forms of innate masculine authority, though it does involve a rejection of patriarchy strictly defined as an equation between God-given kingship and fatherhood, between filial love and the unshakeable obligations of the political subject. In chapter 1, I show how the anti-Lockean romances of such early-eighteenth-century Tory women as Behn and Haywood demonstrated the failure of Providence to create in particular men and women the disposition, respectively, to wield and to accept authority. The Tory romancers' claim to expose the "secret" particulars of British social history, and so to discredit what contemporary political philosophers claimed was the God-given shape of their classed and gendered British society, required a defensive response.[30] In chapters 2 and 3, I locate this response in the writings of David Hume, Adam Smith, and their popularizers in periodicals, practical economic tracts and, most influentially, romances such as Richardson's. Such works displaced the suspect notion of created or predestined social and political status and substituted sentiment and sympathy – naturally shared human feeling and its means of production and circulation. Demonstrated within romance narratives, communicated through sympathy between readers, writers, and characters, sentiment united romance-writers with readers. Sentiment and sympathy served together as theoretical sources, though not always as historical guarantors, of identically gendered and inevitably hierarchical social effects. Chapters 1 through 3 demonstrate how this new focus on economies and second causes, not least in the romances that bolstered theoretical claims about "human nature" with practical demonstrations of its operation, inaugurated a related turn in political historiography – from biblically tracing the divine origins of political authority to theorizing and historically confirming the operations of contemporary society. To outline the role of second causes in British society was thus to describe a new, political economic order, reliant for its stability on interlocking conceptions of nature and gender.[31]

This conception of the shift in the description and modelling of political order is not inconsistent with Whiggish and other historical arguments about the progressive "secularization" of eighteenth-century society.[32] Certainly the new weight political economists placed on second causes – theoretically universal but in practice as variable as the experiences, circumstances, and education of people themselves – made their claims for the role of divine intent in British politics less and less a matter for blind leaps of faith. Yet it can also be argued (as I do in chapter 1) that one consequence of God's demotion from the traditional role of British society's puppeteer was that the influence of a systematic intelligence became increasingly easy to believe. It is possible to read the new focus on second causes as strengthening the political philosophers' theodicy by explaining disorder and suffering as human aberrations consequent on the historical corruption of human nature, products of free will permitted to unfold by a *laissez-faire* Providence. Thus the changes are equally consonant with J. C. D. Clark's insistence that those actually in power in eighteenth-century Britain – the aristocrats, landlords, and most politicians – as well as their tenants and constituents continued to observe Church of England rules and rites in public and in private, and to accept the essentially providential character of social organization.[33]

Given the equivocal political and ontological status of second causes in theorizing social order, it is not surprising that contempories complained both from the left and the right about the "abstraction" – the social and historical detachment, and therefore the potential injustice – of political economy precisely as "human nature" became a prominent factor in it, and as romance-writers began to defend it on sentimental grounds. Their complaints were motivated, variously, by religious orthodoxy, sociopolitical conservatism, gendered grievance, and radical dissent. Yet all these motives, as chapters 2 and 3 suggest, could find voice by detailed restatement or burlesque of previous romance-writers' political and historiographic claims – in a further blending of fiction with political economy: a new version of romance. As some conservatives, including Burney and Sheridan, demonstrated in their ironic or tragic rewritings of earlier romances, political economy's emphasis on second causes, and especially on the Richardsonian romances that illustrated their particular social workings, meant denying the real, visible motions of society. Sheridan's romances insist that few natural laws restrain the economic behaviour of the British, and Burney's heroines suffer endlessly from the compensatory sentiment their fractious society requires them to demonstrate. Equally, insisted the radical Wollstonecraft in her mixed parodies of political economy and Richardsonian romance, romance apologists for political economy cast a veil of nature and necessity over its established injustices, upholding gender and class inequities. Finally, to generalize human nature, as Burke and other late-eighteenth-century "New Whig" writers argued in romances and in political tracts inflected or pocketed by romance, was to hollow, flatten, or harden the human heart. Britain required natural, local emotional ties and individual ideological commitments for the economy and polity to function without disorder. Thus British political economy itself at last paved the way for Wollstonecraft's "English Jacobin" critique of the British society it justified, a critique mounted, like the complaints of her conservative contemporaries, in parodic anatomies of those romances whose illustration and promotion of sentiment upheld the theories of Hume and Smith. The combined result of these romance critiques was, by the turn of the nineteenth century, a broad-based abandonment of "systematic" political economy, and a concerted effort to construct a replacement. Political economy was rejected, and alternatives sought, even by politicians and philosophers, such as Burke, who continued to embrace the market-liberal socioeconomic principles it inculcated.

Diversely intermingled, since Richardson's *Clarissa*, with political economy, romance provided the means to a concerted, critical, but politically various socioeconomic critique directed toward Richardsonian romance and thence toward political economy itself. Yet even as it fulfilled this role, the genre remained closely tied to British political history. Nor did all romance-writers use the putatively "historical" particulars of private lives and motives to expose the inaccuracies and corruption of political economic generality. Some continued assembling such details to prove the theoretical perfection of political economy in the face of social diversity, and, through sympathy, to inculcate the "natural," "human," gender-inflected sentiment that was needed to keep social order running in accordance with political economic rules. Wollstonecraft made "romance" disreputable, and Burke discounted the value of the "systems" she exposed and attempted to dismantle. Nevertheless, the intertwining of the discourses both criticized meant that the workings of romance resembled the logic of the system closely enough to provide, once self-reflexively reworked, an appealing and theoretically convincing Romantic alternative to it. Having exposed the discrepancies between real British history and theoretical political economy in the 1790s, romance became, by the early nineteenth century, the surprising means of reconciling the two. In the hands of Austen and Scott, as chapters 4 and 5 contend, the bond between romance and political economic description gave way to a new commingling of romance with national prescription. Romance, in its new, self-avowedly fictional form, was advertised as the saviour of Britain. Its writers marketed themselves to particular readerships and trumpeted the influence of their romances over those readers, whose consequent power to renovate British social order was the much-celebrated result. At the same time, these writers presented an innovative conception of British society as a union ordered by the systematic, even mechanical, production and circulation of romance rather than by political system itself. Yet they represented their romantic Britain as a return to legitimate traditions: of familial, social, and, above all, *national* authority.

A UNITED KINGDOM: FROM POLITICAL ECONOMY TO BRITISH NATION

Because of their position on the generic border between political philosophy and the details of private life, eighteenth-century romances often tell stories of societies' formation and cohesion. With equal ease, aided by the allegorical connections their politicized readers forge between their private narration and publicly oriented thematics, they portray communities held together by natural ties or disrupt idealized community portraits by exposing their dependence on an arbitrary authority that has hidden itself behind the mask of human nature.[34] After the turn of the nineteenth century, pressed by too many such generic confrontations, political economic assertions about the universality and naturalness of the laws governing human nature began giving way within the generic hybrid of romance to the details of British national sentiment and political history. Nationhood, therefore, appeared as a product as well as a theme of Austen's and Scott's fiction, as Scott's readers have long argued and as Austen's have recently asserted.[35]

To identify the increasing stake in national sentiment within romances is not to imply that political economy lost all its force on Britain and its letters, though I do want to argue that claims for the naturalness of human character and its predictable role in social cohesion could no longer be convincingly upheld by a coalition between romance and political economy: generic competition outweighed generic cooperation. Nor do I mean to suggest that Britain did not exist as a national construct, or that it lacked a sense of national character, before late-eighteenth-century conflicts called the naturalness, pertinence, and propriety of political economic constructs into unanswerable question. Rather, as the recent histories of Gerald Newman and Linda Colley and the historical sociology of Benedict Anderson demonstrate, the "rise," emotional "imagining," or ideological "forging" of a nation was a process that evolved throughout the eighteenth century in Britain, responding to socioeconomic, religious, and political dissensions within and between England, Scotland, Ireland, and Wales, and defending against pressures from without.[36] In particular, I want to argue that a national dimension lay latent from the first in political economy, and so in its romance intertexts as well.

This argument builds on the recognition that from the mid-eighteenth into the nineteenth century the bonds between political economy and the social order it normalized and claimed to describe were disrupted by more than the counter-romances of conservative and radical critics. Although romance, as I suggested earlier in this introduction, did not always function, as Godwin, Edgeworth, and Barbauld would have it, as a force for social order, those romance writers who did claim to regulate the private character of British readers put their fictions to work in tandem with public history, as an aid or alternative to it. At the same time, however, romance had a history of its own, founded on its longstanding association with the private and particular life of British society. Thus the genre enabled critics and promoters of political economy alike to isolate those details of British history and socioeconomic practice that refused to conform with the general rules of human nature that Hume and Smith set out. The effect of such explorations of wayward sentiment or passion, or of calculating cold-eyed greed, was often to open a gulf between the theoretical ordering principles of society and the actual disjunctions and inequities of Britain, whether the details of corruption emerged as an effect of openly political parody or whether, unwittingly self-exposed, they became easy targets for burlesque. Romance had this effect in part because eighteenth-century Britain was ideologically fragmented, and in part because Britain's instability was explored and often deepened in conversations between romance-writers and producers of ephemeral genres, such as pamphlets, periodicals, and conduct manuals, who sought to affirm or replace the laws political economy advanced.

It may seem tendentious to emphasize the internal divisions of late-eighteenth-century Britain. For after the turbulence of the Civil War and Interregnum, the 1688 change of monarchical succession, and the Jacobite rebellions of 1715 and 1745, which had successively polarized British society in the seventeenth and earlier eighteenth centuries, Britain had become relatively calm. While Britain pursued the numerous foreign wars of the period, its domestic peace between 1746 and 1790 – or, as Whig historians from the late-eighteenth-century Adam Anderson onward would argue, between 1688 and 1790 – was interrupted only by riots, with no real threats of civil war.[37] Even the Jacobite threat was historiographically dismissed, until recently, as lacking in socially and geographically broad-based support, and thus visibly doomed from the start. Competing explanations have been proposed for this Britain quieted by consensus. Traditional Whig-historical views describe a post-1688 Lockean Whig accord under which economic, industrial, and political modernization were able to march forward essentially, or at least practically, unopposed. This account has been disputed in intellectual history by J. G. A. Pocock's insistence that a continuing opposition, at its height in the reign of George I, espoused civic republican virtue as an antidote to commerce, and by Pocock's resulting demotion of Locke from the height of ideological influence – an account that Newman's discussion of the masculinist British patriotism of George II's reign also upholds.[38] More recently, the classic liberal account has been challenged in the social historical field by Clark's assertion of a consensus governed not by Whiggism, commerce, or a classical code of *virtus*, but rather by the shared commitment of powerful Britons to a state church, with an embedded ideal of a monarchy inherited "by the grace of God" as expressed in the will of the Church of England – a widespread faith that was, according to Clark, shaken only by the proliferating religious diversity of the early nineteenth century.[39] What all these histories share, however great their disagreements, is a sense that the mid-eighteenth century was a time of developing consensus among the wielders of power.

Yet the contemporary intellectual history of the interlude between rebellion and Reform reveals no persuasive ideological union of the Hanoverian succession's diverse supporters – Whigs, anti-Jacobite Tories, and disillusioned former Jacobites – in any broad-based Protestant consensus.[40] At the same time, the recent work of Clark, Paul Monod, Murray Pittock, and Howard Erskine-Hill in social, intellectual, and literary history has recovered the widespread influence of the Jacobites on the British polity and on Britain's sense of its own unity, and has emphasized the continuing unease their presence created.[41] Pittock suggests, indeed, that Jacobitism survived into the nineteenth century, sometimes as an independent political faith and sometimes as a dress for "English Jacobin" and other radical beliefs – a continuity that Newman hints as well.[42] Taken together with the force of the Jacobite threat, the range of Protestant political writings in the period discloses, despite the pragmatic conjunction of most Protestants in support for the Hanoverian succession (or at least in opposition to the Catholic Stuarts), a disconcerting vacuum where it is ideologically imperative that proofs of the succession's legitimacy should reside. This lack, I argue in chapter 1, was a necessary result of the broad-based turn away from theological exegesis of political events in the wake of the 1745 Jacobite Rebellion and in response to the writings of its adherents.

The most logical response to the problem of monarchical legitimacy, and a potential solution to the ideological void in mid-eighteenth-century Protestant Britain, seemed at first to have appeared in the classic liberal political theory of the late seventeenth century. Such depths of national and historical instability, that is, demanded broad, deep, even universal, philosophical remedies. The appeals to God and biblical history that had justified the claim of William of Orange to the throne could be recycled to promote the legitimate claim of the Protestant George II, whose avowed ancestral right was derived by means of a similarly circuitous path from James I. Thus the theocentric but anti-absolutist political philosophy of Locke's *First Treatise of Government* – in which William III implicitly became the most virtuous among the naturally authoritative husbands and fathers of Britain – won a brief renewed popularity amid relieved Protestant celebrations of the Hanoverian monarchy after the defeat of the Jacobite army in 1746.[43] But Locke's orientation toward first causes ensured the rapid displacement of his political philosophy. Not least, the heterosexual ideological

force of legitimacy – a notion centred on birth and its rigorous regulation – combined with the lawless heterogeneity of British private life and
power relations to make Lockean first causes an unreliable source of
gendered authority. Locke's brief retrospective vogue gave way to the
political economy of Hume (in *Essays* oriented toward an economic and
social order rooted in human nature and its drives, and in the *Treatise of
Human Nature* that provided their base), Smith, Burke, and Paine, whose
writings centred on the immediate effects of human nature and their
consequences for human custom. Hume and his successors offered
signposts for a genealogy of authority that was moving rapidly away
from direct appeals to Providence even as it remained rooted in Protestant assumptions about the existence of a divine creator, the historicity
of Genesis, and the consequent naturalness of heterosexual couplings
and gendered character.

   As it turned out, however, these philosophers were equally unable to
offer solutions, for their guidance was grounded in the same national
historical uncertainty that had impelled the initial return to Locke and
the search for successors to his political history. Seeking alternatives to
divine fiat in their drive to explain the dangerously incomprehensible,
even meaningless twists and details of Britain's social order, Hume and
those who came after him appealed to the new abstract constants of
natural law, which they sought to illustrate not in the ruptures of
monarchical, political, or biblical history, but in the continuity and
predictability that, they avowed, had characterized *homo economicus* (male
and female) and economic Britain from the start. The political economic solutions they proposed are thus usefully seen as a recourse to
private character and behaviour in explaining socioeconomic acts, and
thus as a move to privatize the arena of economic relations as well as to
naturalize the public sphere they increasingly modelled on economic
order. For at the heart of their focus on human nature was the single
myth their new political economy shared with Locke's political philosophy. This myth took the form of continuing faith in a private, natural,
and gendered authority. The complex product of perfectly balanced
relations between the created superior mental and physical strength of
the human male, his intrinsic desire for the female, his sympathy with
the desires of other males, and the female's natural "sentiments" of
domestic feeling for and submission to him, this form of authority was
shaped by the heterosexual couple's collisions with the economic society
that succeeded and realized the theoretical tumults of the state of
nature.

The essential character of heterosexual union, the heart and source of political economy, thus came theoretically to underlie and regulate political economic activity in every arena from the laws of marriage to the rules of consumption, uniting the series of similarly functioning social systems that history had produced. At the same time, the heterosexual domestic character of human nature was said to govern not only the families of commoners, but also the private family of the king, instituting a nationwide series of similarly ordered households tied together by symmetry and sympathy. In this way, political economists laid the groundwork for Austen's production of British nationhood in a series of families linked by parallel relations to orderly writing, reading, and literary consumption – a community-in-isolation that Adorno and Jürgen Habermas were later to elaborate as an effect of the modern "culture industry."[44] But these political economic claims for the naturalness of gendered character and its necessity in social order were also bitterly attacked in romances in which Burney and Wollstonecraft showed that a society founded on naturalizing assumptions about gender – or, in the English Jacobin Wollstonecraft's case, that gender itself – was a corrupt or unjust economic fiction.

At the turn of the nineteenth century, Edward Coxe wryly proposed that the many seditious activities imputed to eighteenth-century Jacobites and Jacobins were merely invented justifications for legal, religious, and economic oppression, fictions set out by a powerful national interest "To make the wrong appear the right,/ And keep our rulers in." For Coxe, in consequence, the different motives attributed to the two groups were deceptive products of Britain's political history, which periodically required refurbished rhetorics for its own legitimation: "In Walpole's time, 'twas Jacobite,/ In Pitt's, 'tis Jacobin!"[45] Chapter 3 addresses this dismissive response to British radicalism as it appeared in the writing of Wollstonecraft, a disaffected radical who had gradually concluded that the English Jacobins and French revolutionaries were dedicated as strongly to the protection of existing economic rights and privileges as were the Old Whigs and *ancien régime* they opposed, though the radicals defined those rights differently. As Wollstonecraft consistently argued by the mid-1790s, the social and political changes the radicals called for were limited to superficial rearrangements of the present order's details. But the generic mutations of the romances of the mid- and late-eighteenth century, including Wollstonecraft's, and their echoes in competitor genres suggest, nevertheless, that a legitimation crisis in Britain's social and political order stretched from the Jacobites to the English Jacobins before being resolved by an explicitly textual and artificial redefinition of legitimacy in the romances of Austen and Scott.

This legitimation crisis was literary in character and gendered in rhetoric and focus. Jacobite propagandists, whose work appeared in broadsides, pamphlets, and caricatures throughout the first half of the century, had tended to ridicule the effeminacy of the Hanoverian kings and question the legitimacy of their ancestry and offspring.[46] The most radical writers among the Jacobins were those who questioned the roots of Britain's social order rather than the present distribution of parliamentary representation and property rights within it. These radicals used similarly gendered and sexualized rhetorics, employing Jacobite fictions to denature what Wollstonecraft called "the prevailing opinion of . . . sexual character" that upheld the claims of political economy by entrenching the gender differences on which society was said inevitably and naturally to be founded.[47] Romance was an especially effective genre for Jacobin attack because of its entanglements with political economy: the genre had long been received as an apt way to demonstrate and teach the private sensations, experiences, and assumptions that political economists had taken as their own foundation. Once refracted through literary history, however, the consequences of this dialectical critique of romance escaped the limits Wollstonecraft set for the rewritten genre. It was, ironically, her own ironic romances, which discredited gender and the gendered laws of Britain's political economy as ideological products propped up by romance, that made room for Austen's and Scott's recuperation of gender and romance in explicitly nationalist and self-consciously fictional form.

What Wollstonecraft made available to Austen and Scott was her exposure of the artifice and the commercial implications of romance. As her quoting knowledge of Burney's *Cecilia* suggests,[48] Wollstonecraft had learned from Burney's conservative romances, with their critique of market ideology, to recognize parallels between the literary marketplace and other British markets. She moved beyond Burney to attack directly not only the cooperation of Richardsonian romance with political economy, but also the ethical failures of the political economy that placed feminine sentiment in its regulating role in Britain's parallel markets. Her own works, in consequence, not only reproduced Burney's critical anatomy of the intersections between romance and the British economy, but also extended the consequences for gender relations. In 1790, as she began outlining her critique of romance in response to Burke's ideological history of the British constitution, Wollstonecraft remarked that feminine "sensibility" – that gendered and codified complex of feelings and responses naturalized and taught by Hume and Smith as "sentiment," and rendered at once more instinctive and more popular by the romances of late century – had become "the *manie* of the day."[49] Her pun (*manie*/money) united the obsessional psychic experience that contemporaries called "mania" with the reliance of economies on symbolic tokens of value. Her explication of sensibility as the shared regulatory standard uniting social and economic exchange was played out in her analysis of the ways in which contemporary "ladies" were induced to "retail," or unwittingly traffic in, the ideological character produced in them by political economists and their conduct- and romance-writing allies. Wollstonecraft's blurring of the lines between ethics, emotion, and economics, a blend that parodies the mingling of moral philosophy and political history that characterized contemporary political economy, established the role of her romances in relation to the political economy with which they compete and to which they respond. Mixing the media of exchange, that is, Wollstonecraft sets up something more than an analogy between the circulation of feeling and economic circulation: the last is founded on the first, and the two meet in the romance genre.

Made explicit by Wollstonecraft's irony, the paired processes of illustration and critique or supplementation had unfolded in romance from the Jacobite aftermath throughout the eighteenth century. In their detailed descriptions of their characters' gendered sentiments, the putative constants of Britain's otherwise anarchic economy, the writers of romance had concurrently demonstrated the ideal effects of proper feeling and taught it to their audience. By simultaneously naturalizing and inculcating sentiments that conformed to the specifications of political economy, providing a gold standard for the intertwining laws of human nature and the marketplace, romance made producible and reproducible commodities of its readers. It acknowledged its own socioeconomic agency, even as it insisted on the innate character and absolute worth of sentiment. As I show in chapters 2 and 3, and as Burney and Wollstonecraft demonstrate, the late-eighteenth-century young lady who coded her delicate sensibility by weeping over *Clarissa*, or her mid-century counterpart who proved her virtuous sentiment by hiding her secret histories beneath a stack of conduct books, responded to the entanglement of the literary arena and marriage market in a Britain whose social and political orders were economically defined, and whose political economy demanded a predictable set of emotional responses. Romance and its readers were self-conscious about the mingling of the genre with the other discourses that regulated Britain's economic and social circulation. Their generic reflexivity propels Austen and Scott as they renovate romance as a medium for the production of a national social and literary legitimacy.

The nationalist recuperation of romance, founded on open acknowledgement of its artifice and commodity status, is the focus of the two final chapters of this book. Bought from booksellers or rented from circulating libraries, as Burney and Wollstonecraft illustrate, romances circulated widely between households and cities, carried by stagecoach, steamboat, canal, and turnpike road.[50] The vicissitudes of romance as books moved through the networks of production and distribution, and their consequences for the fashion, corruption, or sensibility the buyers of romance demonstrate in national historical context, reappear explicitly and affirmatively in Austen's and Scott's novels. For, in commingling with political economy, romance, whether despite or because of its status as a circulating commodity, had become a genre *about* circulation. As such, it upheld or undermined as it illustrated the social, political, and economic logics the political economists had established.

For Austen and Scott, romance and the systems that circulated it – the emerging means of cultural production – provided ideological foundations and practical infrastructure for an explicitly national unity in which political economy played no role. Austen founded her Britain on engaged reading and commentary among family members living within a private but consuming household, a code of conduct that her fictions and others were expected to reproduce wherever distribution systems took them. Scott based his national order on the social and cultural authority of the professional man of English letters, a figure replicated across Britain by the individual imaginative responses of Romantic poets and historical romance-writers. Detached from the political economic intertexts that had supplied it with self-conscious powers of national circulation, cut loose from the human nature that earlier writers had sought alternately to regulate or disrupt, British romance established its own national character in the act of producing Britain. The genre of romance became more national as Britain, and British letters, became increasingly – and lastingly – romantic.

CHAPTER I

Marketing agreement: Richardson's romance of consensus

When Samuel Richardson published *Pamela; or, Virtue Rewarded* in 1740, he wrapped his text in several prefaces. One prescribes consumption of the book through "use" of its "practical examples," which make Richardson "confident of a favourable reception." Two unsigned letters supplement these instructions, lending the middle-class Richardson as weighty and established an authority as his readers were willing to imagine. "This little Book," one pronounces, provides a "hitherto much-wanted Standard or Pattern for this Kind of Writing" and "an Example of Purity to the writers of a neighbouring Nation; which now shall have an opportunity to receive English Bullion in exchange for its own Dross, which has so long passed current among us."[1] The second declares that "a Piece of this Kind is much wanted in the World, which is . . . debauched by pernicious *Novels*" that "reduce our sterling Substances into an empty Shadow" and "Frenchify our English solidity into Froth" (*P1* 8). In contrast to Richardson's claims for the use and exchange value of the text, the anonymous backers value *Pamela* on neither "use" nor "reception," but on "virtue": the text's and its heroine's intrinsic merit. Taken together, the three prefaces reconcile use-value and exchange-value with absolute worth. *Pamela* becomes the "bullion" or "sterling" standard against which all other works in circulation must be valued. Putting Richardson's text to the proof, the prefaces specify the "want" it fills in the literary "World," but their blend of economic and ethical rhetoric also specifies a role for *Pamela* in a broader British arena. As the prefaces define it, Britain's lack is textual, ethical, and monetary, and unease alone unites the conflicting discourses of order and value by which British society is structured. *Pamela* is offered as a text that fulfills Britain's desires and supplies its deficiencies: it bridges desire and moral lack and unites the competing wants of a diverse body politic.

What kind of text is Richardson's "little Book"? It is no "pernicious novel," but no factual treatise: a "Pattern for this Kind of Writing" whose "kind," species, or genre is never named; a substantial "piece" that fills a want even as its specific dimensions remain undefined. Every genre, as Ralph Cohen and Franco Moretti theorize, defines itself dynamically in competition with others, its borders fixed by the contiguous claims and assumptions of particular writers and readers.[2] But the vagueness of Richardson's correspondents, and the series of comparisons, locations, and synonyms they marshal to name and place Richardson's text, also mark the newness of the particular genre to which *Pamela* belongs.[3] In the chapter that follows, I will argue that it is the fluid composite character of Richardson's fictions that allows him to intervene in Britain's troubled public and private spheres, where successive but competing discourses clash on the field of British social order. The genre label he finally gives his texts is a name for their interventionist bent and intertextual character.

A generic history of Richardson's writing begins by discriminating three eighteenth-century spheres of writing: the political and literary public spheres and the private space of the family. It also requires a conceptual disentangling of political history, political economy, and two sub-species of fiction, none of which is exclusively assignable to any one discursive sphere, and each of which existed in inextricable combinations with the others. The political and literary public spheres of eighteenth-century Britain are not, as Jürgen Habermas proposed for Europe, identical. Their imperfect overlap is perhaps made most visible by noting the access that non-citizens (women, servants, labourers, and colonial subjects) had to the field of letters without being permitted to participate in avowedly political oratory or action or – at least without condemnation – in commentary.[4] To define Richardson's relation to the literary sphere, therefore, is also to define the borders and rules of the sphere itself. I will suggest that the literary and political public spheres were intersecting sets. Some of the players and issues were the same, that is, in each, and the two arenas and their players met over the paradoxically public question of the function of private feeling. In the shape as well as in the content of his works, Richardson offered one of the eighteenth century's most influential answers to that question, so that his works came to mime on the level of form the mingled workings of the domestic and social tenets they thematically advanced. In so doing, I will suggest, Richardson's works defined a genre at the intersection of private and public discourse, where political history, political economy, and fiction met and clashed.

The printing, reviewing, and selling of Richardson's works was long subordinated in criticism to private subjectivity. From Ian Watt's reading of Richardson's fictions as documents of middle-class "private experience" through R. F. Brissenden's and John Mullan's discussions of sentiment in *Clarissa* and Michael McKeon's explication of the upward mobility attained through Pamela's subjective letters, readings focused on the intimate spaces of Richardson's narratives.[5] His treatment of privacy is often linked to the "rise" of an "affective" sociopolitical structure in Britain and the consequent displacement of "patriarchy" as a prevailing ideology.[6] At the same time, however, his epistolary fictions are read for their thematization of writing, which not only permitted but made explicit the existence of competing versions of reality – some of which triumph over others and naturalize themselves.[7] Recent discussions of *Pamela* and *Clarissa* unite these perspectives to suggest that Richardson was instrumental in defining a mid-eighteenth-century literary public sphere, and that the works with which he shaped it reflected changing contemporary conceptions of privacy less than they helped invent and order new forms of private life. Such readings help to explain how the logic of the literary sphere provided models for political order without collapsing the two together. Thus Elizabeth Heckendorn Cook suggests that epistolary fictions formally mimic the literary sphere as Richardson envisioned it: a "quasi-public" space "modelled on the relations of the affective family," with domestic ideology as a private counterpart to the shaping public myth of a social contract.[8] Or, as David Kaufmann argues, fictional accounts of domestic relations produce a self-consciously private supplement to the logic of political and economic order, naming and correcting the aporias of political economy.[9]

Even when the generic process is complicated in this way, restoring the division between letters and politics tends to insulate Richardson's fiction from political discourse. Yet – as the diverse rhetorics arrayed in the prefaces to *Pamela* suggest – Richardson's works confront and intertwine with political history and political economy as well as with literary intertexts. Moving among these competing genres, staging confrontations between them, Richardson marks out in his fiction a stable, shared ideological terrain for the political and literary public spheres: the private and subjective, grounded, as his fictions demonstrate, in an invariable and natural kind of virtue. As it appears in *Clarissa*, in particular, the epistolary privacy of the heroine and her correspondents is Richardson's own invention. But the virtue at its heart, the avowed anchor of the domestic as well as the social order he portrays, exists in complex, sometimes competitive relation to other privacies and other virtues, invented by such political philosophers as David Hume and Adam Smith, and by popularizers of their tenets, including Hester Chapone and John Gregory in conduct books, Richard Cumberland in the polite periodical, and Adam Anderson in "light" political economy. At the same time, in writing at the intersection between politics, letters, and private life, Richardson opens his fiction to political critique couched in literary, particular, and ostensibly private form.

Richardson's works do not, then, only promote the growing influence of classic liberal political philosophy on domestic ideology, and they do not work to segregate the ordering principles of the household from those of the marketplace.[10] Rather, as their diverse and shifting inter-texts suggest, they intervene in a crisis within the interlocking political and literary spheres of an already entrenched liberal politics, and between the kinds of writing circulating through each. The critical event was the sudden establishment of internal peace in 1740s Britain, and its paradoxically disruptive ideological consequences. Although the degree of influence won by the Jacobites in England was for years dismissed by historians as lacking in popular roots, and is now the matter of ongoing debate, what seems indisputable is that with the final defeat of the Jacobites in 1745, British Protestants found themselves in general agree-ment about the direction of the British succession.[11] The surviving leaders of their opponents were deprived of land and power, often banished, and – what Gerald Newman insists was more crucial – painted as "savage" alien agitators or "frenchified" servants of a Cath-olic foreign power.[12] But the new Protestant unity, as Linda Colley has argued, was a coalition founded on pragmatic assent to the now-established Hanoverian succession more than on any shared philosophi-cal certainty about the principles of its establishment, or about its relation to British social order.[13] J. C. D. Clark's assertion that Church of England members were overwhelmingly theocentric and dynastic in justifying the Georges does not negate the divergent motives and com-peting justifications upheld by their Dissenting allies, nor does it unify the diverse genealogies of authority that existed, as we will see, even among Anglicans.[14]

Among these Anglicans were the followers of John Locke. These Whig apologists had argued since the Williamite Revolution of 1688, and especially in the debates surrounding the 1714 succession of George I and the failed Jacobite rising of 1715, that a stable foundation for

Britain's social relations, and thus for its political practices, could be found in universal principles and biblical dictates. In particular, Locke's acceptance, in the first *Treatise of Government* (1690), of the Logos-driven creation narrative of Genesis allowed his *Second Treatise* to equate *vox populi* literally and historically with *vox dei*. Locke argued that the universal political rights of male adults progressed inevitably out of Adam's gender-based authority over an innately weaker and submissive Eve, which eventually resulted in the split of society into public and private spheres. Thus the public was inhabited by a fraternity of equals, who forged a contract establishing laws and a system of government. These men were perpetually reconstituted as political and economic subjects by their authority over the wives and families whose privacy, or insulation from the social contract that gave birth to government, was also produced by the created private authority of men over women.[15] Locke's theoretical history gave the political consensus in favour of a particular British monarch's rule a doctrinal predictability that transformed *de facto* kingship into a mark of divine and popular assent, and so guaranteed the virtue and order of the reign. It comes as no surprise, therefore, that Lockean thinking won a brief renewed popularity, even among Tory Hanoverian supporters, after the Jacobite crisis of 1745–6.[16]

But the same historical events that temporarily widened support for Lockean ideology finally forced Britons to choose between acknowledging the precarious arbitrariness of their political order and thus its potential for further fragmentation, or seeking some new source of meaning and stability. Even within the broad-based rhetorical context of the Anglican anti-Jacobitism of the 1740s, debate raged about the sources of Britain's political authority and legitimacy. One 1745 tract insists that the Act of Succession forever established the crown in the Hanoverian line; another warns that a Stuart victory will deprive Britons of their right, established in 1688, "to shake off the Yoke" at will "and chuse new Rulers for themselves."[17] In consequence, British Protestant supporters of the Hanoverian monarchs needed either to unite their histories of political succession and social order by binding them to a single, invariable standard, or to allow them to reveal themselves as equally contingent – as fantasies or fictions. The dilemma may thus be read in literary as well as in political terms. The traditional theocentric histories of political and social order faced a problem of narrative credibility and, what was much the same thing, of narrative dysfunction. The solution, too, had to be found in narrative. The result was a new social, political, and economic gold standard, occupying by its very nature some stable ground shared between the public and private spheres. It was this ground that Richardson's narratives helped define.

Faced with memories of the Jacobites, and thus of a breakdown of consensus within their political narratives, British Protestant writers defined a unifying principle to stabilize the private and public spheres and the relations between them. As these mostly Anglican writers presented it, British society was the product of an ongoing natural history rather than a concluded biblical teleology. Philosophers such as Hume, in the *Treatise of Human Nature* (1739–40) and *Essays, Moral, Political, and Literary* (1741–58), and Smith, in the *Theory of Moral Sentiments* (1759), produced a moralized physiology of the British community, making virtuous sentiment at once the natural origin and the ideal model of social order. This universal, natural form of feeling, with its empirically predictable circulation through the processes of sympathy mapped and theorized by Hume and Smith, together comprised what Eagleton has characterized as a "law of the heart."[18] Thus in the philosophy of social order and of political history after mid-century, sentiment replaced the Jacobite first cause of divine election as well as the surprisingly similar divine first cause that, for Locke and his followers, had created the intrinsic rights and the necessary heterosexual impulses and duties of human nature. At the same time, as claims for "typical" human character replaced the generalizations of biblical history, the turn to second causes compensated for the unpredictability of real events by insisting on the invariable laws of human nature that lay beneath them. Above all, philosophers turned for their illustrations and guarantees of social order from the political to the economic arena, where private traits rather than public consensus could be said to provide a coherent, lawful base for Britain's admittedly fluid, even fractious society.[19] Political economy, in short, took up its social role where theoretical political history had left off. But although Hume and Smith theorized that shared sentiments were the motive of all human action, assuring a consistent theoretical base for a political economy otherwise all too apparently at the mercy of individual caprice, the events of recent history remained incapable of proving their claim. The gap dividing their theory from real history is also the "want" outlined in the *Pamela* prefaces. It demanded the supplement of an explicitly British genre that could simultaneously illustrate and inculcate the sentiment theorized in the new political economic philosophy.

That genre, I will argue, is romance. The claim needs a brief caveat, for romance, which remains notoriously difficult to define, was by the end of the 1740s often used baldly to indicate all that "the novel" was not.[20] As McKeon has shown, genre labels for fiction had become unstable, so that "romance," "true" and "secret history," and "novel" – which had once meant, and have since come again to mean, distinct, even historically successive kinds – were often used interchangeably.[21] The fluidity of labels is, arguably, the mark of a wider kind of generic fluidity, in which genres were in flux both in their definitions and in the dynamic expansion and shrinkage of their borders. To discriminate some conventions and transformations of mid-eighteenth-century romance, therefore, is not necessarily to accept McKeon's view that romance had by 1740 hardened into a category unbreakably tied to aristocratic and conservative ideologies.[22] The conventions of Richardson's fiction were recognizable to contemporary readers because he explicitly revised and responded to recent works that were often named "romances" and never called "novels," as well as to the political historical works that informed them.[23] The "true and secret histories," as Ros Ballaster demonstrates, were written mostly by Tory women with visible political aims.[24] Yet when these writers invoked Locke's justifications of the 1688 Revolution in order to counter them, they laid the foundation for reflections on Whig political history, such as Richardson's romances, whose writers sought rather to supplement or succeed than to oppose. Richardson's works share with the secret histories a treatment of courtship at once intimately and sentimentally detailed and socially resonant, the result of a generic mingling of fiction with political tracts. Both he and the secret historians mark their plots, conflicts, and characters as moral, political, economic, or national exemplars. The significance of their romances is private and public both at once.

Occupying a generic bridge between politics and fiction, Richardson's romance eases the ideological transition of Protestant Britain as it traded creation mythography for metonymy, vesting social order and authority in avowedly representative examples of the human heart. At the same time, his narratives help usher the theoretical justifications of British social order into the economic arena by demonstrating on the levels of form and its readerly consumption as well as of plot the workings of private invariables to unify an economically and socially chaotic Britain. In its presentations of sentiment, romance thus provides the missing economic, ethical, and literary "standard" heralded in the

Pamela prefaces: it supplies Britain's lack. This nationally remedial role places Richardson's fictions in the vanguard of new liberal justifications of Britain's social order and radical revisions of the genre of romance. Yet the same faults in the Protestant consensus that demanded the reconditioned genre continually threatened to undermine it, exposing the contingency or coercions of its ideology of sentiment. By redefining romance for mid-eighteenth-century Britain, Richardson produced what would become, increasingly explicitly, a generic battleground for critics of liberal ideology and Whig justifications of authority, in the eighteenth century and after.

THE GOLD STANDARD AND THE THREAT OF THE PARTICULAR: LOCKE, HAYWOOD, RICHARDSON

The practical workings of Richardson's sentimental gold standard are traceable in the techniques that shaped his audiences to the demands of political economy, and in the alacrity with which his readers responded, at least at first. The letter Sarah Fielding sent on first reading *Clarissa* in 1749, and its intertextual entanglement with Richardson's text, exemplifies the force of this shaping. "When I read of" Clarissa, Fielding wrote, "I am all sensation; my heart glows; I am overwhelmed; my only vent is tears; and unless tears could mark my thoughts as legibly as ink, I cannot speak half I feel."[25] This emotional shorthand has since become cliché – sympathetic speechlessness and tears are the distinguishing marks of eighteenth-century sentiment – and it is likely that Fielding's anatomy of response would have seemed theatrical even to a late-eighteenth-century reader.[26] But it is one of the contentions of this book that the theatricality modern readers associate with sentiment is itself the eighteenth-century product of parodic critiques of Richardson's fiction and its complicity with political economy. Moreover, the conventions Fielding marshals take on new significance when they are read through her double status as reader and writer. This role appears not only in the breathy immediacy of her encounter with *Clarissa* ("written," like Richardson's texts, "to the moment"), but also in the fact that Fielding is herself the writer of fictions influenced by Richardson. Her posture replicates the dual role of the disparate letter-writers whose productions make up the text of *Clarissa* as they engage in moral comment and critique and, by the narrative's end, come emotionally together. In the quasi-private, semi-public exchange that develops among Richardson, Fielding, and other readers, a model community

shaped by shared feeling is enacted in response to Richardson's sentimental text.

A modern reader will suspect that Fielding's form and content have
been carefully orchestrated, and they have indeed been shaped – not
only by the function of letters within *Clarissa*, but also by the use
Richardson makes of his composite, epistolary texts. Their form, the
sentimental letter gone public, had been singled out and developed by
Richardson soon after writing *Pamela*. In the Prefaces to that earlier
work, Richardson publicizes his private letters of congratulation for a
purpose at once moral and commercial – that is, a political economic
purpose. In *Pamela . . . In Her Exalted Condition*, his 1742 sequel, the
heroine mimes Richardson's ways of circulating "her" epistolary text.
In drawing rooms and at dinner tables, Pamela advertises her intent to
print and bind her letters and her reflections on them – the text of *Pamela*
– offering each reader "one side of the Leaf blank for your Corrections
and Alterations."[27] Richardson himself had already bound several interleaved editions of *Pamela* and his other works, which he bestowed on the
country baronet's wife Lady Bradshaigh, the poet Edward Young, and
the teenaged daughters of his friend Aaron Hill, encouraging their
return to him with each reader's handwritten comments interspersed.[28]
He also published a *Collection of the Moral and Instructive Sentiments* (1755)
extracted from his fictions, boasting of their "material . . . use for the
conduct of life and manners."[29] His romances assume a shaping force in
the literary public sphere; he is imitated by his heroines and so by his
readers. The homogeneous sentiments that circulate sympathetically
through his relatively heterogeneous literary community provide a
proof and model of what Hume and Smith theorized about the political
economic operations of British society.

This cultural authority is granted only in retrospect, however, and
Fielding's proud exposition of "glows" and "tears" wholly differs from
the behaviour of Clarissa herself. The pre-Jacobite, pre-Humean heroine, lacking the cultural authority of Richardson's *Clarissa* – necessarily
incomplete, for she is herself engaged in writing it – does her best to
deny the "*throbs* and *glows*" that Fielding sees and mimics.[30] *Clarissa*
makes sentiment respectable, indeed desirable: Richardson shapes a
market for the sentiment he purveys. The recognition is a reminder of
the commercial entanglements of sentimental ideology. Equally, it testifies to Richardson's skillful selling of his text and of the homogenizing
ideology of sentiment that it produces and by which it is demanded.

Among the striking consequences of Richardson's shaping of a reading market are the predictability of the response he required and the willingness of readers to give it. With *Clarissa*, Richardson united Whig- and Tory-leaning, court and country, commercial, leisured, clerical, female, and male writers in assimilating virtue to sentiment and so to natural law. Thus as Fielding paraded her moralized bodily reactions to a work itself discreetly fraught with such reactions, Samuel Johnson circulated a paean to the social utility and moral worth of such sentiment, despite his own Toryism, pronounced enough to raise Jacobite suspicions, his hostility to Humean second causes, and his ambivalence toward romance.[31] In a *Rambler* essay of 1750, Johnson remarked that "Our passions are . . . strongly moved" by narrative sympathy: "we . . . adopt the pains or pleasure proposed . . . by recognising them as once our own." But only a narrative of "domestick privacies, and the minute details of daily life" can so move its readers:

Histories of the downfall of kingdoms, and revolutions of empires are read . . . tranquilly . . . the imperial tragedy pleases common auditors only by its pomp of ornament, and grandeur of ideas; and the man whose faculties have been engrossed by business, and whose heart never fluttered but at the rise and fall of stocks, wonders how the attention can be seized, or the affection agitated by a tale of love.[32]

The narrative of private sentiment, fictional or otherwise, is especially necessary, Johnson claims, in a world whose factions and commerce insulate citizens from one another and from the traditional public discourses of history and political philosophy. Johnson elsewhere exhorts readers to "read [Richardson] for the sentiment."[33] Like Fielding's letter, his essay assists Richardson in bringing the social importance of private sentiment to light. It is perhaps attributable to Johnson's role in Richardson's sentimental community that even the country conservative Bradshaigh, who in 1748 asked "the meaning of the word *sentimental*, so much in vogue amongst the polite," complaining that "every thing clever and agreeable is comprehended" in a word "so common," became the recipient of an interleaved *Clarissa*. She responded with copious notes and tears.[34]

The marketing of sentiment in *Clarissa*'s epistolary exchanges points to an ideological difference between Richardson's practice in *Clarissa* and in *Pamela*. The contrast is only partly concealed by the "Editor's" Preface to *Pamela*, in which Richardson makes an "Appeal from *his own* Passions" to "the Passions of *Every* one who shall read" it (*P*1 3). The sentimentalizing puff provides an odd gateway into a plot that famously banishes the desires of its heroine to lurk half-recognized around the edges of the text and treats the passions of its hero as immoral and politically corrupt. An audibly and sometimes explicitly intertextual work, *Pamela* illustrates a conception of social order derived from Locke, for whom "God-given reason" was the motive guiding virtuous behaviour, rather than from Hume's emphasis on natural passion or his foundation of social order on sympathetic sentiment. In contrast, the Preface, written after the narrative text, hints at the influence of Hume, whose account of sentiment and sympathy in his philosophical *Treatise* and political economic *Essays* did not begin to appear until *Pamela* was nearly complete. Nevertheless, the "passion" that the Lockean conclusion to *Pamela* proudly terms "unreasonable" "Deformity" is transformed, in a Preface that echoes Hume's *Treatise*, into a source of moral improvement (*P1* 410). *Clarissa* intervenes in the mid-century crisis of legitimacy in British Protestant political economy, whereas *Pamela*, largely written before the legitimacy crisis, was completed, prefaced, and sequelled as it began. The survivals of Lockean political history in *Clarissa* are attributed, as we will see, to the heroine's ethical traditionalism. In contrast, the romance of *Pamela* is hybridized not only, as in *Clarissa*, by the generic cooperation of romance with political philosophy, but also by the competing genealogies of social order in Lockean and Humean politics.

Thus although *Pamela*'s first critics praise Richardson for providing a bullion standard for Britain and its fictions, the genre does not itself yet demonstrate that standard, nor does it model the responses enacted in Fielding's reading of *Clarissa*. The readers' ways of promoting Richardson's first romance, like his own preface to it, mark the changing conditions in the literary field. Richardson wrote *Pamela* during a period of more vociferous polemics but, paradoxically, of greater ideological calm. In the 1730s no sentimental standard – no alternative to Lockean political history – was required among Hanoverian supporters. The Lockean order was contested by Tories, but their disruptive power seemed limited to debate. Locke's was, as Joyce Appleby argues, the standard discourse of early eighteenth-century urban Whiggism, which had already reached its Hanoverian- and market-oriented consensus.[35] What *Pamela* provided, therefore, in its triumphal account of God-given reason defeating aristocratic corruption, was a supplement to Locke's political history that illustrated the applicability of Locke's general theological claims to particular private families and so helped Whig arguments hold their own against Tory critiques.

What was desirable, above all, was a kind of romance that could stand against a series of protofeminist Tory romances that had attacked the theocentric history of Lockean political narrative. Aphra Behn, De-larivière Manley, and Eliza Haywood in particular contested Locke's political history by transporting his universalized narrative of natural rights and necessary authority into the most individuated domestic situations, threading his narratives through theirs and exposing the jarring gaps between the particular instances detailed in their own texts and Locke's generalizing claims. Their romances cooperated with the Tory and "country"-Whig discourse of civic republicanism and, even more than these explicitly political rhetorics, helped render human passion politically and socially suspect.[36] What was needed to answer their "true and secret histories" was a generic blend of domestic rights with social authority and their discourses, a mixture that resembled their romances as faithfully as their romances translated the narrative moments in Locke – but one that rendered the irruptions of passion irrelevant.

Bolstering Locke's authority was particularly desirable because the symmetry between Locke's Whiggish history of authority and Filmer's Tory one promised to advance the incipient Hanoverian rapprochement between their followers. For although *Two Treatises of Government* opened a rhetorical gulf between "Political" and "Paternal Power," often read as a rigorous separation of domestic and familial from political authority, Locke limited "political authority" to the "Right of making Laws" and the forceful defence of the polity against domestic or foreign rebellion.[37] "Political and Paternal" forms of authority are "perfectly distinct and separate," Locke argued, but his proof undermines their distinction:

every Subject that is a Father, has as much a Paternal Power over his Children, as the Prince has over his. And every Prince that has Parents owes them as much filial Duty and Obedience as the meanest of his Subjects do to theirs. (*T*2 314)[38]

Locke does not deny the authority of the *paterfamilias* in the household or in society, but advances that authority by extending it from the cottage to the palace. His differences with Filmer nearly disappear when the subjection of women is considered. Filmer had argued that "patriarchal" rights extend from the created relation between fathers and sons to the ties of king and subject. But Locke's paternal authority is gendered rather than generational in character. It is derived by a process of historical necessity from the created superiority of the biblical Adam to Eve and therefore from the innate superiority of all subsequent males, "as the abler and the stronger," to all females, by which means masculine authority is perpetually and "naturally" reconstituted (*T*2 321). God does not mandate Eve's subordination, Locke suggests, yet Eve's created character leads inexorably to her subjection: "God . . . foretels . . . how by his Providence he would order it so, that she should be subject to her husband, as we see generally the Laws of Mankind and customs of Nations have ordered it so; and there is . . . a Foundation in Nature for it."[39] Thus Locke's theoretical genealogy of masculine authority is also a theocentric affirmation of the existing socioeconomic order.

Such a generalizing narrative was especially vulnerable to critiques mounted from a perspective shaped by gender. To pose unanswerable questions to Locke's theoretical social history of Britain it was only necessary to produce counter-narratives illustrating particular cases of masculine weakness, or of feminine strength, willfulness, or rebellion, within particular British families. Haywood's "true, secret history" of *The Mercenary Lover* (1726), for example, mingling narrative whispers and transcribed letters with political and legal commentary, exposes what Haywood claims are the motivating passions of certain ambitious businessmen and genteel heiresses, presented under pastoral aliases. Desire for the married Clitander, a "Trader" in "the metropolitan City of this Island," overcomes the "Principles of Virtue" guiding his ward, the "extreamly cautious" young heiress Althea.[40] Clitander, meanwhile, has an equally disruptive ruling passion. He aims to gain Althea's fortune as well as her sister Miranda's, and he has already taken the first steps toward consolidating their resources by marrying Miranda – hence his guardianship of Althea. Unlike her sister, Miranda is a Lockean woman, who begins on her marriage "to dress, look, speak, and act in every Thing as became a Person of the Station she had taken on her" (11). But the ingrained submission she shares with Locke's Eve is undercut by Clitander's answering "Passion for the Enjoyment of her Wealth" – an ironic rewriting of the socioeconomic authority of the Lockean *paterfamilias* – and by Althea's destructive "Passion" for Clitander (19). Evident in this narrative, as in the related incest-and-politics plot of Behn's *Love-Letters between a Nobleman and his Sister* (1685), is the coincidence of sexual and financial desire – "the two worst Passions of deprav'd Humanity" – as disruptive forces inherent in private and so in social life (17).[41] Both romances challenge Locke's, in which all family life, and society, begins with rational interest and affection that can be tracked along empirically predictable paths. At the same time, the incest on which Haywood centres her narrative, as Clitander marries one sister and impregnates the other, roots the passions that overthrow natural law in the heart of the family, the source of all Lockean social order and authority.

In answering Behn and Haywood, Richardson reshaped romance and so revised its relations with intertexts in political history. *Pamela* retained the focus on private, heterosexual domestic life, and especially on the process of courtship, that had formed the point of contest between Locke's political history and its Tory romance critiques. But Richardson's new narrative made universal instead of particular claims for its presentations of family narrative, and it allowed virtue to emerge triumphant from domestic and sexual battles instead of being exposed as lascivious and corrupt. His romance inhabited the anti-Lockean romance of Haywood and Behn, dialectically transforming it in ways concordant with Lockean ideology. Famously centred on the "virtue" of the young servant Pamela Andrews in rejecting the many advances made by her employer, the rakish Mr. B, *Pamela* "rewards" its heroine with marriage, social advancement, and the management of her aristocratic husband's "Family Oeconomy" (*P1* 226). As the central location of Richardson's romance and thus as the meeting place of fiction and political history, the "Family Oeconomy" is also the intersection, as for Haywood and Locke, of the public and private spheres. Pamela's "reward" is the product of B's equation of her public value with private virtue: her prize is as much ideological as social and sexual. What Richardson names "virtue" is his heroine's dogged attachment, upheld by her horror of class miscegenation, to the conventions of her social and gender position. Pamela's fidelity to the existing hierarchies she believes to be God-given is the quality that through Richardson's dialectical irony fits her for a rise in rank and power. It allows Richardson to confirm the general rule of social hierarchy and domestic authority precisely by allowing – as Behn and Haywood allowed – the particular instance to subvert it.

Pamela's triumph not only justifies the existing social order, but also sets aside B's corrupt power as the product of an irrational passion that is readily overcome. The romance of *Pamela*, like Locke's account of civil society, allows passion to interfere with social order only so long as it can stand against God-given reason and virtue – which is to say, not long. Richardson's narrative begins in a domestic disarray reminiscent of Haywood's before moving with an unstoppable logic to establish the natural order Richardson, like Locke, ascribes to domestic and heterosexual relations. It is the logic of romance itself that upholds Pamela's virtue against B's passion, reassuring readers that political power and rank are, in the end, legitimate public expressions of virtue; that even in the apparently radical case of Pamela's dramatic social rise an unseen hand sets in motion, and maintains, the order of British society. Romance transforms class confusion, already marked as an instability caused by aberrant circumstance, into the exception that confirms divine rule. To say that the central struggle in *Pamela* is ruled by romance is to express in generic terms the providential rule on which Locke's political theory is based, and to which Pamela's success, in turn, is subject. *Pamela* does not create a new socioeconomic ideal, but legitimates, in Richardson's romance of necessity, the origins of Britain's social order.

PAMELA'S NECESSARY ORDER: BRITISH ROMANCE AND TORY CORRUPTION

The necessitarian romance of *Pamela* unfolds through cooperating processes of generic competition and genre history, but it is by means of a nationalist – and Francophobic – polemic that Richardson renders its endpoint natural and inevitable. The outcome of his narrative leaves his readers with an unshakeable sense that God and right reason are on Britain's side, and are therefore in support of the present constitution. Transforming the generic debate into a battle between British virtue and foreign corruption, he impugns the Tories and their romances as tools of a French subversion of British order. Not only does he counter Haywood and Behn by reclaiming their generic ground, but he also assails the legitimacy of their hold on it by demonstrating their bad English – their failure to read and write British romance properly, whether Richardson's, Pamela's, or their own.

The narrative begins with a crisis of authority and a debate on its legitimacy. The benevolent dowager Lady B, Pamela's employer, has died and her son, Mr. B, has returned from his travels to assume his majority and the control of his inheritance. Richardson precipitates heroine and reader into the immediate aftermath of the death, a period of extreme uncertainty in the aristocratic household now headed by her son. The temporarily masterless Pamela is the central register of this uncertainty. She is caught, as mid-eighteenth-century Britain is caught, between two "rulers" with divergent accounts of the origin and justification of their rule. The battle between servant and master that follows, taking up most of the plot and narration of the novel, is a struggle to reconcile Pamela's intrinsic worth, as Richardson and Lady B establish it, with the social value the powerful B is willing to grant her, and with legitimate social authority. Richardson's romance plot may thus be read as a contest between competing conceptions of Britain's social order and their ways of reconciling absolute with social worth.

Although the rival claims to authority in *Pamela* centre on household government, they are strongly identified, rhetorically and generically, with particular positions in the contemporary debate on political order and its history. Lady B argues that domestic virtue, including charity, chastity, marriage, and religious observance, is both a divine injunction and the only source of order in British society. Hers is an assertion associated with Locke, but it is also rendered traditional and legitimate by becoming a bequest to her son along with his more material inheritance. The competing view is upheld by the young B himself, who clings to it doggedly for most of the novel. His exaggerated mixture of rakishness and obsession with inherited rank and the public display of its symbols ironically recasts the corrupt desires of Haywood's city Whig trader, Clitander, as the sexual and economic self-interest of a quasi-Jacobite country Tory. Despite B's youth, that is, Richardson dismisses B's troublesome claims as an anachronistic delusion, to be exposed as the corruption wrought by a foreign education.

When the very young B returns to Britain to inherit his estate, his lingering affinity with France associates him with the absolutism of the *ancien régime* – and thus with the French "Levities" that the *Pamela* prefaces urge British romance to amend (*P1* 5). Looking back on his Frenchified self, the mature B recalls that having "dress'd, [he] grew more and more confident, and became . . . insolent withal, [having] . . . but too much [his] Way with every body" (*P2* III: 189–90). His affection for power based on birth and deportment heralds Adam Smith's portrait of Louis XIV as "the most perfect model of a great [hereditary] prince":

what were the talents and virtues by which he acquired this great reputation? . . . It was by none of these qualities. But . . . "he surpassed all his courtiers in the gracefulness of his shape, and the majestic beauty of his features . . . He had a step and a deportment which could suit only him and his rank" . . . Knowledge, industry, valour, and beneficence, trembled, were abashed, and lost all dignity.[42]

In the early stages of the narrative, B embodies what Habermas calls the "representative publicness" of an absolute monarch, enacting what he is convinced is a divinely ordained and unshakeable bond between a king's (or aristocrat's) body natural and the body politic he rules.[43] Such a powerful figure effectively has no private being, for his presence, power, and worth are inextricably tangled up together. His rule, at the same time, is above the law, and transcends all expectations for his behaviour. But B's politics and his domestic actions simultaneously echo the Stuart notion, expounded by Filmer and rebutted by Locke, that royal right, of which every man's household authority is a legitimate domestic type, descends from an absolute rule granted in Genesis to Adam – a right independent of virtue, irrevocable even after the Fall.[44] In portraying B's domestic politics, Richardson collapses positions typical of Jacobite Toryism with those of French absolutism, making the influence of the last responsible for the errors of the first. That neither can stand for long against the influence of Pamela's virtue suggests at once the inevitable effects of intrinsic feminine virtue on society, and the ease with which acquired foreign corruption can be overcome by British nature and the romance that conveys it.

Richardson does not deny that a significant faction among Britain's landowners shares B's Franco-Jacobite political beliefs: he is explicit in equating that rural ideology some historians have considered as a bipartisan "country" interest with the kinds of passion Haywood and Behn represent, and thus with the Jacobite authority he himself rejects.[45] His treatment of B's Lincolnshire neighbourhood supports Clark's claims about the sizable influence of Jacobite Toryism, and Richardson is himself, insofar as he sympathizes with Lockean history, embroiled in an ideology campaign against a substantial group of British Tories.[46] But, like Locke, he casts his opponents – however dangerous, however many – as the unfortunate victims of a miseducation that is necessarily foreign in origin. Although Locke acknowledged that Britons had sometimes failed to conform with the theory of "natural" virtue and authority he outlined in the *Treatises*, he also argued, in his *Essay Concerning Human Understanding* (1685), that the virtue God bestowed survives only in those "least corrupted by Custom, or borrowed Opinions," or "foreign and studied Doctrines," which erase the "fair Characters Nature had written."[47] His claim may assist Richardson to demonstrate that B falls from virtue only because his French education has taught him to misuse authority at home. Richardson positions B and his Tory neighbours, and thus the Tory romances he rewrites, within what Whig political philosophers from Locke to Thomas Paine saw as an exotic disease sending threads of decay through the native moral fibre of England.[48]

In *Pamela*, the squires of Lincolnshire are all country Tories. All uphold the absolutism that Richardson brands artificial and corrupt in B himself. Once reformed, B fears being "deem'd a *Whig*" by his neighbours for endorsing Locke's doctrine that kings, like their subjects, are subject to the law (*P1* 336). But he has nothing to fear in his unreformed days, as he tries to seduce Pamela, for his neighbours readily uphold the fence he erects dividing his family's magistracy, parliamentary seat, and authority in the church, from his private moral failings. Indeed, Pamela despairs, "All the Gentlemen about are as bad as he," and all "keep Company . . . with our fine master" (*P1* 72). Like Haywood's and Behn's Whigs, Richardson's Tories are careless disrupters of private families.⁴⁹ This ironic reordering of Tory romance extends self-reflexively to Richardson's own construction of a narrative and readership, for B and his neighbours initially misread, and fail to make use of, Pamela's – and Richardson's – romance. As their domestic conduct predicts, and as Pamela herself fears from the start, they favour a reading of Pamela's letters that supports B's authority and detaches it from virtue. "What is all this," says Sir Simon Darnford, whose help Pamela begs, "but that the 'Squire our Neighbour has a mind to his Mother's Waiting-maid? . . . He hurts no Family by this" (*P1* 122). B's neighbours read his pursuit of Pamela as a purely private event that requires no notice until, at length, it leads to a cross-class marriage with Pamela, which they see as a transgression of the established order of the neighbourhood and country.

On this ground of B's "family oeconomy," invoked only to be dismissed by Darnford, Richardson establishes the crucial distinction between his Lockean Whigs and his Lincolnshire Tories – and, by extension, caricatures such Stuart apologists as Haywood and Behn. It is only to the Tories that B's "family" is a purely legal institution for the transfer of rank and property. For Lady B has long since, during B's stay in France, transformed the meaning of "family" to reflect Locke's theological and political historical definition. B indeed harms "a family" by pursuing Pamela, and that family is his own. Good kings, says Locke, are "nursing Fathers tender and carefull of the publick weale" – their domestic virtue motivating their successful political rule (*T2* 342). In turn, the dying Lady B warns her son, "I hope my *Pamela* would not be in Danger from her Master, who owes to all his Servants Protection, as much as a King does to his Subjects" (*P2* III: 204). It is under such an influence that Pamela, on the morning after B's first seduction attempt, is confident in "the Concerns and Wishes of the Family" (*P1* 68).

That the family is at the very heart and source of Richardson's, as of Locke's, British social order, and that it is at once vulnerable to French attack and immune to destruction by it, appears in the converted B's frequent references to the broadly social role of a British *paterfamilias*. An unvirtuous head of household, he declares, in the most Lockean terms, is "ruinous in the End to the whole Publick, in which his own Private is included" (*P2* III: 107). In contrast, his imperious early complaint that Pamela's "Letter-writing of all the Secrets of my Family" has been "injurious to my Honour and Reputation" (*P1* 74, 90), and has made "a Strange Racket in my Family" (*P1* 92), not only misrepresents the private and public role of the British family, but also misconceives the British romance with which Richardson seeks to regulate it. Like Darnford, that is, B consistently places Pamela's letters in the wrong literary and political contexts. Both men's errors confuse the relations between romance and Britain's social order.

What B does share with Richardson, and with Pamela, is a sense of the considerable social weight wielded by Richardson's own romance, and by the letter-writing Pamela within it. B attacks Pamela by constraining her power to write, but Richardson's subduing of B, as McKeon and Nancy Armstrong in particular have noted, is equally founded on limiting the ways of reading and writing he initially represents.[50] When B condemns the letters in which Pamela desperately reveals his bids to enforce the *droit du seigneur*, damning them as "treasonable Papers," he reads her protests through his French absolutist misconceptions, so that what to her is an unjust attack and an unjustifiable mixing of classes appears to him to be a master's inherent right (*P1* 199). At length, however, her letters influence him to rethink his asserted power, not as a right of his noble birth, but as a failing in social order. To B, the letters prove the universal influence of the natural traits outlined in Locke's political history. His conversion takes place in a series of paired scenes that contrast his early, "tyrant's" view of household events with his later desire to read these events in Lockean terms, assimilating Pamela's appearance, her exchange-value, to her use-value and her virtue. On first seeing Pamela in the peasant costume she puts on to mark her independence of him, he accuses her of social and sexual pretension: "you . . . disguise yourself, to attract me . . . like an Hypocrite as you are" (*P1* 62). But by the end of the book, he parades Pamela in her pastoral clothes before his neighbours, eager to ensure their conformity with his new ways of reading. He has come to insist that Pamela, like *Pamela*, be read as heroine and author demand: as a narrative testimonial, like his own conversion, to the weight of Pamela's (Lockean) virtue (*P1* 62).

More crucial still is B's changed approach to Pamela's letters. He initially views these documents as Haywood's Clitander and Behn's

Silvia read their own and their lovers' correspondence: as mannered
and public artefacts rather than elements in romance, inseparable parts
of a genre that intervenes between political history and private narrative, social order and family life. Resenting Pamela's letters as treason-
ous, he refers to the borders they breach between domestic intimacy
and political significance: "so I am to be exposed, *in* my House, and *out*
of my House, to the whole World, by such a Sawcebox as you?" (*P*1 41).
Yet his final "tyranny" is to take the hidden letters from her, furthering
Richardson's hybridization of generic conventions:

> it is my Opinion they are about you; and I never undrest a Girl in my Life; but I
> will now begin to strip my pretty *Pamela*; and hope I shall not go far, before I
> find them.
>   I fell a crying, and said, I will not be used in this Manner. Pray, Sir, said I, (for
> he began to unpin my Handkerchief) consider! Pray, Sir, do! – And pray, said
> he, do *you* consider. For I will see these Papers. But may-be, said he, they are
> ty'd about your Knees with your Garters, and stooped. (*P*1 204)

His old oath – "by G-d I will have her!" (*P*1 64) – yields to the new: "I
will see these Papers" (*P*1 204). Tyranny turns to earnest interpretation
in mid-grope, revealing B's new understanding of political authority as
the legitimate product only of a God-given private morality. By the end
of the book, B is circulating Pamela's narrative to his friends to educate
them in virtue, and it is he, like Richardson himself, who encourages her
to have the letters bound. The impassioned will to power is overcome by
a will to take part in a Lockean interpretation of courtship and family
life, and self-display in dazzling French dress gives way yet again to a
public rendition of Pamela's virtue.[51]

  Yet it is not Pamela's will as expressed in her bound letters, it is crucial
to note, that conquers B and his neighbourhood, improving Britain
estate by estate (*P*2 III: 52, IV: 228). A Lockean wife has no will, but
naturally assumes her husband's as her own. Before her marriage,
therefore, Pamela willingly gives in to B's sexual-textual threat – not by
submitting to be stripped, but by bringing him the letters he demands.
And B's friends praise the married Pamela's lack of self-will in Lockean
terms: "You have your own Will in every thing," they tell her, "Because
you make your own Will his" (*P*2 IV: 2). Even so, Richardson emphasizes
the effect of letters on "will" in B's conversion. Locke argues in his *Essay
Concerning Human Understanding* that virtue and corruption equally employ the receptive human will, and in yielding her will to B, Pamela
expects that romance will reform him with its unconquerable "Effect
upon your Temper . . . in my Favour" (Locke, *Essay* 252–7, 281–2; *P*1

207). B himself declares that his marriage to Pamela is "so much the Act of my own Will, that I glory in being capable of distinguishing so much Excellence" (*P1* 283). Richardson's romance divorces B's will from corruption (read Filmerite Toryism) and realigns it with virtue (or Locke's necessitarian history), and thus with Pamela herself. Pamela makes a "Convert" of B only to the degree that her letters realign his vitiated will with what she, with Richardson, insists is his own intrinsic nature.[52]

Lockean family values prevail as Locke himself insisted they must, but they also conform with the logic of romance as Richardson writes it. *Pamela* dialectically inverts the Tory romances of Haywood and Behn, denaturing the "natural" passions they attribute to their scandalous characters and universalizing the Lockean domestic order they dismiss as anomalous, deceptive, or impossible. In this way, Richardson brings romance back to Locke. In holding out even for a moment, however, B and his Tory neighbours call the inevitability of Locke's consensus into question. Their resistance, and the passions that motivate it, herald the Jacobite crisis of 1745–6, and produce the ideological unease audible in the sentimental prefaces to *Pamela*, and visible in their three-way generic hybrid.

THE PROBLEM OF LOCKEAN REASON: FROM PASSION TO SENTIMENT

To suggest that the memory of B's Tory dissent shadows the restorative conclusion of *Pamela* is to identify the problem that passion – in Tory fiction, and later in Jacobite polemic and action – poses for Locke's history of Britain's social order, as well as for the triumph of "virtue" in Richardson's romance. That Richardson increasingly confronted the resulting instability in the British community appears from the sequel, in which the "reformed" B's marriage to Pamela is repeatedly disrupted by his desire for other women. But the problem of passion was not confined to Richardson or romance. The events of *Pamela . . . in her Exalted Condition*, already foreshadowed in the haunted closure of *Pamela; or Virtue Rewarded*, reproduce what J. G. A. Pocock calls the crucial political debate of early-eighteenth-century Britain: a clash between "virtue" and "commerce," which not all participants regarded in Richardson's partisan political terms. Although Pocock does not explicitly address the heterosexual dimension of "commerce," or the association between commerce and femininity that Laura Brown, in particular, identifies, he argues that members of a growing "court" commercial interest promoted the dictates of feeling, or the fulfillment of personal desire, as a source of pleasure and a means to socioeconomic progress.[53] Rural landholders, in contrast, who advocated classical republican ideology, insisted that desire caused corruption, and promoted the virtue of *civitas* above the wants of the self.[54] According to Pocock, Locke's political history is marginal to these debates. Where political comment unites with private emotional description, however – in romance and in the feminized domestic "virtue" of Richardson's title – their union has little to do with *virtus* and everything to do with Locke. As Richardson ironically inverts classical republican rhetoric in *Pamela*, the "virtue" he pits against passion expresses neither civic manliness nor its associated traits, right reason and stoicism. It inaugurates his realignment of Whig anti-Jacobitism with proper feeling and with Britain's unity. Moving between publicity and privacy and the changing genres associated with each, Pamela's virtue, like Richardson's romance, provides a battleground for ideologies of social order that were simultaneously competing and evolving.

It was in part because of the Tory romances *Pamela* answered that feeling was suspect in early-eighteenth-century political thought, and that it was so often arrayed against virtue. Such popularizers of Lockean morality as the conduct writer Richard Allestree, a favourite of Henry Fielding's "Shamela," insisted that Britain's "Estate . . . hangs on private families, the little Monarchies . . . composing and giving law unto the great," and "the disposall of Families and all Domestic concerns therein lies chiefly on the Wife."[55] Women's role as *aides de camp* to domestic patriarchs meant that if their passions failed to conform to masculine expectations and authority, the political history recounted by Locke and Allestree would fall apart. The lines of authority in families would be exposed as arbitrary, the Hanoverian crown would be forced to stand without historical aid, and the British social order would be without legitimate bases. Thus although the unrestrained feminine desires depicted in Behn's "secret histories" provoked distasteful memories of the courts of Charles II and James II, whose Stuart reigns had needed no popular legitimation, they were strategically dismissed rather than rebutted by critics. Whether Haywood was a fair prize in the urinating contest in Pope's *Dunciad*, and whether Behn lived the "licentious" life described in Clara Reeve's *Progress of Romance*, are tangential to the point of such claims. Because Behn and Haywood had depicted the natural passion of particular women in order to disprove the universality of Locke's political history, their romances were best countered by biographies that represented their fictions as anomalous, short-lived outgrowths of the female writers' own unnaturalness or monstrosity.[56]

Richardson's predatory Tories have their rakish ancestry in Behn's *Love-Letters*, in which passion appears as the most dangerous of Whiggism's many destructive forces. Behn's *roman à clef* is an unusual secret history with referents in the real Whig family of Ford Lord Grey and intertexts in the records of Grey's trial for seducing his sister-in-law, Lady Henrietta Berkeley.[57] In this cautionary romance, passion is masculine in origin but spreads to infect Behn's heroine, her home, and Britain as a whole, corrupting them and countering Locke's claim that female virtue and submission inevitably characterize the post-lapsarian polity and the British family. Silvia elopes with Philander, the friend and supporter of Cesario (a veiled Duke of Monmouth) in his rebellion against his father and king. Philander insists, his pious Lockean speech marking his hypocrisy, that it "shocks ones Nature to find a Son engag'd against a Father."[58] His political and sexual passion easily override the Whig principles he continues to declare. The results extend to his own family life as well as the king's, causing gender indeterminacy and ambiguous sexuality of a kind that Locke deems to be impossible. Seduced, Philander's wife's sister transforms herself into his nephew or son, cross-dressing to elope without attracting her father's notice, but also in large part because of Philander's pleasure in her boyish appearance. She becomes a female rake, beginning with an affair (according to trial records, historical) with Philander's valet, "without Controul, forgetting all Respect of Persons or of Place" (Behn 161). Ceremonially cutting her ties to virtue, she laments her seduction in a Tory rhetoric that upholds Behn's narration and echoes Filmer's *Patriarcha* as well:

> how dreadful is the Scene of my first Debauch, and how glorious that never to be regain'd Prospect of my Virgin Innocence, where I sate inthron'd in awful Virtue . . . 'till thou, O Tyrant Love, with a charming Usurpation invaded all my Glories . . . which I resign'd with greater Pride and Joy than a young Monarch puts 'em on. (Behn 158)

Whiggism produces feminine passion and political disruption – twin perils categorically excluded from the Lockean political history Behn's Whigs espouse. In the wake of Berkeley's elopement and Behn's *Love-Letters*, the threat of what Carole Pateman names "the disorder of women" became a weighty argument against the Lockean Whig consensus and the 1688 Revolution and Hanoverian succession it upheld.[59]

In an echo of *Love-Letters* that marks a contrast to it, Richardson's Pamela, unlike Silvia, is resolute about "person" and "Place," as the prefaces re-emphasize (*P1* 5, 25). Although B's seduction attempts are infinitely cruder than Philander's, Pamela's resistance to them is motivated less by outraged virginity than by horror at B's decreasing "the Distance that Fortune has made between us" (*P1* 35). Thus Pamela's lack of passion, her preoccupation with social rules, and her lack of self-will make her the surprising anchor of Richardson's romance and the guarantor of class stability. At the same time, as Richardson represents it, B's civic republican claim that private passion is outside his community and national interests serves merely to mask the self-interested waywardness of his passions. Richardson's representation of the struggle between Pamela's passionless, socially normative virtue and B's corrupt desire suggests that a classed and gendered rhetoric of "virtue" could be employed as efficiently in Whig and anti-Jacobite as in Tory romancé and polemic. Pamela's "virtue" – or "vartue," as Fielding transcribed "Shamela's" labouring-class dialect – was the feature of the novel most attacked by opponents of Richardson's Lockean Whiggism. Even such anti-Jacobites as Fielding saw it as a code-word for a disguised upstart desire.[60] What Fielding attacked in *Pamela* were the marks of Richardson's debates with Haywood and Behn, and of Richardson's opposition to B's Toryism. What Fielding opposed was Richardson's appropriation of a Tory romance discourse that had itself appropriated an ironic version of Locke's political history.

But not all the political intertexts of *Pamela* are mediated through Behn's or Haywood's romances. A second source for Richardson's representation of the problem of passion emerges in Appleby's argument that the debates on Britain's social order and "virtue" had begun, after the turn of the eighteenth century, to be structured by two rival discourses or genres, one focused on political history and the other on economic order.[61] In the first, as Filmer and Locke debated it, admitting the existence of diverse passions disrupted the legitimacy and stability of the existing order. In political economy, however, a chastened feeling and its sympathetic transmission became a source of cohesion and stability to the precise degree that passion appeared capable of disrupting British society. In prefacing *Pamela*, Richardson blurs his references to these rival discourses by edging political history closer to Hume's emergent political economy. But the matter of feeling on which he focuses "editorial" attention is also the point where Hume's political economy emerges from the theoretical history of Locke.

Much as Johnson read Richardson "for the sentiment," Hume read Locke for the role of the passions in Britain's economic history, and he retold Locke's contractarian history of Britain in his *Treatise of Human Nature*. Hume agreed with Locke's first *Treatise* that a rational "convention," or implicit consensus, had come to regulate property accumulation and transfer in Britain, and so to govern its social relations, but he also insisted that the origin of such economic and social exchanges, and the source of their rules, lay in "natural passion," or the predictable laws of human feeling, alone.[62] Reason itself, Hume argued, can be called into action only by passion: thus "nature provides a remedy" for whatever is "irregular and incommodious in the affections" (*T* 489). The example Hume offers in the *Treatise* and *Essays* is the marriage compact, in which laws institutionalize a bond begun by passion, and uphold tendencies and patterns established by gender differences inherent in natural feeling.[63]

Yet although Hume presents his response to Locke as a corrective and critique, his remarks voice tendencies already latent in *Two Treatises*. Even as Locke published his creation myth for British society in the first *Treatise*, that is, he provided – as Genesis provides – a competing myth of origins. His second *Treatise* traces the establishment of commerce and order not to contract but to "*Labour*," which "puts the *difference of value* on every thing." Labour produces stable protocols for assigning value because, like all productive activities, it is ruled by a universal human reason, which is used by each member of society to identify personal needs and wants. In turn, reason directs a pre-existing, unstoppably forceful, but aimless passion toward the fulfillment of personal needs (*T2* 296). The value of goods derives from the cost of labour, which depends, in turn, on the willingness of consumers to work as producers, manufacturing some goods in order to satisfy their desire for others that they do not or cannot produce (*T2* 296–7). The value of people also derives from work, which establishes "*a Right of Property*" by setting aside portions of land, goods, and wealth originally "common" to all. Although property rights, like the other laws of society, finally harden into "*Compact*," therefore, it is finally passion, however directed by reason, that motivates labour and so the order of property as well (*T2* 299).

Read against the history of British society in the first *Treatise*, Locke's labour theory of value hints that shared feeling holds the social fabric and its system of value together. Beginning with nature and backed by custom, differences in degrees of passion and in its proper objects, coupled with the universality of passion itself, produce differences in wealth and property and finally create different ranks. In this way, natural passion provides an origin and model for the development of social order and political authority. The fundamental model for Britain's order is heterosexual desire, which produces what the first *Treatise* stipulates is the original division of labour, the first property contract, and the earliest hierarchy of rank. So too, in Hume's political economic retelling of Locke's creation myth, its two versions are united by feeling: by the innate submissiveness of women, which renders them subjects of rule in political history and "goods" to be transferred in political economy, and the intrinsic desire of men for authority and ownership.

To reconcile the economic logic of British society as Hume and Locke describe it with its Lockean theoretical history – to unite feeling and commerce with the rules of virtue – it was necessary to codify, predict, and regulate the consequences of feeling. In particular, reconciling B's demand-based notion of Pamela's value with her sense of use-value, and finally with intrinsic worth, became, as Richardson's prefaces point out, a crucial task for romance. Something very like a reconciliation between demand, use-value, and worth begins to redirect B's desire in the last stages of *Pamela*, shaping it to Hume's political economic account of British society. That Pamela's attractions for B exponentially increase as she makes herself scarce in effect legitimates his developing desire. While Richardson denies his heroine's passions and transforms his hero's, that is, he demonstrates that virtue and commerce, passionate demand and innate worth can work together. His technique, which replays Hume's reading of Locke, and which is more fully realized in *Clarissa*, is to re-gender the passion whose gender Behn and Haywood had rendered unstable, and so to make it safe.

In *Pamela*, only unvirtuous, and therefore de-gendered, women experience passion: the housekeeper Jewkes's hinted desire for Pamela, which Fielding parodies, or the imperious violence of B's sister Davers, which earns her the epithet "Captain Bab." Yet although Pamela is passionless, she is neither unfeeling nor especially rational. Her arguments with B are founded on Lockean principle upheld by the pleading speeches and welling tears that would come, after *Clarissa*, to be the hallmarks of sentiment in Richardson's readers, and there is something about the character she thus expresses that appeals to some intrinsically "reasonable" element in B's own feeling for her. Although B begins by reading Pamela's letters ironically and as a political ploy, he cannot resist their appeal to his passions, which parallels the claims Richardson makes for romance in his "editor's" preface. Thus Richardson represents the effects of Pamela's virtuous sentiment on B's rational passion in generic terms.

On first demanding Pamela's letters, B ridicules their corrupting influence. "I long to see the Particulars of your Plot," he insists, "For you have so beautiful a Manner, that it is partly that, and partly my Love for you, that has made me desirous of reading all you write." "Besides," he adds, "there is such a pretty Air of Romance, as you relate them, in your Plots, and my Plots, that I shall be better directed in what manner to wind up the Catastrophe of the pretty Novel" (*P1* 201). But rhetorical and generic suspicion soon give over to fascination with the "Romantick Girl" and her "very moving Tale" (*P1* 208). B advertises Pamela's "wondrous Story" as a text with the potential to make people "perfect," and when he muses, "who knows but my Happiness may reform another Rake," he equates sexual desire with moral yearning; fulfillment with moral rectitude. "I know," replies a rakish friend, "for I am more than half reform'd already" (*P1* 402). Once Pamela's story begins to move him, B never again refers to her romance as a novel. Richardson has redefined romance, meanwhile, as a privately moving but publicly orderly genre. Reclaimed from Haywood and Behn, romance, newly associated with the use-value of stably self-regulated sentiment, and masculine aristocrats, now linked with predictable demand, are recuperated side by side. That exchange-value and absolute worth are naturally inseparable is manifest, according to Richardson, in B's response to Pamela's letters and in the selling and reading of Richardson's romance.

I am suggesting that a third term – a tentatively distinguished sentiment, feminine in origin and influence, desirable without itself desiring – emerges between the binaries in *Pamela*, making possible the reconciliation of masculine passion with reason, and easing the transition from political history to political economy. B's rational transport, produced by the retailing of Pamela's sentiment within Richardson's romance, marks the emergence of a distinction between (virtuous, natural) sentiment and (corrupt, unnatural) passion that becomes increasingly central to Richardson's fiction. The effects of this emergent sentiment are graphically illustrated in the interleaved edition of Locke's *Some Thoughts Concerning Education* in which Pamela writes "the Sentiments of a Young Mother" between the lines of "Prescriptions of a Learned Gentleman" (*P2* IV: 314). Thus Richardson's romance harmonizes Hume's natural history of Britain with Locke's political history. Yet it may be here, in the saving transfer of influence from qualities gendered masculine to those gendered feminine, that the most persistent ambiguities of *Pamela* reside.[64] For sentiment, as well as the romance that begins to promote it, works to reconcile reason and passion – and so calls the passive, private nature of femininity into continued question, in ways that turn Britain's theoretical uncertainty into historical instability.[65]

CLARISSA, GENDER, AND POLITICAL HISTORY

In *Pamela*, Richardson begins the translation of Locke's foundation myth into a sentimental vocabulary on which Hume also drew for his political economy. Locke's first family becomes Britain's every-family, to be recreated when necessary by a reading experience that awakens reason and chastens feeling. But real British history bore out neither Locke's theoretical history nor the stable sentiment of its Hanoverian beneficiaries, and debates in the political field exposed the blind spots and faultlines in the field of letters just as romance-writers had corrected and defended Locke's political history.[66] The unease produced by Richardson's recalcitrant country squires – that imperfectly answered question haunting the edges of *Pamela* – soon found mirrors in political events and in the literary interventions that alternately promoted and protested them. The Jacobite rebellion of 1745–6 conclusively proved, Locke notwithstanding, that British women did not naturally obey men, and that British men harboured no intrinsic desire to submit to the magistrates that represented and governed them. It also showed that too few British Protestants could be counted on to uphold the Lockean correspondence between popular consent and legitimate kingship. Yet Locke's political history persisted, whether approved or reviled, as a focus of debate. The result was a nascent bipartisan political consensus.[67] Protestants disagreed among themselves about the source of political legitimacy, and Jacobites and anti-Jacobites disagreed on the succession itself.[68] But they expressed their competing anxieties in consistently gendered and generic terms.

In responding to the Jacobites, the pamphleteers of Hanoverian consensus employed a catalogue of generic allusions in which Richardsonian romance mingled with Locke's British political history. In particular, Richardson's gendered reading of Lockean family history, and his re-gendered responses to the earlier romances in which Tory writers debated with Locke, circulated through the narratives produced as British Protestants attacked the 1745 rebellion. As Jill Campbell has shown, Whigs attempted to prevent a recurrence of Charles Edward

Stuart's revolt by caricaturing its female participants as Amazonian warriors and prostitutes and its men as effeminate or monstrous hags.[69] Their rhetoric spread to anti-Jacobite pamphleteers of all political stripes after the 1746 rout of the Jacobite army at Culloden, and provided models for English response to the French Revolution half a century later.

The kind of "termagant" figure exemplified by Richardson's Lady Davers, and the attacks on Tory, Francophile, and feminine passion such portraits embodied, became a popular model for anti-Jacobite writers. In one broadside, an executed rebel's wife confesses an unlawful seizure of household authority that drove her husband into Jacobite rebellion.[70] Pamphleteers depicted other women, notably Jenny Cameron, Stuart's reputed mistress, as hyper-masculine soldiers. Parodic portraits of Cameron were sold along with scandalous tracts about her life: to Whig readers, Lockean and otherwise, Cameron became a byword for Jacobite enthusiasm and the unnatural influence of France.[71] Caricatures represented her straddling in tartan trews, a pendulous sporran placed suggestively before her and a scabbard drooping disconsolately between her legs. The portrait recalls Cameron's youthful elopement, in which the masquerading cross-dressed "boy" "ravished" her illicit lover more than the woman could – a scene in turn referencing Silvia's masquerade in Behn's *Love-Letters*.[72] These images make Cameron less a martial woman than an emasculated man, and Whigs accused Jacobite men of more anomalous sexualities – "private use" of "*Spanish* Padlocks," and "Sodomy after the *Italian* Manner."[73] Gender and sexual fluidity mime the disorder of the body politic and economic but are readily banished by the return of political and social normalcy: a Richardsonian conclusion to the anti-Jacobite tracts.

Yet although the anti-Jacobites borrowed Richardson's generic logic, finding in socially desirable gendered sentiment the irresistible effects of nature on the British polity, the tract writers also realigned Jacobitism with an intrinsic, even physiological unnaturalness. Even the moderate Andrew Henderson, in his 1748 *History of the Rebellion*, pronounced Jacobites "estranged by Nature from the Body of the Nation."[74] Such attacks drew added weight from the participation of Jacobite women in literary as well as military battles – from Cameron and Flora Macdonald to the anonymous poets whose mixed declarations of love and military zeal for "Bonnie Charlie" were tinged with transgendered homoeroticism. "Retract thy Face," one urged, "lest that so fair and young,/

Should call in Doubt the [martial] Orders of thy Tongue." She added, "I on no other Terms a Man would be,/ But to defend thy glorious Cause and thee."[75] Anti-Jacobite reaction was further bolstered by Stuart's escape to France, disguised as a maidservant, after fleeing Culloden's carnage. These texts lay out a Richardsonian array of references to gender rebellion, political rebellion, female passion, and France, which define the "natural" character of Jacobitism. The anti-Jacobite tracts unwittingly kept alive, and in Britain, the spectre of natural passions that cross gender bounds and that refuse either to be controlled by reason or to respond to feminine sentiment. These were kinds of passion that Richardson had marked as foreign and artificial.

Taken together, Jacobite and anti-Jacobite discourses undermined the universality of Locke's edenic history of British society. In consequence, the existing story of the social contract, with its irresistible progression from God-given private affiliation to social order and political authority, could no longer be viewed – even by its adherents – as a necessary historical event. The lack of ideological cohesion grew deeper as the eighteenth century progressed and Protestants united behind the newcomers to the British throne on a generally though tacitly accepted *de facto* basis.[76] A century of debate on the nature of royal right subsided into pragmatic acceptance of a habitual monarchy, leaving Britain's social order without a stable centre – without either one true monarch or the people's righteous decision to set him in place.[77] *De facto* rule, for which Locke's legitimating myth had proved too easily contested by gender rebellion, needed narratives to transform it into a stable and predictable source of political legitimacy.

Britain needed a history that would hold it "naturally" together, affirming its union of countries and citizens even in the face of real disagreements – replacing Locke's creation myth with a less programmatic conception of national cohesion. The generic conventions of that history were more crucial than its particulars, for what was required was a persuasive ideology of British identity and unity, dependent in turn on a generic integration of fractured narrative threads. To this legitimacy crisis, sparked in part by anti-Jacobite refractions of his own romance, Richardson's romance was uniquely qualified to respond, and he responded with a further renovation of romance in *Clarissa* – that work uniquely fashioned for "an age *like the present*."[78] In his 1740 critique of Locke in the *Treatise*, Hume had insisted, provocatively but prophetically, that the social contract was "a mere fiction, not unlike that of the *golden age*, which poets have invented," for the "first state and situation" of "man" "may justly be esteem'd social" (493). After 1745, as Richardson rewrote romance by writing *Clarissa*, Hume's sceptical comments pinpointed the crucial problem with Lockean ideology and provided the germ of an answer to it. Following Hume, Richardson recasts Lockean theory, and embeds it in his romance alongside Humean sentiment, explicitly as a fiction. He retains the domestic outcome of Locke's *Two Treatises* as Britain's ideal, but simultaneously enacts Hume's new emphasis on second causes over God-given universal laws. *Clarissa* portrays a Britain held together by sentiment and sympathy, the sameness-indifference of human bodies created and equipped, but neither fated nor forced, to live a social life.[79]

An ideology of the body is an ideology of natural feeling. As Richardson and Hume re-envision Britain in the political economic terms of second causes and natural law, physiologically driven emotional responses produce and shape all social practices, and therefore unify and regulate Britain's body economic. *Clarissa* not only participates in but also represents in miniature this public space, where the relations between social order and private character, while ideologically crucial, are both theoretically disputed and challenged in practice.[80] In *Clarissa*, a multitude of writers comment on the "history of a young lady" – an "affecting story," but thin in comparison with Richardson's "useful" work (*C* 36). The rival perspectives the correspondents express gain currency within *Clarissa* by means of the utility of their letters, their frequency and breadth of circulation, and the credit that accrues to the writers – a process recapitulated in the literary marketplace as the letters reach, and provoke the sentiment of, the external readers of Richardson's fiction. Underlying these fluctuations in use- and exchange-value, however, is an unchanging source of worth in sentiment and its origins in the common structures of the body. Composed of letters and underwritten by sentiment, the romance Richardson writes in *Clarissa* becomes the characteristic literary form of a new British order, teaching Britons to be economic subjects in a liberal polity and illustratively granting the new role of *homo economicus* a natural, innately social foundation.

Whereas *Pamela* is partly about the clash between successive political histories, therefore, Richardson rewrites this conflict in *Clarissa* as the competition between three contemporaneous accounts of political economy. His romance maps the violent confrontations between them. The work opens with Clarissa Harlowe already caught between opposing modes of economic practice upheld by her upwardly mobile relatives and by the aristocratic Robert Lovelace, her would-be seducer. The mercantile Harlowes propel Clarissa across a treacherous financial and sexual landscape to further their expansionist economic ends, while Lovelace, a protectionist in social and economic life, uses her to resist their goals. Spurred on by their son's fierce desire for advancement, the Harlowes work at *"raising a family"* (*C* 77), bartering what Lovelace contemptuously calls their *"acquired* fortunes" for a title for the heir (*C* 426). To gain entry into an aristocracy they hope will close firmly behind them, they must consolidate the family wealth through entails and marriage settlements. Thus the Harlowes impel Clarissa, with beatings, starvation, confinement, verbal abuse, robbery, and blackmail, to marry the illiterate, "sordid," but solvent Solmes. As they promote their family's rise, Lovelace, as narrowly genealogical in his economic faith as the Harlowes are ambitious, works to lower the "sordidly imperious" family once more (*C* 145). He hopes, by seducing Clarissa to live with him in a libertine commerce unbound by legal or financial settlements, to return the Harlowes to their "natural" level (*C* 161). His lowering desire, like the Harlowes' desire to rise, is sexual and economic both at once.

Richardson's careful typing of his characters divides the bourgeois sheep from the aristocratic goats: *Pamela*'s party politics, and the inevitable defeat of Francophile Toryism, give way to the entrenched domestic class conflicts of *Clarissa*. However, Richardson discriminates class categories only to emphasize the economic similarities of the moneyed and landed classes, and to highlight generically the common ground they share in political economy despite their social, religious, and partisan differences. *Clarissa* upholds Newman's claim that the social authority of the aristocracy was at once envied and emulated by the upwardly mobile, whose goal, even in opposition, was a share in the power the aristocracy wielded.[81]

Yet Richardson's approach to his competing class fractions is marked by a stern dramatic irony: the Harlowes and Lovelace are unaware of their similarities.[82] Unselfconscious about their preoccupation with economic power, they are victims, in Richardson's view, of a bodily dysfunction that is at once natural (that is to say, organic) and unnatural (that is, anomalous and corrupt). Richardson's treatment of the competitors recapitulates the portraits of the "emasculated" Jenny Cameron, taking up anti-Jacobite rhetorics of natural anomaly or mutation to suggest that the socioeconomic fractions at war in his fiction are unnatural by nature. The bodies of the apish Harlowes and the libertine Lovelace, like Jacobite bodies, are intrinsically deformed, producing what Richardson and his Whig contemporaries saw as incorrigible deformities of social organization. The anti-Jacobite portraits themselves, however, began with Richardson's own earlier romance, which cast political passion as gendered physiological deformity. In injecting his partisan romance conventions with a more generalized political economic discourse of human nature, Richardson recruits the literary forms of party politics for use by a less partisan liberal ideology and for Britain's post-Jacobite unity. He places the debate on political order and its legitimation squarely within the economic arena and insists on a natural sociability uniting British subjects, even those whose anomalous bodies disrupt their natural sentiment.

The Harlowe family is fractious, at once profligate and miserly, and riddled from beneath by insubordinate plots. These rebellions, and the domestic and social conflicts that result, stem from excesses of the body that appear first in the children before spreading – an order-inverting contagion with disorderly symptoms – to the father and others in authority. Domestic, social, economic, and bodily disruption alike originate in the excessive "passions" of James Harlowe, the heir who sparks the family's desire to sell Clarissa. James's "natural imperiousness and fierce and uncontrollable temper" spring, as Clarissa's correspondent Anna Howe suggests, from a surplus of blood to the heart, and abate only once, before the plot commences, when he loses a duel with Lovelace. His own "blood gush[ing] plentifully down his arm" gentles James for the first and last time, lasting only until "fever," brought on "by the perturbation of his spirits," replaces the lost heat moments later (*C* 39). Anna's words trace James's political economic faults to the malfunctioning economy, or balance, of his body. This anatomy of economics and ethics recurs as Clarissa places her family's passions within a taxonomy of unbalanced circulating humours. Arabella, Clarissa's sister, expresses her "ill-nature" (*C* 37) not in "violence" like James's, but in "virulence," its female counterpart: her passions, even more than her brother's, are a disease endemic in the Harlowe family (*C* 52). A "gouty paroxysm," a surplus of misplaced fluids, makes Clarissa's father James Senior equally vulnerable (*C* 55). Affected by excess blood and his children's excess passion, he is disabled by disease where his son is innately deformed. Even Lady Charlotte, his docile wife, contracts "a very violent colic": she literally lacks the stomach for passion, but once immersed in the tumult of James's and Arabella's "fierce" and "masculine spirits" she quickly becomes infected (*C* 54). As Clarissa represents it, an excess of passion – however socioeconomically destructive – is the result of a tragic pathology rather than a cause for denunciation. At the same time, the traditional analogy between economic circulation and the blood in the body is traced, in *Clarissa*, to the natural foundation of one on the other.[83] Even where sentiment is corrupt, that is, its sympathetic circulation remains in place.

By expressing the battles for social and economic power in bodily terms, Richardson traces the economic preoccupations of the Harlowes and Lovelace to a single source. For diseases of circulation are not confined to the city characters, but terrify and harm Clarissa most in Lovelace himself. In his moments of self-assessment, Lovelace unwittingly confirms the democracy of passion, a circulating disease that knows no class borders or boundaries. He sets himself above the Harlowes and Solmes on the ground that his own "predominant passion is *girl*, not *gold*" (*C* 417), but he also boasts that raping Clarissa will gratify "imperial" passions that are at once social, economic, and sexual (*C* 719). These desires and the "imperious" commands of young Harlowe mirror each other: as Clarissa herself warns, "the workings of passion, when indulged, are but too much alike" (*C* 641). There is little to choose between the aristocratic and bourgeois-expansionist economic aims of Lovelace and the Harlowes, for both derive their force from physiological excess. In a diseased heart, passion overcomes the natural sentiment that, according to mid-century political economy, makes *laissez-faire* economics, post-Jacobite politics, and social cohesion compatible.

The third among the political economies that meet in Richardson's romance is Clarissa's own, distinguished from the economic practices of the Harlowes and Lovelace by the stable touchstone of the heart. Her sentiment is the inflexible gold standard underlying the fluctuations within and clashes between competing political economic practices and beliefs. It is her "heart" that "recoil[s]" from Lovelace and Solmes, yet her feeling is not merely personal and private, but the monitor of virtue (*C* 153). "My *heart* is less concerned . . . than my *soul*," she declares (*C* 221). She argues against the compulsions exerted from two opposing directions, appealing to inborn sentiments that provide an infallible rule:

Principles, that *are* in my mind; that I *found* there; implanted, no doubt, by the first gracious Planter: which therefore *impel* me, as I may say, to act up to them . . . let others act as they will by *me*. (*C* 596)

Passion overcomes Clarissa's sentiment only once, when she elopes with Lovelace in order to escape Solmes.[84] Although she later condemns her "presumptuous" decision to "rely so much" on her native "knowledge of the right path," she continues to maintain that all Britons share her internal emotional monitor. Lovelace's economic and sexual bullying are contrary to *"human nature"* in placing passion above natural senti-ment (*C* 566).[85] The violence Clarissa experiences and its inverse, her continuing sympathy with her family, allow Richardson to avow the theoretical universality of sentiment while acknowledging practical his-torical differences among Britain's people, with consequences amount-ing even to tragedy or revolution.

Like *Pamela*, *Clarissa* represents social structures in universalist terms shared with a political philosophy that traces an unshakeable British order to the laws of natural morality. Departing from his practice in *Pamela*, however, Richardson trades Lockean mythic history for the practical conflict between particular circumstances and the general laws of personal, political, and economic life. In his preface, he argues that the merits of *Clarissa* lie in sentiment alone: "story or *amusement*" are "little more than the vehicle to the more necessary *instruction*" taking place, as Johnson was to reiterate, through appeals to sympathetic feeling (*C* 36). This statement makes an instructive anti-Pamela of Clarissa Harlowe, who cannot survive, let alone transform, a world disfigured by other people's passions.[86] *Clarissa*, accordingly, becomes an anti-*Pamela*, for the logic of Richardson's sentimental revision of romance not only admits the possibility of conflicting passions, but allows passion the practical victory as well. Yet the general claim – the ordered public sphere as the endpoint of divine teleology – persists despite its particular failures in Britain. The Lockean narrative of necessity also persists, as an elegiac social fiction, a romance to be longed for, not least by Clarissa herself.

CLARISSA AND HUME'S SENTIMENTAL ECONOMY

Clarissa portrays not virtue rewarded, but virtue dismissed, misread, made tragic. Where sentiment is what counts, and where "virtue" is emphasized over "reward," romance appears non-teleological because it represents a forever unrealized teleology. What matters is that the impulse to order and community exists in Britain, whether or not this natural tendency finds fruition in real order. In emphasizing cause, the sentiment intrinsic to and general throughout British society, over the particular consequences of sentiment, Richardson echoes the post-Jacobite Hume, whose *Treatise of Human Nature* combines critique of

Locke's writings on social and political human nature with a political economic supplement to them.

The generic character of romance underwrites Richardson's Humean narrative. Often considered alongside Hume's philosophy, Richardson's fiction is not often read in its intertextual dialogue with Hume, perhaps because biographers have stressed Richardson's ignorance of contemporary political philosophy.[87] Yet although nothing in *Clarissa* approaches the extended reading of Locke's educational philosophy in *Pamela*, Richardson nevertheless shapes his romance to enact something very similar to Hume's economy of sentiment, and to chasten it with generic memories of Locke. At the same time, in the interaction with Richardson's readers, his production of sentiment moves beyond questions of self-interest and benevolence to become a response to Britain's real history as it is promoted, criticized, and otherwise mediated through political philosophy. In responding in romance to the politically sceptical Hume and his critique of Locke, Richardson also responds to the Britain the two proposed to shape.

Richardson first mentioned Hume directly in a 1756 letter, as a "very mischievous writer," full of "absurdities and contradictions of himself."[88] The self-contradictions that troubled Richardson concerned the influence and accessibility of first causes, on which Hume's *a priori* avowals often contradicted Hume's *a posteriori* conclusions. Although Richardson's response to Hume was ambivalent, his mistrust seems to have been founded on rhetorical more than on philosophical disagreement, for even as Hume's sometimes sceptical assertions raised Richardson's mistrust, the two writers engaged in closely related, though generically different tasks: producing a post-Jacobite Britain that could, in the political economic order it declared, supersede Locke's theological history of the British social contract without sacrificing Britain's natural unity. Jerome Christensen argues that Hume at once helped define a lack in Britain's social order and supplied the lack through letters. Hume's offering of texts written in a personal style, and assuming a literate, responsive, but not usually learned reader modelled an exchange of sentiment through sympathy that united the writer with his readers. In this way, Hume, like Richardson in the *Pamela* prefaces and *Clarissa*, offered an ideology of union that would overcome Britain's lack – and created a market for his own texts as well.[89]

But Hume did not originate the gaps in British social practice to which he responded. Rather, he rewrote, and so remedied, an ideological failing that the earlier debates on Lockean political history and real history had produced, and for which the shaky post-Jacobite consensus had made an answer critical. He added his voice, that is, to those of Behn, Haywood, Manley, and Richardson, and his political economy adapts to the consequences of their romances. If Locke's narrative of edenic origins was necessary to hold British society and government together, then the British polity, proved susceptible to passion and the fluidity of gender roles, held a giant emptiness at its centre. In response, Hume set his theory of British social cohesion in the economic field and, beginning with the "family economy," he founded his economics not on labour, but on desire itself. His normative sentiment, coupled with his sceptical recognition that its teleological origin and endpoint were necessarily speculative fictions, took on new life in the aftermath of Jacobite faction and anti-Jacobite fiction.

Whereas Richardson, as a writer of romance narratives, in *Pamela* drew out the historical narrative threaded through Locke's *Treatises of Government*, the philosopher Hume founded his revision of Locke's history on a critique of his epistemology, taking the *Essay Concerning Human Understanding* as his study text. He began with the fundamental Lockean principle that ideas proceed from experience. For Hume, this empiricist stance has one crucial corollary: that human minds can neither experience nor imagine first causes, and can never, therefore, be certain that any chain of events includes a causal relation. On these grounds Hume rebuts the Cartesian claim that because human minds cannot directly know causality, "a supreme spirit or deity," with a divinely capacious mind, must be "the immediate cause of every alteration in matter" (*T* 160).[90] But he also attacks Locke's derivation of the laws of nature from the experience of causality, his "finding from experience, that there are . . . motions and variations of body, and concluding that there must somewhere be a power capable of producing them" (*T* 157). In Hume's view, Locke contradicts himself, for if, as Locke argues, "All ideas are deriv'd from, and represent impressions," it is also the case that "We never have any impression, that contains any power or efficacy. We never therefore have any idea of power" (*T* 161). Consequently, not only the being of God, but also the bond between divine and human nature necessarily remains unperceived and unconceived. Hume is categorical: "nothing in any object . . . can afford us a reason for drawing a conclusion beyond it . . . even after the observation of the frequent or constant conjunction of objects, we have no reason to draw any inference" (*T* 139). Belief in cause and effect is therefore simply a "habit," and the "ideas of necessity, of power, and of efficacy" are derived from "custom" rather than from nature (*T* 154–5, 164). The claim to find divine order in human history, then, is a custom – or, to name custom's narrative genre, a fiction – as well.

Here Hume's logic performs the oddest of the contradictions that made Richardson uneasy. Yet it is also at this point that Hume, contrary to Richardson's complaints, offers an irony useful to Richardson. People cannot experience causality by means of reason, Hume insists, but they *can* know through reason and experience that custom causes belief. On a purely theoretical or fictional level, as Hume only implicitly concedes, first causes may be conceived and understood. His theory teeters on the brink of the imaginary here, but there is nothing unreal about his "instinctual economizing of the mind."[91] Scepticism about first causes turns over to expose its other side: Hume's biological essentialism, his reliance on second causes. He avows doctrinal certainty that custom and habit proceed from "human nature," for "Nature may certainly produce whatever can arise from habit: Nay, habit is nothing but one of the principles of nature, and derives all its force from that origin" (*T* 179).

Hume's recourse to human nature and the body as a second, knowable cause lets him argue that although "rules of morality are not conclusions of our reason," and that consequently no "immutable measures" exist "of right and wrong," "Morals" nevertheless "excite passions, and produce or prevent actions" (*T* 456–7) and "reason . . . can never oppose passion in the direction of the will" (*T* 413). Hume's warnings about the folly of attempting to know causality are here entirely forgotten. At the same time, he avows, "sympathy," the "communication" of "sentiments," produces natural moral law, a shared and emotionally compelling sense of rightness "denominated Virtue," even in the absence of the externally verifiable absolutes he associates with first causes (*T* 316, 499). Hume upholds the homogeneity of sentiment, and opposes it to individual passion, as firmly as Locke proclaimed the universality of reason. He insists that despite "the difference of sexes, ages, governments, conditions, or methods of education; the same uniformity and regular operation of natural principles are discernible" in "mankind" (*T* 401). Although he turns away from Locke's theological absolutes, therefore, Hume replaces God and God-given reason with the common sentiments of "human nature" as the source of social order (*T* 318).[92] Trading epistemology for ideology, Hume lends British society a new, political economic absolute.[93]

What makes Hume's political economy especially useful in theorizing mid-century Britain is his treatment of sentiment as a theoretical gold standard needing no support from political history. Hume allowed considerable space for incorporating, and so disarming, disjunctions among the feeling, desiring subjects who make up the British polity. Because Hume founded his theory of sentiment on species-specific traits of the body, bodily variance offered Richardson a natural explanation for the real differences passion makes in spite of the theoretically shared workings of sentiment. Hume remarks that "we never remark any passion or principle in others, of which . . . we may not find a parallel in ourselves. The case is the same with the fabric of the mind, as with that of the body" (*T* 318). Thus he traces the individuality of passion to bodily differences – sex, class, race, or anomalies within each – that struggle against the theoretical sameness of human physiology. Class, Hume suggests, is both a natural physical distinction and a potentially disruptive social difference:

The skin, pores, muscles, and nerves of a day-labourer are different from those of a man of quality: So are his sentiments, actions and manners. The different stations of life influence the whole fabric, external and internal; and these different stations arise necessarily, because uniformly, from the necessary and uniform principles of human nature. (*T* 402).

Sex similarly lends "force and maturity" to men, and "delicacy and softness" to women, but also ensures that women experience stronger sympathies than men (*T* 401). Thus bodily differences, and the passions they produce, disrupt the consonance of hearts with natural law, requiring a supplemental legal and political control.[94] Echoes of Hume's contradictory view of the naturalness of gendered sentiment and the gendered obstreperousness of passion are audible in the conduct books of Gregory, who urges women to live by rules he also insists are women's inescapable nature.[95] Just as it is "human nature" for shared sentiments to provide firm foundations for social and economic exchange, it is human nature for contingent events and gendered nature to disrupt the workings of the sentimental standard. Sentiment theoretically produces, but cannot in practice guarantee, the cohesion of British society.

But romance, which narratively incorporates such political economic conundrums, can also represent general theory on a level of concrete particularity. Read allegorically, it can supplement theoretical claims with representative practical examples. The concreteness of its encounters with political economy are reinforced if the relations between the romance and its reader can be said to fulfill political economic aims. In representing variation as a kind of excrescence or cancer – a naturally occurring but anomalous disease of the heart – Richardson accepts

Hume's sceptical theory of sentimental sameness and his reluctant histories of passional difference. But Richardson's romance also patrols the edges of the sentimental philosophy it incorporates, loading with moral condemnation whatever slips away from the rules sentiment outlines. *Clarissa* is, finally, less indeterminate, less open and polyglot than its epistolary structure implies. Rather, the conjunction of epistolarity with a romance plot allows Richardson to focus the broadest range of differences into the single category of deviance and disease, even as Richardson admits that the differences exist and, sometimes, flourish. Richardson's "strength," as Nicholas Hudson puts it, is "making a focussed act of rhetoric *appear* dialogic."[96] In illustrating and annulling the variations of desire within *Clarissa*, Richardson cultivates uniformity among his readers, producing the horror at corruption and the sympathy with sentiment, demonstrated by readers from Fielding to Bradshaigh, that are needed to sustain and to prove the truth of Hume's political economy.

As Richardson puts it, *Clarissa*'s tragic romance "is designed" for the demands of *"the present"* (*C* 1495). It is suited to the uneasy consensus of the post-Jacobite years, when the spectres of self-willed women and lustful men give rise to suspicion that Locke's – and thus *Pamela*'s – account of naturally consonant wills had described not Britain's real history, but an idealistic fiction or deceitful political dogma. While Hume established his theoretical model of an orderly Britain, Richardson illustrated and enacted a related but competing model – one in which not only consonance of sentiment, but also rigorous sympathy for the "victims" of differing passions holds writer and readers together. To buy and read *Clarissa*, as the work itself demonstrates, is to participate in a demonstrative agreement of sentiments that is projected – in however limited a corner of Britain's newly sentimentalized economy – to overwhelm all lapses into deviance. In *Clarissa*, Richardson not only upholds and models, but also markets sentiment.

CLARISSA'S ROMANCE AND THE DREAM OF NATURAL CONSENSUS

Discerning the success of Richardson's marketing tactics is made difficult by a retrospective irony: the too-great popular success some late-eighteenth-century critics deplored was in fact the visible result of Richardson's not having been successful enough. In 1788, the popular moralist Cumberland objected that young ladies learned from *Clarissa* a usurped authority of feeling: "more artificial pedantic characters [are] assumed by sentimental Misses in the . . . desire of being thought Clarissa Harlows, than from any other source of imitation whatso-ever."[97] Cumberland's reading pits Richardsonian sentiment against rightful authority, and daughters against their father's right. Recent readings confirm his analysis, though not his indignation. Thus John Zomchick suggests that the violent conflicts in *Clarissa* exemplify the dilemma of British subjects caught between new individualist ideologies and an older, theocentric, and patriarchal vision of British society.[98] But Caroline Gonda points out that the voices raised against the father in *Clarissa* – however seductive – are uniformly discredited by self-inter-est.[99] (The aristocratic Lovelace, who mingles libertine and absolutist rhetorics in suspiciously Jacobitical ways, is in any case no convincing representative of revolution or modernity.) At the same time, although Clarissa defies her father's wishes, she does so unwillingly. She quickly reveals a rigorous obedience to another paternal rule, which is literal and earthly, but which is also, in her mind, the type of divine authority and law.

For every clash between Clarissa's sentiment and her father's author-ity, an equal and opposite consonance connects the "will" of the dead grandfather Harlowe with hers. Clarissa obeys her family's *über*-patri-arch, and her economic practices and ethical comments imitate his. Underlying Cumberland's complaint is Richardson's unwillingness or failure fully to generalize the sentimental community that Clarissa and grandfather Harlowe represent. For by allowing Clarissa to be de-stroyed by the violence of the Harlowes precisely because she makes her grandfather's will her own, Richardson allows sentimental practices to remain the endpoint of an unrealized teleology. The Harlowes prefer parricidal infanticide to sentimental unity, and Clarissa's "reward" is the projected conclusion of an inconclusive romance. The problem Richardson's text poses for contemporary Britain is not that Clarissa is rebellious, but that the real, particular failures of sentiment that sur-round and overwhelm her overshadow her conformity with Hume's sentimental political economy. It is the corrupted sentiment of others, and not Clarissa's own rebellion, that turns Richardson's romance to tragic ends.

The struggle that catches Clarissa is a contested transformation *within* a Britain already ruled by a Protestant Whig consensus. She suffers because her society has moved from a political history founded on first causes toward a sociology of the second cause and a political economy based on nature. She suffers because her trust in a God-given reason borne out by British history has been proved to depend on a precarious natural sentiment that can only be theorized and can never be empirically proved. Her code of conduct reads very much like Hume's first renovation of Locke, for it is sentiment, she argues, that leads to such Lockean social effects as property and economic laws, and to a consequent social cohesion. Ordered to sacrifice her heart to "family views," she replies with a redefinition marked not only by confidence in the unity of sentiment and virtue, but also by a Lockean trust that the coherence of British society, and thus of every human society, is historically inevitable (*C* 101). "The world is but one great family," she declares, "originally it was so; what then is this narrow selfishness that reigns in us, but relationship remembered against relationship forgot?" (*C* 62). Clarissa states her views in the scriptural terms of the Lockean Whig orthodoxy as it existed before the mid-1740s.[100] But by 1747 Charles Edward Stuart's revolt had shown that the passion for power could override the bonds of sentiment even among the royal family, and Hume had insisted that Lockean ideals of the family of man are fictions. History suggested to Hume, and he suggested to his readers, that there never was a "state of nature," and that bodily failings would always forestall the universal consonance of human sentiment (*T* 316–17, 493). Reproducing in Clarissa's mingled philosophies Hume's transformative reading of Locke, Richardson's plot sets Clarissa's sentiment sparring with her family's violent passions. Clarissa's narrative role, and the generic role of Richardson's romance, is to reconcile the two.

Thus Cumberland is right to suggest that Richardson opens a rift between the will of a patriarch and the heart of a woman, a daughter within his household, a division of sentiments impossible in Locke. But Richardson defends and contains the breach between Harlowe and his daughter. Cumberland is wrong to suggest that *Clarissa* recommends filial rebellion, and Richardson's letters more forcibly deny the charge.[101] The conflict of daughter and father, as Clarissa recognizes, begins with, and should remain, a clash between the daughter's natural sentiment and her brother's excessive passion. It is only, as Clarissa laments, because "my brother has engaged my father" in his private passion against Lovelace, that "it is become my father's will that I oppose" (*C* 96). James's anomalous passion intrudes on the sympathy of brother and sister; at the same time, it forges a diseased, competing sympathy between father and son. It is because Harlowe Senior permits

James's passion to corrupt his own heart that Clarissa, despite what Richardson calls "the strictest notions of filial duty," dissents and disobeys (*C* 37). Accused of wilfulness, she retorts in terms borrowed from Milton's and Locke's Eve or Richardson's Pamela: "what was my will till now, but my father's will . . . Has it not been my pride to obey and oblige?" (*C* 305). Even in disobeying her father, Clarissa acts in sympathy with him, for her dissent is a product of his own. Wilfully allying himself against his daughter, Harlowe disobeys his own father, whose written "will" in Clarissa's favour preserves his sentiments. "A second childhood was attributed to him," Clarissa says: accusing the grandfather of a kind of inverted filial defiance, reflected in Clarissa's proxy rebellion, allows the terms of his will to be easily set aside (*C* 104). Arabella celebrates this overthrow of family sympathy, declaring that "My papa's *living* will shall control my grandfather's *dead* one" (*C* 198).

Like Clarissa herself, and like the Richardson of the pre-Jacobite period in which Clarissa's romance is set, grandfather Harlowe is a theoretical Lockean.[102] But his will, like Clarissa's letters, is a sentimental document, showing in its rhetoric and intent the blurring of private sentiment and public order under the sign of natural law that characterizes Hume's political economy. Placing sentiment above the letter of the law, he urges that his family obey his written will "as they value my blessing, and my memory," although the bequest is "not . . . strictly conformable to law" (*C* 53–4). The James Harlowes, Senior and Junior, are troubled that their father and grandfather has made Clarissa, through inheritance, a *feme sole*: a holder of property outside her father's or husband's jurisdiction, with rights of contract, command, and self-determination as unusual as they are uncomfortable.[103] But the grandfather intends to bestow "favour" rather than freedom on Clarissa: he rewards her "matchless duty," and does not intend to liberate her from paternal control. The duty he rewards consists, first, in obedience, and second, in the consonance of Clarissa's sentiment with his own. Clarissa's first "act of duty" as an heiress is to yield her grandfather's estate to her father's legal and financial control (*C* 78). Her belief that the world is a family united by sympathy makes her the only Harlowe who continues the patriarch's charities (*C* 161–2).

Clarissa is caught between patriarchs and the competing rhetorics of duty and sentiment they marshal to compel her obedience. Quoting Walter Scott's epigraph to his 1814 novel of Jacobite nostalgia, *Waverley*, Robert Gordon suggests that "Under which king?" was the crucial question facing mid-eighteenth-century Britons.[104] Not just Jacobite and anti-Jacobite soldiers, but also the political philosophers, moralists, historians, and novelists who explained or defended these were forced to choose allegiance to some national "father." All needed to be prepared, however sceptically or unwillingly, to justify this father's rule. That Britons made different choices raised a spectre of national fragmenta- tion with doubly damaging effects, for an internally divided body politic also meant a lack of stable justification for the rule of a contractarian or *de facto* king. In *Clarissa*, Richardson faces the Harlowe family with precisely such a choice between fathers. Read in this context, where historical choices shade into literary and political allegory, the implica- tions of their allegiance bear a representative force that extends beyond the private sphere.[105]

This is not to suggest that *Clarissa* should be read as "a" post-Jacobite political allegory. Nevertheless, that sentiment must meet the challenge of such divisions of allegiance intimates the tasks to which Richardson commits sentiment as he reconstructs the sources of Britain's cohesion. Clarissa's feminine sentiment, like the wifely, maternal, and daughterly virtue of Elizabeth and Sophia of Hanover, which in the Act of Suc- cession justifies the Hanoverian inheritance of the British crown through the Protestant female line, confirms her allegiance to an *über*- patriarch and renders that loyalty right. Her consoling obedience, however threatened by the passions of the Harlowes, suggests that the subject who is true to natural sentiment has, like a virtuous wife or daughter, no real choice to make. Instead, paternal sentiment chooses the subject-daughter as, in Hume's political economy, it guides the British subject. Sentiment gives subjects natural obedience and simulta- neously guarantees their "free will" (*C* 149).

The same sentiments that, for Hume, provide theoretical common ground for economic exchange theoretically ensure that all Britons, through similarities of sentiment and its sympathetic exchange, will always choose the same king. Real history, however, proves that they will not, exposing the fictionality, the utopian romance, of sentiment. One king and father, in this schema, becomes a dream or a ghost: he is the shadow of a missing consensus, the last theoretical common ground that is the earliest forgotten among a series of shifting and conflicting positions with a greater appeal to the choosing subject and his anomal- ous, passionate body. In the Britain of Locke's political history, theoreti- cal order is undone by historical disjunction. Similarly, in Hume's philosophy, the sentiment that adheres to social and economic stability is cast into the shadows by the variations and violence of human passion and desire. In *Clarissa*, the ghostly grandfather – represented in the text only by a sentimental document that has lost its connection with the writer's loving, dying body – is a nexus for political history and political economy, an epitome of romance. What Arabella names the father's "living will" is the point at which the histories unfolding in politics and economics converge. In *Clarissa*, coherence and consent, whether centred on property transfer or on the authority it enacts, are as ghostly as the vanished patriarch. History, as Richardson represents it, is discordant and compulsive, doing violence both to Hume's theoretical anatomy of sentiment and to sentiment itself. Both are figured by Clarissa, who is repeatedly the victim of violence.

The epistolary shape of Richardson's text allows Clarissa to outline her sentimental ideals in extended written form, but it also permits the Harlowes and Lovelace to attack her sentiments as economically and politically subversive fictions. The resulting alliance between romance and Clarissa's sentimental gold standard expresses the ideological role of *Clarissa* in microcosmic form, but the violence done to Clarissa's own narratives simultaneously calls the mediating efficacy of romance, and the cohesion it upholds, into question. Lovelace and the Harlowes explicitly deride Clarissa's sentimental view of society as a romance, and their derision marks the point of impact between Humean theory and post-Jacobite British history. When Clarissa writes demanding that Solmes cease his courtship, James remarks that her letter is one of many "pretty romantic flights you have delighted in," and her aunt laughs at her "romantic picture of a forced marriage" (*C* 159, 322). Lovelace is even more explicit, lamenting the "romantic value" Clarissa places on chastity and filial obedience, and complaining that no "hero in romance" was ever "called upon to harder trials" (*C* 146, 885). The segue from "romantic" to "romance" in Lovelace's speeches marks the adjective as shorthand for a genre, one that is associated with a particular brand of moral sentiment, and the family and Lovelace are quick to condemn Clarissa's reading and writing in much the same terms as Cumberland employs in his critique of Richardson's influence on female readers. Clarissa's "reading," one uncle accuses, makes her "a stranger to nothing but what you should be most acquainted with" (*C* 150). Another remarks that "reading and writing, though not too much for the wits of you young girls, are too much for your judgements" (*C* 155). His comment forges a self-reflexive bond between Clarissa's reading and writing of the letters that comprise Richardson's romance, and the romance itself. *Clarissa* holds out, in its heroine, a sentimental gold standard, but the dissenting letters of her family demonstrate that Britain lacks cohesion as badly as ever.

Somewhere beneath the excesses of the Harlowes' violent passions lie vestigial traces of sentiment, instinctive responses to what Clarissa calls "the voice of nature" as it is mediated through the grandfather's written will (*C* 987). Yet the Harlowes' fluency in the rhetoric of the heart establishes a counter-romance to Richardson's, Hume's, and Clarissa's, even as it marks a generic symmetry between them. When the Harlowes rail against Clarissa's "stand in opposition to us all in a point our hearts are set upon," they redeploy Clarissa's sentimental language, evoking the genre in which it plays a crucial part (*C* 107). When Clarissa laments that her family "are resolved to break my heart," the servant Betty Barnes responds, "you are resolved to break theirs: so tit for tat, miss" (*C* 119). That the Harlowes' servant speaks for their economic and emotional affairs registers Richardson's disapproval of their passionate motives, marking how far they have come from their natural sentiment, and how much distance they have allowed to open between their transactions with money and with feeling. But Betty's retort also suggests that only dangerously subtle differences separate sentiment's guiding role in Britain's intersecting economies from its inverse – from allowing economic wants to determine the movement of sentiment, the sign of Richardson's corrupt society. Barnes's speech is a bad parody of Clarissa's Lockean equation between sentiment and economics: the "romantic" language of the heart fails to control the legal rhetoric of contract, jarring violently against the unfeeling yet impassioned Harlowe language of exchange.

Violence overtakes Clarissa and her texts long before the end of the work. Clarissa's family browbeats her, Lovelace rapes her, and the narrative fails to reach any teleological end. William Warner points out that Clarissa resists Lovelace's attempt at closure after the rape, despite his insistence that "The affair is over": Richardson grants Clarissa the authority to define the ways in which the romance should be read (*C* 883).[106] But Clarissa's own texts, especially her letter to Lovelace immediately after the rape, register the vivisections that passion performs on sentiment and the sentimental body. Lovelace perceptively acknowledges that he regrets Clarissa's Humean sentiment, her "LOVE OF VIRTUE," because it is "*principle*, native . . . so deeply rooted that its fibres have struck into her heart, [and] . . . there is no separating of the one, without cutting the strings asunder" (*C* 657). Confronted by violent passion, her sentimental principles produce anorexia and self-obliteration. In a letter she compares herself to a woman whose pet bear has "tor[n] her in pieces" (*C* 891). But Clarissa, as much as Lovelace, has become the bear, nature turned by human corruption against nature. "What she writes she tears," Lovelace notes to his confidant Belford, enclosing letters "*Torn in two pieces*," "*Scratched through, and thrown under the table*," or, in the series of commonplace quotations Clarissa writes out to comment on her state, scattered around the page like dismembered limbs (*C* 889–90, 893). Clarissa's violence against her text recapitulates Lovelace's own against Clarissa, both bodily ("the affair is over") and textual (his "*interception*" of some letters and "extraction" of a deformed text from others) (*C* 808, 811).

The one narrative that reaches Clarissa's correspondents intact is her coffin, famously annotated with self-designed inscriptions. Told of the coffin, and receiving Clarissa's last will, Arabella responds that "nobody could help being affected," but adds "that it was [Clarissa's] talent" to move her audience or readers. It is only on seeing the coffin itself – "the receptacle that contained the glory of their family . . . driven thence by their indiscreet violence" – that Clarissa's "talent" for sympathy works on her family's vestigial sentiment and yields a proper return (*C* 1322, 1398). Yet even as sentiment comes to dominate interpretation of Clarissa's romance, Clarissa herself, like her grandfather before her, becomes a ghost haunting Richardson's narrative. Richardson turns Jacobite nostalgia to Lockean liberal ends, but only at a price, for violence overtakes the text, overshadowing the ghosts of sentimental theory.

Sentiment produces social and economic cohesion only in Clarissa's and Richardson's dreams – and in romance, the immediate field of sentiment's operation. In the text as a whole, a Mandevillean practice prevails in which not sentiment but excessive passion becomes the British norm, and self-interest the sole trait that British subjects have in common. Richardson's defensive insistence on the embattledness of sentiment has the effect of producing, in romance, a generic playing field on which economic and political debates can be conducted, pursued not least by parodying Richardson's own fictions. Yet the counter-romances of Frances Burney, in which sentiment yields financial corruption and ruin, or of Mary Wollstonecraft, in which sentiment and gender are themselves exposed as violent economic fictions, look in some ways more like *Clarissa* than like a parody of it. For coercion shadows cohesion throughout Richardson's work. Unlike *Pamela*, *Clarissa* can extricate its heroine from the corrupt field of British history only in the shadow-world of saints and ghosts, the aftermath of violence, which is said, in *Clarissa*, to resemble the heroine's Lockean utopia. Richardson emphasizes Britain's ideological lack in order to supplement it with natural sentiment. But precisely in anatomizing the workings of sentiment in the service of British history, his romance highlights Britain's fractures and its losses.

CHAPTER 2

"Summoned into the machine": Burney's genres, Sheridan's sentiment, and conservative critique

In February 1774, the case of Alexander Donaldson, an Edinburgh bookseller accused of violating perpetual copyrights held by the London booksellers' monopolies, was debated in the House of Lords and the salons and coffeehouses of Edinburgh and London.[1] During the eighteen days it took to decide the case in Donaldson's favour, Frances Burney, aged twenty-one, met the pamphleteer John Shebbeare, who had published an attack on Lord Hardwicke's Marriage Bill in sentimental fictional form. Burney sat silent as Shebbeare dissected *Donaldson* with her father's guests, but she recorded in her diary that "what most excited his spleen was Woman, to whom he professes a fixed aversion; and next to her . . . the Scotch; and all the satire which he levelled at them, consisted of trite and hackneyed abuse." Burney concluded that Shebbeare's marriage of libertine misogyny and English nationalism with a cynical disregard for copyright made him and his novel an "antidote" to any woman's desire to marry, though she conceded, "I must read 'The Marriage-Act' . . . nevertheless."[2] Burney's fictions would later demonstrate that what underlay such *laissez-faire* thinking about sexual and literary commerce, and its accompanying defensive nationalism, was Britain's rejection of absolute standards of value and its embrace of the newfangled tyranny of the marketplace. In sacrificing the orderliness of families, the security of property, and the traditional Tory equation of birth with worth, Britain was imperilling internal unity as well.

Enacted in 1753, the Marriage Bill dictated that all marriages take place in the established church, in one party's parish of residence. No marriage could proceed in England without the sanction of banns or, among the aristocracy who were willing to pay for such decorous privacy, the authority of a special licence. Reviled by Catholics, Dissenters, and liberal believers in the natural virtue of sentiment, as well as by the fraud artists and impoverished younger sons whose hopes of

73

enrichment it curtailed, the Act deterred such once-frequent practices as Fleet marriages and heiress abduction by granting control and protection of women and their fortunes to fathers and husbands until widowhood should release them to their own authority.[3] The one remaining alternative to church and state scrutiny was elopement to Scotland, which had retained its own marriage laws after the Treaty of Union. Such elopements posed distinct dangers for both women and men, provoking cautionary narratives from supporters and opponents of the Bill.[4] In theory at least, Parliament made English marriage a transfer of real property between a woman's husband and father. The free circulation of goods (that is, women) and capital (their dowries) through Britain was, at least in the marriage market, effectively curtailed. In a significant sense, the Act proposed limits for Whiggish thinking about the social and economic value of individual desire, and Burney was to become a staunch defender.

The suspicion of unregulated capital and commerce that Burney demonstrated in preferring Hardwicke's Act to Shebbeare's abuse extended equally to copyright. Burney supported neither the *Donaldson* decision nor the new Copyright Bill that resulted from it. For although the Bill limited bookseller copyright to fourteen years, and although it thus disestablished the London congers that had hitherto restricted the ability of writers to profit by their own works, it did not much increase authorial control over the publication process. Rather, by redrawing the copyright laws for England, it lifted restrictions on the reproduction and circulation of literary capital in the provinces, Scotland, and Ireland, and increased the likelihood that "pirate," or illegitimate, editions would circulate as well. Like Samuel Johnson, as James Boswell recollected his response to the Bill, Burney favoured lifetime copyright for writers. This ideal system of copyright law was to operate analogously to a father's and a husband's control of a woman from spinsterhood through marriage, governing letters, like courtship, as a matter in which real property was at stake. Texts would be circulated by booksellers who contracted with writers to produce particular editions under authorial consultation. Copyrights would no longer be bought outright, by monopolistic *or* by entrepreneurial booksellers. After a writer's death the right to make books of his or her work would enter the public domain.[5]

In her diary, Burney associated Shebbeare's carelessness toward copyright with his opposition to Hardwicke and his desultory support for Donaldson: she tied his hatred of women and Scots to his *laissez-faire* commercial stance. Thus, in judging Shebbeare, she established a precocious suspicion of individual feeling as an ethical guide and a basis for marriage or social cohesion. At the same time, she began forming what was to become a lifelong but unsatisfied preference for subscription – genteel and limited in character, and allowing a writer to retain control over the circulation and pricing of her literary products – as a mode of publication.[6] Taken together, the romances in which she approached these two commercial arenas offer rules, deducible from the heroines' representative encounters with the various forms and figures of the marketplace, for uniting England and Scotland in Britain. Based on the demonstrable warrants of labour and "parentage" – in *Evelina* Burney was to apostrophize her father as "the author of my being" – authorial copyright would, like the Marriage Act, help forestall the social uncertainties, national animosities, and gendered cruelties consequent on imperfectly regulated commerce.[7]

The conjunction of courtship and the book trade with national unity in Burney's diaries – and, as we will see, in the romances that followed them – is one representative instance of a broad but cohesive critique of commerce by late-eighteenth-century conservative writers, many of whom were women. Samuel Richardson's fictions and other romances of mid-century, together with David Hume's political economy, had established the fields of letters and commerce as intersecting public spaces. The practices of circulation and exchange that characterized both fields were said by these writers to originate in the privacy of family relations, which provided the model for both larger, public spheres. In the "family economy," and so in the widening circle of economies it anchored, all social and economic relations moved in relation to a gold standard – natural sentiment – reproducible by the genre of romance.[8] In consequence of this pyramidal conception of society, in which sexual, industrial, and literary commerce rest on a shared standard reference point, Burney and her conservative peers could not, in rebuking contemporary market practices, separate economic activity from cultural production or domestic privacy – as historians of commerce and of Parliament's approach to economic regulation then tended, and still tend, to do.[9]

Accounts of late-eighteenth-century courtship fictions often suggest that the audible ambivalence of these works, or their ironic undercutting of their own sentimental resolutions, marks a covert or even unconscious opposition to contemporary expectations about the role of sentiment in marriage.[10] At the same time, historians of eighteenth-century fiction draw attention to the large numbers of women writing in the last quarter of the century, and to their uncertain response to the (resultant or underlying) marginal status of the romance genre.[11] I propose that a close connection existed between these forms of ambivalence, and that this closeness is the mark, within Tory romances at least, of a political economic protest with implications extending beyond domestic rules and the writing of particular women. As conservative writers recognized from the 1750s forward, the sentimental romances of mid- and late century unite political economic ideals with emotional expectations. The heroine's happy marriage, the often unrealized teleological end of sentimental romance, is contingent not just on her rightly feeling heart, but also on her demonstration of virtuous sentiment.[12] Sentiment, in consequence, becomes not only the cornerstone of narrative resolutions, but also a touchstone for the solution of social, economic, and some-times political conflicts that such closures often enact. Romances pro-duce among readers, as well as illustrate among characters, the senti-ment that, according to Hume and Adam Smith, lent cohesion to modern Britain.

Late-century conservative writers of romances, embodying their questioning of the marriage market in such a doubly market-oriented genre, united in a generalized assault on the unregulated commerce that, they feared, was the real end of sentimental romance. Often, they conducted their attack by questioning or parodying the genre itself. Such an assault was already incipient in the response of Frances Burney – barely of age and not yet a published writer – to the writings and conversation of the New Whig John Shebbeare. As a Tory writer of romance, Burney found her generic protest against commerce and sentiment paradoxically enabled by the triumph of the market in the *Donaldson* decision – a victory for the kind of cultural free trade, and for popular sentimental fictions, that the heroines of her romances find especially damaging. But her anti-commercial romances had deeper, more specifically generic roots: in resistance to Richardson's *Clarissa*, which had established the sentimental gold standard in romance and upheld it for political economy, and in romances written in the 1760s and 1770s by conservative writers who could neither escape the generic confines Richardson had established nor bring their own sentimental fictions to the restorative conclusions he projected.

CONTINGENCY AND NATURE IN SHERIDAN'S ROMANCES

The uneasy relations between Frances Sheridan's fictions and Richard-son's *Clarissa* exemplify the ambivalent state of conservative protest in the romances of the 1760s. In her romances, Sheridan directed her critique not only against Richardson's generic influence, but also, by extension, against the Humean political economy of sentiment that his romances upheld. To highlight Sheridan's conservatism requires a brief caveat. I discuss under that name the unease her fictions demonstrated with political economy through her criticisms of the market and the sentiment that, as Richardson insisted, provided Britain's economy with its natural laws. But Sheridan was also an Anglo-Irish Protestant who had married into a family of outspoken and increasingly prominent Patriots turned Anglo-Irish Whigs.[13] A similarly double relationship to Whiggism, and specifically to political economy, shapes Sheridan's romance narratives. Domestically and in letters, Sheridan's ambivalent position marks the ideological fragility of the Protestant post-Jacobite coalition to which Humean sentiment had offered a unifying theory, and for which Richardson's *Clarissa* had provided a generic basis. The Protestant consensus continually threatened to crumble – not, as might be expected, around the political-historical question of George III's monarchical legitimacy, but rather in consequence of political econ-omic questions about the naturalness of gendered sentiment and the legitimacy of commerce. These questions arose, as Sheridan's romances suggest, in response to persistent assumptions about first causes and their relation to Britain's political history, which the political economic renewers of political thought in the wake of the Jacobites sought, for the most part, to defend.

Sheridan published her first work of fiction, *Memoirs of Miss Sidney Bidulph, Extracted from her own Journal*, anonymously in 1761. Its distin-guishing quality, as Margaret Doody points out, is the unrelenting, irredeemable hopelessness of its heroine's history.[14] The narrative be-gins as Sidney Bidulph is forbidden to marry Orlando Faulkland, whom she loves, because he has apparently seduced another young lady. The Richardsonian introduction of Sidney's rival as "Miss B" warns the modern reader, but not the pre-*Pamela* Bidulphs, that she is a female rake, no victim of Faulkland's blandishments.[15] Soon after, Sidney submits to her mother's demand that she marry the sedate Arnold. But Arnold is already emotionally and financially entangled with B's aunt, the courtesan Gerrarde. He betrays Sidney, publicly banishes her, and squanders her fortune before dying and leaving her and her daughters penniless. After several fruitless attempts to earn her living by em-broidery, Sidney is rescued by a rich cousin and reunited with the widowed Faulkland, who has obeyed her demand that he marry B.[16]

They marry only to learn that Faulkland's wife has been mistakenly reported dead. The epistolary narrative ends with Sidney's "adieu" to her confidante Cecilia: "nothing but my death should close such a scene as this" (421).[17]

Coupled with the unending mishaps that befall her, Sidney's unwavering demonstrations of sentiment and the "strictest principles of virtue; from which she never deviated, through the course of an innocent, though unhappy life," comprise a tragedy that contemporary reviewers found particularly troubling (9). Some objected because Sidney – as most reviewers insisted, unlike Clarissa Harlowe – suffered through no fault of her own. Such a plot distressed reviewers avowedly because of its deterministic view of human suffering, though the accusations of predestinarianism that greeted Sheridan may well have been rooted in suspicion that scepticism and blind contingency were the real motives of its plotting. One reviewer in the *London Magazine* opposed Sheridan's tendency to promote a Calvinist form of predestination among its impressionable and sympathetic readers, on the grounds that such fatalism could lead to atheist despair.[18] Other readers, including Samuel Johnson and the *Critical* reviewer, viewed *Sidney Bidulph* more approvingly as a version of *Clarissa*, and its heroine as "a type of Miss Clarissa Harlowe," though these readers also wondered, as Johnson put it, whether Sheridan had "a right, upon moral principles, to make [her] . . . readers suffer so much."[19]

There was also, however, the possibility of a wholly different critical approach. Reading Richardsonian romances and the ongoing literary responses to them, many of Sheridan's conservative contemporaries described a dialectic between feminine sentiment and the printed text that they saw being cooperatively promoted by political economists and practical moralists. The tears of a virtuous young lady, as the philosophers and Richardson suggested, and as their female readers understood, guaranteed the virtue of the narrative she was reading, while her heartfelt response to moral fictions simultaneously testified to her own moral fitness. In the introduction to *Sidney Bidulph*, Sheridan reproduces this discourse in the approval expressed by the work's young male "Editor" as his two female companions respond to a tragic history with "that true testimony of nature to its merit, tears" (3). Contemporary critics of such exchanges between tears and texts often identified their roots in the modern marketplace. Writing in late life about the 1770s, the editor and biographer Lady Louisa Stuart recalled her youthful avoidance of reading sentimental fictions in company "lest she should not cry enough to gain the credit of proper sensibility."[20] Stuart's remark ironically marries the language of political economy with the rhetoric of conduct books. "Proper" sensibility, as distinct from the "true" and "false" sensibility debated at the end of the eighteenth century, is a retrospective synonym for Richardsonian, or for Humean, moral sentiment.[21] As a young lady's virtuous sentiment shades into the register of emotional sensitivity, it gives its possessor "credit" in the eyes of her audience, who assess the value of romances in tandem with their reader's value – socioeconomic as well as emotional and sexual – on the marriage market. After mid-century, that is, the sentiments displayed in a young lady's reading move past Richardson's idealistic portrayal. They are revealed as the feminine complement to the slippery coins and easy tears with which the "men of feeling" portrayed by Henry Mackenzie and Laurence Sterne in the 1760s and 1770s prove the equivalence of their own emotional and economic worth in their encounters with (usually female) distress.[22]

Sheridan's Sidney, who is well-read in "romances," describes an experience similar to Stuart's as her brother first tries to "draw [her] out" for Faulkland's contemplation (18, 21). Sir George Bidulph's carefully crafted conversational sallies teach her, as she puts it, to see herself as "a piece of goods . . . to be shewn to the best advantage to the purchaser," though she protests only when he talks of her in an openly "*bargaining* way" (14, 18). When Sidney, who often acknowledges her own position as "a Heroine," jokingly declares that the hero she marries must combine "generosity, valour, sweetness of temper, and a great deal of money" – his sentiment best proved in his manner of sharing his estate – she is corrected by her mother not for her irreverence, but because "a *great deal* is not necessary; a very moderate fortune with *such* a man is sufficient" (13, 49). In making her readers "suffer" what her sentimental heroine suffers, therefore, as even her "innocent" heroine recognizes, Sheridan gave Britain's marriage market, as well as its literary market, precisely what those who established gold standards for those intersecting economies continued to demand (9). On this view, Sheridan's romance, with its mingling of suffering, money, and tears, does not alone induce despair in its readers. Rather, despair arises from the demand for sensibility her fiction answers: from the chaotic unruliness of markets, the condition of Britain itself.

In highlighting the singularity and powerlessness of Sidney's sentiment, and its easy falsification by B and Gerrarde, Sheridan differs audibly with Richardson. Yet as if to guarantee assessment of *Sidney*

Bidulph by Richardson's sentimental standards, Sheridan's "Editor" dedicates "the following sheets" to "THE AUTHOR OF CLARISSA AND Sir CHARLES GRANDISON" (n.p.). "His" dedication identifies Sidney's narrative with the sentimental epistolary romance that Richardson had shaped to the demands of post-Jacobite Britain.[23] In forging this connection to Richardson's hybrid genre, "the Editor" evokes Richardson's political economic intertexts as well, declaring Sheridan's fiction more faithful than Richardson's *Pamela* to "real life," "probability," and "general experience" (5).[24] Like Richardson's Clarissa, Sidney Bidulph is never "rewarded" for her virtue, although her submissive patience during her marriage more than rivals the married Pamela's fidelity. *Pamela*, Sheridan's allusive rhetoric of "virtue" and "reward" hints, misrepresents the "nature" that *Sidney Bidulph* illustrates so "justly" (5). But *Pamela* is not the only target of Sheridan's implicit criticism. In revealing Richardson's "editorship" of *Clarissa* as a mask for his authorship, Sheridan's anonymous "editor" dismisses Richardson's claims for the historicity and representativeness of *Clarissa* as well. Sheridan presents her own work as a fictional editor's compilation, and she insists that the similar claim Richardson makes is a fictive device framing what must, in consequence, be read as another fiction.

Nevertheless, the sentimental epistolary form of Sheridan's romance resembles more than it departs from *Clarissa*: Sheridan's detachment of Richardson's romances from real history is not founded on any neo-Puritan suspicion that fiction writing is tantamount to deliberate untruth. Neither is her uneasy relation to Richardson's generic example the result of any clear sense of rivalry or desire for distinction. Rather, her push-pull relations with Richardson's romance may ultimately be seen to derive from political economic differences. Sidney exchanges Pamela's and Clarissa's Lockean faith in natural law for a pragmatic Hobbesian pessimism: "I have acted agreeably to the dictates of my duty; that must be my consolation: life is in itself a warfare, *my* life has been particularly so" (304). The contrast is highlighted in the moralizing preface with which, like *Clarissa*, Sheridan's narrative is framed. In this "Editor's Introduction," Sheridan's man of letters describes his receipt of Sidney's manuscript correspondence from Cecilia Rivers, the Anna Howe of the narrative, who seeks in old age to make sense of her long-dead friend's unremitting sorrow and distress. Cecilia couches her solution to the problem of suffering in a review of John Home's *Douglas*. She asserts that the tragic fall of a "blooming hero . . . adorned with the highest virtues" is more faithful to real life, and more productive of faith in "providence," than the "poetic justice" that "rewards" such heroes with earthly happiness (4–5). Her phrasing marks her reading of *Clarissa*, in which Richardson famously insists that resisting "*poetical justice*" teaches "the great lessons of Christianity."[25] In drawing her analogy between Sidney's letters and Clarissa's, Cecilia asserts the errors of Richardson's political economic theology.

Cecilia asserts that "an equal distribution of justice" can be found in heaven, but she dogmatically avows the inscrutability of first causes. Human suffering results from "strange misfortunes," which are "no more dispensed by the great ruler of all things for punishments, than the others are for rewards" (4–5). The disasters Sidney faces are undeserved, but desert is irrelevant: "God does not estimate things as we do" (5). Thus "It is ignorant, as well as sinful, to arraign his providence" by lamenting the random cruelties of human existence as though they have pattern and meaning, and thereby condemning God's nonintervention in the affairs of human life (5). Notwithstanding her reviewers' accusations of Calvinism, Sheridan couches her references to "providence" (unlike the comments of Richardson they imitate) wholly within the retrospect of a narrator who is herself involved in the tragic events of the work (5). That character is convinced that God causes no human events, and she seems by no means certain that God intervenes in earthly affairs at all.[26]

That Sidney does not curse God and die, therefore, is largely because an interventionist God is absent from the landscape of this work. The absence of providential order is most marked in the disappearance of that unshakeable natural law that Richardson, Hume, and Smith attach to sentiment. The sentimental logic of Richardson's romance ensures, in *Clarissa*, that despite the heroine's socioeconomic sufferings, the reader is reminded that the virtuous sentiments of her "heart" are the natural human norm. In chapter 1, I illustrated how Richardson attributes the corruption of the Harlowes and Lovelace to an excess of passion stemming from disease or deformity, which overwhelms their still-visible natural sentiment. Virtue, however unusual it might be in practice, is for Richardson the normal state of British society, and sentiment the rule. In contrast, the "best purposes" of Sidney's feeling heart, such as convincing Faulkland to marry Miss Burchell, are invariably "perverted from their ends" by "some unseen power" of "evil" (362). This figure resembles the "malignant demon" that Descartes proposed as the only epistemological alternative to a controlling providence.[27] Unwilling to accept the contingency that marks the events of her life and the plot, and denies them a natural logic or pattern, Sidney seeks the supplementary, imperfectly consoling explanation of a diabolical intelligence.[28]

Sidney's sentiment is neither powerful in practice nor theologically translucent. Unlike the world of Richardson's *Clarissa*, Sidney's social and economic world is without consistent laws or ethical and social constants and thus without natural means of self-regulation. Sentiment guarantees nothing beyond the "inevitability" of "social victims."[29] In exposing the fictionality of Richardson's sentimental law, Sheridan shows, by extension, that the natural "sentiment" that in Hume's philosophy creates fixed rules defining "Virtue," and the "*sympathy*" that creates a natural human desire to comply with them, are fictional as well.[30] At the same time, she resists the more explicitly political economic claim, most prominent in Smith's *Theory of the Moral Sentiments*, that "an invisible hand" shapes human feeling to accord with social order, and that a natural "love of system" promotes "sympathy" with the human happiness the "invisible hand" guarantees.[31] There is no system in *Sidney Bidulph*. As Todd puts it, in this novel "sentiment" – in political economy and its romance supplements – "suffers its logical worldly defeat."[32]

A world that looks to sentiment for its rules, Sheridan shows, is a world given up to disorder, for the impulses of a virtuous heart are not all-seeing. Nor are they stable or general enough to produce the stable order that Richardson had insisted, even in *Clarissa*, was the natural consequence of sentiment in private and public life. That Sidney Bidulph's last words are despairing, and that Cecilia's conclusion ends with an ellipsis, trailing off into irrecoverable loss, further indicates the work's absolute refusal of even the most idealistic, most theoretical teleology. This narrative is extended in *The History of Nourjahad* (1767), Sheridan's more popular and more sceptical posthumous romance. In *Nourjahad* the hero's excessive passions are chastened by tragic experience and restored to their sentimental nature, but the providential sufferings that befall him are revealed as a complex "machinery" worked not, as in Smith's ideal Britain, by individual "sentiment" and "sympathy" as the self-regulating "machine" of "system," but by the command of an absolute monarch, a man born to rule and to command great wealth irrespective of the feeling and virtue his education of Nourjahad displays (*TMS* 185).[33] Reading *Sidney Bidulph* retrospectively through *Nourjahad*, one could argue that the earlier romance portrays a society not only in want of unshakeable points of ethical, legal, and economic reference, but also in need of regulation from without: in desperate default of the wholly impersonal standards guaranteed by absolute kings.

That Sheridan, like Sterne and Mackenzie, continued in the Richardsonian mode of sentimental romance, varying direction only with *Nourjahad*'s swing into the geographically removed and politically cautious form of the Oriental tale, suggests the generic and political impasse she had reached. To yearn for monarchical absolutes in contemporary Britain was not only to break with the post-Jacobite consensus, but also to do battle with Sheridan's family and her Anglo-Irish upbringing, in which the hereditary Stuarts were anathema from a national, religious, and political point of view. Sheridan, like her Anglo-Irish and Scottish contemporaries, lacked a way to be critical of Britain's political economic consensus without dangerously criticizing the newly unified British polity with which political economy had become intertwined. The *Donaldson* v. *Beckett* case and the resulting changes in copyright would provide a focus for late-eighteenth-century conservative protest among Sheridan's acquaintances, including Johnson and the Burneys. But when Sheridan died in 1767, the *Donaldson* decision, which was to offer a means of holding anti-commercial and anti-sentimental complaint safely within the literary public sphere, was still seven years away.

COPYRIGHT AND COMMERCE: *EVELINA* IN THE AFTERMATH OF *DONALDSON*

When Burney published her first work of fiction, *Evelina*, in 1778, she reprised the epistolary romance narrative that introduced Sheridan's inexperienced heroine into sophisticated social life. This was still a relatively new subset of romance. Its intersections with Hume's sentimental political economy sprang in part, like Richardson's debates with his readers on women's marital choice, from those marriage-market conditions of increasing circulation and selection that the Hardwicke Bill sought to restrain. But Burney further modernized the genre by orienting it more firmly to the contemporary marketplace. Sidney Bidulph, like Clarissa Harlowe, saw "the world" come to her. Her suitors, like Clarissa's, were introduced into her family's private space by a brother or a parent. Burney's heroine, in contrast, leaves home to make her "entrance into the world," an innovation emphasized in the subtitle of the third and subsequent editions.[34] As this subtitle indicates, *Evelina* does not merely reproduce, but deepens and extends Sheridan's narrative of a young woman's worlding, and Burney shares Sheridan's suspicion of the intertwining ideologies of personal heterosexual feeling and commercial order that were said to regulate social life. *Evelina* provides an optimistic resolution – optimistic, however, only in its anachronistic impossibility.

At first, Burney's romance promises to recapitulate the unhappy experiences of *Sidney Bidulph*, although frequent eruptions of satire directed against city merchants, foppish commoners, and the French and Francophile English prevent the heroine's misadventures from unfolding so painfully. The pseudonymous Evelina Anville – "Evelina" suspiciously echoes her mother's maiden name, Caroline Evelyn, and "Anville" is its invented acronym – plunges rudderless into the marriage market, claimed only by her mother's distant relations, the Branghtons. These merchants become the targets of Burney's satire for the Scotophobic intolerance they direct against their lodger, Macartney, as well as for their ill manners and pretensions to fashion.[35] But as her mother's friend Lady Howard puts it, Evelina has "natural grace," and "nature has blessed her with an excellent understanding": "that politeness which is acquired by an acquaintance with high life, is in her . . . well supplied by a natural desire of obliging, joined to a deportment infinitely engaging" (21). Evelina circulates in public only until her father, Sir John Belmont, can be brought to confirm the claim to legitimacy and aristocracy that is already evident to the world in her natural gentility. Her legal claim, supported by her guardian, the clergyman Villars, and upheld by Howard's influential circle, is conveniently documented not only in a series of letters between Belmont and Caroline, but also in Evelina's resemblance to her mother.

Perhaps the most telling register of this work's opposition to Richardsonian sentiment and the logic of the marketplace is that the only sentimental scene in *Evelina*, reported to Villars by Evelina herself, details the emotional encounter between the heroine and her father as he recognizes Caroline Evelyn in her face:

"Poor unhappy Caroline!" cried he, and . . . burst into tears. Need I tell you, my dear Sir, how mine flowed at the sight? (383)
"Gracious Heaven!" looking earnestly at me, "never was likeness more striking! – the eye, – the face, – the form, – Oh my child, my child!" (385)

Confronted with Evelina, her mother's "resemblance" and "representative," Belmont proclaims his willingness to "own her," taking her instantly off the market (383, 385).[36] In Burney's anachronistic utopia, sentiment does not uphold the market's power, but rejoices at a rare opportunity of averting it. Reinvented as real property instead of consumer goods, Evelina escapes the market and its logic, transferred by contract and "settlements" from her father to her aristocratic suitor in a way that fulfills her own desires, as she writes ecstatically, "without" her "being consulted" (377). Evelina incidentally brings Belmont to acknowledge Macartney as his son by another woman, confirming Evelina's ready acceptance of him as a "dear brother" (382). Thus Burney's utopian return to the aristocratic past through a rigorous enforcement of Hardwicke's principles resolves not only Evelina's problems, but offers a local, familial remedy for the problem of Britain's internal disunity as well.[37] In Burney's early romance, the joyous affirmation of genealogy and birthright is also the source of Britain's national harmony. Both are the best evidence of "Providence" (405).

Evelina escapes into an aristocratic world of settlements and special licences. Her conservative romance marks the beginning of Burney's extended critique of copyright, and of markets generally, for which the circulation of texts, like Evelina's circulation, is a synecdochic type. What transforms Evelina's evasion into evidence of Burney's critique is the chiasmic relation that, as Catherine Gallagher points out, links the heroine's market experiences to those of the writer.[38] Burney's romance declares that the intrinsic worth of Evelina Belmont derives from kinship and is expressed in "natural" virtue, and only requires paternal acknowledgement to be irrevocably established. Burney herself, however, produces a narrative whose value is by no means so certain or stable as the worth of its eponymous heroine. First rejected by the bookseller Dodsley, *Evelina* was offered to Lowndes, a publisher and distributor of ephemeral texts. Lowndes, in his turn, rejected Burney's suggestion of serial publication and assumed control of the book's circulation, deciding how many editions to issue and paying Burney 20 pounds for the copyright (*ED* II: 213).[39] Burney's response in her diary is torn between pride in her good sales in England, Scotland, and Ireland, and an "odd sensation" of conservative discomfort at losing control of *Evelina*, which it "is now in the power of *any* and *every* body to read" and "may now be seen by every butcher and baker, cobler [*sic*] and tinker, throughout the three kingdoms, for the small tribute of three pence" (*ED* II: 214).

Evelina shares its avowedly factual epistolary form with Richardson's *Clarissa* and Sheridan's *Sidney Bidulph*. However, the introductory claims of its "Editor" are superadded to the admissions of a self-proclaimed "Novelist" acutely aware of the "inferior rank" she and her work are likely to be accorded, as a woman and a romance, within "the republic of letters." Burney acknowledges her romance in a way that Richardson and Sheridan do not. In so doing, she questions the efficacy of its utopian conclusion and, at the same time, uneasily names the work's subjection to the book trade. In the prefaces to *Evelina*, Burney acknowledges commercial anxieties that the text itself denies. As she outlines the future of her romance in prefacing *Evelina*, the work, like the copyright law that governs it, remains at the mercy of commerce throughout Britain and Ireland. That the text was eventually pirated in Ireland validated Burney's fears, and confirmed her early opposition to the *Donaldson* decision as well.

That *Donaldson* was a landmark in British literary and political culture, and especially in the relations between romance and political economy, is evident in the passion that spills out in Burney's reaction to Shebbeare, in her anxious prefaces to *Evelina*, and in other contemporary responses. Its influence may be felt, in particular, in the new political alliances that were defined by writers' degrees of support for or opposition to commercial freedom, as expressed in their reactions to the competing claims of Donaldson and the London congers. For refocusing British liberalism and conservatism, and thus for reconfiguring the nature of the British union, the effects of *Donaldson* v. *Beckett* may be compared in character, though not in historical duration or geographical extent, to those of the 1745 Jacobite Rebellion.[40] Copyright created strange bedfellows and opened strange rifts. The New Whig conservatism of Edmund Burke, for example, stood firmly against Scotland's "pirate" printers and in support of established trade, and he vigorously defended the London congers' claims in the House of Commons (*ED* 1: 288n). Attorney General Thurlow, on the other hand, damned Beckett and his colleagues as "impudent, monopolizing men."[41] Meanwhile, the conservative literary professionals Johnson and Burney, while benefiting mildly from the break-up of the London monopoly, took a third position, opposing the decreased regulation of literary commerce with Scotland and the provinces while continuing to revile the law that permitted the London congers to absorb authorial copyright in the first place. Their disagreement with Thurlow and Burke measures the break some late-eighteenth-century conservatives made with the rhetorically Whig but practically bipartisan economics that had come to represent conservatism in the political arena, replacing the older, Jacobite-tainted Tory traditionalism. Yet equally, Burney broke with the Richardsonian romances that had promoted this political economic consensus.

Late-century conservatives, including Burney, represented commerce as a diffuse force that penetrated into and destabilized the safest corners of private life. They often paired letters and courtship in their criticisms, as imperfectly regulated and increasingly commercial fields of social action, couching their critique in generic terms. In his journal *The Observer*, for example, the playwright Richard Cumberland, an acquaintance of Burney's, attacked the pervasive influence of Richardson's romances, especially *Clarissa*, on letters and the conduct of young women. Lamenting the increasing influence of "puffery" on literary commerce, he compared it with the ubiquity of fashion in courtship. Together, he insisted, these forms of consumption and show allowed upstart servants and tradespeople to buy their way into social and ethical respectability independent of their moral or financial worth.[42] His parallel between cultural goods and young women on the marriage market reproduces the relation Burney's *Evelina* prefaces establish between her heroine and the text that bears her name. While the new Copyright Act gave writers a limited nominal right to their own productions, it also subjected texts to the competition of booksellers and thus to the vagaries of consumer demand. So too, Burney's romances suggest, the desires that drove the marriage market, aided by sentimental propagandists such as Shebbeare, have supplanted the written rule of the Marriage Act. If fathers and clergymen can, by law, prevent elopements, they also encourage their daughters and parishioners to compete for the notice of potential husbands. The double critique of the marriage market and the culture market contested what conservative women writers, and some of their male colleagues, feared was the triumph of commerce, and its justifying ideologies of sentiment, in Britain. They observed a world in which desire had gained even more influence than Richardson, in *Clarissa*, had admitted it to wield. They thought, as Sheridan feared, they were watching the breakdown of British society – the overthrow of British institutions by individual desire; the defeat of British laws and customs by the unchained human will.

Collectively, Burney's romances form a detailed response to these contests. They uphold the Tory longing for absolute and unshakeable measures of human worth – the world conservatives believed Britain had lost – and they reject the overriding rule of supply and demand that, conservatives feared, had usurped the place of social, political, and economic absolutes. The three romances Burney published between 1782 and 1814, following her first experience in the literary marketplace, pioneer the new conservative subgenre of economic romance. The characteristic mode of their plotting is a parodic irony that wells up between the cracks in what at first appear to be romances of sentiment resembling Richardson's or Sheridan's. Burney's irony, the product of a generic parody that takes aim at Richardson by imitating Sheridan, inundates the heroines of her romances before chastening them with a lesson in the advantages of absolute standards and established authority. Burney directs her critique toward "sentiment" and "taste," which in Richardson's *Clarissa* and Hume's *Essays, Moral, Political, and Literary* and *Treatise of Human Nature* had established the rule of "natural" human dispositions that were to supplement the capricious logic of commerce in courtship and the book trade. As in Louisa Stuart's reminiscences, the "credit" of Burney's heroines unites two principal fictions that sanctioned the law of demand and the circulation of women, books, and other goods, bringing together the institution of trust between buyer and seller with the conventional physical signs of sentiment that signalled a woman's worth. An equally inefficient sign of sexual, ethical, and economic worth, credit undergoes a thoroughly ironic split in Burney's romances. She examines the ambiguous tendency of "credit" to reduce worth to appearances. She addresses the ease with which writers following Richardson's example, and seeking to reconcile worth with demand-value, too often exchanged the former for the latter. Except for her beleaguered heroines, Burney's characters rigorously exclude questions of birth from marriage, of worth from cultural production and consumption, and of ethical absolutes from both, replacing them with financial credit and "the credit of sensibility."[43] The ironies of "credit" thus parody the workings of the political economy whose claims for the trustworthiness of natural sentiment had come, as Burney represented it, to dominate commerce, courtship, and the field of letters that intersected both.

Burney's heroines are renovated Clarissas and Sidney Bidulphs, extricated from their struggles and saved from tragedy only by a magical and arbitrary restoration, heralded in *Evelina*, of Tory standards of socioeconomic and ethical worth. In Burney's works, unlike Richardson's *Clarissa* or Sheridan's *Sidney Bidulph*, the romance of rescue is permitted to complete itself. Burney's romances, however, offer a conservative wish-fulfillment that is the antithesis of Richardsonian romance, and that is not even considered by Sheridan. Following each heroine's desolate journey through a cross-section of British society, the damaged moral absolutes and economic standards are restored by what Burney represents as a return to a world in which birth, character, appearance, and moral and financial worth perfectly coincide. In Burney's utopian world, value is upheld by paternal and conjugal authority, fenced round and protected by formal contracts, and supported by the principled obedience of women whose virtue and feeling have nothing to do with the shows of sentiment they are often obliged to make.

FEELING, ETHICS, AND THE MARKETPLACE

As Sheridan and Stuart recognized, feminine sentiment had long been not only a sign of female worth, but an invitation to masculine taste as well: sentiment contained within itself the seeds of sensibility. Writing to Richardson in 1751, for example, one of his friends, a merchant named Edwards, remarked that *Clarissa* has "given me a touchstone by which I shall try the hearts of my acquaintance, and judge which of them are true standard."[44] In his Prefaces and Postscript to *Pamela* and *Clarissa*, Richardson suggested that his romances demonstrated, and produced among their readers, the sentiment that alone could provide his fractious British society with the economic and ethical gold standards necessary to hold it together.[45] Edwards is a compliant reader. Like the "Editor" of Sheridan's *Sidney Bidulph*, and like Richardson himself, he equates the signs of sentiment in response to sentimental texts with the reader's moral worth, her value in society, and her price on the marriage market. At the same time, however, his letter raises a question that Richardson, caught up in the problems of real history, and of sentiment's ideological fragility and practical powerlessness, did not wholly anticipate: the problem of theatricality.[46] For, as Burney demonstrates in *Cecilia* (1782), *Camilla* (1796) and *The Wanderer* (1814), the equation of sentiment's signs with real feeling, and so with worth itself, allows doubly for slippage. Thoroughly investigated and mourned in *Sidney Bidulph*, and partly conceded even in *Clarissa*, the possibility that sentiment has little practical force and only a theoretical, even fictive relation to social order is fully and tragically realized in Burney's romances. Yet these works also deplore the consequences that follow when sentiment is falsified by those who would increase their market value without the backing of inheritance or investment in moral labour. Burney shows that sentiment opens itself to charges of relativism as well as of fictionality: to suspicions that an economic fiction alone holds a lawless Britain, corrupted by *laissez-faire* self-interest, in check.

Burney first united the problem of true and false sensibility with credit in 1778, in a series of sceptical vignettes written soon after the publication of *Evelina*. Writing to her sister Susanna, Burney described the two competing qualifications of her bluestocking acquaintance Sophy Streatfield: a talent for translating Greek and the ability to weep at will. Cynically aware of the social capital Streatfield manufactures along with her tears, Burney pays a sly homage to her theatrics with the prima donna's title "the S.S." Burney's friend Hester Thrale invites Streatfield to her salon, where she enters the presence of Burney, Johnson, and other conservative women and men of letters. When Thrale, familiar with Streatfield's talents, commands her to weep for the pleasure of her guests, Burney watches as "Two crystal tears" appear in "the soft eyes of the S.S., and roll . . . gently down her cheeks." But Burney's sentimental diction soon gives way to sardonic analysis. No one will marry an impoverished bluestocking, according to Burney, so Streatfield has developed control of her tears to compensate for her learnedness and poverty. Displaying her sentimental self, she is "very well satisfied" that she is "only manifesting a tenderness of disposition, that increased her beauty of countenance."[47] Streatfield assumes, correctly, that her absurd tears will buy more desire than condemnation. Burney records Thrale's witty wager with her male guests – an offer to "'insure [Streatfield's] power of crying herself into any of your hearts she pleased.'" Gleefully quoted, this figure of speech shrewdly names the economic force of Streatfield's performance: as good as coin to buy herself a husband, the canny S.S.'s tears are a sure thing – so sure that Burney and Thrale offer a financial guarantee.

Middle- and upper-class women like Burney and Thrale, Streatfield, Sheridan, and Stuart received clear messages from many sources about the essential social purposes of sentiment. More covertly, they also recognized the growing market for it. From Richardson forward, economists, educators, and writers of sentimental romances alike urged their readers to cultivate visibly feeling hearts, to gain the "credit of proper sensibility" in the eyes of the world. Their exhortations, however, often registered what the writers themselves would deny: that sentiment was neither universal nor intrinsic, and that its signs were by no means stably attached to the feelings they stood for. In attempting to provide unstable markets with an unchangingly virtuous and feeling anchor in the privacy of the home, the most popular conduct writers of the day reintroduce market logic into courtship and domestic morality.[48] In *A Father's Legacy to his Daughters* (1774), for example, the physician turned conduct writer John Gregory is torn between marketing and preaching to his unmarried daughters, the immediate addressees of the conduct book he published for the young women of Britain. His wish for them to develop "in whatever can make a woman amiable," including sensibility, conflicts with his "father's quick apprehension of the dangers that too often arise . . . from the attainment of that very point."[49] To mediate this conflict between propriety and demand, proper sentiment and the ambiguous signs of emotional responsiveness, Gregory exhorts his daughters to cultivate "your modesty . . . the natural softness and sensibility of your dispositions" (10). He begs his daughters to employ sensibility against itself, attracting men by the very device that guarantees their virtue. Yet his warning that "I do not want you to affect delicacy; I wish you to possess it" jars against his concession, immediately following, that "it is better to run the risk of being thought ridiculous than disgusting" (36). In seeking a husband, it is better to assume false modesty than to be caught with one's sensibility down altogether.

This collision between natural and cultivated feeling tends to reproduce, even in such preventive discussions as Gregory's, the feared infiltration of virtue's laws by desire and demand. Burney acknowledged this mutual contamination of market and morals, taking an especially sardonic delight in the bold conduct of Gregory's daughter at their first meeting. She wrote to Susanna that "Miss Gregory, though herself a very modest girl, quite stared me out of countenance, and never took her eyes off my face" (*DL* i: 42, 44–6). Like Streatfield's tears, the stares of Gregory's visibly modest daughter belie his claim that women are governed by natural sentiment, or that the evidence of sensibility may be trusted. Assumed as a flirtatious veneer to be dropped in female company, the girl's apparent blushing propriety allows Burney to demonstrate that Gregory's lessons create demand rather than bolstering his daughter's virtue – and that Miss Gregory has learnt her father's lessons well.[50]

Nor was this infiltration by the market unique to Gregory's work. Other conduct writers were less subtle in their market orientation. In a tract reprinted throughout the 1790s, and parodied by Burney, William Kenrick unapologetically, if in part metaphorically, outlines an economics of sensibility and social perception: "Fairer than polished silver, more valuable than virgin gold, more precious than the oriental pearl, or the diamonds of golconda, is reputation to a female." Kenrick directs his instructions entirely toward the appearance of virtue, and of feeling in particular, arguing that a valuable woman is easily identified by the visible signs of sensibility. Her "tears mingle with those who weep, and she laugheth with those who are cheerful; she shareth the calamities of her neighbours, and she partaketh also of their joys."[51] In *Cecilia, or Memoirs of an Heiress*, Burney's distaste for this doctrine appears as a series of escalating disasters that follow the mad moralist Albany's coercion of the sentimental heroine – ironically named for Sheridan's calmly wise Cecilia – to charities she cannot afford.[52] The speeches of Albany, Cecilia's tutor in charitable endeavours, draw equal attention to the social expectations of the marriage market and to the literary markets in which Burney's romances, and thus her characters, participate. Albany " 'runs into blank verse perpetually,' " as Cecilia's urbane acquaintance Gosport notes satirically.[53] More often, he speaks in the portentous couplets of biblical proverbs or wisdom books – or of Kenrick's conduct book. " 'Are you proud? are you callous? are you hard of heart so soon?' " he asks Cecilia, " 'yet seest not that thou art marked for sacrifice! yet knowest not that thou art destined for prey!' " (68, 204).

Albany's prophetic couplets mask his equation of worth with wealth. Yet his beliefs recapitulate those of Cecilia's guardian, the miserly tradesman Briggs, although Albany advocates freespending charity. To highlight the resemblance, Burney gives Briggs a bent for metaphors of sensibility and a tendency to speak in couplets that resound with de-based mimicry of Albany's – and Kenrick's – psalmodic style. " 'Is he a *good* man? that's the point, is he a *good* man?,' " Briggs asks in evaluating the economic power of another of Cecilia's three guardians. " 'Is he *warm*? that's the point, is he *warm*?' " (751). Neither Cecilia's legal guardian nor the moralist who becomes her financial guide is distin-guishable from the fortune-hunting denizens of the marriage market, who watch Cecilia, in a passage that echoes *Sidney Bidulph*, "with the scrutinizing observation of a man on the point of making a bargain, who views with fault-seeking eyes the property he means to cheapen" (34). The shared belief of the men in Cecilia's world that her financial liquidity and credit can and should signal her sensibility and so her worth discredits Albany's lessons in feeling, the popular romances and conduct books he quotes, and the values of the contemporary marriage market all at once.[54] Sir Robert Floyer, one of Cecilia's corrupt suitors, is more accurate than he knows in complaining that " 'there's no going upon trust with women, any more than with money' " (230). Burney makes the consequences explicit as Cecilia's sufferings culminate in madness and loss. She is doubly circulated, her value up for grabs, listed in the *Daily Advertiser* among the goods of a pawnbroker who finds her wandering in the City – "a crazy young lady, tall, fair complexioned, with blue eyes and light hair," and "no money about her" (901).

This account of "sensibility" and "credit" is extended and rendered more bitter in *Camilla* (1796), a romance structured as a conduct book, offering "Specimens of Taste" alongside "Modern Ideas of Duty," "The Computations of Self-Love," "Juvenile Calculations," and "Tuition of a young Lady." There, as these chapter titles hint, Burney joins political economic analysis of the marriage market to a more explicit discussion of "taste" in the cultural marketplace. To the elite world of the "ton" into which the innocent Camilla is thrown, spending – of coins and of tears – is the register of sensibility and value in both spheres. Burney plays on that Richardsonian notion the conduct writer James Fordyce approvingly called "generous sensibility," a standard trait that limits the possibility of false feeling by linking women's taste and character with the money they spend on charities, accomplishments, and elegant items of dress.[55] For Fordyce, whose much reprinted *Sermons to Young Women* was the most influential of mid- and late-century conduct books, courtship explicitly divides its players into consumers and consumed. Camilla's fiancé Edgar Mandlebert learns from the clergyman Doctor Marchmont, his tutor, a Fordycean *caveat emptor* approach to courtship. Marchmont exhorts him to examine Camilla with "positively distrustful" eyes; to scrutinize her as a wary purchaser – or as Sheridan's Orlando Faulkland – is expected to do:

Whatever she does, you must ask yourself this question: "Should I like such behaviour in my wife?" Whatever she says, you must make yourself the same demand. Nothing must escape you; you must view as if you had never seen her before; the interrogatory, *Were she mine?* must be present at every look, every word, every motion . . . even justice is insufficient during this period of probation, and instead of inquiring, "Is this right in her?" you must simply ask, "Would it be pleasing to me?"[56]

However stringent Edgar's standards might be, his taste remains self-interested. Nothing prevents the "pleasing" and "liking" that replace "justice" from shifting at his pleasure. As products of a fickle taste, the consumer judgments that drive his courtship of Camilla, and thus the romance Burney devotes to it, visibly mime the relativism of a social order based on the cooperation of taste and sensibility.

Camilla's displays of feeling figure largely among the determinants of Edgar's taste for her. Thus when Edgar angrily condemns Camilla's loss of "sensibility," she desperately sets out to regain it in his eyes (705). She promises *"upon her honour"* to redeem the credit of a failed shopkeeper and his family, though she herself is penniless. Although her honour, or probity, is compromised by giving way to feeling, her "steadiness" cannot "withstand her compassion," and it is compassion that she must prove to Edgar's satisfaction (711–12). At the same time, however, she purchases an expensive ballgown, to impress Edgar with her beauty and her naturally exquisite taste. Charity and fashion alike require Camilla to spend money she does not have. Burney stages a set-piece in which Camilla looks "now at the pleading group [of the tradesman's "interesting" children], now at her expensive dress . . . and with a blush turning from the mirrour, and to the children with a tear . . . consented" to pay the family's debts (713–14). Camilla's alms and "expensive dress" are acts of mirror-gazing directed outwards, a response to her awareness of a public opinion that continually judges her sensibility, and so her value, by her spending. Acutely aware of her reputation for taste and feeling, she compromises both again and again. The credit of her sensibility shades literally into financial credit as, like Cecilia before her, she at last becomes entangled with the moneylender who bankrolls her charitable and fashionable pretensions.

Like Sheridan and Richardson before her, Burney places her heroine at the centre of a web of demands, her credit fluctuating wildly in relation to men's competing claims. As Camilla encounters it, however, fashionable society is a giant marketplace, with no law save the law of appearances and the desires to which semblances cater. The artificially inflated or unfairly deflated values caused by the unstable balance of supply and demand play out, on an uncomfortably personal and feminized level, the entrapment of courtship and cultural production within the field of commerce. Thus Camilla's rescue of an abused pet bird and her care for her spendthrift brother Lionel attract the eye of Sir Sedley Clarendel, a rake who assumes postures of delicate feeling, but who privately pokes urbane fun at the sensibility he mimes in women's presence. He remarks to Edgar, for example, that "We are at such prodigious expence of sensibility in public . . . that if we suffered much for our private concerns to boot, we must always meet one another with tears in our eyes" (473). Burney hints at Clarendel's exemplary status within a corrupt cult of sensibility by nicknaming him "Clary," a diminutive he shares with Richardson's Clarissa, notwithstanding Richardson's careful distinction of virtuous sentiment within the varieties of instinctive, delicate feeling. Like Clarissa, Clarendel proves his feeling through finance, responding to Camilla's profligate charities with illicit offers of money. To the feckless Lionel, in turn, Camilla becomes a circulating currency, a limitless order on Clarendel's banker. "'What will [appealing to Clarendel for funds] cost you,'" he asks his sister, " 'except a dimple or two the more?' " (523). Edgar Mandlebert completes the triangle of male demands. Like Lionel he equates women with coin: if a man's credit depends on his honour, then a woman must "guard . . . the honour of her husband," which is, like her pin-money, a "deposit" in her hands (476). Like Clarendel, Edgar desires Camilla most when he watches her sacrifice herself.

Burney stringently ironizes the excessive self-sacrifice Camilla has learnt from earlier romances and conduct books – from Richardson, from Fordyce, and even from Sheridan. *Camilla* climaxes in an embedded parody of the death scenes in *Clarissa*, in which Burney treats Camilla's longing for death as a fit of petulant "egotism" (872). Like Clarissa, Camilla writes a series of "farewell" letters, with "the direction . . . with difficulty added, '*Not to be delivered till I am dead*'" (870). Like Clarissa, she begins a process of "self-examination" before falling in "an aguish shivering fit, while her eyes seemed emitting sparks of fire," declaring, " 'It is certainly now . . . over, and hence I move no more' " (871–2).[57] Unlike Clarissa, however, who never doubts that God's "mercies" will come to her, and who says of death that "a very few moments – will end this strife – and I shall be happy,"[58] Camilla finds her own "joy" rapidly "converted into an awe unspeakable" (872). As Burney's narrator puts it, Camilla realizes that "The wish of death is commonly but disgust of life," and "Conscience" regains "the reins from the hands of imagination," which have "concealed from her view the cruelty of this egotism" and the "wilful" sin of "self-murder" (872–3). Camilla, perhaps, has read too many romances: she wishes, as Cumberland fears young women wish, to become a Clarissa Harlowe. Now, as the "mist" that has "hidden from her own perceptions the faulty basis of her desire" is "cleared away," she takes up a "prayer-book" instead (872–3). As in *Evelina*, a stern but elegiac Burney rescues her heroine from the rules of the market, and from the sentimental romances that, as her parody suggests, convey them – this time by redirecting her taste from the heart and its sensibility toward the soul and its Church of England laws.

Burney's conclusion stabilizes Camilla's value and social position, but it cannot wholly foreclose the circumstances from which Burney rescues her heroine. At once a standard of value, her taste signalling her fitness for the taste of men, and an object of fluctuating and unsettled worth, Camilla is dependent on the caprices of consumers. In each case her worth, like the worth of a literary work subjected to the logic of commerce – and like the rules of social order, or so Burney and other conservative women fear – depends solely on masculine demand.

Camilla is severely critical of the reasons and motives behind that demand, of women's excessive desire to comply with it, and of the Richardsonian romances and conduct books that teach both.

THE THEATRICALITY OF CREDIT

I have been arguing that a homology is visible in Burney's romances between courtship and credit, and that a mirroring relation unites the Marriage Act of 1753 and the Copyright Act of 1774. The key to their connection, in Burney's texts as in the romances to which her works responded, is the established intersection of sentimental romance with political economy. For the doubleness of credit – its simultaneously economic and ethical valence – derives from two distinct sources that meet in political economy: the moral philosophy Hume and Smith derived from Francis Hutcheson, and the political and economic history they inherited from John Locke.[59] In turn, the popular economists and conduct writers who circulated their ideas, and the romance writers who demonstrated their use, share responsibility for the coexistence of moral and financial ideals within the late-eighteenth-century understanding of credit, and thus for their mutual contamination as well. As a woman's reputation for sensibility appears to popular moralists as an economic matter, so the writers of political economic pamphlets view financial credit as a moral issue. In Burney's romances, which reproduce this interpenetration, the exchange signalled the inescapability of the laws of commerce even in the so-called private spheres of literary consumption and marital choice.

The word "credit" appears frequently in romances written after 1780. Its sources lie in conduct literature, in Richardsonian romance, and in the rising anxiety that conservative writers of popular economics expressed about public credit and private debt, especially after war with France terminated Britain's issue of specie.[60] To Jane Austen, for example, credit unites personal relations with financial dealings, Elizabeth Bennet's willingness to believe George Wickham's slanderous gossip and the Meryton tradespeople's indulgence of his consuming and gambling.[61] Credit plays a similarly ambidextrous role in Burney's romances, but her works also register, centrally, deeply, and morally, a critical view of *her own* uses of "credit," which her works represent, in both its economic and ethical senses, as falsehood. In Burney's economic romances, credit is characterized by displays of sensibility and socioeconomic power by those without equity, and by a value for reputation over such older Tory concepts as kinship, honour, and birth. Austen's economic terminology ("credit," "interest") has been explained as the result of willingness to engage with a commercial society "in its own terms" rather than a latent critique of commerce.[62] I argue in chapter 4 that Austen embraced commerce as an inescapable fact capable of being turned to the uses of national character and British social stability. But Burney represents such acceptance of financial thinking in daily life as a product of commercial corruption and a sign that traditional determinants of worth have been supplanted by financial expediency and demand.

In Burney's texts, in short, credit is more than a metaphor: it is the crux in romance where ethics and finance shade into one another, where tracts about money and morals become indistinguishable in the aims of political economy. Just as conduct books made good consumers of their readers in order to make them good choices for prospective husbands, works of popular political economy tended to double as conduct books. In 1763, for example, Adam Anderson, a career merchant, civil servant, and one of the Scottish Enlightenment's popularizers, recounted the economic history of Britain as a triumphant tale of moral and commercial progress. Anderson writes for the improvement as well as the instruction of his middle-class readers, attempting to instill a sense of the benefits of taste, including private spending even where personal debt is involved.[63] He preaches a definition of wealth that includes all the circulating money in Great Britain, not excepting money owed by one party to another (xxv): he shares the enthusiasm of Smith or Hume for circulating credit as a motor and proof of expanding trade and a contributor to growth. To Anderson "The immense increase of our . . . plate, jewels, furniture, paintings, equipages, libraries, medals, coins, shipping, horses, and other cattle, &c.," regardless of the debts of the buyer, is visible proof of Britain's economic health (xxiv).

Particularly troubling was this insistence of Whiggish Scots political economists that the increasing circulation of funds in the British "national" economy – a form of financial success that rests atop a precarious pyramid of credit relations – is a sign of Britain's moral progress. The 1688 Revolution, for example, becomes for Anderson a defining moment in the triumph of Britain's national character, precisely because Britain has since then "increased in . . . almost every part of our general commerce" (111). In his *Letters on a Regicide Peace* (1796), Edmund Burke was to attack Anderson's teleological account of credit and financial history for its indifference to national unity, to public spirit, and to Britain's interests abroad – matters newly relevant in the face of the "regicide peace" with France that the increasingly conservative Burke was then endeavouring to forestall.

As he wrote the *Letters*, Burke was simultaneously, though unsuccessfully, attempting to establish a subscription for Burney's *Camilla*. That work confirms Burke's suspicion of credit, but whereas Burke condemns the ill effects of credit on British commerce, and the clash between self-interested private lenders and the national interest, Burney illustrates the displacement of "real" financial equity by private credit agreements, and the supplanting of government rules by self-regulating networks of lenders and borrowers.[64] For Burke, Britain's government suffers at the hands of private financiers, but the government's own policy on private finance appears by its absence in Burney's romances. Chaos in Britain's social order is the consequence. The *laissez-faire* policies of a market liberal administration permit the internal ethnic hatreds of *Evelina*. Equally, they fail to control the financial amorality that Burney's villains, from Harrel and Sir Robert Floyer in *Cecilia* to the minor confidence tricksters who populate *Camilla* and *The Wanderer*, employ in their dealings with her heroines.

The wars of the 1790s brought financial chaos, and Whig apologists attempted to defend on moral grounds the government's lack of interest in legislating credit more tightly. Sometimes their arguments took up a pessimistic resignation to human desire, noting that "there are few acts of parliament tending to restrain the selfish interests of man, which his ingenuity has not evaded."[65] Others invoked early-eighteenth-century civic republican Tories to justify commercial policy by appealing to natural moral laws, producing, for example, a cheap reprint of Robert Harley's *Essay Upon Public Credit* (1710), which had optimistically defined credit as "the offspring of universal probity," immune to the incursions of artifice.[66] But in the 1790s this repackaging of Harley's optimistic claims must have sounded to Burney, as to other Tories, more consolatory than truthful, offering little security to those whose powers of discrimination failed to protect them against the tricks of the seductive but impoverished credit seeker. The last decades of the century abounded with these dupes. Conservative pamphleteers deplore an increase of counterfeiting, that consummately artful means of gaining unfounded credit, and condemn the wielding of financial clout by those without hard cash as robbery for driving up the price of essential commodities.[67] Burney's own portrait, in *Camilla*, of the heiress-hunting Bellamy (*né* Nicholas Gwigg, ambitious son of "the master of a great gaming-house") epitomizes conservative fears of the confidence trickster sprung from beneath to undermine Britain's socioeconomic safety, and to spur the anger of England's propertied classes against Scotland and the Scots by eloping to Gretna Green.[68] For despite prohibiting elopements within England, the Marriage Act does nothing to protect Camilla's sister, the heiress Eugenia, from the ambitions of the seemingly sympathetic Bellamy. What Burney shares with the pamphleteers is a terrifying image of the ubiquity of credit, and a sense that the internal logic of credit has fully supplanted the laws that nominally regulate marriage and commerce.

As Burney recognized and lamented, credit depended largely on the fashionable appearance of the debtor – an appearance easily assumed through pretense, which meant that credit could be founded on nothing more solid than the credulity of a previous seller. The conservative belief that not only romance writers, but also Britain's Parliament, did too little to protect its citizens from such artifice derived added weight from events Burney described in *Cecilia* and *Camilla* – the tendency of the credit edifice to come crashing down, crushing those at its base. With the 1760s had commenced a time of increasing worry over liquidity, public and private, in Britain – a shortage of coin or, in conservative minds, of "real money," that the policies of the 1790s only intensified, as Burke's *Regicide Letters* suggest. The government's permissive attitude to private finance had led to proliferating mortgages and third-party bills of exchange even among small tradesmen, many of whose assets were already tied up in consumer credit, subject to the uncertain likelihood of payment by a contracted date. The default of one link in these networks of circulating promises produced a chain of escalating claims. The bottommost participant, faced with unpayable debt, was often precipitated into financial ruin, starvation, and prison – a state of affairs that Burney's virtuous tradeswoman Mrs. Hill faces at the hands of Cecilia's guardians before being rescued, at great risk, by Burney's heroine.

Private credit, like the increasingly demonstrative sensibility that rose alongside it and with which it was socially entangled, was by definition indeterminate, unlegislated, and dependent upon subjective perception.[69] Thus the fears hinted at in Burney's romances – for the state of Britain's economy, and so of Britain's national unity and national character – reflected the belief that artifice was rapidly supplanting birth and virtue in social relations. Her romances appealed to a fashionable reader, yet what they mourned in their treatment of credit was the apparent triumph of public opinion and personal appearance over law, social tradition, and the longstanding Tory ideal of absolute, inborn worth. Conservative moralists in general began to treat credit as a figure for the destruction of the old hierarchies of British society. Burney, too, ridicules the attempts of the middle class and minor gentry to ape their social betters in ways beyond their means, but the intertextual traces embedded in her romances help to indict political economists, moralists, and romance-writers for their complicity in Parliament's failure to protect the victims of credit. Among those crushed are Burney's heroines, too quick to demonstrate their sensibility, and the tradesmen who call in bills the gentry never mean to pay.

SEX TRADE, BOOK TRADE, BRITISH ECONOMY: HUME'S ECONOMIC THEORY

By demonstrating the moral and financial perils of their heroines in terms of "credit" and sensibility, Burney's economic romances replicate ironically the cooperation of earlier romances with conduct books and *laissez-faire* popular economics. But the sources of the critique run deeper, to the intellectual foundations of British political economy. Hume's sentimental empiricism, with its systematic and general account of Britain's social relations, lies behind the complicity of the conduct-writer and romancer with the writer of financial pamphlets. His self-regulating account of Britain's political economy underlies Anderson's faith in credit, and his belief in natural sentiment as a reliable anchor for a marketplace otherwise ruled only by desire foreshadows the conduct books' insistence that women demonstrate sensibility. Indeed, conduct-writers inevitably urged young women to read Hume's *History of Great Britain*, and Burney herself had read it at sixteen (*ED* 1: 30).[70] By simultaneously assailing the political economy of sentiment and senti-mental political economy, Burney's romances mount a comprehensive assault on the cooperating discourses that would endlessly reduplicate Hume's account of sentiment and promote his sentimental view of Britain's social order by inculcating a demonstrative sensibility in women.

It is the consoling influence of sentiment, circulated by sympathy, that holds Hume's theories about aesthetic taste, economic organization, and Britain's social history firmly together and halts their slide into relativism. His essay "Of the Standard of Taste" (1742), for example, equates sympathetic sentiment with a natural love of particular kinds of beauty.[71] Hume forestalls all possibility of disagreement by submerging the social explanation of human differences. He insists that the literary, the aesthetic, and even the sexual tastes of the privileged classes are the only living representations of "the common" – that is, created or God-given – "sentiments of human nature." These crucial second causes of Britain's social order develop properly only among those fortunate individuals who are unhindered by exhausting work or faulty education (*ST* 232). Beauty is a gendered and socially loaded term in eighteenth-century aesthetics, and Hume associates beauty with femaleness as well as with the sources of human sociability.[72] The association with women allows him to extend the operation of sympathy – a process of "infusion" in which sentiment must be seen to be communicated – beyond the immediate "friends and daily companions" who provide the best examples of its effects. For sympathy, when it circulates heterosexual sentiments, is also avowedly universal, in the same sense that universal (manhood) suffrage was universal. All men (at least in theory, or in Eden) desire Woman.[73]

Thus a natural God-given desire establishes the common ground sexual relations share with the consumer marketplace. The passion to accumulate goods, according to Hume, results from a similarly "original principle," a social drive for reputation, and not from inherent desires for particular kinds of goods – a view that Smith reiterates in *Theory of the Moral Sentiments* (*T* 281; *TMS* 51). In the same way, men's general desire for Woman creates specialized tastes for different kinds of women. Sentiment and sympathy work together to naturalize Hume's demand-theory of economic value and social order, which might otherwise threaten the stable relations between objects and their value, or among the various ranks in British society. For although it is labour that immediately determines value, an underlying mechanism of sympathy controls the demand for particular goods, and so for particular kinds of labour. For Hume, consumption and sexuality share a common root: "our passions are the only causes of labour."[74] All men desire Goods, but each community of men establishes its own competition for particular goods, just as all men want Woman, but different women – and, implicitly, their distinct displays of sensibility – please different men. Sympathy, among men and with women, assigns a class-inflected character to men's consumption and sexuality, and to this sympathy Hume gives the primary responsibility for social regulation. It was this equation, produced by Hume's general theory of sentiment and taste, that conservatives most feared in the popular guise of the cult of sensibility, and that conservative women, including Sheridan and Burney, opposed in gendered as well as political economic terms.

Hume's biological theory of demand undergirds his definition of the social contract: "a convention enter'd into by all the members of the society to bestow stability on the possession of . . . external goods, and leave every one in the peaceable enjoyment of what he may acquire" (*T* 489). By defining society as a set of laws governing desire among sympathetic subjects, Hume gives women an obvious place among the goods that, if allowed to pass with "looseness and easy transition from one person to another," destroy the bonds and hierarchies of society. Women are both bearers of their own potentially dangerous sensibility and objects of masculine choice. An implicit "sexual contract," controlling the movement of women, thus implicitly precedes the all-male social contract.[75] At the same time, however, Woman and the operations that surround her provide crucial ground for sympathetic community, not only binding men together in shared desire, but also absolving them from the softer forms of sympathy. Sympathy in men confines itself to judgment and desire, but women have stronger imaginations and are more subject to empathic sentiment (*T* 370, 388). They have custody, that is, of sentiment where it enters the realm of sensibility and its sympathetic circulation by romance. They bring communal feeling into the lives of citizens without becoming citizens themselves. Sentiment, as Hume employs it, positions Woman at the junction where the gold standard encounters demand-based value. In Hume's political economy, women's bodies, their emotions, and their conduct are all scored across and across with the competing demands of "human nature."

Conduct-writers also argued that the essential sensibility of women required simultaneous cultivation and control, and that it justified in its very nature the control it required. Yet they nevertheless attempted to *produce* women whose piety and skill at "making puddings and pies" – qualities Burney's elderly gentlemen are fond of demanding – play second fiddle to demonstrations of sensibility and taste.[76] In teaching women to become the marriageable objects of masculine desire, the conduct books confirmed the "natural" desire for feminine beauty and sensibility on which Hume had insisted. One area persisted on which Britain's consumers could agree; in one arena consumer agreement could produce competition without riots or inflated value. But Burney repeatedly demonstrates that this agreement is itself a fiction produced by apologists for an uncertain and unregulated marketplace. Sensibility, in her romances as in Sheridan's, guarantees neither moral rule nor social order. At its worst, it bears no traces of the Richardsonian ideal of virtuous sentiment: it is no more than a mask for the unrestrained desire contemporaries called "luxury."

CREDIT, LUXURY, AND CLASSICAL REPUBLICANISM IN THE 1790S: BURNEY'S NEW CONSERVATISM

Luxury, in its sexual and financial senses the evil twin of credit, had been the standard bugbear of classical republican philosophers, whose stern promotion of the national interest over individual desire in the first half of the eighteenth century placed them among the ancestors of mid-century liberals and conservatives alike.[77] Hume was among the first moralists to re-examine luxury. He did not argue, however, the established Mandevillean defence, that private vices produce public benefits, but rather upheld the essential virtue of desire itself – and therefore the worth of luxury and credit – as impulses toward the expansion of Britain's hearts, minds, and economy.[78] His argument began with the needs of British society as a comprehensive and organic whole, but his belief in the compatibility of personal appetite with public spirit threatened classical republican tradition from within.[79] To attack credit after the 1740s, then, was to defend traditional hierarchies against encroaching commercial interests; to defend the cause of Tory absolutes against conceptions of economic and moral value that were subject to individual desire.

By the 1790s, however, classical republican claims, and even the stoicism sometimes extolled by Sidney Bidulph, had become unreliable for conservative purposes. The English Jacobins had assumed the attack on luxury as a weapon against the excesses of the rich, while defences of public spirit gave way to a Burkean insistence on private virtue, including virtuous commercial practices like those, or so Burke insisted, of the London booksellers' conger.[80] Burney's developing response to the naturalized and demand-based ethic upheld by political economy places her alongside Austen, Joanna Baillie, and Hannah More, among others, in the post-Burkean dialectical swing that updated or opposed Hume and his popularizers not with a return to classical republicanism, but with new ways of thinking about Britain that based national security, in politically diverse ways, on the character and order of British households. Although Burney is still generally considered an eighteenth-century novelist, and although her works respond to Richardson and his competitors, she wrote and published two of her four romances after 1795, and her career extended well into the second decade of the nineteenth century – an extension not merely chronological, but ideological as well. An increasingly elaborated relation to political economic tenets can be identified in Burney's approach to commerce, from her first desperate attempts, in *Evelina* and *Cecilia*, to forestall the approach of sensibility and credit, to her exposure in *Camilla* of the dangerous belief that sensibility and taste defend traditional socioeconomic relations and ethical absolutes. It culminates in the fully outlined commercial spheres of *The Wanderer*, in which, as in *Evelina*, Burney can counter the triumph of commerce only by a thorough retreat into the bosom of the genteel family – a romance conclusion with the fragility almost of Sheridan's theatrically utopian *Nourjahad*.

In emphasizing the role of families in regulating society, Burney joins the nineteenth-century promoters of what Nancy Armstrong calls the "domestic ideology" of middle-class Britain.[81] But Burney's romances are generically and philosophically rooted in eighteenth-century debates on sentiment and sensibility. The generic character of her romances, along with her suspicion of commerce and her anachronistic mourning for lost law, sets her apart from these novelists. Unlike the Victorian domestic ideologue and her early-nineteenth-century forebears, Burney never resorts to the family for an idealized natural social order. She sets her sights not on sympathy between family members, but on absolute rules held in place by the authority of the British state. These rules are not the same as the socioeconomic power that masquerades as morality in the domestic novels Armstrong discusses: Burney makes no attempt to situate her families outside history. In responding to commerce and to political economy, not least through the romances that had responded to Hume, she counters in romance the naturalized social order and idealized commerce that most novelists of the early nineteenth century, like Hume himself, approved. Even within the developing domestic ideology, then, Burney is a conservative.

Nor is Burney a feminist or English Jacobin novelist. Superimposed on the market trials of her heroines, the marriage endings of her works refuse to fulfill without questioning the desires of her readers. Neither, however, is romance imposed on a resistant or subversive Burney by the demands of the book trade. Such views arise from the assumption that late-eighteenth-century social criticism is necessarily of a radical character, an assumption that has sometimes led to the conflation, for example, of Mary Wollstonecraft with More, and which implies that the genre of romance and the critique of liberal society can rarely coincide.[82] Burney's novels exist within and actively contribute to a conservative political context, the same context that produced an Edmund Burke. I propose that there is little ambivalence in Burney's uses of romance, without seeing her works as radical in their treatment of women's position in late-century society, or in their critique of British society generally. Her economic romances are coherent wholes. Taken together, they form a unified body of social comment and, sometimes, of social protest. Burney's simultaneous investment in and generic critique of courtship responds to the contemporary yoking of marriage with the market – not in contradiction of her essential conservatism, but precisely in keeping with it.[83]

The marketplace in Burney's romances does not escape the defining rule of consumer societies: that goods exist in part to cement social relations and demarcate the character and value of their possessors.[84] If this function of goods in modern societies is universal, however, the "particular" values they convey differ from society to society – or even from day to day within a single society. In *Cecilia*, *Camilla*, and *The Wanderer*, Burney conceives society's wrongs as somehow "new," another stage in an ongoing process of corruption. Her heroines suffer not because values are changing, but because *value itself* is shifting, pitting family status and fortune against the socially defined and ever-changing beauty, fashion, and accomplishments each heroine is expected to achieve.[85] When Burney describes the mingled anxieties and desires of her characters in response to the marriage market, she does so because the market is conflicted in its exactions, and because its wavering valuation of Burney's heroines renders their self- and social worth equally unstable and fluctuating.

Burney's critique of credit in her economic romances indicates more than dissatisfaction with courtship customs, however destructive their consequences. Each heroine's debts result from moral and social dilemmas imposed by a society whose stable hierarchies, bonds, and information networks are shown to have collapsed. But it would equally be a mistake to view Burneyan economics as merely a metaphor for Britain's fragmentation or lack of fixed standards. Rather, each heroine's "credit" failures stem from commerce, represented in the pairing of courtship and the culture market. As Burney suggests in her intersecting parodies of sentimental romance, conduct books, and political economy, economic and moral relativism – and thus the social fragmentation of Britain – arise together.

THE WANDERER: WRITING AND READING CREDIT IN CRISIS

To read Burney's *The Wanderer* is to discover that the luxury and credit relations of commercial society have now, in the early nineteenth century, become thoroughly entrenched. The most forceful conservative pamphleteers of the time were headed by Burke, whose critique of Hume and his popularizers focused on the dangers of public credit. While Burney evidently shared this anxiety, she explicitly objected to Burke's acceptance of other commercial relations that he made part of conservative belief. Her letters to Susanna Burney in the 1780s explore her divergences from Burke, whom she admired and with whom she differed very reluctantly. She could not agree that Britain's history, as Burke was to argue in *Reflections*, and had begun arguing in Parliament, had integrated commerce into existing social categories and accommodated it to traditional means of determining worth. For her, in contrast to the representations of Richardson and Hume, sentiment could not chasten the fluidity and disruption caused by consumption and credit. One recent example struck Burney especially forcibly, and she disagreed violently and at length with Burke's prosecution of the Indian governor Warren Hastings, which she had attended, seeing her own faith in Hastings and disagreement with Burke as support for her country's intrinsic "honor" as an imperial power against Burke's ill-justified regard for Britain's commercial interests abroad.[86] Added to this opposition to Burke, Burney's experience of the book trade reinforced her suspicion of the effects of commerce on British national and imperial unity, and her views of literary property follow Johnson's Tory views rather than Burke's more commercialized conception.

The trials of Juliet, heroine of *The Wanderer*, stage numerous versions of the issue Burney's earlier romances also engage in their intersections with commercial history and political economy: the fluctuating worth of a young woman perpetually in danger of betrayal *into* extravagance and *by* luxury or fraud. *The Wanderer* revisits Burney's earliest reflections on sentiment and social worth by re-examining the scene of Sophy Streatfield's tears. The orphaned and disowned Lady Juliet Granville – deprived, like Evelina, of her real name till novel's end – supports herself by performing on a public stage, under the name of "the L.S." That this displaced heroine must survive by displaying her sensibility in music and feeling suggests that Burney has at length come to sympathize with Streatfield, acknowledging in retrospect that Streatfield's, too, was a command performance. But the despairing tone of *The Wanderer* is new:

among the powerful persons represented, none stands up against the new law of sensibility and desire. Among all levels of society in Juliet's world, a "'fashion' system of consumption" may be seen to have supplanted landed wealth and ancient name.[87]

An incipient dread of the contemporary upper-class acceptance of commerce, and of its workings in culture and courtship, appears in Juliet's nameless, penniless situation, and her forays into genteel and commercial life. Burney's critiques of credit and sensibility yield to an overwhelming preoccupation with the intersecting markets through which Juliet must travel, and *The Wanderer* may thus be read as a fully integrated analysis of a consumer society in which Burkean conservatism is the rule among the ruling class, and in which sensibility rules several social spheres at once. The closed system and standards of a traditional aristocracy have given way to the question-begging of credit and taste that, in Burke as in Hume, shapes a new tradition of defences of commerce. Burney's narrator condemns the "imitative custom . . . of patronizing those who had already been elevated by patronage; and of lifting higher, by peculiar favour, those who were already mounting by the favour of others."[88] Juliet needs a genteel appearance and connections in order to find employment, but can gain neither without first acquiring both. She must be able to consume luxuries in order to be able to consume essentials, and, all the while, her survival and her place in society remain dangerously and painfully unresolved. In order to enter the credit system, one must already have entered it: credit circulates without end in this novel, founded solely on successful representations. True worth (that is, Juliet's innate virtue, the unchallenged product, as in *Evelina*, of her noble birth) get lost in the system of financial and social credit.

Because *The Wanderer* unfolds through the same categories of analysis that Burke adapts from Hume and Richardson, and that Sheridan had explored before her – sensibility and taste – it can be read as a companion text to Burney's letters on Hastings, an intertextual rebuke to Burkean conservatism. Not least, the text's distinction from Burkean politics marks the latter's inadequate response to Hume. In this romance, the patronage of artists and the collecting of art unite taste and charity, since Hume and Richardson the most visible branches of sensibility.[89] Characters assume these moral qualities like clothing in order to gain social – and therefore economic – credit. Such performances recur throughout *The Wanderer*: with the exception of Juliet, nearly all the female characters emulate Streatfield's interested sensibility. Their quests for a show of softheartedness and taste often cooperate, to the special detriment of the female object of patronage. When Juliet turns harp teacher, she finds a patron in the "accomplished" Miss Arbe, who compensates for her own lack of fortune with the taste and sensibility she displays in serving as a kind of artistic pimp for other fashionable women: as Arbe notes, "nothing [is] so commodious, as . . . patronage" (316). Even Lady Barbara Frankland, whose name reflects her sincere nature, learns the harp from the underpaid Juliet because "curving, straightening, or elegantly spreading her fingers upon the strings; and . . . the general bend of her person" as she plays are effective courtship tools. The harp, which "shews beauty and grace to advantage," is an apt means of "exhibiting" young women (230).

From Arbe to Frankland, women spend (or promise to spend) to show their sensibility and taste. Financial credit cannot be separated from social reputation. Hoping to keep rigid social distinctions intact despite their disappearing bases, these women construct a system of acquirement and display that exploits those at the end of the financial chain. The mothers of Juliet's harp students refuse to pay her, condemning her in moral terms for providing the luxury accomplishments they require for their daughters, and making her the subject of a public debate about conduct. Paying for services rendered, one claims, is " 'to pamper a set of lazy dancers, and players, and painters; who think of no one thing but idleness, and outward shew, and diversion' " – that is, of luxury (324). The place of the literary producer in relation to aristocratic consumption and the capricious logic of the book trade is one obvious subtext here. Recalling the *Evelina* prefaces, in which the writer "without Name" finds herself the object of public scrutiny, the patrons of the still-nameless Juliet force her into the marketplace, although she teaches music in order to support herself in privacy. They draw off condemnation of their own theatrical ambitions by clothing Juliet in a "vivid" and "shewy" "sarcenet of a bright rose-colour" (313–14). To make Juliet a scarlet woman is to " 'distinguish us *Dilettanti* from the artists,' " as a white-clad patron puts it (314). Likening cultural labour to prostitution, fashionable society burdens the artist with its own enslavement to commerce.

The credit system claims its victims from the bottom of the chain. For fashion victims are also credit victims, and the inevitable failures and falsities of sensibility and taste are at the root of both conditions. When Juliet's employers counter her requests for payment by attacking her character, she loses her employment and her credit: reputation and fashion cannot be distinguished from each other. Her career as a seamstress, which follows her failed attempts at surviving by teaching the harp, revisits and amplifies Sheridan's most sceptical scenes of sentiment's inadequate substitute for financial probity. Like Sidney Bidulph, Juliet is "an artificer" who is "pretty dexterous at her needle," and she too finds refuge as the tenant of a milliner, for whom she sews fashionable ornaments.[90] Unlike Sidney, however, Juliet has known the milliner in her former life on the sidelines of aristocratic society, and her credit is already suspect. Unnerved by Juliet's sudden decline in status, her landlady demands immediate payment, and although Juliet's noble blood takes immediate offense, she cannot pay, because her patrons will not pay her (276). On Juliet's eviction, no relative surfaces to help her, as Sidney Bidulph is rescued by her cousin Ned Warner. Instead, Juliet escapes the public eye in the impoverished room of her friend Gabriella, who is, like her, a banished noblewoman. Together they start a sewing business, to protect themselves against public suspicion as well as to support themselves, but financial disaster quickly looms, "from the difficulty of accelerating payment for what [they] sold, or procrastinating it for what [they] bought" (623).

The victimization of cultural producers is not the sole destructive consequence of the system of sensibility and consumption. The female consumer's familiarity with cultural goods becomes a sign to potential suitors of her position on axes of "cultural" and "economic capital."[91] The objects of fashion, those that demonstrate currently desirable taste, change as the bearers of sensibility choose and reject them, and the status of the consumer and producer rises and falls in tandem with them.[92] The traditional worth of the young lady and the artistic skill or charitable act disappear into the fluctuating desires that structure the markets of culture and courtship. Thus Lady Barbara acquires taste and skill from Juliet, but raises the stakes by participating in a system that dresses Juliet, as a social inferior and a cultural entrepreneur, in the garb of a prostitute. A system in which the desirability of other women depends on her *and* on her exclusion overdetermines Juliet's access to credit. Her "real" noble status remains invisible in a world of layered representations.

As worth becomes fashion-dependent, the marriage market confronts another, related issue, apparent in the acquirements even of the virtuous Barbara: that of theatricality and falsehood. Fashion systems remain exclusive only insofar as participants can distinguish the impostor from the privileged member – a distinction that is obvious only where the social actors are few, unchanging, and known to each other.[93] But one of the major marketplaces in contemporary courtship, for example, was the masquerade, where open boundaries and identities masked beyond recognition meant, or so its critics feared, that intruders could "get in," threatening the virtue and value of the young lady participants.[94] These anxieties appear in the labelling of Juliet as an "impostor" and the demand that she name herself before anyone will help her. Even her uncle Lord Denmeath refuses to believe her proofs of her legitimacy. He tries to bribe her to return to France, promising that "The road is still open for you to affluence and credit" – imperfectly concealing his fear that this "impostor" has already been granted credit, in both senses, as a member of his family (616). Another acquaintance, meeting Juliet without the blackface she wears to escape Robespierre's France, accuses her of a kind of commercialized witchcraft: "'What a fine fortune she may raise, if she will take up a patent for beauty-making!'" His public exposure of Juliet as a manufacturer of masks drives off her supporters, "alarmed . . . for . . . [their] own credit" (252–3). To participate in a system of hierarchies based on sensibility and credit is to dread the presence of impostors. Indeed, this society attempts to exclude Juliet from the credit system because it fears she has already infiltrated it.

BURNEY'S ECONOMIC ROMANCE

Like the sceptical Sheridan, but unlike the English Jacobin women she was to influence (Wollstonecraft, for example, had a quoting knowledge of *Cecilia*), Burney does not object to the equation of women with men's worth or to their role as bearers of value.[95] Her economic romances question instead the loosely Humean calculus of conduct books, economic pamphlets, and sentimental romances, their growing investment in sensibility, and the mismanaged Burkean conservatism that has gained them a social and intellectual footing. She conceives her ideal society, from *Evelina* to *The Wanderer*, as a return to a world in which a woman's recognized value corresponds with her moral, genealogical, and financial worth; where marriage is a private agreement between a woman's father and the suitor he approves. This is the world of Hardwicke's Marriage Act, respected and rigorously enforced.

The end of *The Wanderer* is the culmination of these returns. Juxtaposed to the market misadventures of the sentimental Juliet, it appears even more utopian and contingent. From having appeared as nameless as Evelina; having circulated through the French and English countryside, been promoted as a musician, and threatened with the public stage; having worked, like Sidney Bidulph, as a milliner, and become, like Cecilia, goods "advertised in a news-paper," Juliet at length becomes the cherished object of private contract (663). Inside a "bathing-machine," itself a contrivance for protecting modesty, Juliet's uncle, brother, and guardian, representing the church, navy, and nobility of Britain and France, contract with her only suitor, a private English gentleman with a significantly Tory name.

Harleigh . . . was speedily summoned into the machine; his proposals were so munificent, that they were applauded rather than approved; and, All descending to the beach, the Bishop took one hand, and the Admiral another, of the blushing Juliet, to present, with tenderest blessings, to the happy, indescribably happy Harleigh. (864–5)

Juliet does not enter this masculine bargaining machine, but neither do her guardians parade her through the marriage market. The privacy in which they keep her counteracts the unseemly publicity of her journeys through Burney's romance. Only after the contract do they present Juliet to the public, issuing from the machine to bestow her, literally, on her husband. Her blush, the sign of modest sensibility, marks her stable virtue. The safe conduct that concludes *The Wanderer* is at once the most unequivocal and the most unlikely of Burney's endings. As a formal legal contract between husband and father, Juliet's marriage reinstates a pre-sensibility, indeed a pre-sentimental, courtship tradition: unlike Richardson's sentimental ideal, which submerges its market interests in virtue, nature, and the heart, the aristocratic agreement acknowledges its base in contracts and the law.

Driven by French revolutionary appropriations on the one hand – Napoleon, with his radical vocabulary of state and citizenhood, had taken up the language of civic virtue to declare England a nation of shopkeepers – and betrayed on the other by Burke's defence of commerce, conservative women adapted without moderating conservative rhetoric. Like Napoleon, they despised the division of Britain between "selfish vanity and cringing cunning," "the insolent, vain, unfeeling buyer" and "the subtle, plausible, over-reaching seller," yet they equally feared the French Revolution and the radical critique of commerce (*Wanderer* 428). In this nineteenth-century context, a civic republican rhetoric could no longer oppose the long-feared decline of rank and family and the absolutes they stood for. Burney responds with an ancient ideal of marriage, a traditional contract between gentlemen, replacing circulating women and fluctuating worth with a stable system of value and exchange.

Burney revives the Great Chain of Being as a great chain of families. The elegiac overtones of her conclusion may well derive from a sense of impossibility, as Burney's own career makes plain. In order to get *The Wanderer* into print, after months of internal debate and family discussion, Burney signed a profit-sharing contract with her publishers. Longman's would take the work only if Burney agreed to participate in their commercial speculation on its success. Her insistence that she "had far rather lose a little interest of Money, than any I can avoid of something better" – her reputation as a writer or creative control of the text – did not protect her, and in ceding control of *The Wanderer*'s production, she forfeited the critics' approval as well.[96] Despite its ironies at the expense of earlier romances and the commerce in which they are invested, *The Wanderer* remains an economic romance: precisely because of its immersion in the literary marketplace, it is as thoroughly trapped as Sheridan's romances had been by their insulation from market history. Its heroine's escape from the march of commercial history, the commodification of written works, and the pervasiveness of the ideology of sensibility is as unlikely as Sheridan's mid-century scepticism had made it: possible only through a fictive historical return.

CHAPTER 3

Wollstonecraft and the revolution of economic history

In the summer of 1795, Mary Wollstonecraft, with her infant daughter Fanny and a nurse, travelled to Scandinavia as the agent of the merchant Gilbert Imlay, Fanny's father and Wollstonecraft's soon-to-be former lover. Wollstonecraft embroidered the outline of the journey in a series of sentimental letters, addressed to Imlay as if from Scandinavia but written in London after her return, and intended for publication: the *Letters Written during a Short Residence in Sweden, Norway, and Denmark* (1796). The *Letters* image the lone woman travelling bravely, cradle at her side, ignorant of the languages spoken around her, her sorrow at Imlay's absence relieved only by the beauty of the northern landscape. At the same time, however, in ways that seem informed by the equivalences Frances Burney established in *Cecilia* among the circulation of feelings, currencies, and bodies, Wollstonecraft's self-portrait of her sensibility is juxtaposed, often jarringly, with critical analysis of commerce and of Imlay's relation to it. The result is a divided work that divided its contemporary readers into two distinct camps: those who saw Wollstonecraft's text as an escape from the cruelties of commerce and politics, and those who found in her sensibility a critique of liberal political economy and commercial society.

Wollstonecraft had long understood sentiment and sensibility less as emotional fact or philosophy than literary convention: the hallmarks of a genre bearing, as we will see, the weight of British cultural and political legitimacy. In her *Vindications of the Rights of Men* (1790) and *of Woman* (1792), she had outlined and protested not merely the social and economic role of sensibility, but the genres and literary institutions that promoted it. In *Letters* she put her theoretical anatomy of sensibility into practical play, parodically enacting the generic conventions that her fissured text broke down. Sensibility, sentiment, and their parodies, her *Letters* suggest, like the divided responses of her critics, are at heart the same: products of economic ideology. Like Burney, Wollstonecraft set

the genre of sentimental romance to expose its own illegitimate engagements – its work in the pay of market-liberal ideologies – and to reveal
her own economic and ideological dependence on the genre in which
she wrote. Taken together, Wollstonecraft's self-reflection and generic
parodies held out unrealized potential for a new, even a non-ideological,
model for engagement with, and transformation of, Britain's economic
history.

Wollstonecraft's parody in the *Letters* extends outward from genre to
disrupt commerce as well as sensibility, in ways that reveal the contribution of sensibility, commerce, and their genres to late-eighteenth-century social positions and identities. Not only does her text set the
relationship of economics and sensibility in flux by destabilizing and
questioning the interests and motives of the text's implied writer, as
Mary Favret suggests, but it insists on the fictiveness of sentiment,
commerce, and gendered identity as well.[1] In addition to her equivocal
placement on the cusp of publicity and privacy, a function of her
epistolary text, Wollstonecraft strikes a double pose as a sentimental
narrator and a "concubine" with her bastard, according to the reactionary critics of the *Anti-Jacobin Review*, or her "brat," as Wollstonecraft puts
it.[2] Her masquerade is reduplicated as she appears to those who aid her
as a *feme sole*, an economically independent widow, before revealing
herself, in a revelation that is itself a fiction, as a *feme couverte*, a wife and
her husband's business agent.[3] Read from the retrospect of 1798, when
Wollstonecraft's posthumous works appeared, these layered unmask-
ings, disguises, and misrecognitions bear forcefully on the text of the
Letters. The moments of sentimental self-disclosure disclose nothing
more nor less than the equivalence, and equal emptiness, of each
legitimate or illegitimate pose Wollstonecraft strikes. There is no depth
beneath the tectonic shifts that mark the surface of Wollstonecraft's text:
the forms of sentiment, sensibility, and scepticism, commerce and feeling, the public and private, the madonna and the whore, give way only
to pastiche itself.

I here invoke Fredric Jameson's account of pastiche as an empty
formal mimicry and an irony that has lost its concrete referents amidst a
barrage of images and commodities in consumer society, because Wollstonecraft's *Letters* comprise such a mixture of texts and generic conventions, an early instance of such an assemblage.[4] In the *Letters* and her
other late work, the posthumous *Wrongs of Woman; or, Maria* (1798),
Wollstonecraft assembled her pastiche from competing discourses,
genres, and written works. But, read now, Wollstonecraft's pastiche also

evokes Judith Butler's recuperation of such bottomless parodies by highlighting the "trouble" layered and parodic performances can work on the artificial structures and ideologies in which they intervene, and which they further denature by revealing the "original, the authentic, and the real . . . themselves" as textual "effects" or "regulatory fictions."[5] Each of Wollstonecraft's works takes part in a specialized intertext: the analysis of contemporary revolutionary events, and of their historical effects, that went on between 1790 and 1820. Responding to the French Revolution and to social unrest at home, and upholding competing justifications of socioeconomic authority and cohesion, British writers as politically and professionally diverse as Edmund Burke, Frances Burney, Elizabeth Inchbald, Thomas Paine, Helen Maria Williams, William Godwin, and Walter Scott founded their readings of history on theories, explicit or implicit, of generic change and competition.[6] At the same time, they supplemented theory with a historiographic practice that gave a shared generic shape to their own interventions and those of their opponents. Invoking and normalizing the Richardsonian plot at the same time as they made their political economic and political historical investments increasingly explicit, these writers established a characteristic battle to the death between "sentiment," or "true sensibility," and "legitimacy" on one side and the forces of "gothic" barbarism and "monstrosity," their textual shadows, on the other. The dialectic of enlightenment, in Theodor Adorno's terms, was invoked generically and played out in competing ways within these romantic texts.[7]

In the highly schematized and self-referential context of the late-eighteenth-century "Revolution debate," sentimental and gothic romance, romance and historical novel fall into place not as the prefigurings and successors that traditional genre theorists tended to see in them, but as the actively mixing, clashing, competitor forms that such historians of genre as Clifford Siskin, Franco Moretti, Michael McKeon, and Ralph Cohen have made them.[8] The competing genres of romance, novel, and political economy overlapped one another's boundaries as writers sought to evict their antagonists from the shared social space each writer, with each genre, attempted to enclose.[9] Taking shape under the flaunted banner of sensibility, Wollstonecraft's *Letters* and her posthumous novel are nevertheless fissured throughout by eruptions of gothic isolation, terror, and grief, which take place at the moments of most excessive pastiche, and which often threaten entirely to usurp and transform the text. For Wollstonecraft, as for her more conventional gothic-writing contemporaries, the gothic haunts and discredits "natural" propriety and legitimacy and the romance genres that invoke them.[10] But she affirms what her conservative colleagues, and some others, disguise or override: the basic *equivalence*, or interchangeability, of genres that together, through their history of fruitless, endless mutual opposition, make up what is, finally, an ideologically cohesive late-eighteenth-century historiography. I will argue that not just the sliding equivalencies of social postures and positions but also the competing genres embedded within her texts mark Wollstonecraft's critique of contemporary markets and market ideology. For Wollstonecraft, the market is the origin and *raison d'être* of class and gender ideologies and of the romance and anti-romance histories that promote them.

The generic investments of the late-eighteenth-century British conversation herald François Furet's assertion that French Revolutionary events were "political and even ideological in nature."[11] But Wollstonecraft contradicts Furet's claim that ideological events refuse causal analysis directed toward economic change. By 1792, responding to the Girondist, Montagnard, and Sans-Culotte phases of the Revolution, which, as Albert Soboul argues, temporarily aligned the mercantile and industrial lower-middle classes of Paris with rural peasants in a shared cause and set of practices, Wollstonecraft had come to associate ongoing events in France with the commercial life she condemned.[12] She shared this analysis with Burney, but unlike Burney found little to choose between the Revolution and its royalist and British enemies. In their intertextual traces, which enact the continuity of romance among "English Jacobin" and "anti-Jacobin" writers, Wollstonecraft's *Letters*, and the work that followed, her *Wrongs of Woman*, reduced Burkean and Paineite alike to market-economic ideologues and thus to wielders of a single romance genre. Taking feminine and masculine social functions for her analytic focal point, Wollstonecraft centred her critiques of economic ideology on two interlocking terms – gender and sexuality – that had consistently posed problems for political economy since the appearance of John Locke's early liberal theory, debated on gendered grounds by writers including Aphra Behn, Eliza Haywood, and Samuel Richardson. In re-engaging with gender in a generic analysis that parodies Richardson's genres as recognizably as Burke's, Wollstonecraft extended her critical use of the romance genre beyond Burney's "red-Tory" critique. For Wollstonecraft, as in Jameson's theory of pastiche, ideology and reality are indistinguishable – lost in competing layers of texts without a "natural" or real-historical foundation. Contemporary gender, like contemporary romance, is revealed as at once all-pervasive, naturalized, and wholly conventional: a successful ideology of the marketplace.

In the *Letters* and *Wrongs of Woman*, within and behind the narrator's and heroine's ambiguous, sentimental, and yet self-consciously dubious affairs of the heart lie *les affaires*: marriage, courtship, sensibility, and romance conventions of all kinds imperfectly conceal their origins and investment in business and the marketplace. And for every legitimate market, there is a "black" market, its illegitimate double. In the *Letters* and in *Wrongs*, *couverture* and legitimate paternity, the counting house, the Custom House, and the moral text, linked together under the authority of the law, appear alongside the female economic agency, prostitution, unmarried motherhood, under-the-table commodities trading, and under-the-bedclothes reading they depend on for their legitimacy. Especially refractory, as Wollstonecraft's fissured texts and travels demonstrate, is the easy interchange between official, legitimate commerce and its shadowy opposite, the trade in contraband bodies and goods and disreputable books. It is this exchange, revealing the fictiveness of genre distinctions and the gender and class distinctions they enact and sustain, that drives Wollstonecraft's collapsing of legitimate and illegitimate identities, markets, and literary forms in a single act of textual pastiche. Her levelling of genre hierarchies and differences in response to historical events should prompt us to rethink the kinds of force that genres, in veiled cooperation with markets and other economic forces, have exerted on history.[13]

Wollstonecraft's *Letters* and her *Wrongs of Woman* summarize the critiques of economic institutions and their ideologies of genre that engrossed her earlier works. At the same time, the works enact the contemporary generic competitions that Wollstonecraft attacked. Thus, while these texts provide an often ironic synopsis of Wollstonecraft's career, they may simultaneously be read, in their wide-ranging generic parody, as critical synecdoches for the debates on socioeconomic order and its political economic legitimations that continued throughout the 1790s. To read in this way, synecdochically, is to acknowledge the allegorical character of the debates themselves, with their investments not only in genre reform but also in a characteristic moral and political plot. To work at a tangent to the fields of late-eighteenth-century debate and criticism is also to recognize the movement in Wollstonecraft's last major works from criticism to parody of contemporary socioeconomic and political argument and the genres of its "regulatory fictions," which allowed her to make imitation an unconventional means of protest.[14] This chapter examines the *Letters*, in which Wollstonecraft first converted earnest analysis to parodic performance of gender and its genres and (economic) institutions, before turning to the more extended pastiche of *Wrongs of Woman*. In outlining Wollstonecraft's interlocking parodies of genders and genres, and their roots in her critique of political economy and contemporary economic practice, I consider the reasons why Wollstonecraft's genre theory proved essentially unreadable in her own time and, until relatively recently, in ours – the reasons, that is, why the potential she offered for an economic history unmediated by genres remained unrealized. I begin by reconstructing the generic mediations of the Revolution debates through the critical lens of Wollstonecraft's genre theory.

THE GENRES OF THE REVOLUTION DEBATE

In his notorious 1798 *Memoirs of the Author of the Vindication of the Rights of Woman*, Godwin lamented the weakmindedness of Elizabeth Inchbald, who had cut Wollstonecraft socially on learning by her marriage to Godwin that she had never been married to Imlay. Inchbald was presumably untroubled by the love affair between Wollstonecraft and Godwin, which had culminated in marriage only after a year of literary and sexual partnership and, latterly, Wollstonecraft's advancing pregnancy. Even so, on the *Memoirs'* publication, Inchbald won widespread public support for her position. As the *European Magazine* succinctly put it, in an opening statement in what one reader calls "the Great Wollstonecraft Scandal of 1798," Inchbald "will be acquitted in the court of propriety." But Wollstonecraft herself is a "warning to those who fancy themselves at liberty to dispense with the laws of propriety and decency, and who suppose the possession of perverted talents will atone for deviations from rules long established for the well-government of society."[15]

Favret points out that Godwin's *Memoirs* in part explains the inability of contemporary readers to distinguish Wollstonecraft's life from her texts, particularly in the *Letters*.[16] Godwin's title conflates biography with textuality, juxtaposing his "memoirs" with "the author," and "the author" with her *Vindication of the Rights of Woman*. Yet Inchbald's cut came before the *Memoirs'* publication. There was already something illegible about Wollstonecraft and her ideas in 1796, or perhaps – if the *Monthly Review's* response to the "too many ideas" combined "too much together" in her *Rights of Men* is representative – as early as 1790.[17] Wollstonecraft's works could not be read for the same reason that their historiographic potential went unfulfilled: she cast off the generic conventions of contemporary political debate by inhabiting them. Her critique of sensibility undistinguished from sensibility, Wollstonecraft's deviations from sentimentalist ideology were treated in the press as the product of excessive feeling and, at the same time, as a drastic fall from feminine sensibility, perhaps itself only falsely displayed.[18]

Inchbald's inability to read Wollstonecraft is especially ironic given her generic influence on Wollstonecraft's late works and her own first novel's illegibility. In 1791, Inchbald – playwright, editor, "English Jacobin," and former actress, a popular and representative figure within the intersecting circles of British liberalism and letters – published *A Simple Story*, a translation of contemporary political debate into domestic fiction. The four-volume novel was unprecedented in hinging structurally and thematically on the continuity of sentimental with gothic romance. Its two opening volumes outline the sentimental romance of Miss Milner and her guardian Lord Elmwood, from the first "flow of . . . passion," as one reviewer remarked, to marriage.[19] Instead of stopping there, as traditional romance stops, Inchbald follows their daughter Lady Matilda through two volumes of gothic adventures, brought on by the breakdown of the Elmwoods' marriage in adultery and hate. Elmwood is transformed in the last line of his romance with Milner from Abelard to "tyrant." His transformation literally turns on the ring he "put upon her finger, in haste, when he married her," revealed in the volume's final portentous sentence, to Milner's "excruciating shock," as "a – MOURNING RING."[20] The fulcrum-figure of the ring makes a segue into the gothic terror of the final volumes. This rapid parallel evolution of character and genre convinced contemporary reviewers that the "picture of Lord Elmwood" was "the main design" of Inchbald's narrative, yet even as they praised the "unity of design" that Elmwood's presence lent the work, they expressed unease at the turn in Elmwood's character.[21] In her brief comment on the novel, Margaret Anne Doody defends the inconsistency by emphasizing Inchbald's feminist critique of the all-pervasive power of patriarchs and inheritors by means of the text's generational and historical continuity.[22] It was less Inchbald's chiasmic approach to history, however, than her genres that contemporaries found shocking, for it was Inchbald's unified generic approach to the apparent diversity of her contemporaries' historical and political discourse that set Elmwood centre-stage and yoked the genres of the work together.

This hinging of the novel's paired volumes made it a pioneer in the emerging genre of historical romance. Inchbald's mother and daughter heroines are linked by a sentimental history that turns, through time and the vicissitudes of masculine desire, to tyranny. But the continuities are literary as well as genealogical and gendered: Terry Castle points out the structural resemblance of the novel's halves, dominated by each heroine's movement towards marriage.[23] Inchbald's historical process from mother's life to daughter's through the janus-headed figure of the patriarch is marked by genre as well as gender. That the continuity of genre conventions coincides with continuous gender oppression in Elmwood's history allows Inchbald to demonstrate what Wollstonecraft also claimed: the continuity between gothic oppression of women and sentimental admiration. For women, at least, Inchbald suggests, sentimental and gothic romance are two faces of a single social fact, and the origins of tyranny are present in sentimental gallantry as the seeds of Matilda's story lie latent in Milner's: the most feeling of lovers, or so the novel threatens, may be a gothic tyrant under the skin. In distinguishing by genre different stages in one character – that of a man whose single person unites moneyed, aristocratic, parliamentary, and clerical authority – Inchbald's novel mirrors the French Revolution debate, establishing its genres in purely personal biographical relation: as contingently rather than qualitatively distinct. Thus, not at all in the sense that the reviewers understood it, Elmwood served as a crux in the doubled narrative of *A Simple Story*. In drawing her genres together around a public man and his history, Inchbald was not so much inventing a new historical plot for the novel as representing synecdochically the generic symmetries that shaped the late-century discourse on revolution and social change from the start. It is only in this way that Inchbald's *Simple Story* is "simple": in reducing to the homogeneous conventions of romance the arguments of French and English revolution opposer and sympathizer alike.

As a public woman, who had both embodied and resisted the conflicting expectations in contemporary economic ideology and political debate that women be publicly visible, visibly feeling, yet silent and inactive in politics and trade, Inchbald was uniquely positioned to attack the gendered fulcrum on which the Revolution debates and their genres turned. Her turncoat portrait of Elmwood registered the ideological shifts that had shaped the career of the foremost Revolution debater, Burke, the former Whig defender of the American Revolution turned "New Whig" opponent of France. Even for his contemporaries, as Elmwood's centrality to Inchbald's novel hints, it was a commonplace that Burke changed late-century political debate forever when he co-alesced the anti-revolutionary sentiments of the rich and the landed into one document: the *Reflections on the Revolution in France* (1790).[24] That Burke rewrote contemporary political events as a romance narrative, set in the moralized domestic arena and opposing "virtue," "nature," and legitimacy to "corruption," usurpation, and monstrosity, is rapidly becoming critical convention as well.[25] But the atmosphere of banality that soon began to linger over Burke's romantic text hid something less stable, and thus more fruitful for contemporary opposition. As Inchbald's *Simple Story* emphasized, Burke framed his text as a *double* romance: a tale of not one, but two families, English and French, told in the sentimental terms of domestic harmony and the disruptive images of gothic terror. The natural endpoint of Britain's "gothic" political and cultural inheritance, according to Burke, is happiness in the family. In Europe, in contrast, the repressed gothic threat of a monstrous illegitimate progeny, revolution, returns to destroy the sentimental domestic peace of France and its royal family.[26] Because the generic sequence of Britain's economic and political narrative diametrically opposes that of France, Burke's opposition between gothic horror and sentimental pleasure perpetually threatens to turn back on itself, revealing the continuity between Britain and Europe, sentimental and gothic romance.

In describing Britain, Burke is a presentist – even, like the radical Godwin, a perfectibilist. He subscribes to the liberal ideology in which, as Ian Duncan puts it, a history defined by constant advances finally "comes to a stop," placing the apex of Britain's upward progress at the date of its 1688 Revolution.[27] Burke redefines the Williamite Revolution as the endpoint of evolution. Domestic sentiment now upholds social order and social customs, Burke argues, and the English state, from that time, has continually sprung anew from "family affections":

we have given to our frame of polity the image of a relation in blood, binding up the constitution of our country with our dearest domestic ties, adopting our fundamental laws into the bosom of our family affections, keeping inseparable and cherishing within the warmth of all their combined and mutually reflected charities our state, our hearths, our sepulchres, and our altars.[28]

As a metaphor for the British polity, the passage is well known. Yet the passage is more literal than metaphorical in Burke's text, for Burke uses sentimental romance to draw the discourses of British history within the private, natural space of family life. For the heroine of his British romance he takes Sophia of Hanover, granddaughter of James I and object of the 1701 Act of Succession that promised England's crown to the legitimate " '*heirs* of her body, being Protestants' " (20).

In the early liberal philosophy of Locke and David Hume, political and economic order depended on the natural, pre-political submission of English wives to husbands, and the original consent of communities united by sentiment to ancient, or "gothic," forms of representation and rule.[29] Once proved "natural," class and gender hierarchies and property arrangements based on birth were thus proved inevitable without the traditional recourse to divine grants of power to patriarchs and kings. Natural worth and its historical consequences, not absolute donation, became for Locke and Hume the theoretical, and for Locke the historical, source of human authority. To Burke, such a natural history of authority – a sentimental journey out of and up from the founding traditions of the gothic past – theoretically justifies *and* is literally confirmed by the Act of Parliament that re-established the British crown's succession, permanently filling the throne left vacant by James II. Unlike James's childless daughters Mary and Anne, Sophia of Hanover is a mother of kings: a fertile "*stock* and root" whose Protestant wifely virtue ensures the legitimacy of her offspring and her offspring's power, regardless of who her husband is (21). She gives birth bodily to a new succession, and, Burke argues, the British people submit themselves and their children to her heirs forever, freezing her national maternity in time. It is this alliance of physical with political maternity that for Burke sets Britain's "political system" in "just correspondence and symmetry with the order of the world" and "the method of nature" (30). By couching the history of the Hanoverian monarchy in the form of sentimental romance, Burke transforms the philosophic history and liberal economics of Locke and Hume into a conservative national romance for the nineteenth century. As Duncan puts it, Burke's texts represent "a complex transition between Whig and 'Conservative' cultural hegemonies."[30]

Implicit in Burke's romantic enactment of philosophical history, then, is a claim about the natural origins of sentimental romance and Britain alike. For in updating the political and economic theories of Locke in his polemical political history of Britain, Burke draws on an aesthetics that shares the nativist assumptions of his historiography: the aesthetics of Horace Walpole, William Gilpin, and Richard Hurd, whose celebration of gothic as England's native style, and romance as its characteristic form, opposed the "corruption" they found in France. Their gothic revival imported into literary and artistic criticism the politically volatile myths of England's Gothic Constitution, which treated the 1688 Revolution as a restoration, definitively casting aside the "Norman Yoke" that was said to have replaced Britain's own natural, native forms of government with French artifice and absolutism.[31] In shaping his sentimental account of the English state, Burke, too, offers a contrasting history of France – and, by extension, of contemporary English radicalism – incorporating Hurd's and Walpole's literary-generic account of history as well as Locke's progressivism. Thus, Burke insists, the French, unlike the naturally virtuous English, are easily seduced by radicalism's gothic romance, a "monstrous fiction" that has "perverted all the well-placed sympathies of the human breast" (36, 52). His rhetoric recalls Walpole's claim to have discovered an ancient blackletter work of European clerical monstrosity locked away in the bookcases of an English country house, and to have reproduced it for the pleasure of a sceptical English audience entirely distinct from its original French readers, whose "vulgar minds" it can readily "enslave."[32] Burke's account of corrupt and unnatural French "fictions" – a modern revival of Walpole's avowedly ancient gothic romance – transforms virtue into prostitution and legitimacy into bastardy, explicitly inverting the progress of romance from gothic to sentiment that, for Walpole and Burke, characterizes English government and culture. Burke's reading throws a pall of illegitimate, Frenchified foreignness over the "literary caballers and intriguing philosophers" who introduce radical discourse into Britain, while, aligning his own often-gothic romance with the "method of nature," he exempts it from the field of modern letters that threaten Britain and its native romance traditions (9–10). It is this opposition between gothic and sentiment, this progressive, generic historiography of Britain, that Inchbald's *Simple Story* mimetically refuses.

In particular, Inchbald's portrait of Milner, Lady Elmwood, answers the most famous scene in Burke's *Reflections*, the march on Versailles, which pits the gothic forces of sexualized revolutionary violence against an "almost naked" Marie Antoinette, making her sword-pierced bed a sentimental icon violated by gothic intrusion (62).[33] In Burke's text, the invasion, incited by "the horrid yells, and shrilling screams, and frantic dances, and infamous contumelies, and all the unutterable abominations . . . of the vilest of women," erects absolute boundaries between sentimental heroines and gothic whores or hags (63). Yet Linda Zerilli points out that framing revolution as a sexual assault on the national family life – pitting prostitutes against legitimate domesticity – destroys the ideological force of "natural" feminine virtue.[34] The loss is limited to France, and there is a corollary gain: the contrast between the "elevated" French queen and the gothic hags proves that what happened in England in 1688 was not a revolution (66). In France, the "gallery is in the place of the house" and prostitutes usurp the marriage bed: gothic violence displaces sentiment and political order. In England, conversely, political legitimacy is strengthened and confirmed by a monarchy founded on the "dearest domestic ties" and grown out of the gothic past. Nevertheless, Burke's ideological reversal opens the way for a re-reversal. Inchbald's *Simple Story* stresses the instability that haunted Burke's political and aesthetic narrative from the first. Burke's reverence for "gothic" archaism sat oddly against his celebration of the Enlightened present as the natural and uniquely English successor to a barbaric, "gothic" past that still persists in Europe. More crucially for Inchbald, the dichotomy between sensible, naturally submissive women and monstrously unruly hags prompted Burke's opponents to find one lurking behind the other, destabilizing the opposition of chaste wife and gothic whore. Pornographic depictions of Marie Antoinette in particular exposed Burke's opposition between sentimental and gothic women as less absolute than Burke pretended.[35] Inchbald's portrait of Milner explores her journey in and out of "whoredom," and her romance's easy turn to gothic. The novel's generic slippage, and the slip of its central figure from heroine to magdalen, makes Inchbald's later inability to read Wollstonecraft's works appear surprising as well as, perhaps, deliberate.

ECONOMIC CONTINUITY AND GENERIC REVERSAL: BURKE AND PAINE

The generic doublings Inchbald traced in her *Simple Story* lay waiting within Burke's *Reflections*, although Burke's rigid opposition between Britain and France denied the tension between genres by insisting that the generic transitions he described moved only one – evolutionary – way. Inchbald's portrait of Elmwood hints at the latency of gothic within sentimental romance. Wollstonecraft would expand on the hint in her *Letters* and *Wrongs of Woman*. Yet even as Wollstonecraft learned genre critique of the contemporary debates on political authority from Inchbald, she benefited from a negative example, as her review of *A Simple Story* suggests. Wollstonecraft praises the novel's coherence and its critical account of female socialization, but laments its closure in harmonious marriage between Matilda and her cousin Rushbrook, Elmwood's heir, as a capitulation to the sentimental view of women the novel earlier parodies and exposes.[36]

Wollstonecraft's dissatisfaction with Inchbald's novel points toward the differences between her own generic analyses and Inchbald's. Although Inchbald astutely describes the contemporary ideologies of genre, discriminating two competing positions in the contemporary field of debate on political order before reducing them to sameness within the genre of romance, the causes and production of the discourses she examined remained outside her analysis. As her educationalist rhetoric suggests – it is Matilda's "PROPER EDUCATION" that singlehandedly arrests the generic reversal in *A Simple Story* – she proposes to mend gender ideology by the simple means of teaching women to transcend its expectations: to become less "feminine," less the victims and more the controllers of their sensibility (338). What she does not offer is a material analysis of sentimental femininity, a reaching behind genre for its ideological motivations. What is missing from Inchbald's text, that is, is a sense of historical process. Milner's transformations, like her husband's, take place in the half-page of white space between volumes, which represents seventeen years. Inchbald does not comment on the ease with which her heroine of sensibility becomes the victim of "passions tumultuous" and flees Elmwood's castle for a "large gloomy apartment" "by the side of a dreary heath" in "a lonely country on the borders of Scotland" (106, 194, 195–6, 199). The novel does not explore the conflict between the narrator's command that readers "tremble" while reading the tale of Milner's fall, and her sympathy for the "susceptible heart" and "thousand virtues" of the "dying penitent" – any more than Inchbald applies such an analysis of generic continuity to Wollstonecraft's life and *Letters*.

Where Wollstonecraft differs most abruptly with Inchbald is in her analysis of economic history. In prefacing her *Simple Story*, Inchbald claims "NECESSITY" as her literary motivation (2). In the plot, however, a gendered essentialism displaces the economic and historical force of "necessity." The word comes to stand for a kind of Enlightenment "general nature," in which genders are "species," instead of a particular, personal or national, economic history.[37] Inchbald's model of female education, in which restriction teaches self-control, tempering natural sensibility to virtuous domestic sentiment, reproduces Burkean assumptions about naturally gendered spheres of action and the symbolic importance Burke attached to gender. In rewriting Burke's gendered genres, Inchbald decontextualizes his account of political history, for even as his generic antagonisms made a symbolic event of Revolution, they were framed within an economic philosophy that extended well beyond France and 1789. Burke's uses of romance in writing political economy have been less well-analyzed than the generic conventions themselves,[38] perhaps because Burke's role in transforming conservatism from a mystical to a modern discourse – what R. J. Smith calls a "reversal of polemics" that saw Hanoverian and commercial apologists borrowing Jacobite Tory rhetorics of nature and inheritance – is so well known.[39] Tom Furniss and Gary Kelly highlight the economic investments of Burkean genre theory, but Kelly suggests that Wollstonecraft, like many more recent readers of Burke's *Reflections*, debated only by ignoring them.[40] Yet it is arguably because of Burke's association with the long and uncertain history of British liberal political economy that his genres shaped the Revolution debates *and* Wollstonecraft's response. It was Inchbald's refusal to engage Burkean economics in her Burkean text that dissatisfied Wollstonecraft with Inchbald's generic analysis of sensibility and the ideology of sentiment.

As J. G. A. Pocock demonstrates, Burke's new politics was largely a renovated economic and political Whiggism. Clothing old liberal economics in new generic garb, a rhetorical act consistent with his conservative political and cultural doctrines, Burke refurbished his theory as a conservative orthodoxy for the nineteenth century.[41] Each component of the political narrative of *Reflections* finds its correlative in the economic narrative: revolution is not only unvirtuous politics, but corrupt trading practice as well. Burke's denunciation of revolutionary economics has two objects. He attacks the appropriation of money and property from monasteries and landed estates, which the French National Assembly justified by the need to make good on the national debt, as an overthrow of property rights and a dangerous lesson to the labouring class that money and goods may be had without work (94, 215). At the same time, he condemns France's issue of "a currency of their own fiction in the place of that which is real": a paper circulation whose *assignats*, he insists, could not be rooted in specie (48, 134). "Compute your gains," Burke exhorts France: "see what is got by extravagant and presumptuous speculations" (33). France's speculations are without substance, detaching property from the labour and inheritance that had, since Locke, justified and lent it value, establishing a circulating national credit in isolation from the nation's "real" economic resources and its hopes. Above all, Burke condemns the collapse of "chivalric" manners – the "manly sentiment" and "sensibility of principle" that unite "veneration" for women, property, and states – as the force depriving property and trade of substance (66–7).[42] Burke's revolutionary gothic romance is also an economic gothic, for the monstrous actors who disrupt France's affection for its queen are the same "sophisters, economists; and calculators" who destroy France's economic probity: as a disregard for real value, substanceless trading mirrors violence toward Marie Antoinette (66). In contrast, Britain's economic probity corresponds to its settled lines of succession through the reassuring maternity of Sophia of Hanover. Domestic sentiment, the "sensibility of principle" that motivates the labour and inheritance underlying British property, guarantees, as in Hume's economics, a consistency of worth. The gothic monster in Burke's text is an economics and politics cut loose from gendered sentiment, for Burke as for Hume the fundamental gold standard. Unlike Inchbald, Wollstonecraft would highlight the homology linking the gothic turns in Burke's economic and political narratives. Thus Wollstonecraft would expose what for her was the real monster: the gendering of sentiment itself.

Most opponents of Burke, however, opposed his *Reflections* on different grounds from Inchbald's or Wollstonecraft's. They neither equated Burke's gothic and sentimental romances nor exposed the economic roots of his generic history of France and Britain. Rather, Burke's claim about Britain – that its gothic past, including the destruction of monasteries and their property rights by the "tyrant" Henry VIII, to whom Burke compares the French Assembly, had produced a satisfying sentimental present (101) – provoked opponents to argue that complacency had blinded him to the modern "gothic" barbarisms of aristocratic profligacy and corrupt inheritance at the expense of "natural" English liberties. Casting himself as the defender of ancient freedoms against the barbarous present, Thomas Paine produced a counterplot to Burkean romance, charging Burke with the "monstrous," "horrid" excesses for which Burke attacked the Revolution.[43] Against Burke's equation of the French Revolution with gothic horror, Paine argued in *Rights of Man* (1791–2) that Burke's sentimental politics and economics, in deploring the replacement of "real," affective representations of value with horrifying "false" ones, were themselves a gothic fiction usurping the "general" representational ideal enshrined in ancient common law and the "general" wealth produced in Britain by "the natural operation of commerce."[44] Economically and politically, Paine did not parody, but inverted Burke's generic narrative.

Whereas Burke views history through the generic lens of "Quixote . . . chivalry nonsense," Paine counters Burkean romance in avowedly "plain" style (1: 62–4).[45] Resembling Burke even in denouncing Burke, he sets up a correspondence between "natural" government and "natural" writing, making himself representative of both:

As the republic of letters brings forward the best literary productions . . . so the representative system of government is calculated to produce the wisest laws . . . An hereditary governor is as inconsistent as an hereditary author. (II: 166)

Britain's attorney general argued at Paine's sedition trial that "children's sweet meats were wrapped" in pages from his *Rights of Man* "in the hope that they would read it."[46] In reading it, Paine suggests, the people take part in the evolution of political from literary representation, culminating in a putatively "natural" but generically mediated end to Britain's monstrous, gothic present.[47] Paine, like Burke, produced a political economic romance that busily denied its own generic shape and literary origins.

For Burke's French narrative, in which gothic hags usurp the prerogatives of the sentimental heroine, Paine substitutes a movement from "monstrous" "hereditary despotism" into "manly . . . sentiments" (1: 54, 59, 61). At the same time he replaces Burke's British narrative with its converse, the turn from sentiment to gothic. To Burke only "the vilest of women" wish to overthrow aristocracy. Paine counters that aristocratic and monarchical succession are "the vilest systems" of government (II: 184). Paine reminds Burke that William I, the *"head of the list . . . the fountain of honor"* of his loved succession, which distinguishes Britain from France, was himself a French "plunderer of the English nation" and "the son of a prostitute": William's mother, Paine's ironic riposte to Burke's Sophia of Hanover, imperilled the *"honor"* of the English succession in the very act of giving birth to it (1: 120). Paine raises the stakes by accusing Burke of "unnatural" sympathy with the queens he admires. Aristocracy, he argues, "reduces man into the diminutive of man in things which are great, and the counterfeit of woman in things which are little."[48] As in government so in narrative, and as aristocrats go, so go their apologists.

Implicit in Paine's accusations of Burkean effeminacy is the view that what makes men "monstrous" is natural in women. Paine counterposes "natural" feminine character to the chaos of effeminate men and faithless wives, taking the naturalized figures of women and their sensibility as stable referents. Like Locke, he founds his liberal politics on a gender inequity that is only in part effaced. Paine argues that Burke sets up a "political Adam, in whom all posterity are bound for ever," without proving "that his Adam possessed such a power or . . . right" (1: 57). He returns to Locke's study-text, the book of Genesis, in which "the distinction of sexes is pointed out, but no other distinction is even implied" (1: 77). Paine denies the eternal submission of the British people – the text of the Act of Right – because natural law forbids anyone to "bind or control the personal freedom . . . of an individual beyond the age of twenty-one years" (1: 56). Only marriage justly demands such submission, because gender hierarchies alone exist prior to legal contract and political history (see 1: 80–1). Paine's revision of Burke restores the chaste private wife to historical and natural precedence over "the monster aristocracy" – whose "equivocal generation" makes "bastards" of female and later-born children – and its chief figure, the prostituted queen (1: 89, 91). But the grounding of gendered character, family life, and the roots of British history in nature remains, as do the competing categories of prostitute and wife. Sentimental romance and gothic romance discriminate France from Britain: only their heroines change places.

Despite all denials, Paine's inversion of Burkean narrative committed radical discourse to a Revolution debate ruled by notions of political representation that depended on literary representation – on gendered metaphoric embodiment – as well as on the naturalness of history. Reversing itself again and again, the crucial ideological binary of sentiment (or "chivalry") and gothic – shared by "conservative" and "radical" versions of British Enlightenment economics and political philosophy – locked political discourse into the sterile holding pattern of romance. Inchbald's unwillingness to dispense with sentimental romance in concluding her *Simple Story* testifies to the generic power of the Revolution debates, but Inchbald's entrapment was not unique to her cultural criticism. In opposing Burkean conservatism, the radical corresponding societies of the 1790s, from London to Liverpool and Leeds, adhered to Paineite natural law. Thus their member rolls "read . . . like a radical 'Who's Who'" without including any women.[49]

Even so, following generic conventions established by Burke and Paine, radicals used feminine figures as counterweights to Burke's Sophia of Hanover and Marie Antoinette, replacing his gothic portraits of female radicals as prostitutes or hags with their own virtuous daughters, wives, and mothers. They turned Burke's genres to their own advantage. John Thelwall, for example, ironically termed Burke a "*preux chevalier*" for neglecting working- and middle-class women's rights at the

demand of aristocratic women's prerogatives.[50] Yet Thelwall excluded
women from the London Corresponding Society, and he objected to
Burke's use of romance "metaphor" and "allegory."[51] Nor was radical
romance merely textual: it shaped political practice as well. Sometimes
women, much as they had in France, assumed allegorical parts in
"English Jacobin" risings or rhetoric.[52] Others participated in the demonstrations against food overpricing and undersupply that provided one
forum for popular criticism of the state.[53] As participants in crowd
action, female demonstrators provided press accounts with a symbolic
focal point, and male radicals with romantic roles as defenders of nature
and the family. Helen Maria Williams wrote of the French Revolutionary *fêtes* that the "leaders of the revolution engaged beauty as one of
their auxiliaries," and a similar engagement took place in England.[54]
This stalemate pattern of double reversals, predicted by Inchbald and
enacted by Burke, Paine, and their sympathizers, at length gave birth to
Wollstonecraft's pastiche.

WOLLSTONECRAFT'S ECONOMICS: THE *VINDICATIONS*

Soon after its publication, the *Monthly Review* discussed Burke's *Reflections*
in a long essay that Wollstonecraft – employed as an *Analytical* reviewer
while writing her book-length response to Burke – undoubtedly read.
The *Monthly* emphasized the dichotomies between Burke's "sublime
and grovelling" images. Burke's narration, the reviewer wrote, moves

> from the decent drapery, furnished from the wardrobe of a moral imagination,
> to the huge full-bottomed periwig of a bedizened monarch; from the purity and
> delicacy of a Roman matron, to the filth and nastiness of a village pig-stye; from
> the sweet fragrance emitted by the bloom of a young, lovely, and beautiful
> female, in the morning of her days, *decorating the horizon of life*, to the foul stench
> exhaling from the mental blotches, and running sores, of an old, rotten,
> ulcerated, aristocrat.[55]

According to the *Monthly*, it is because of its fluctuation between these
poles that *Reflections* is "extravagantly extolled by one party, and extravagantly abused by the other."[56] The *Monthly* reviewer names the two
poles against which Burke's text may be read: acquiescence or diametri-
cal opposition. The reviewer's own recognition of this polarity comes in
a rational but politically toothless third. Paine falls into the category of
"extravagant abusers" who recapitulate Burke's "exuberant . . . effu-
sions."[57] Whereas Burke argues against a compulsory paper circulation,

Paine promotes the real circulation of wealth in European commerce: a shared economic history produces their shared economic emphases and thus promotes the generic symmetries of their narratives. This shared political economy may explain their considerable cultural influence. Certainly it resonates through Wollstonecraft's double critique of both.

Excluded on gendered grounds from the corresponding societies and the official politics of the public sphere and, more important, driven by exclusion to recognize the economic-historical logic that underlay it, Wollstonecraft found herself in the *de facto* position of the *Monthly Review*'s moderate observer – shut out of the Burkean dichotomy. Following Inchbald, however, and moving beyond the neutrality the *Monthly* recommends, Wollstonecraft began what amounted to a rudimentary generic analysis of the Revolution debate and its consequences. Wollstonecraft is often attacked for offering education as an antidote to the "effeminacy" of female character – at the expense of sexuality, as Cora Kaplan argues, or in the unwitting service of gender ideologies whose promoters wished to hide their systemic character, as Moira Ferguson claims.[58] Yet, unlike Inchbald, Wollstonecraft did not substitute biological necessity for the contingent forces of economic history and historiography. Genres for Wollstonecraft revealed the material conditions that produced them, even as their writers sought to obscure their material history or found it already hidden beneath generic layers. Wollstonecraft's *Vindication of the Rights of Men* pinpointed Burke's attempt to naturalize in romance the English obsession with property and wealth. Her *Rights of Men* predated Paine's *Rights of Man*, but by 1792, in her *Vindication of the Rights of Woman*, Wollstonecraft extended her analysis to Paine's text as well.

In *Rights of Men*, Wollstonecraft remarks that Burke's cynical version of romance "confine[s] the term romantic to one definition – false, or rather artificial, feelings."[59] A train of ritual disenchantments leads Wollstonecraft from this "romantic" fascination with feminine beauty and weakness, which shapes Burke's *Reflections*, to his underlying love of property, which Wollstonecraft satirically personifies as royal, feminine, and chaste. Sentiment masks sensibility, but it is economic interest that produces both. Concluding his vignette of Marie Antoinette's invaded bedroom at Versailles, Burke laments that "the age of chivalry is gone" and "the decent drapery of life is . . . rudely torn off" (62, 66–7). But Wollstonecraft counters that Burkean chivalry is a "Gothic drapery" "stripped" away by revolution (48). She exchanges his gothic portrait of rape for a complex unmasking of property as a monster veiled in sentiment, in a series of unveilings that is itself a bottomless parody of sentimental discourse. Behind the French queen's sacred majesty, Burke's metonymic substitute for the money and estates he venerates, lurks "the sacred majesty of Property inviolate," Wollstonecraft's own pastiche version of Sophia of Hanover (48). Property's undraped figure is found, paradoxically, to be composed of nothing more than drapery. When Wollstonecraft asks Burke, "Must every grand model be placed on the pedestal of property?," her narrative uncovers not only what she identifies as Burke's "real" interests, but also the allegorical logic that gives such interests symbolic flesh (48). Wollstonecraft accuses Burke of preserving the "demon of property" by sentimentalizing wealth: his romance helps property, and the gendered conventions that uphold it, to masquerade as nature (9).

Hence Wollstonecraft's economic reading of Burkean romance leads to an indictment of liberal political economy and its attempts to subsume economic self-interest in natural history: "Security of property! Behold, in a few words, the definition of English liberty" (14–15). Her reading is not merely ironic: it also reveals the shared interests that produce the competing and ultimately unproductive generic mediations of Burke and Paine. Wollstonecraft's *Rights of Men* heralds some aspects of Paine's rhetorical analysis of *Reflections*, ironically exposing, as Paine would do, the monstrosity of Burkean sentiment. But already incipient in Wollstonecraft's first response to Burke was a tactic Paine did not take up, which was to be central to her later sophisticated works of radical pastiche. Wollstonecraft's rhetoric of masking and unmasking hints, as Paine does not, at the symmetry of gothic and sentimental romance – a symmetry produced by the process of subordinating illegitimate economies and sexualities to a legitimated, gendered, and naturalized symbolic code. Wollstonecraft charges that Burke "sacrifice[s] the many" to a "gothic" ideal of property encased in a romance founded on "gothic notions of beauty": "the ivy is beautiful, but . . . it insidiously destroys the trunk from which it receives support" (10). Wollstonecraft turns on Gilpin and Hurd here: their ivy is no longer the instrument of aesthetic naturalization, but is exposed as the tool of ethical decay. The trappings of sentiment, in covering the weakness of the British "liberty" Burke supports, weaken the real lives and real communities of Britain. Surfaces invade what lies beneath them, exposing depth itself as surface; sentimental romance and gothic romance interpenetrate, becoming indistinguishable; symbols undermine the reality they subsume. Economic romance itself, Wollstonecraft begins to hint, is the monster its writers fear.

Even in 1790, before her critique of genres in history was fully realized, Wollstonecraft rested the guilt for this romantic politics not just at Burke's door, but with the Revolution and its sympathizers as well.[60] Rebutting Burke, she stressed not his difference from French revolutionaries and their English allies, but the "fondly cherished romance" he shares with them: "had you been a Frenchman," she tells Burke, "you would have been . . . a violent revolutionist," impelled by "romantic enthusiasm" (44). To Wollstonecraft, it seems, an economic revolution was an economic revolution, and a romance a romance, regardless of party allegiance and the order of genres within the competing revolution historiographies. In her *Rights of Woman* Wollstonecraft's critique of contemporary dependence on the varieties of romance became an extended political theory. Tracing Wollstonecraft's roots in Enlightenment liberalism, Zillah Eisenstein identifies the seeds of a new radicalism in her treatment of women as a social class rather than a *lusus naturae*, a special case of "man," as prescribed by Genesis, Locke, and Paine.[61] By rejecting essentialist theories in favour of a socioeconomic history of gender, Wollstonecraft broke with the social-contract liberalism of Locke and Hume. Eisenstein suggests that Wollstonecraft was finally limited by the ideology of individualism that accompanied Locke's social contract. But Wollstonecraft went farther than Eisenstein allows, analyzing and later parodying femininity as a political fiction serving the varieties of liberalism and their promoters and mouthpieces, from Burke to Paine and Inchbald. Although recent readers recognize Wollstonecraft as a precocious deconstructionist of gender, they less often – Claudia Johnson is an important exception – emphasize the material dimension of her attacks on gendered sensibility and sexuality.[62] For Wollstonecraft, gender has a history: as Wollstonecraft argues, a philosophical history that "turn[s] . . . the charge on Nature" when accused of injustice; an economic history with literary pretensions (*RM* 45). Wollstonecraftian gender, then, has a literary history rooted in liberal political economy and the practices it upholds.

According to Wollstonecraft's provocatively materialist account of gender, "Woman" must appear to be " 'in herself complete,' " a holistic token of her own worth.[63] It is worth recalling that Wollstonecraft borrows this conception of femininity from Adam Smith's account of absolute French monarchs, who for Smith exemplify the "naturalness" of ambition and respect for rank – sentiments, among others, that anchor the comparative *laissez faire* Smith advocated in the British economy.[64] As in Smith's account of the visibility of *noblesse* and natural sentimental responses to it, the gendered behaviour that "preserve[s]" middle- and upper-class women's pedestalled "station in the world" has a second function, a foundation for the first (*RW* 202). It upholds their husbands' and fathers' stations and attracts the sentiments of other men, without which their own value must suffer. It is in this ironic sense that, in Wollstonecraft's memorable phrase, "The many become pedestal to the few" (*RW* 109). By visibly enacting the delicate sensibility that gives them self-sufficient yet referential value by drawing masculine sentimental reverence their way, Wollstonecraft's women acquiesce in a pre-existing sentimental romance of gender that naturalizes not just their own reduction to property, but property's very existence. Thus the "constitution of civil society" – liberal society's origins and the acts that ensure its continuity – bears final responsibility for "prevailing" ideologies such as gender, sentiment, and sensibility (*RW* 88, 116). The official "constitutions" of the liberal state – including France's "NEW CONSTITUTION," which, Wollstonecraft argued, denied women's "legitimate rights" in order to uphold the illegitimate property rights of men – give explicit form to a textuality, a generically overdetermined representativeness, already implicit in liberal political economic convention (*RW* 68). In promoting a "REVOLUTION in female manners," Wollstonecraft called for broad-based rejection of the ideologies, including the "prevailing opinion of a sexual character" – now called gender – that upheld the liberal state (*RW* 88).

In the second *Vindication*, Wollstonecraft's anatomy of the empty symbolism that justifies economic "freedom" recalls Paine's claim that a "change in the moral condition of governments" must do away with government by "effigy." But in devaluing inheritance, Paine promotes increased respect for *earned* property.[65] At the same time, he exchanges false sensibility for true, replacing Burke's texts with his own. Such a preoccupation with signs and surfaces, Wollstonecraft suggests, reduces political debate to empty symbols and competing genres, and distracts participants from the economic realities that shelter behind generic conflicts and symbolic differences. It is for this reason – the role of sensibility in naturalizing property and concealing the illegitimate commerce of money, sex, and sentiment – that Wollstonecraft, in *Letters* and *The Wrongs of Woman*, will bring down, by means of pastiche, the purely literary barriers separating wifehood from prostitution. She will demonstrate that society legislates "female manners" to protect its property relations, for "property" is ideology's "poisoned fountain," and the "sexual distinction which men have so warmly insisted upon is arbitrary," whether between man and wife or wife and whore (*RW* 211, 265). But so long as "wealth renders a man more respectable than virtue, wealth will be sought before virtue"; "women's persons" will be "caressed," and "the mind will lie fallow" (*RW* 264). Not "their minds," but "*the*" mind: bodies here are strictly feminized, but "mind" is genderless and general. Men and women alike suffer the disjunction between romance and property, and the obsession with simulacra that hides the real of economic history. Economic self-interest and self-justification produce an unstoppably self-creating yet apparently natural cycle – not a natural, but a *historical* necessity.

CIRCULATING PASTICHE

By the time Parliament passed its Reform Act in 1832, the New Whig account of the French Revolution – Burke's account – had triumphed, at least within the field of letters. This version of the story, popularized by Williams, Scott, William Wordsworth, Thomas Carlyle, and Charles Dickens, among others, is heavily weighted toward gothic, with a corresponding alliance between Britain and sentiment.[66] Judging from the rarity of generic analyses of Paine, the success of Burke's version, as measured in degrees of circulation and imitation, with the anathema attached to Paine in early-nineteenth-century Britain, obscured the generic allegiances Paine shared with Burke as well as the economic assumptions that undergirded both versions of romance, the loser as fundamentally as the winner.[67] The outcome of debate between Wollstonecraft and Burke – the overarching triumph of the Burkean account, with its displacement of its own literary and ideological *bricolage* onto the political action of the revolution it describes – prefigures late-twentieth-century debates on the right ways of reading revolution. In turn, Furet's, Mona Ozouf's, and Lynn Hunt's theories of revolution as symbolic practice, and the challenge they pose to materialist histories such as those of Soboul, echo Burke's presentation of the French Revolution as a work of genres independent of their material conditions.[68]

One oblique but lasting consequence of the semiotic focus of cultural histories of the 1790s written in the 1970s and 1980s has been the bracketing, until recently, of radicals such as Paine from the generic, or "literary," component of the Revolution debate. Recent readers of Paine's style discuss his plainness of language, or the degree to which his forms and narration helped hail a "common" reader.[69] But such readings of Paine's rhetoric remain uncommon: Paine has not been investigated in a specifically generic context. Thus even as literary histories of the British 1790s have become more dialectical, investigating the "historicity of texts" in dynamic relation to the "textuality of history," the symmetry of "radical" with "New Whig" revolutionary romances has continued almost undiscussed.[70] The bracketing of the literary Paine has had the collateral effect of contributing to render Wollstonecraft's gendered generic critique of Locke's and Hume's economic descendants almost illegible.[71] Wollstonecraft's radically critical rewritings of sentimental and gothic romance have come to look to their readers more and more like the sentimental and gothic novels of Inchbald, Ann Radcliffe, and Hannah More, Burney's economic romances, or the romantic tracts of Burke and Williams – all sources and targets for Wollstonecraft's pastiche. Her economic-historical radicalism is only now beginning, by such readers as Johnson, to be untangled from her generic method.[72] Readings of Wollstonecraft's works have for the most part overlooked the pastiche that forms the crucial *matter* of her fiction: the parodic detachment of signs from "real history" and the dissection of "legitimate" genres that conceal their own illegitimate investments.

The irony in Wollstonecraft's illegibility is that pastiche alone forced contemporaries to read her works within the Revolution debate in which she intervened. So firmly were generic accounts of the Revolution entrenched, even by 1792, that in reviewing the straightforwardly polemical *Rights of Woman*, Revolution sympathizers and opponents alike failed to read beyond its ironic analysis of sentiment, sensibility, and romance to its deeply revolutionary implications.[73] Although *Rights of Woman* addresses men and property-holders, setting their continued hold on power in England and in France in ironic contrast with the egalitarian claims of English liberals and French revolutionaries, the *Monthly Review* promoted Wollstonecraft's work as an Enlightenment liberal conduct book for women: a kind of nonfictional imitation of Charlotte Lennox's *Female Quixote* and a descendant of Hester Chapone's *Letters on the Improvement of the Mind*. The reviewer maintained that "The *sum of* our fair philosopher's doctrine concerning the degradation of the female character is, that it springs *entirely* from the want of a due cultivation of the rational powers."[74] He argued that women may become more "agreeable" and "respectable" through education, but he dismissed as "romantic" Wollstonecraft's call for economic and political change.[75] Wollstonecraft's text had collapsed into the sentimental politics she theorized and sought to replace.

What Wollstonecraft's readers, from Godwin forward, have read as her greatest political weakness or psychological strength – her wavering dance with sensibility – she turns to polemical advantage in the *Letters*, exposing at once the shallowness and the seductiveness of sentiment. It was only by literalizing accusations about her romancing in a pastiche romance – turning the genres of historiography in on themselves, enacting in self-consciously excessive form the generic continuity of British radical and conservative discourses within the Revolution debates – that Wollstonecraft attracted widespread attention, and condemnation, from the public and the press. For pastiche is founded on imitation, albeit imitation from off-centre. In her first embryo pastiche, the *Letters Written during a Short Residence in Sweden, Norway, and Denmark*, Wollstonecraft mingled imitations of romantic aesthetics, romance plotting, and sentimental form. Mixing these brought together the crucial texts of the Revolution debate as Wollstonecraft had read it: Burke's *Reflections*, which reappeared as a tale of sentimental heroines, abandoned women, and sadistic villains, and a set of variations on his earlier theory of the beautiful and sublime; Paine's *Rights of Man*, with its reflections on "human nature" and its appropriate genres of representation; Williams's two series of *Letters from France* (1790, 1793), from which Wollstonecraft borrowed the epistolary mode that expresses the writer's sentiments and describes her sentimental journey through the scenes of revolution; and the contemporary novels of Burney, Radcliffe, and Charlotte Smith, whose feeling heroines flee from persecution, suffer misreadings of their virtue, or go in search of an errant husband's heart. That the *Anti-Jacobin Review*, in 1798 and 1799, would expose the "prostitute" and "monster" behind Wollstonecraft's sentimentalized texts speaks to the success with which she chose and reanimated her quotations from sentimental convention, but also to the rapidity with which her pastiche became illegible.

Above all, Wollstonecraft brought new currency to the generic continuities of Inchbald's *Simple Story* with a dialectical and seemingly endless series of generic exchanges and substitutions. Inchbald exposed the gothic undertones of sentimental romance. Wollstonecraft, equally and alternately, revealed the sentimental pretences of gothic, so that the *Letters* refuse to arrive at a stable generic resting place. At the same time, Wollstonecraft's generic analysis goes deeper than Inchbald's, reaching behind generic interchange to expose, not just the gendering of genres in the Revolution debate, but the ideological necessity to contemporary market culture of sensibility and legitimacy. Like Inchbald's *Simple Story*,

Wollstonecraft's *Letters* embodied a generic cross-section of the Revolution debate. But more important, and more threatening than Inchbald's novel or Wollstonecraft's own *Vindications*, the *Letters* for the first time explicitly analyzed these tropes, traditions, and genres as, at bottom, economic: as generic mediations aimed at preserving a commercial *status quo*. The most fundamental difference between gothic and sentimental romance, the *Letters* demonstrate, rests on the temporal priority the writers give the genres of Britain's economic history. Sentiment gives way to gothic or gothic to sentiment: Wollstonecraft reveals that both orders, and thus many of the oppositions within the Revolution debate itself, "inhere in the [narrative] surface."[76] In miming generic difference, Wollstonecraft's *Letters* reproduce generic – and economic – resemblance.

The generic logic of the *Letters* is a double process of equivalence and disenchantment. Behind each wife, Wollstonecraft shows her reader a whore; for each heir, she reveals a bastard; for kings, she gives her reader tyrants; and for beautiful landscapes she offers the debased sublime of wastelands created by commerce and industry. In each revelation of legitimacy's illegitimate real, what is revealed appears not as an opposite, but rather as a hidden face of the legal, the normal, and the expected: gothic and sentiment, as in Inchbald's *Simple Story*, turn into each other. Gothic gives way to sentiment: Wollstonecraft's paradigmatic example comes from the Norwegian justice system, converted from horror to chivalry by the interposition of Norway's Prince Royal. Easily swayed by the pleading female prisoners who "f[a]ll at his feet," the prince "pardoned a girl condemned to die for murdering an illegitimate child": the young woman herself "is since married, and . . . the careful mother of a family" (274–5). But sentiment, in turn, produces several forms of gothic romance and monstrosity. One kind, a vaguely comic, proto-Byronic narrative, comes from the decay of gendered categories established by sentiment. The prince's bounty, in Norwegian eyes, complies so fully with sentimental convention as to rupture the gender-bounds that sentiment dictates. His chivalric rescues of female prisoners effeminate him, so that "the people like to make a kind of mistress of their prince" (274). Wollstonecraft literalizes Paine's accusations of Burkean effeminacy, conflating Burke's narrating subject with Marie Antoinette, his royal mistress and central object of desire.

A second, more conventional but more explicitly feminist metamorphosis from sentimental to gothic narrative turns on the epistolary narrator's meeting with a young "widow," a wet nurse. On hearing "a melancholy ditty sung by this poor girl," the quasi-autobiographical narrator finds her own "heart writhing" in sentimental "anguish" (283). Her sentimental response only intensifies, however, when "Wollstone-craft" learns that the woman has been "abandoned" by a man who has "run away to get clear of the expence" of his "illegitimate child," for whose support he is legally responsible only if he remains in the immediate vicinity and has agreed to pay (283). The widow, that is, is a fallen woman, her child a bastard, and her song, like the songs of mad mothers in gothic novels and romantic poems, provoked by the mutually metaphoric horrors of sexual guilt and economic distress. So too, as the narrator's half-veiled identification with the widow and her "tears of disappointed affection" lead her reader to suspect, is the narrator's own "song," although she continues to claim "widowhood" for the situations of both (247, 283).

To avoid "the pangs arising from the discovery of estranged affection, and the lonely sadness of a deserted heart," her own as well as the widow's, "Wollstonecraft" declares her intention to digress. The digression brings economics, and its connection with "gothic" ideologies, further into the heart of her sentimental text. Although "wages are low," and those of a wet nurse among the lowest, the law forces the deserted mother of a bastard to "maintain it herself" despite her poverty (80). And all this to absolve the state of responsibility for the welfare of its citizens, who are thrown, as Paine demands, on their money-making resources and, as Burke recommends, on charity. Although the narrator frames this discussion with economic claims resembling Paine's, a reminder of gendered injustice haunts her hymn to freedom: "the rich," she says, are "all merchants" – *earners* of fortunes – and are "obliged to divide their personal fortune amongst their children, the boys always receiving twice as much as the girls." It is because of this gendered principle that Norwegian "property has not a chance of accumulating till overgrown wealth destroys the balance of liberty" (273). Wollstonecraft's pastiche, quoting Paine's *Rights of Man* and her own *Rights of Men*, ironically reframes her attack on Burke's "definition of English liberty" (*RM* 14–15).

As Wollstonecraft's twinned narratives of unmarried mothers suggest, sentimental claims mask illegitimacy and justify the *laissez-faire* policies of Norwegian economics, which Norwegian justice promotes. The ideology of sentiment works in Norway as in Burke's acount of Britain, masking the gothic consequences of financial, political, and domestic policy. Yet to crown these destabilizing turns in Wollstonecraft's narrative, the Norwegians' Revolution sympathies lie with the French (255, 274). In Wollstonecraft's rewriting, then, the generic reversals of the Revolution debate blur into inextricable generic identities: gothic and sentimental romance, legitimacy and illegitimacy collapse into a textual heap. The initial, sentimental mood of her text rapidly gives way to admit an irony that folds, in turn, into a destabilizing whirl of ironies. Even the "beauty of the situation" she finds in Sweden, its rivers seen against "thickly wooded rising ground" where "loveliest banks of wild flowers variegated the prospect, and promised to exhale odours to add to the sweetness of the air, the purity of which you could almost see," is destroyed by the "intolerable" smell of "putrifying herrings, which they use as manure" to cultivate their woods (261).

This gulf between mode and matter repeatedly reasserts itself: the "fine effect" of trading ships on German rivers, for example, is juxtaposed with the "speculating merchants," their owners, whose "mean machinery" in turn reminds Wollstonecraft of the slave trade and its ships (343–4). In Scandinavia, "slavery," along with "the gigantic evils of despotism and anarchy," is being pushed aside (346). Lost, however, are the "good-breeding," the "sentiments of honour and delicacy," that mark the aristocracy, which "appear the offspring of greatness of soul, when compared with the grovelling views of the sordid accumulators of *cent. per cent.*" (340). It is impossible to distinguish which is preferable, or which Wollstonecraft prefers: aristocracy's appearance of greatness, which succeeds only when contrasted with commerce, or economic freedom united with unshakeable sordidness. Sentiment and slavery are partners, yet republicanism is reduced, politically, socially, and (punningly) economically, to interest. Money, manners, sentiment, and sensibility are interchangeable, and imperfectly hide their underpinnings of slavery and other forms of illicit commerce, sexual and financial: this blandly noted spiral, cutting recurrent paths through the text, is Wollstonecraft's pastiche.

Slavery, the pre-eminent gothic event in Wollstonecraft's text, is the point at which pastiche erupts most often. Like romance, slavery holds within itself the competing discourses of legitimacy and illegitimacy, emotion and exchange. Behind the discourses of slavery, with their rigid divisions within and between the categories of the enslaved and the free, real bodies appear, along with a common experience of disenfranchisement and violence that the ideologies of economic history deny. Wollstonecraft's collapsing of sentiment with gothic demands such *exempla* as the two modes of contemporary enslavement, domestic and foreign: prostitution and colonial slavery, homologous acts of illegitimate buying and selling. Both are homologous, too, to the respectable counterparts – servitude and marriage – that represent each act of commerce within the sanction of the law, much as sentimental does gothic romance. In her recent work on Caribbean colonialism, Ferguson argues that Wollstonecraft, with other late-eighteenth-century British women, uses African slavery as an exaggerated metaphor for women's sexual status in Britain.[77] For the eighteenth century, however, *couverture*, the perpetual minority of (white, British) women – growing out of a sexualized politics that placed women's age of sexual consent in childhood while keeping legal and economic consent forever out of reach – provided colonial slavery with a theoretical justification and produced the paired rhetorics of de-gendering and ultra-gendering that underwrote it.[78] Wollstonecraft argues that enslaved "men stand up for the dignity of man, by oppressing the women" sexually and economically, but she also directs her irony toward "ladies of the most exquisite sensibility" who "forgot that their attendants had human feelings" (*Letters* 253–4). Both claims differ markedly from the observations of Olaudah Equiano and Aphra Behn.[79] But Wollstonecraft's comments refuse a hierarchy of oppressions and destabilize all economically efficient identities. They recall the dramatic irony against "virtuous" women in *Rights of Woman*: that the ideology of sensibility teaches them to "hug their chains, and fawn like the spaniel" on men who control them sexually and economically – grateful for the legal and ideological sanction that saves them from being prostitutes or slaves (*RW* 152).

As Wollstonecraft knew, it was at the point of exchange between genres, where sentimental convention blurred into gothic oppression, that slavery and the illegitimate sexuality contemporaries called "whoredom" came together to reunite the avowedly natural categories of "sex" and "race" with the history of the marketplace they naturalize. Wollstonecraft's text occupies and so undoes the suture linking nature and culture, the place where genres overlap and defend one another's borders. Thus it was here that the discourses of privacy and prostitution, femininity and monstrosity, descended on Wollstonecraft herself. These discourses tied her "sentimental" protest against the doubled market to her illegitimate sexuality and fiscal activities, including her shocking solitary pursuit of "*men's questions*" on Imlay's Scandinavian business, in the public eye (*Letters* 248). Even as it silenced those who might otherwise have followed her, the public condemnation of Wollstonecraft marked the success with which she united Revolutionary genre criticism with material critique of its own conventions.

PARODY AND ILLEGIBILITY IN WOLLSTONECRAFT'S *WRONGS OF WOMAN*

In a letter of August 1795, with Wollstonecraft's *Letters* forthcoming, Burke privately began the charge against her writings, which would soon be taken up concertedly by the conservative press. His description names "Mrs Woolstencroft" the chief of a "Clan of desperate, Wicked, and mischievously ingenious" female rakes who bring "Ruin" on Britain by seducing its "providant and virtuous Wives and Mothers of families" away from their domestic – household and national – duties. Sexually and politically deviant, Burke's Wollstonecraft insidiously appeals to the natural sensibility that makes women their country's best moral legislators by veiling her "foreign" threat in soothing, sentimental terms.[80] Burke's (mis-)reading of Wollstonecraft and her works alongside the sentimental heroinism of Williams and Germaine de Staël, as the worst in an increasing breed of "Jacobin" conduct books designed to produce the revolutionary heroines they describe, set the stage for a broad-based condemnation of Wollstonecraft as a "philosophical wanton" – an unnatural hybrid of sexual licence and "cool, calculating, intellectual wickedness," less excusable than passion.[81] Figuring Wollstonecraft's growing *œuvre* as offspring of her monstrous promiscuity, Burke and the British press defined her works as yet another illegitimate gothic detour within the Revolution debate and the generic battle for Britain's sentiments.

Uneasily acknowledging the economic substrate of her generic and social criticism, public attacks on Wollstonecraft highlighted the question of "calculation" and, as Vivien Jones suggests, they generalized the question to other "radical women" as well.[82] The double focus of Wollstonecraft's hostile readers on money and sex, epitomized by the *Anti-Jacobin*'s *double-entendre*, accusing Wollstonecraft of "illicit commerce" with Imlay and Godwin, implies that her texts were manifestly more critical in their use of gothic and sentimental convention than such apparently supportive readers as Godwin admitted, or were able to recognize.[83] The gothic intrusions through the sentimental surface of her early works, and the gothic and sentimental pastiche of her later ones, seek neither their reader's imitation nor desire. Rather, they enact the complicity between legitimate and illegitimate commerce, sexualities, and letters. Generic interchange, within and between the texts of Wollstonecraft's career, is not merely the means, but the substance, of her critique of political economy.

Wollstonecraft made only one position statement on the writing of romance. It was published posthumously, edited to an unknown degree by Godwin. Yet her statement, designed to preface her unfinished *Wrongs of Woman*, disclosed her use of generic models in the novel and reversed the abstraction of persons and economies into genres that had shaped Britain's debates on Revolution since 1790. The novel sentimentalizes bodies, but the preface claims to "have embodied" the novel's "sentiments." Wollstonecraft's reversal reminds her readers of the real female bodies – bought, sold, married, abused – behind genres and sentiments. By means of its paired heroines, her text, she says, will enumerate "the wrongs of different classes of women, equally oppressive, though . . . various" (74). Her "classes" are distinguished by financial specifications that create distinct ideological categories from a single economic reality. Her middle-class heroine, a merchant's daughter, is married for her dowry and prostituted by her husband, while her working-class heroine, the abandoned daughter of a tradesman, turns desperately to prostitution. At the same time, however, her claim to have "embodied" "the sentiments" in *The Wrongs of Woman* invoked the classical definition of allegory to define the work of romance, drawing attention to the process in which the shadowy needs of the economic *status quo* take on comfortable generic shapes in her own, as in her contemporaries', textual interventions.[84] The pastiche that forms the plot and narration of the novel exists only within the more explicitly gendered and economic critique of the prefatory frame.

Tilottama Rajan emphasizes the contrast between Wollstonecraft's novel and the sentimental and gothic conventions it invokes and reanimates, a difference she links to Wollstonecraft's thematization of hermeneutics in the network of intratextual autobiographers and readers whose interpretations make up the novel. For Rajan, the incomplete closure of each interrupted narrative within Wollstonecraft's novel marks an imperfect correspondence, a "gap," between "narrative" and "life." Each narrative thus calls for the supplementary participation of a reader – one who unites to an understanding of history's constraints on the desire for completion and community embodied in the text, an awareness of desire itself.[85] The texture of *Wrongs* fully supports such a reading: the broken stories of the three protagonists actually usurp the "finished parts" of the novel, as Godwin's Preface put it, overthrowing even Wollstonecraft's aggressively intentional "Author's Preface" and the third-person narrator who presides over the novel's beginning.[86] That the novel was itself left unfinished appeals for a reader willing to read past the imperfect closure of the foreshortened text to supply the deficiencies of history. Yet however literally open-ended such an incomplete and indefinite text might be, and however resistant to definition by the periodical reviewers who condemned it, the novel nevertheless remains enclosed – within "its historical moment," as Rajan concedes.[87] But it is also, and more problematically, trapped within interpretive frameworks that locate the real action of the late-eighteenth-century public sphere in representation and generic competition.

Nevertheless, *The Wrongs of Woman* is not easily held within a representative frame, and it is at once more open and more circumscribed than hermeneutic readings imply. Nancy K. Miller argues that "the plots of women's literature" frequently concern "the plots of literature itself," and *Wrongs* certainly interrogates contemporary narrative conventions.[88] Yet in parodying and undermining her characters' narratives as often as she presents them, Wollstonecraft introduces a second kind of openness into her novel. At first this openness is easy to miss, for it looks deceptively like entrapment. Recent readers emphasize, for example, that the bond between Maria and Jemima, celebrated in earlier feminist accounts of the novel, remains no more than the distantly hierarchical relationship of a servant and mistress. The heroines' stories forge no real connection between them.[89] But Wollstonecraft sites her heroines' failed communication within an exchange of genres that pantomimes the generic shapes of Burke's *Reflections* and Paine's *Rights of Man*, and reflects the paired narratives of Inchbald's *Simple Story*. More explicitly than Inchbald's heroines, and in ways unremarked by Burke or Paine, Maria and Jemima are prisoners of genre. One is condemned to weep theatrically over Rousseau and lament her misfortunes in terms borrowed from sentimental and gothic romance, the other to narrate herself into the dual role of gothic jailer and whore with a heart of gold. Jemima's sentimental "tear of social enjoyment" impels her to aid Maria's doomed love affair with her fellow prisoner, the Rousseauist "Prometheus" Darnford, transforming the "Horror" of their "mansion of despair" into what the narrator sardonically calls "Armida's garden," where all three are "lapt" in a seductive "Elysium" (*Wrongs* 75, 89, 101). It may be significant that Wollstonecraft quotes Milton's *Comus* here, and that Darnford is named for Mr. B's sexually and politically corrupt neighbour in Richardson's *Pamela*: gothic becomes a classic-liberal sentimental romance as easily as its victims hug their chains. More than in *Letters*, gothic and sentimental romances meet, intertwine, and undermine one another, but in *Wrongs* romance visibly forestalls political and economic transformation as well. Even the sentimental Maria thinks "how difficult" it is "for women to avoid growing romantic, who have no active duties or pursuits" (87). The tyranny of generic convention counterweights the possibilities held open by the incompleteness of Jemima's and Maria's narratives.

The generic pastiche of Wollstonecraft's text is both profoundly limited and anarchically unstable, as if to show that genre selection is both overdetermined and arbitrary. The sensibility Maria demonstrates in her meditations on female misfortune – " 'Woman, fragile flower! why were you suffered to adorn a world exposed to the . . . stormy elements' " – is not only inadequate to the circumstance she describes (the confinement of women in madhouses) but also participates in a layered sequence of ironic allusions: to Anna Barbauld's assertion that women "copy" flowers in escaping "the stormy wind" and "rougher tasks" "assign'd" to "loftier forms"; and, more directly, to Wollstone-craft's attack on Barbauld's "ignoble comparison" in *Rights of Woman* (*Wrongs* 88; *RW* 122–3). Jemima's choice of framework for her narration, beginning with her mother's seduction by a fellow servant and the "incessant" insistence on virtue by which her mother won marriage at the expense of arousing her lover's "hate," ironically rewrites the failed seduction of Richardson's *Pamela* (*Wrongs* 102). What appears, however dimly, in the inappropriate but inevitable generic conventions em-ployed by Wollstonecraft's paired heroines is the determining force of history – covertly economic, and consequently ideological. It renders the two women unable to see or speak beyond the genres assigned to them, which they themselves uncritically embrace.

In emphasizing the literariness of the ideologies she criticizes and the historical entanglements of her own text, Wollstonecraft highlights the paradoxical *normalcy* of her competing genres: the success of her generic montage in representing a public sphere shaped by competing represen-tations. When Maria becomes an imprisoned gothic heroine, her thoughts mimic Radcliffe's *The Italian*, a new novel this sentimental heroine has likely read. Jemima's gothic tale of sexual oppression raises, as the "Letters" of Henry Mayhew would do fifty years later, a pity more often reserved for the heroines of sentimental romance. Hence although it is possible to read the transformation of gothic prison into sentimental community as a feminized utopia, the novel's excessive side-by-side rhetorics of gothic and sentimental convention demand a different, less sanguine and more historical, reading.[90] The contrasting terms in which Maria and Jemima reflect on gender – Maria's soliloquy on " 'Woman, fragile flower' " and Jemima's lament that "virtuous" women see prostitutes and victims of rape as monstrous "creature[s] of another species" – register their generic entrapment, but, like the elements of postmodern pastiche, the subgenres of romance are rendered all alike (*Wrongs* 107).

At the same time, Wollstonecraft's heroines can be seen enacting and naturalizing differences among experiences that actually stem from a single source: a British economy that treats both women as currency, and its ideologies of gender and genre. Jemima is "a slave, a bastard, a common property," and so she thinks of herself as monstrous (109). But her mistreatment as a "whore" and "bastard" by her stepmother and in the streets hides a resemblance between illegitimate and legitimate sexualities and their markets: between, that is, the monster and the wife. For Maria, too, sells herself – marrying Venables to escape an abusive stepmother; married by him because her uncle "promised him five thousand pounds" – and it is Maria who notes that "By allowing women but one way of rising in the world, society makes monsters of them" (137–8). As in *Letters*, Wollstonecraft short-circuits the expectations of the Revolution debate and its readers by exposing the likeness of wife and whore, revealing the symmetry of the genres to which these figures "belong," and allowing a troublesome materiality to surface in the generic exchange.

Even the way in which the avowedly divergent gothic and sentimental genres are consumed is the same: Maria is "absorbed by the sublime sensibility" of Rousseau's *Nouvelle Héloïse*, but the horror of her gothic confinement has even more power to "absorb the wondering mind" of Wollstonecraft's reader (75, 89). With this connection, Wollstonecraft definitively implicates her own text, and its consumer, in the ideologies of genre that entrap her characters. The only difference between gothic and sentimental romance lies in readers' belief in their difference. It is this belief alone – a product of ideology and, at a distance, of the political and economic demands of the historical moment – that keeps Wollstonecraft's heroines apart in the novel and the minds of its readers. On their liberation, Jemima "insist[s] on being considered as" Maria's servant: "On no other terms would she remain with her friend" (191). The symmetry and disconnection of wife and whore are not commercial only because the two are linked by economic transactions, or by their role in a fiction produced and circulated by entrepreneurs with an interest in liberal economics. Rather, gender and its subcategories and markers – legitimacy and illegitimacy, virtue and prostitution, sentimental and what Jane Austen and the nineteenth-century book trade will call "dreadful" gothic romances – are produced and exist in the context of a market economy that assigns pre-set roles in pre-existing genres *and* convinces women to believe their own performances.[91]

In the course of the *Wrongs*, then, Wollstonecraft's critique of representation becomes auto-critique, directed not merely at *Wrongs*, but at the embryonic pastiche of her *Letters* as well – and not just as texts, but as books in the hands of their readers. Believing herself free of Venables immediately before he incarcerates her, Maria departs with her baby for "an excursion on the continent" (181). Unlike the similarly encumbered Wollstonecraft of *Letters*, however, Maria finds her tour and narrative cut short. Drugged and robbed of her child (and trapped in England), she wakes to feel herself carried by a man with a "murderous visage" and lantern, into a "gloomy pile . . . half in ruins" and guarded by "a monstrous dog" (184). In a stylized "terror," she lapses into an aphasic series of gasps; the narrator interposes to supplement a narrative that is "broke[n] off abruptly" (170). Such breakages enact the entrapment of Wollstonecraft's narratives within the genres of romance, for Maria's terror forestalls a sentimental narrative that has, in its turn, appropriated and forestalled Wollstonecraft's. Ultimately, Wollstonecraft's novel, like Maria's memoir, is a fragment.

The courtroom scene that supplements the novel's "finished parts" contextualizes and encloses this fragment, enacting the symbolic relation between what Wollstonecraft names "the partial laws of society," economic custom and the gender convention that upholds it, and what Mary Jacobus, revising Jacques Derrida, calls the gendered "law of genre."[92] The scene unites two kinds of representation, "partial" in the sense of incompleteness as well as of bias: legal and ideological definitions are doubly incommensurable with the lives they regulate. Just as Wollstonecraft can be heard only in sentimental texts and then only by opponents, Maria's written brief on her "nature" and "feelings" is her only voice in her *in absentia* defence against charges of adultery (195). Her paper quotes Wollstonecraft's theory of gender as an illusory but constraining economic fiction: "the policy of artificial society," intent on preserving property, produces the "false morality" that reduces women to be capable only of passive "virtues" such as chastity (*RW* 196–7). In demanding divorce in economic and sexual terms, Maria's paper enacts the economic register of her transgressive desires and her "strange" and "atrocious" affair with Darnford (194–5). The judge responds by reducing Maria's "feelings" to "notions" and "French principles" and by defending the rights of husbands to retain the bodies and fortunes of their wives. His reading of Maria's narrative at once recapitulates Burke's charges against Wollstonecraft's *Rights of Woman* and foreshadows the attacks of the *Anti-Jacobin* and other late-century reviewers, from Burke to More, who were to condemn Wollstonecraft's novel on identical economic and ideological grounds.

THE END OF *THE WRONGS OF WOMAN*

Wollstonecraft's text necessarily fades into silence. For women in 1798, as the *Anti-Jacobin* attacks make clear, to act or speak economically and politically was to act the whore. Attempts to escape the ideologies of romance led to identification with the monstrous prostitute of Burkean gothic, and Wollstonecraft herself draws the monsters and madonnas of her novel from contemporary economic and historical representation. Her courtroom scene, like her pastiche-text generally, harnesses the disorderly energy of the gothic monster – but only for a moment. That brief instant of Wollstonecraft's historically specific claim on contradiction and disorder works to reveal the contingency of her society's ways of reading and the arbitrariness of its sentimental texts and ideologies. In damning Wollstonecraft as a *lusus naturae*, substituting the novelist for the novel and its heroine, the periodical reviewers closed off her fragmented text as the court supplements Maria's. Yet in conflating the representation with the woman, the reviewers, like Maria's judge, added a textual dimension to the revolutionary whore. The assertion that Wollstonecraft is a prostitute and monster because she writes monstrous fictions discloses the literary process of contemporary political discourse. The evident alliance between literariness, gender, and politics that resulted, of course, was what Wollstonecraft had argued all along.

Maria's critique is not, like Wollstonecraft's *Rights of Woman*, misread. In this woman's desire to speak, the judge recognizes a potential breach of the laws of gender, genre, and Britain, which dictate that women be represented instead of speaking, and therefore uphold the intrinsically figurative character of women's relation to public discourse. He forecloses Maria's narrative by re-translating economics into sensibility, condemning Maria's feelings as excessive, and re-consigning her to the "private mad-house," noting that "the conduct of the lady did not appear that of a person of sane mind" (*Wrongs* 199). Yet his reading of

Maria's incipient "innovation," like Maria's romantic text itself, is temporary and arbitrary, visibly trapped in the moment (198). In working at cross-purposes, Maria's plea and the judge's response expose each other's contingent historicity. The text's generic confinement mirrors not just Maria's and Jemima's "real" economic and sexual confinements, but the judge's ideological confinement as well.

Juxtaposing the force of economics and politics on representation with the inadequacy of texts to embody the real dynamics of status and oppression, bargaining and exchange, that underlie and motivate the competing kinds of narrative, Wollstonecraft opens her text to readings shaped by a historical self-awareness, as Rajan argues. At the same time, she opens the novel to forms of readerly consciousness that are informed about literary history, in its textual and economic components, and resistant to generic confinement. Re-reading the romances of the Revolution debate, Wollstonecraft insists on the arbitrariness of genres and so unveils the process that selects them and sets aside their material history (20). Her pastiche registers the intransigence of the historical matter – the real bodies and real economies that lie behind and beneath the sentimental text – that the writers of the Revolution debate subsume in generic wrangles. She reveals, indeed, that the economically damaging effects of difference, protest, and a stubborn materiality are the very conditions that drive the Revolution debate's discursive coherence. The resolution of the real into genres remains perpetually unrealized, despite the attempts of writers and readers to impose determinate and comprehensive genres and interpretations. By marking and voicing the multivalent matter beneath the genres, Wollstonecraft incurably troubles their virtual coherence.

CHAPTER 4

Romance at home: Austen, Radcliffe, and the circulation of Britishness

In 1791, the sixteen-year-old Jane Austen, literary muscles cramped by what *Northanger Abbey*'s heroine calls the "torment" of reading David Hume's and William Robertson's massive histories, wrote a short *History of England*.[1] This *History* stands the narratives of hegemonic liberalism daringly on their heads: Britain has neither progressed from Stuart absolutism to Hanoverian liberty nor recovered a golden age of Saxon autonomy.[2] Instead, Austen writes Jacobite history. She avows, even more explicitly than Frances Burney, her "attachment to the Scotch"; she declares herself "partial to the roman catholic religion," and closes by exonerating Charles I from charges of tyranny with a defence "certain of satisfying every sensible and well disposed person" – "that he was a Stuart."[3] By turns imitating and parodying her Scottish Enlightenment predecessors, she appropriates the varieties of Scottish attachments and Stuart sympathies for Britain as a whole, making herself, a young Englishwoman, the united Britain's historiographic representative.[4] Yet Austen ignores traditional Jacobite *jure divino* justifications as completely as she disregards the New Whig doctrine of Hanoverian legitimacy, and there is nothing teleological about her narrative. Her Tudors gain the throne by "good luck"; the "Adoration" of monarchs, though a "Duty," is rarely performed. Henry VIII's dissolution of the monasteries, while no Protestant apogee, is "of infinite use to the landscape of England in general, which probably was a principal motive for his doing it" (137–8, 144). The *History* declares its author "a partial, prejudiced, and ignorant historian," writing "to vent . . . Spleen *against*" everyone "whose parties or principles do not suit with mine" (135). Austen writes with an ironic consciousness of generic conventions and with national self-consciousness. Framing and commenting on her text, coupling wit with self-reflexion, her irony registers the artifice and arbitrariness of historical writing and event alike. History and historiography take their places among the aesthetic practices by which Austen's modern Britain defines itself.

I will argue that the conjunction of Toryism, parody, and history already apparent in the juvenile *History* shapes a crucial place for Austen's fiction among the early-nineteenth-century ideologies of British social and economic cohesion. That Austen was an ironist has been much discussed; that she was, in her ironic way, a Jacobite has received less attention.[5] Yet had Austen published the *History* she would have become publicly what she was in private manuscript: one of those Tory writers of Romantic history, among them Walter Scott, whose "lavishly" praised Stuarts and "vilified" Whigs drew the ire of the *Edinburgh Review* in 1820. "A strange sort of spirit [has] lately sprung up," the *Edinburgh* protested, a "speculative Jacobitism," "twin brother to the newfangled doctrine of legitimacy."[6] The reviewer complains that Scott and other Tories rest their excessive support for Hanoverian prerogative on a sentimental base of literary Jacobitism, as fictive as prerogative is unjust.

Clifford Siskin and Robert Crawford have recently commented that the early-nineteenth-century resurgence of Jacobitism in literary and political debate, as well as its late-twentieth-century resurgence in scholarship, make Jacobitism a shorthand figure for the problem of "British culture" generally.[7] Indeed, Austen's support for legitimacy is as ironic as her historiography, as aware as the *Edinburgh* of the contingency of history. *Northanger Abbey*'s Catherine Morland insists that as "'a great deal of [historiography] must be invention,'" it has no right to be "'tiresome'" to its readers (84). Even so, she admits its value in teaching children to read, the first step toward literacy and access to romance (85). Bored by the history whose utility she unwillingly concedes, Catherine finds fiction more entertaining and more useful. Austen's own *History* educates its reader in Toryism, mounting a rigorous defence of "establishment" – from its jeer at Henry VIII for dismantling the Catholicism "for Ages . . . established in the Kingdom," to its faith in the secular scripture of gothic nationalist aesthetics with which William Gilpin and others replaced it. But she relies on no earlier conservative claims about human nature and God-given social rules. Her narrative is self-consciously artificial, witty, and explicitly polemical even when it is sentimental, taking Mary, Queen of Scots, as its beleaguered gothic heroine. It assigns similar aesthetic motives to historical actors, including Henry VIII. In her early writing of history, Austen began working out an ideological and generic model for her novels and for British

nationhood. Her aesthetically and historically self-conscious conservatism was as radical an account of the past's influence on the present as
any by Wollstonecraft or Paine.

Beginning with *Northanger Abbey*, written in 1797–8 but not published
until 1818, Austen renovated romance. By marketing and circulating
her reconditioned version of that markedly hybrid and historicized
genre, she renovated Britain's history as well. The effects of her generic
reconsiderations are noticeable even before their first publication in
Northanger Abbey. While reviewing Austen's *Emma* for the *Quarterly Review*
in 1815, Scott first drafted a formal pedigree for British fiction, establishing Austen's primacy as a mother of the novel. In keeping with the
interests of the Tory *Quarterly*, he treated literary history as the consequence of a Burkean inheritance. Itself "the legitimate child of the
romance," a French, courtly, extravagant though highly honourable
form of fiction, the modern novel begot two children. One was the
prodigal firstborn, whose descendants flourish in France, devoted to
sensibility and to the dishonoured shade of the fantastic parent-form.
The other, the cadet, is serious, dependable, and domestic, British to the
bone. Its favourite children are Austen's works, the modern novel's
legitimate, though late-born, inheritors.[8] In 1832, in his Magnum Opus
preface to *St. Ronan's Well*, Scott lent concreteness to this family history
by recounting his own literary genealogy, casting himself as Austen's son
and (implicitly) as the inheritor and improver of her literary dower. In so
doing, for the first time, he granted literary history an explicitly national
importance. The best novelists, from "the authoress of Evelina" to
"Edgeworth, Austin [*sic*] . . . and others," he argued, seek "*celebrare
domestica facta*." The succession of celebrants culminates in Scott's *St.
Ronan's Well*, "the most legitimate" of British novels.[9]

Scott's account of the novel's romance heritage draws unattributed
on the literary histories of Richard Hurd and Clara Reeve, but his
shaping of overtly nationalist rhetorics of legitimacy to literary criticism
is striking.[10] He invokes what William Hazlitt condemns as a "bastard
interpretation of divine right," Edmund Burke's legitimist claim that
Britain's economic and political practices are a patrimony transmitted
from fathers through virtuous mothers to deserving sons, bypassing any
weak or wayward heirs.[11] Employing Burkean rhetoric in defiance of
Hazlitt, Scott draws the ideological heart of post-Napoleonic conservatism into his literary history. The history of the novel as Scott writes it
recapitulates the history of the monarchy, upholding and naturalizing –
as in new Tory justifications of Hanoverian government, now in the

hands of the Regent who Tories believed would soon become a senti-mental-Jacobite king – the superior claim of a younger branch to an English (literary) throne kept warm for them by women. The domestic novel, Scott's name for the youngest, most British, most distant branch of romance, has the best right to fill its place. Significant here is Scott's magistral notion of the place of romance. Precisely because their doubly "domestic" interests unite the intimate sphere of the family with the nation's needs, novelists, as Nancy Armstrong and others have recog-nized, become acknowledged legislators – of Britain, if not the world.[12]

In the early nineteenth century, as Jon Klancher and others demon-strate, "genre reform" in letters occupied all parts of the political spectrum, directed both toward and counter to the socioeconomic and political reform for which Catholics, Dissenters, artisans, and radicals were agitating.[13] Working from the proposition that the hegemonic powers of texts were double – capable at once of illustrating and reproducing desired social practices and their justifications – writers from Percy Shelley, William Wordsworth, Joanna Baillie, Hannah More, and Scott to the earnest William Bowdler and George Croly produced works at once to teach and to produce their audiences or readers. In making a literary ancestor of Austen, Scott subsumed her novels in his own ongoing project of cultural renovation and preserva-tion through fiction. His genre reforming was "domestic" in both senses implied by his quotation from Horace: its work was carried out for the homeland *and* the home.[14] For Scott, it culminated in the pageantry he orchestrated for the 1822 visit of George IV to Edinburgh. With a whirl of plaids and bagpipes, he sought to convince all Britain, including Edinburgh, that Scotland was " 'a nation of Highlanders' " – by means of the reflexive exercise that urged his fellow citizens to bring his early Waverley novels to life.[15] Whereas Scott worked from the homeland toward the home, Austen's novels, as Claudia Johnson argues, were directed from the private toward the national public sphere.[16] It was by naming the new role Austen helped forge for romance as one of the movers and shakers of cultural history that Scott reconciled generic self-reflexion with his naturalized, avowedly evolutionary, and genetic legitimation of romance.

Austen, however, engaged in genre-reform of a different kind from Scott's, writing romances of British national identity without attempting to palliate or disguise any portion of the genre's or the nation's artifice. She confronted the problem that had faced patriotic conservatism since the economic and political upheavals of the 1790s: the suspicion that its conceptions of authority, history, and value in politics, letters, and the household were unnatural and therefore illegitimate. In her domestic novels, which are also national romances, Austen rested the full weight of legitimacy – not, like Hazlitt, on representation or consent; nor, like his opponent Burke, on virtue, chastity, and nature; nor even, like the gothic revivalists Hurd, Gilpin, and Horace Walpole, on Britain's native cultural inheritance – but on cultural construction: the artifice of romance itself. Threats of generic instability and "illegitimacy" surface frequently in Austen's novels, most often as the *verso* side of parody. Her reformation of romance, seen retrospectively from the position of generic solidity romance achieved in part through her work, enabled Scott to naturalize literary history as the teleological result of a legitimate generic inheritance, rendering the descent of romance linear, uncontested, and smooth in the service of British nationhood.

THE NATIONAL TALE AND NATIONAL ROMANCE

Austen's national romances reveal an often overlooked English thread among the early-nineteenth-century fictions of national character produced by such Scottish and Anglo-Irish writers as Scott, Susan Ferrier, Edgeworth, and Sydney Owenson. Generically and historically engaged, feminist as well as Tory in sympathies, Austen's conservatism was subtle in its tactics, willing to incorporate and recirculate the energies of New Whig political economy and political history, female radical and colonial resistance, and the tropes and genres of Britain's colonies and subject kingdoms. Among the discourses that commingle in her romances, Austen refashioned and recirculated the conventions of the so-called "Jacobin novels" and "national tales" – the fictions, respectively, of English radical and colonial nationalist protest – as well as the New Whig gothicism of Burke, Gilpin, and Hurd. Meeting these writers on their own ground, defusing the social protests and preachments, generic conventions, and disruptions that served as their vehicles in order to reclaim romance for cultural-Jacobite Tory ends, she established herself as a model for conservative novelists, and the national importance of domestic fiction for the nineteenth century.[17] Her works stretch the borders of the genre Owenson named "the national tale": it was not only England's colonies and dominions that produced fictions of resistance to "foreign" usurpation and cultural conquest, but also England itself. As Austen defined it, the British national tale was a conservative genre of resistance to radical discourse, portrayed as a "foreign" corruption of natural, native English romance. Her explicitly literary engagement with New Whig conservatism and radical critique was ultimately more ideologically successful than anti-Jacobin polemic, volunteerism, or demonstrations for king-and-country, as Scott's parallel turn from militia-drilling to romance-writing and pageantry suggests.

In important discussions of the kinds of historical and political fiction that existed at the turn of the nineteenth century, Ina Ferris and Katie Trumpener outline the conventions of the national tale, a colonial novel of national identity preserved in the complex exchanges between home and nation.[18] While this description in some ways resembles Scott's account of the "legitimate" novel, it also updates, politicizes, and accounts historically for his generic taxonomy. Their study examples include Owenson's *Wild Irish Girl* (1806), which concludes with the marriage of its royal Irish heroine to the son of her English absentee landlord. Because traits "both natural and national" attract Horatio to Glorvina, their marriage creates a "family alliance" that is "prophetically typical of a national unity of interests and affections between those who may be factitiously severed, but who are naturally allied."[19] A domestic paragon with talents for historiography and the harp, Glorvina can bring about the Britishness that Owenson, at this early stage in her career, still recommends to Ireland's future: a unity-in-difference best symbolized in the multilayered reconciliations of romance.[20] Thus Owenson's novel partakes in the long generic inheritance of Richardsonian romance, in which symbolic marriage can reconcile allegorically competing solitudes. At the same time, however, Owenson heads, with Edgeworth, a new generic tradition, both akin and opposed to the historical romances of Scott and his imitators.[21] Historically and politically engaged but grounded in the intimate sphere, the "national tale" occupies the more domestic end of the nationalist romantic project. The family, its practices, and ways of representing them in romance become a predominantly progressive – even radical – concern.

In highlighting the nationalist implications of romance, Trumpener removes Austen's novels from the genealogy she shares with Radcliffe, Owenson, Edgeworth, and Scott. In contrast to her politically invested contemporaries, whose ideological engagements Nicola Watson, Ferris, and Trumpener delineate, Austen remains among the shrinking group of " 'lady novelists' " traditionally juxtaposed to Scott's historical fiction and characterized by extreme domesticity of focus.[22] Owenson and Edgeworth, in contrast, form a ground of interchange between the homebound ladies of nineteenth-century criticism and the masculinized historical tradition of Scott and John Galt, revealing the dialectic between the generic histories of history and romance in the resemblances and conversations between historical novel and national tale. Yet the recent readings of Maaja Stewart and Edward Said highlight, in different ways, Austen's national and transnational ideological investments, and Johnson notes that Lionel Trilling remarked on the explicit "Englishness" of Austen's fiction as early as 1957.[23] At the same time, Austen audibly imitated and parodied Owenson's and Edgeworth's works, as well as those of Radcliffe, their immediate ancestor in the writing of romance.

Neither mere burlesque nor limited to her earliest works, Austen's response to Radcliffe's anti-Jacobin gothic romances and Owenson's national tales in *Northanger Abbey* provided foundations for her English version of British national romance. In an 1809 letter, she comments that the "Irish Girl does not make me expect much" from Owenson's later novels, though "If the warmth of her Language could affect the Body, it might be worth reading in this weather."[24] Her winter reading prefigures the scene in *Northanger Abbey* in which Catherine Morland and Isabella Thorpe "meet . . . in defiance of wet and dirt, and shut themselves up, to read novels together." Unlike her characters, whose avid consumption of Radcliffean gothic cements what she sarcastically terms their "very warm attachment" and "literary taste" (37, 39), Austen remains unmoved by Owenson's and Radcliffe's claims that "nature" undergirds their marriage plots. What Owenson treats as a heartfelt union of hero and heroine, Austen dismisses as a rhetorical effect of overpassionate language. Symbolic marriage, however desirable, remains a function of romance. And so, Austen will demonstrate, does the "nature" of the British nation, the national character Austen's romance assembles from the competing voices of Scottish and Irish as well as English writers of history, politics, and romance.

A glance at the nationalist novels of the early nineteenth century reveals the conflicting political positions and generic claims that, according to genre theorists from Ralph Cohen to Franco Moretti, are latent in any new genre such as "the national tale."[25] Just as the character and custody of romance had been under dispute since the mid-eighteenth century, as liberals, conservatives, and radicals fought their ideological battles on its simultaneously sentimental and political economic ground, so too the borders and identity of national tales, and of national character, were continually being disputed.[26] Like the gothic romances and national tales Austen revised, her national romance used symbolic marriages to unite competing cultures and classes and to celebrate what it defined as Britain's national character, under threat from the cultural changes it construes as foreign. But her romances worked, more influentially than their liberal and conservative predecessors, not by linking national character with natural domestic virtue, but by declaring explicitly and joyfully the conventionality and artifice of the heroine's final domestic happiness, and of their own generic conventions. Austen acknowledges, often explicitly, the literariness, the riskiness and contingency of her conclusions. What she recognized was the potential that accusations of artifice held out to a conservative nationalism. Her embrace of the literary was made possible by the very contradictions that Hazlitt and others, in the 1790s and after, had used against conservative discourse.

THE NATURALIZATION OF BRITISH AESTHETICS

To read Austen's novels in their fulness as national romances that engage and ironically resolve problems of national history is to map Austen's position on a chart of contemporary contradiction and crisis. The political landscape has a plurality of notable features, not all of which Austen addressed. The two late-eighteenth-century revolutions that form its main points of convergence, however – the French Revolution and its Napoleonic aftermath, and that English revolution in political and economic authority that Burney and Wollstonecraft protested, and that Neil McKendrick, Philip Corrigan, and Derek Sayer call "commercialization" or "*embourgeoisement*" – are directly relevant to Austen's novels.[27] Austen's specific political loyalties, it should be noted, have proved elusive, fuelling discussions of the novelist as, variously, a proto-Marxian critic of market liberalism, a utopian aristocrat, and a feminist radical, as well as, in more contemporary terms, a Tory.[28] These arguments prove neither Austen's vagueness nor the bad faith of her critics, but highlight the degree to which determining the politics of British female novelists in this period has depended on their often illegible place in the French Revolution debates, or their position on the highly charged and complicated issue of women's role within them.[29] As Johnson points out, irony and ambivalence make placing Austen squarely amid these debates doubly difficult, clouding the debates themselves.[30] Viewing socioeconomic upheaval as Austen most explicitly responded to it, however – as it was embodied in political and aesthetic debates on the legitimacy of England's "gothic" inheritance and on the changes wrought by the Copyright Act of 1774 – helps to reconcile as well as complicate the various conflicting Austens of recent account. To Austen, politics is unavoidably what Wollstonecraft had earlier feared it was: a literary and economic matter. Allowing Austen to appear in the complex role of a generically- and historically-conscious conservative helps to define her national romances as well.

It was only in eighteenth-century France and its colonies and European neighbours that declared political revolutions took place at the *fin de siècle*. Equally importantly for British novelists, however, Britain in the same period underwent a copyright revolution conducted by a coalition of the powerful and the upwardly mobile. The 1774 *Donaldson* v. *Beckett* decision, in which the House of Lords sided with upstart provincial booksellers against the established London congers, replacing the *de facto* perpetual copyrights held by the London trade with time-limited contracts between writers and sellers, brought to light an unsolvable contradiction in the ideologies of inheritance that justified the British aristocracy and, by extension, the monarchical succession.[31] In deciding *Donaldson*, the Lords invoked their hereditary privilege to silence the disputes of their social inferiors. But by finding in favour of the plaintiff, the entrepreneur or "pirate" Donaldson, they simultaneously damned his merchant-respondents as " 'impudent, monopolizing men.' "[32] Casting the respectable middle-class monopoly as a set of oligarchic tyrants, they ended whatever illusions might have remained about the separation of aristocratic power from the commercial sphere. By forcing writers to contract with booksellers for particular editions and sellers to hone their marketing techniques and distribution networks in order to turn a profit within a much briefer copyright period, *Donaldson* institutionalized competition and contract in the republic of letters – now explicitly become, as critics such as Burney and Samuel Johnson lamented, a literary marketplace.[33]

But the *Donaldson* decision also paved the way for the reissue of some quite new "old books" as "classics" in fancy-bound series. By the early nineteenth century, as Austen was writing and publishing her fictions, this impulse toward literary nationalism, defining a British canon, had expanded to include the previously unregarded genre of "the novel." Anna Barbauld's fifty-volume bound and matching set of *British Novelists* (1810), with critical introductions, was the first work to define (and to market) a canon of "great" fiction, as editors had been doing with poems at least since Thomas Warton published his *History of English Poetry* in 1774, and as Elizabeth Inchbald had done with drama in her ten-volume *Modern Theatre* and seven-volume *Collection of Farces* in 1809. The ephemeral genre of the anthology took equal advantage of *Donaldson*, with writers such as the Anglo-Irish New Whig Croly shaping and reshaping teaching canons for commercial or ideological advantage.[34] Not least among editors and printers of novels and didactic texts, therefore, the profit motive gave birth to a self-consciously British literary traditionalism – a canon-forming drive.

The debates on revolution and the ambivalent effects of the new copyright law produced parallel contradictions in late-century England's existing national myths. I have been arguing that the form of liberal ideology then in place had relied from its inception on the natural order of English families, an assumption that undergirds the political history of John Locke's *Two Treatises of Government* (1690) and, more shakily, David Hume's political economic account, in *Treatise of Human Nature* (1740) and *Essays, Moral, Political, and Literary* (1740–58), of sentiment and the passions as a source of human authority.[35] But as Wollstonecraft lamented, the mid-century reliance on the normalcy of family feeling gave place at the end of the eighteenth century to Edmund Burke's fear, expressed in the *Reflections on the Revolution in France* (1790), that traditional reverence for the chastity and beauty of women and the authority of husbands and fathers, which he conceded was a "pleasing illusion," was fast crumbling into scepticism.[36] Burke's lament embodied the discomfort of Hanoverian apologists turned New Whig conservatives, who had long celebrated the forced abdication of James II as a return to English nature – a restoration of "gothic" principles of English liberty and a sign of progress away from Catholicism and feudalism; an end of revolutionary history – but now found their own putatively final and decisive revolution uncomfortably replayed in France. The erstwhile Catholics across the Channel shouted slogans of British Protestant modernity (*liberté, fraternité*) while behaving in ways that, for erstwhile liberals such as Burke, only emphasized the gothic barbarity of the revolution they pursued.[37] In New Whig conservative minds, writing in praise of Britain's "gothic inheritance" had given way to gothic Terror.[38]

The part played in the Revolution Debate by English Jacobin women in particular – often writers of gothic romances, whose incipient feminism cooperated with their reformist politics – revealed the ideological origins of the naturalized, domestically based conception of the state beloved of liberal theorists and their romance-writing apologists. Above all, Wollstonecraft emphasized the artificiality, even the fictionality, of the contemporary ideals of gendered character that grounded political theory and Whig ideology. Her own two treatises of government, the *Vindications*, and her *Wrongs of Woman* dissected the conception of "woman's nature" that underwrote the cooperation of moral philosophy with political requirements in England and in France, terming it a "prevailing opinion" to accompany Burke's "pleasing fiction."[39] At the same time, as I suggested in chapter 3, Wollstonecraft's works outline generic and political links between the "gothic" barbarity that New Whigs such as Burke lamented in the French Revolution and the New Whigs' own ideal of England's "gothic" past.[40] But Wollstonecraft was not arguing in a vacuum. Her position as the most reviled of the female English Jacobins was based on assumptions about her representativeness; the *Anti-Jacobin Review*, Richard Polwhele, and Laetitia Matilda Hawkins, prominent in polemics against female radicalism, targeted Charlotte Smith, Mary Hays, and Helen Maria Williams as well.[41] Wollstonecraft made her ideological connections between New Whig and radical gothic by pressing the self-deconstructive tendencies of the late-century gothic revival as well as of the Revolution, forcing both to expose their latent contradictions. The ambivalences and contradictions of British gothicism, as Gerald Newman describes them, emerged most audibly in aesthetics and literary history. But their appearances repeated an uneasy balance within ideologies of commerce, a truce amid contradiction that appeared, in turn, in the conflicting canonizing and marketing drives that met in contemporary letters and the literary marketplace.[42]

Not only the House of Lords, but also the writers whose works their Booksellers' Bill regulated, found themselves torn between commercial modernity and gothic tradition, and tried to enjoy both at once. Scott, for example, praised Walpole's novel *The Castle of Otranto* (1764) as an "improvement upon the Gothic romance": "a specimen of the Gothic style adapted to modern literature, as he had already exhibited its application to modern architecture." Scott noted astutely that Walpole's renovations to his suburban villa "fit to the purposes of modern convenience, or luxury, the rich, varied, and complicated tracery and carving of the ancient cathedral," just as *Otranto* "blend[s] the two kinds of romance, the ancient [gothic] and the modern."[43] Walpole's aesthetics enacts his personal and political values, and he may, therefore, be seen to live an impossible national fiction. A similar ambivalence appears in Gilpin's treatise of national aesthetics, *Observations Relative Chiefly to Picturesque Beauty* (1788). Gilpin praised British medieval architects for giving up "awkward imitation" to "strike out a new mode

of architecture . . . without searching the continent for models."[44] But
even as he admired the Britishness of indigenous gothic structures, he
took special pride in their ruin, as he pointed out in admiration for the
great abbeys of the North of England: "Where popery prevails, the
abbey is still intire and inhabited" – but England's ruined abbeys are
"naturalized to the soil," a pleasing backdrop for a liberal nation and
its industrious, rational citizens (1: 13–14). The naturalness of gothic
ruination, Gilpin declared, is evident even where the ruins are replicas,
put up to adorn the grounds of England's great houses (1: xxvi).[45]
Hurd's *Letters on Chivalry and Romance* (1762) also reframed literary history as a contest between native and foreign models. Hurd concedes
that neoclassical works are "more perfect," but insists that "Gothic
architecture has it's own rules, by which . . . it is seen to have it's merit,
as well as the Grecian," and that Britain's modern texts and other
cultural objects improve on the gothic ideal (61). Yet Hurd, too, is
uncertain whether to celebrate a modern English canon or to mourn
for lost greatness. Before Burke's elegy on the "pleasing illusions" of
"the age of chivalry" was Hurd's lament for the "revolution" away
from English gothic style: "What we have lost, is a world of fine fabling;
the illusion of which is so grateful to the *charmed Spirit*" (120).

When I call English gothic a "myth," I do not mean that it lacks
historical foundations in either a literal or a symbolic sense. As Austen
herself suggests, Britain built its national wealth as well as its state and
religious structures on the gothic ruins left behind by the dissolution of
the monasteries and the disestablished Catholic church.[46] Because of
this historiographical basis, Gilpin's and Hurd's ambivalent elegies on
English national character resound through Burke's more overtly political *Reflections*, a work of national self-definition in a time of crisis and one
immediate target of Wollstonecraft's protests against English – and
French – gothic. The gothic contradiction created a schism not only in
aesthetic discourses tinged with political nationalism, but also in political philosophy, where, as Newman has shown, it came together in a
single narrative with aesthetic debate.[47] Burke scolds the French, who,
having "possessed in some parts the walls and in all the foundations of a
noble and venerable castle," "might . . . have built on those old foundations" instead of "pulling down an edifice which has answered . . . for
ages the common purposes of society."[48] But the British love of "old
foundations," Burke argues, prevents a revolution from ever taking
place in Britain: "The very idea of the fabrication of a new government
is enough to fill us with disgust and horror. We wish . . . to derive all we

possess as *an inheritance from our forefathers*" (27–8). With the anniversary of Britain's 1688 revolution close in memory, Burke cannot simply advocate tradition for tradition's sake. Instead, he creates a complex alchemy between English aesthetic and political tradition and the laws of human nature. The alchemy kicks in as Burke, like Hume before him, reveals natural "common . . . sense" as the true father and ruler of British tradition: "sense . . . hath built up the august fabric," and wishes, "like a prudent proprietor, to preserve the structure from . . . ruin" (81). Sense keeps British politics true to nature, and "Upon that body and stock of inheritance we have taken care not to inoculate any cyon alien to the nature of the original plant" (28). Legitimacy is a function of primogeniture tempered by a higher nature.

The parallel contradictions in the literary and political public spheres, their gaps exposed largely by Wollstonecraft, produced parallel resolutions. Both resolutions are embodied in Austen's novels, and especially in their distinctive relation to the gothic: to what contemporaries argued was England's native tradition both in letters and politics. As a literary genre, the gothic was favoured by the English Jacobins, including Wollstonecraft and William Godwin, and by antirevolutionary New Whig and conservative novelists, social theorists, and literary historians from Radcliffe to the young Scott and Burke, as well as Hurd, Walpole, and Reeve. As a historical theory and national style it formed an important strand in conservative as well as in radical politics.49 Austen's heroines encounter a variety of gothic forms and structures. Northanger Abbey; *Emma*'s Donwell Abbey; Radcliffe's novels, read by Catherine Morland; Gilpin's aesthetics, quoted by Elizabeth Bennet in *Pride and Prejudice*;50 the entailed estates in *Sense and Sensibility*, *Pride and Prejudice*, and *Persuasion*: all are literary, political, and architectural versions of a single national myth. In every case, Austen's irony reveals the fictionality of the national fiction, and the anxious New Whig self-interest that lies beneath it.

The portrait of General Tilney in *Northanger Abbey*, in which Austen uses indirect quotation to ironic advantage, skewers Gilpin's nativist aesthetics, Burke's faith in inheritance, and the double lives of the House of Lords together. According to Austen's narrator, the General lectures Catherine on British manufactures and taste while showing off the furnishings of Northanger Abbey. Indicating the tea service, he tells her that he

thought it right to encourage the manufacture of his country; and for his part, to his uncritical palate, the tea was as well flavoured from the clay of Staffordshire, as from that of Dresden or Sêve. But this was quite an old set, purchased two years ago. The manufacture was much improved since that time; he had seen some beautiful specimens when last in town, and had he not been perfectly without vanity of that kind, might have been tempted to order a new set. (139)

Although Austen borrows her caricature of the General from eighteenth-century anticommercial burlesques such as those found in Burney's novels, his nationalist approach to consumption and taste and his "luxury and expense" correspond to the self-consciously English "luxury" and "convenience" that Scott found at Walpole's Strawberry Hill. Walpole's imitation Olde English squire blends in Austen's novel into a substantial and extremely powerful English gentleman. In her portrait of the General and his elder son, as in several other novels, Austen examines the darker side of the Burkean national "entail," the passage of particular estates to unworthy heirs. Where Burke sees inheritance as a defence against ruin, Austen's heirs themselves make ruins – of young women (Willoughby in *Sense and Sensibility*) or their own fortunes (Willoughby, *Mansfield Park*'s Tom Bertram, and *Persuasion*'s Sir Walter Elliot). Sometimes, like William Walter Elliot of *Persuasion*, with his violently punning threat to swing the auctioneer's "hammer" against Kellynch Hall, they ruin the estate itself. Austen's heirs endlessly enact the precise transitional stage in British Protestant history when gothic artefacts became gothic ruins. For Austen the ruined, redomesticated abbey never improves on its gothic past.

Yet although Austen recapitulates the critique in which Wollstonecraft parodied British political and aesthetic hypocrisy, she does not reproduce Wollstonecraft's radical remedy. Her own playful account of Henry VIII's aesthetic impulse in dissolving the monasteries, for example, is an admiring quotation from Gilpin.[51] Rather, she shapes taste with the pragmatic conviction that gothic ruins – women, estates, and family fortunes – exist throughout Britain, and the insistence that her readers, by reading her writings, must amend them. In her fictions, Austen burlesques gothic and laughs impartially at its mingled transitional visions of aristocratic corruption and revolutionary tyranny. Yet despite outspoken reservations, she retains and reuses many of the gothic elements she laughs at, countering Wollstonecraft and her Burkean opponents, especially Radcliffe, on their chosen political and literary ground. Thus Austen's self-conscious national romance simultaneously depends on and resolves the contradictions in English romance writing and social theory.

Two sets of scenes – in Radcliffe's *The Italian* (1797) and Austen's *Northanger Abbey* – will illustrate the differences between Austen's self-consciously "speculative-Jacobite" response to Wollstonecraft's counter-romances and the gothic revivalists they opposed, and the responses of New Whig conservatives whose romances supported the gothic visions of Hurd and Burke. Beneath Austen's new way of thinking about privacy and nation lie the urgent problems of nature, fiction, and English tradition that, after Burke and Wollstonecraft, had undermined the conservative force of "nature." Austen's proposed solution, however, is less the symbolic resolution of her novels in happy domesticity, a goal typical of sentimental romance after the mid-eighteenth century, than her reproduction of that resolution in a chain of English households, a process of circulation and re-creation that can be brought about only by literary production and consumption. *Northanger Abbey* begins a process I call domesticating gothic, which at once produces and complicates the separate spheres David Kaufmann assigns nineteenth-century romance and political economy within Britain's national order.[52] Austen brings the most visible conventions of the romance genre home from Italy, where Radcliffe distanced English readers from political instability; home from the turf of the English Jacobins, who assailed the justice of modern English politics and ancient tradition in gothic fictions and narrativized polemic; home from the "natural" aesthetic arena in which Gilpin and Burke employ them: home in the sense of a return to the domestic *and* the national and economic fold. Radcliffe's gothic scenes become landmarks on a map on which Austen traces, with increasing assurance, the ties that unite family, fictions, and politics – and the borders that hold them apart.

GENDER, AESTHETICS, NATURE: RADCLIFFE'S ANSWERS TO WOLLSTONECRAFT

Radcliffe's works are often read for their sceptical revelations of the material base of the supernatural and of aristocratic ideology.[53] Yet her aggressively naturalized reassertion of the sublime and beautiful in *The Italian* also marks a Burkean conservative engagement in the arguments about gender and aesthetics in which Wollstonecraft and Burke conducted their debate on nature, politics, and Britain's gothic inheritance. The most striking set-piece in her politicized aesthetics appears at the centre of *The Italian*, as her hero, Vincentio, son of the Marchese di Vivaldi, and heroine, Ellena Rosalba, escape from the convent where Ellena has been

imprisoned – and "stop," despite fear of pursuit, "to admire the scene."
Each enjoys a discrete segment of the circumferential view:

"See," said Vivaldi, "where Monte-Corno stands like a ruffian, huge, scared,
threatening, and horrid! – and in the south, where the sullen mountain of San
Nicolo shoots up, barren and rocky! From thence, mark how other overtopping
ridges of the mighty Appennine darken the horizon far along the east, and
circle to approach the Velino in the north!"

"Mark too," said Ellena, "how sweetly the banks and undulating plains
repose at the feet of the mountains; what an image of beauty and elegance they
oppose to the awful grandeur that overlooks and guards them! Observe, too,
how many a delightful valley, opening from the lake, spreads its rice and corn
fields, shaded with groves of the almond, far among the winding hills; how gaily
vineyards and olives alternately chequer the acclivities; and how gracefully the
lofty palms bend over the higher cliffs."[54]

Deictics notwithstanding, neither turns to look: Vincentio continues
gazing on sublime power and Ellena on "beauty," fertility, undulation,
and domestic cultivation. Their parallel but distinctive pleasures complement each other as the "beauty and elegance" of the plains temper
the "awful grandeur that overlooks and guards them," or (as this
evocative diction implies) as the bracing sensation of awe produced by
the masculine sublime, with its links to political as well as aesthetic
power, complements the ennervating effect of the feminized and maternal beautiful in Burke's *Philosophical Enquiry into . . . the Sublime and
Beautiful*.[55] This aesthetic division of labour defines the gender of its
participants, upholding the idea of naturally separate spheres for (public) men and (private) women.[56]

In contrast, Wollstonecraft's radically constructionist account of "female nature" exposes such links with "beauty" as a political fiction, a
product of "specious homage," "false refinement," and "the constitution of civil society" (*Rights of Woman* 73, 76), and her *Wrongs of Woman*
will suggest that gallantry does little more than mask sexual and economic violence. As *The Italian* begins, Radcliffe seems poised to counter
Wollstonecraft on her own culturalist ground. Like Radcliffe herself,
and joining a long series of romance heroines from Sheridan's Sidney
Bidulph to Burney's Juliet Granville, Ellena founds her claim to worth
on her work as a professional in "the field of cultural production," a
maker of elegant consumer goods that distinguish the taste of their
owners.[57] She spends "whole days in embroidering silks" to be "disposed of to the nuns of a neighbouring convent, who sold them to the
Neapolitan ladies, that visited their grate, at a very high advantage" (9).

Yet even as Radcliffe emphasizes Ellena's status as a cultural producer, she denies it, emphasizing her heroine's ladylike concealment of her trade "in the veil of retirement" and her shame on Vivaldi's discovering it. Radcliffe replaces the vast, impersonal marketing and distribution network through which she sent her own cultural goods with a polite private commerce among women, in face-to-face encounters in drawing-rooms and at the convent grate (9).[58] Ellena's worker status is entirely recanted when her birth is revealed: as the daughter of the Count di Bruno, she is Vivaldi's social and economic equal (410). As the narration continues, Radcliffe replies to Wollstonecraft – not as Austen will do, by embracing cultural production as a source of useful social fictions, but by reasserting the already shaky Burkean aesthetics that Wollstonecraft had countered (158–9).

The consequences of Radcliffe's denial become especially clear when peasants enter the picture, a third voice in Radcliffe's scenes of taste. Paulo, Vincentio's robust indentured servant, responds to Ellena's cries of aesthetic pleasure as Ellena does to Vivaldi's. Respectful but unempathic, he is pre-engaged with pleasing views of his own:

"Ay, Signora!" exclaimed Paulo, "and have the goodness to observe how like are the fishing boats, that sail towards the hamlet below, to those one sees upon the bay of Naples. They are worth all the rest of the prospect, except indeed this fine sheet of water, which is almost as good as the bay, and that mountain, with its sharp head, which is almost as good as Vesuvius!" (159)

As Paulo gazes on the panorama of mountains and fields, marked in its upper reaches by indicators of the sublime and in its lower limits by the beautiful, he takes pleasure, not in sublimity or beauty, but in signs of habitation and landmarks that recall his Neapolitan home. Vivaldi "smil[es]" at Paulo's "nationality," for the boats Paulo longs for figure in an earlier aesthetic set-piece in the novel (159). Places of picturesque labour as well as objects of peasant desire, they provide an unconscious spectacle for nobles who find aesthetic – and subliminally political – gratification in the peasants' natural enjoyment of their work-day, which is spent, according to Radcliffe, in singing and dancing:

The boatmen rested on their oars, while their company listened to voices modulated by sensibility to finer eloquence, than is in the power of art alone to display . . . they observed the airy natural grace, which distinguishes the dance of the fishermen and peasants of Naples. Frequently as they glided round a promontory, whose shaggy masses impended far over the sea, such magic scenes of beauty unfolded, adorned by these dancing groups on the bay beyond, as no pencil could do justice to. (37)

Singing about their work, the peasant fishers, like Paulo, never transgress the boundaries that separate their "picturesque" labours from the delicate leisured taste of their watchers, which, as in Gilpin's aesthetics, finds in rural labours a supplement to that union of sublimity and beauty that Gilpin names the picturesque (Radcliffe 37; Gilpin 1: 43–5).[59] As Radcliffe organizes her aesthetic scenes, the peasants' lack of taste – a tenet of theorists from Hume to Burke – ensures their obedience and joyous acceptance of their place within socioeconomic and national order.[60]

Accordingly, so long as the upper class remain willing to allow space to the domestic, self-interested, and social taste of peasants, the peasants will continue to participate docilely in the compositions of the picturesque eye, and in the social order the compositions often seem to allegorize. The distance between gentleman and peasant labourer remains firmly in place while the gentleman surveys, as part of his own aesthetic (if not actual) demesne, the peasant's delight in his surroundings. Those who refuse to tolerate the taste of their inferiors are doomed to suffer rebellion, as the monk Schedoni, Ellena's uncle and the usurper of her father's lands and title, finds as he journeys with his niece and their voluble peasant guide through the varied scenes of an Italian country carnival. Schedoni

bade the peasant be silent; but the man was too happy to be tractable . . . Every object here was to him new and delightful; and, nothing doubting that it must be equally so to every other person, he was continually pointing out to the proud and gloomy Confessor the trivial subjects of his own admiration. "See! Signor, there is Punchinello, see! how he eats the hot maccaroni! And look there, Signor! there is a juggler! O! good Signor, stop one minute, to look at his tricks. See! he has turned a monk into a devil already, in the twinkling of an eye!" (274)

Like Paulo's earlier, blissful praise for the near-Neapolitan scene he sees while helping Ellena escape, so does this nameless peasant's need to stake out visual territory represent a reassuringly debased parallel to Vivaldi's and Ellena's pleasure. Listening to his cries of enjoyment, Ellena "consent[s] to endure" his commentary, but the "gloomy" and "proud" Schedoni, intent on quelling the peasant's carnival humour and defending the aesthetic border between them, continues to order " 'Silence!' " (274).

Among the scenes at the fair is a troop of travelling players enacting a domestic tragedy. The peasant seems to mean nothing personal or particular in the cry of " 'Signor, see! Signor, what a scoundrel! what a villain! See! he has murdered his own daughter!' " with which he greets the villain's actions (274). But his careless speech becomes subversive precisely because Schedoni, in foreclosing the peasant's taste, makes himself vulnerable to transgressions of the boundaries of his own. Schedoni's guilt shows on his face: he has himself attempted to murder Ellena, whom he believes to be his daughter; he is, even in his own view, as much devil as monk. Noticing Schedoni's passion, the guide assumes a "significant look" and familiar tone as he recounts a story of murder and usurpation that resembles Schedoni's own. "'You never will let me finish, Signor,'" he says as Schedoni again attempts to silence him. On Schedoni's "impatiently" guessing the story's murderous end, the peasant sarcastically assails him: "'How well you have guessed it, Signor! though to say truth, I have been expecting you to find it out for this half hour'" (282). The aristocrat's haughty disengagement gives the peasant a hold on him – a hold that becomes literal as the peasant takes "hold of his garment, as if to secure his attention to the remainder of the story." Even when Schedoni "rose, with some emotion, and paced the room . . . the peasant kept pace with him, still loosely holding his garment" (283).

Those aristocrats, conversely, who indulge their servants' sociability win the peasants' respectful – and so less literal – attachment. When Paulo offers to amuse Vincentio with a mysterious tale, Vincentio invites his servant to sit beside him, and listens with an attitude of obvious forbearance. His tolerance ensures his control of Paulo's narrative, and Paulo moves around in the story as Vincentio commands him to digress or "proceed" (81–2). But Paulo's loyalty runs deeper than his storytelling for Vincentio's pleasure, its earliest register. Having at length rescued Ellena and arranged to marry her, Vincentio offers to free Paulo and grant him a pension, whereupon the peasant weeps at Vincentio's feet in "a passion of joy and affection" and begs to remain in vassalage (405). "'What use,'" he asks "'are the thousand sequins to me, if I am to be independent! what use if I am not to stay with you?'" (407). Paulo's love for his master shows the benefits of Vincentio's tolerance: his loyalty permits even the Marchese to forget his defensive haughtiness, and makes a reassuring spectacle for the circle of "noble spectators," the Marchese's guests, who applaud Vincentio's "generous" promise that the weeping Paulo "should always remain . . . 'near me'" (407–8).

The text of Radcliffe's gothic romance agrees with Burke that "Good order" requires that "the people . . . not find the principles of natural subordination by art rooted out of their minds" (*Reflections* 215). To Radcliffe, a naturalized aesthetics is the best prevention. Her conclusion makes her work a gothic romance of a particular kind: a work of avowedly ancient moral teaching and allegorical social cohesion of the kind praised by Hurd. In a final tableau symbolizing the idealized social relations heralded by Vincentio's marriage to Ellena, Radcliffe stages "a scene of fairy-land" comprising the "beautiful" Vivaldi villa and the "bold" and "lofty" view it "command[s]," a realm large enough to accommodate all classes (413):

> Vivaldi and Ellena had wished that all the tenants of the domain should partake of it, and share the abundant happiness which themselves possessed; so that the grounds, which were extensive enough to accommodate each rank, were relinquished to a general gaiety. (414)

As the word "general" suggests, all ranks join in the festivities, but without ever meeting to offend each other's tastes: Radcliffe capitalizes on Paulo's loyalty and Vincentio's toleration. Consequently, Paulo and the peasants are the happiest of all the guests as they dance – or " 'frisk,' " as Paulo puts it with an aggressive simplicity undoubtedly not his own, " 'in my own dear bay of Naples, with my own dear master and mistress' " (413).[61] Offered his freedom once again, Paulo refuses to leave his master, continuing to celebrate, in loaded terms, his " 'liberty' " (414). Paulo has the book's last word. Rebellion, or even the literary and cultural encounters Burke called a "monstrous medley of all conditions, tongues, and nations," is less a political than aesthetic, and thus natural, impossibility (59).

GENDER AND THE REWRITING OF AESTHETIC PARODY: *NORTHANGER ABBEY*

Despite her novel's early denaturing of romance through its focus on cultural producers, Radcliffe's self-conscious use of sensibility and taste to realign classes and genders, and the aestheticized romance conclusion that restores them to their "natural" places in the home and the polity, make *The Italian* a forerunner of the early-nineteenth-century conservative novel – a mixture of romance and didacticism that would aim at producing in the reader's domestic life its artificial but essential domestic conclusion. But Radcliffe's retreat into utopias dressed as nature was not a solution to appeal to Austen. To establish domestic harmony, in its national as well as its homely sense, required the kind of "pleasing illusion" that would affirm rather than efface its own role in "Good order": a fiction acknowledging the artifice of its own domestic romance, and of its displacement of gothic terror.

Austen rewrites Radcliffe's and Wollstonecraft's scenes of beauty and sublimity in her mock-gothic romance *Northanger Abbey*, and so in Britain as well. As Radcliffe places her characters atop an Italian summit, a "circle of mountains" below, so Austen's heroine and hero climb a small rise in Somerset, so that "the whole city of Bath" gradually unfolds as a "landscape" at their feet (111). Austen's ironic, domesticated version of Radcliffe's set-piece, a kind of Paulo-esque but knowing reading of the scene, revises Radcliffe's vision of naturally separate tastes and spheres as Henry Tilney gives Catherine – who unlike Ellena knows "nothing of taste" – "a lecture on the picturesque." Like Radcliffe's Vincentio, with his love of blasted scenery, Henry has a taste for the sublime. His rhetoric turns picturesque beauty to sublime grandeur so that Catherine and he can imagine it clearly, demonstrating the desirable effects of sublimity in landscape by invoking "a rocky fragment" and a "withered oak" amidst the "beauty" Catherine admires (87). Less delicate than Ellena, Catherine can appreciate Henry's taste for the sublime, if only because she appreciates Henry. She proves herself "so hopeful a scholar, that . . . she voluntarily rejected the whole city of Bath, as unworthy to make part of a landscape": Austen's combined irony and praise for the naïve Catherine reminds her readers to read the scene as playfully allegorical rather than, like Burke's and Radcliffe's similar scenes, ideologically earnest. Having gained his point, Henry ends the discussion:

Delighted with her progress, and fearful of wearying her with too much wisdom at once, Henry suffered the subject to decline, and by an easy transition from a piece of rocky fragment and the withered oak which he had placed near its summit, to oaks in general, to forests, the inclosure of them, waste lands, crown lands and government, he shortly found himself arrived at politics; and from politics, it was an easy step to silence. (111)

Curiously, Burkean romance and radical political philosophy agree about women's relationship to the sublime. Radcliffe demonstrates in *The Italian* that women naturally admire the beautiful and usually fail to appreciate the sublime, a view that draws on Burke's division of aesthetic labour in his *Sublime and Beautiful*, and which will be enhanced by William Wordsworth's gendering of parental nature in the *Prelude*. Wollstonecraft divides taste into identically gendered categories, but she contends that Britain's romance-fuelled corruption, and the liberal political economy that regulates it, are the efficient causes of gendered character. She insists in *Rights of Woman* that women and servants are tactically denied access to poetic sublimity and "the sublime curb of principle" (105) by a training in sensibility – and romance reading – that teaches them to prefer "the graceful before the heroic virtues" (126) and blinds them to their own "sublime hopes" of an afterlife (100). Austen, however, in her new national romance, takes a radically different position: Catherine *can* gain access to the sublime, and she does so *without* needing "to participate in the inherent [political] rights of man-kind" that Wollstonecraft argues are necessary to overthrow the "arbit-rary" "sexual distinction" (*Rights of Woman* 265–6).[62] Indeed, by the time of the Beechen Cliff scene, Catherine already knows and loves a differ-ent, explicitly feminine kind of sublime, taught by Radcliffe's gothic romances even as Radcliffe declares its impossibility. Her "passion for ancient edifices," and the syntax that describes it, reveals an indepen-dent imagination coupled with a polymorphous but explicit sexuality

> next in degree [not in kind!] to her passion for Henry Tilney – and castles and abbies made usually the charm of those reveries which his image did not fill. To see and explore either the ramparts and keep of the one, or the cloisters of the other, had been for many weeks a darling wish . . . too nearly impossible for desire. (110)

What Catherine must learn is a renovated Burkean political lesson: to discriminate estates from bodies.[63]

Countering Wollstonecraft, Austen answers radicalism with prag-matics. Catherine requires not an explicitly political or economic, but a domestic empowerment that, as Austen presents it, approximates both in a way that is readily attainable and yet subject to a salutary masculine control. In learning to confine her taste for the sublime within certain limits, Catherine gives up her excessive pleasure in gothic novels, which threatens *Northanger Abbey*'s resolution: Austen reconfigures Wollstone-craft's social revolution as a "revolution in [Catherine's] . . . ideas" (171). At the same time, however, the aesthetic learning that Austen promotes wins her heroine the vicarious socioeconomic and political power that places her beyond the reach of such upwardly mobile figures as the marauding and impoverished John Thorpe and his cruelly snobbish New Whig crony General Tilney. Austen reclaims the "femi-nine" traits that Wollstonecraft deplores: the "advantages of natural folly in a beautiful girl have been already set forth by the capital pen of a sister author," she remarks. "I will only add in justice to men, that . . . there is a portion of them too reasonable and too well informed them-selves to desire any thing more in woman than ignorance" (86). Henry

carefully orchestrates Catherine's learning, reintroducing her to sublimity while exerting his authority as a teacher – and as a man – to restrain
her developing taste. His limit is the boundary between private and
public spheres, the point where Catherine famously confuses gothic
novels with revolutions, and he transforms taste into politics by making
a (Burkean) metaphor of his own, blasted, "British oak." Past this point
Catherine cannot, does not, and indeed *should* not, for her own security,
desire to follow – as Henry knows and his direction of their discourse
ensures. In forging her practical aesthetics, then, and embodying and
circulating it in romance, Austen denies Radcliffe's arguments for a
domestic and beautiful feminine nature as fully as she rejects Wollstonecraft's call for political change that will open the aesthetic and political
sublimes without restraint to women.

To aid his disentanglement of politics and aesthetics, gothic and riots,
Henry invokes the materiality of the Radcliffean book in terms that will
shape Austen's conclusion. The "something very shocking" that
Catherine breathlessly expects "will soon come out of London" is

> nothing more dreadful than a new publication which is shortly to come out, in
> three duodecimo volumes, two hundred and seventy-six pages in each, with a
> frontispiece to the first, of two tombstones and a lantern. (88)

Such a "dreadful" duodecimo work, a portable, concealable, and thus
potentially seductive and antisocial volume, is a fashionable item whose
standardized content does not diminish the anticipation of its eager
readers. Yet the book's materiality and commodity status, which contribute to its "dangers," can also be used to contain them. Catherine
calls Radcliffe's *Mysteries of Udolpho* " 'the nicest book in the world,' " to
which Henry retorts, " 'I suppose you mean the neatest. That must
depend upon the binding' " (107). He reduces Catherine's dangerous
admiration for gothic novels to fashion and the desire for something new
by highlighting the commodity form of the book, its status as an
aesthetic object. Claudia Johnson complains that he bullies Catherine,
yet Henry is more agent than target of Austen's irony. The conclusion
reinscribes his weighty influence: Austen stills the voices of her hero and
heroine to remind readers that they, too, hold a duodecimo novel in
their hands.[64] While Henry's and Catherine's romance remains unresolved, Austen says, their "anxiety . . . can hardly extend . . . to the
bosom of my readers, who will see in the tell-tale compression of the
pages before them, that we are all hastening together to perfect felicity"
(250). Like the popular novels that Henry makes safe, Austen's book is

not just a potentially "dreadful" work, but a predictable commodity book, bought precisely for its conventionality, and thereby rendered sociable and harmless.

Northanger Abbey offers more than popular gothic: Austen turns the commercial availability and generic conventions of romance to ideological advantage, even as her irony embraces the contingency of her orderly conservative conclusion. Her final sentence reiterates the book's encounter with a faceless literary marketplace and its subjection to unknown critics and readers, but it simultaneously claims the wide anonymous distribution of the novel as a stimulant to debate in an explicitly public and ideological literary sphere: "I leave it to be settled by whomsoever it may concern, whether the tendency of this work be altogether to recommend parental tyranny, or reward filial disobedience" (252). Rhetorically willing her text to her readers and asking them to "settle" its moral, Austen briefly names their power over the text before reasserting the power of the book to "recommend" morals and shape the ethical discussions of its readers as they "hasten together" toward satisfying conclusions.[65] The novelist limits and directs the reading and reproduction she seeks, with her novel, to produce.

Austen's investment in print culture is crucial to the question of what it means for an English novel to be a British national romance. Like Austen, Henry, the novel's centre of aesthetic education, couches moral choices as literary ones, asking Catherine to choose between competing histories of letters and of England's gothic past:

Remember the country and the age in which we live. Remember that we are English, that we are Christians. Consult your own understanding, your own sense of the probable, your own observation of what is passing around you – Does our education prepare us for such atrocities? Do our laws connive at them? Could they be perpetrated without being known, in a country like this, where social and literary intercourse is on such a footing; where every man is surrounded by a neighbourhood of voluntary spies, and where roads and newspapers lay every thing open? (159)

What has gone surprisingly undiscussed in this speech is Henry's invocation of Britain's traffic in books: the public press and its distribution networks, the turnpike roads and canals that for thirty years had increasingly riddled the island.[66] Readers tend to treat the speech as another instance of Austen's irony, arguing that General Tilney's brutal termination of Catherine's Northanger visit on learning of her small fortune effectively belies the civilizing influence of letters.[67] Yet Henry claims only that legal forms and literary networks create "openness," preventing the kinds of secret, "gothic" tortures and murders that Radcliffe's villains long to commit, and that British anti-Jacobins and Jacobins respectively associated with the French Revolution and *ancien régime*. Austen's conservative aesthetics, it should be recalled, is necessarily limited: as an avowed Jacobite, she desires a political and ideological order that predates the sentimental romances of the New Whigs, an ideological longing long since doomed to failure.[68] *Northanger Abbey* offers only a temporary solution to the ideological bickerings of Burke, Radcliffe, and Wollstonecraft, and to the violence all three deplore and fear. Having discredited the naturalness of English gothic, Henry takes up, makes explicit, and politicizes the submerged artificiality in the gothic revival's celebration of canon and tradition, emphasizing the role of print production in producing a modicum of social order.

Among the more significant implications of this embracing of print culture and romance is Austen's subsequent refashioning of the aesthetic tastes of working people and their effect on social order. In *Persuasion*, for example, published and bound with *Northanger Abbey* in 1818, Austen parodies *The Italian*'s concluding "meeting" of classes. As the Musgrove sisters lie unconscious side by side on the Cobb at Lyme Regis, fishermen gather "to enjoy the sight of a dead young lady, nay, two dead young ladies, for it proved twice as fine as the first report." Their greedy gaze answers the helpless Frederick Wentworth, who, having accidentally dropped Louisa Musgrove on her head, "knelt with her in his arms, looking on her with a face as pallid as her own." They parodically reproduce the hysterical eye of Mary Musgrove, Louisa's sister-in-law, whose screams of " 'She is dead! she is dead!,' " which may well hold a wishful element born of boredom and confinement, first summon the fishers to the scene.[69] But despite the gazers' evident enjoyment, a relish at once erotic and political, "To the best-looking of these good people Henrietta was consigned" without scruple (111). Unlike Radcliffe, Austen acknowledges the overlap of classed and gendered tastes, allowing her fishers to turn the tables on Radcliffe's and make aesthetic objects of the gentry. Yet Austen's heroine easily imposes order on the scene, and Austen's own self-reflexive control of the novel ensures that her working-class characters never think to break it. Austen's self-conscious romance dismisses the dangers of class miscegenation and trespass even as it represents the threat.

In her national romances, Austen couples generic and commercial self-consciousness with admissions of the close ties between ideology and romance. Yet precisely because of her ironically explicit exposures of her own didactic aims, her fictional packaging of taste-forming reading makes her works part of the prehistory of the modern mass culture industry as Max Horkheimer and Theodor Adorno and Jürgen Habermas describe it, as well as a herald of that coming modern world in which, as Fredric Jameson argues, the distinctions between ideology and the real, lost in an all-pervasive irony, can no longer be distinguished.[70] The self-declaredly popular novelist set herself to producing virtuous families who would form a secure web across England, from the metropolis to the provinces; who would absorb and defuse the dangers of reading and of radical critiques of aesthetic and political artifice. A politically conservative yet explicitly feminine counterpart to the radical corresponding societies, Austen's envisioned chain of reading households would ensure, as Henry Tilney enthusiastically puts it, "a neighbourhood of voluntary spies . . . where roads and newspapers lay every thing open," guaranteeing social order (159). Burke's natural families and Wollstonecraft's fictive ones give way to Austen's exuberant trust in the circulation, distribution, and virtuous reading of such explicitly literary romances as her own.[71] *Northanger Abbey* reconfigures the reading public as a foundation for Britain's social order, an aggregate of individual women engaged in moral reflection in the intimate sphere of the family.[72] It makes available the moment at which Tories – once as opposed to commerce as Frances Burney, and as likely to collapse sociopolitical tradition into immutable law – harnessed the privacy of the "popular twelve," its modes of circulation, and the romance genre it circulated, for ideological use.

THE MACHINERY OF THE TEXT: *PERSUASION*

Judith Wilt has argued that even as Austen reconditions "machinery" borrowed from Radcliffe in *Northanger Abbey*, the Radcliffean gothic energies that Austen renders fictional continue to plague her text, a ghost in her own machine.[73] Indeed, in Austen's earliest novel, literal machinery – not just the conventions of late-eighteenth-century romance, but also their mechanical reproduction – escapes her irony or drives it toward indeterminate excess, as in her cavalier treatment of General Tilney's cruelty and the failure of Henry's ecstatic praise of cultural industry to banish the ghosts of corruption. Publishing the novel in 1818, Austen included an "Advertisement" reminding her reader that "thirteen years have passed since it was finished, many more since it was begun, and that during that period, places, manners, books, and opinions have undergone considerable changes" (n.p.). She asks leniency with a text whose machinery, within the plot and in the book's production and circulation, has dated more quickly than the culture in which the work intervenes. *Persuasion*, however, written almost twenty years later but published and bound with *Northanger Abbey*, is the early work's mature companion piece and supplement. It plays out the gothic history and ideology of England in a series of domestic interiors, so that sailors home between Napoleonic battles are as "distinguished in . . . domestic virtues" as in "national importance," and the ruined English estate with which Austen answers Burke's praise of entails and inheritance is less central than the ruined love of the landholder's daughter (252).

Austen's dark, uncertain narrative completes, though with a new recognition of its own limitations, what the earlier work began. Her last novel effects its domestication and mechanization of national literary and political issues because its heroine has a history for the first time in Austen's works, making history, public as well as private, a major topic in the novel. Sir Walter Elliot's near-bankrupt abandonment of his ancestral home, Kellynch Hall – the sign of sociopolitical and economic change or decay – conjures up for the heroine, his daughter Anne, ghosts of a love affair ended by family "persuasion." At Kellynch, unlike Northanger Abbey, the shades of history and its genres are not explained away by parody, but neither do they disrupt the conclusion of the novel. Instead the ghosts *become* Austen's machine. The national history reproduced in Austen's last romance is Anne Elliot's history, and Austen's machinery aids its reproduction for the readers as much as for the heroine herself.

The crucial historical reflections in the novel are Anne's own, directed at her personal past, which becomes synecdochic of her country's changes. Austen's rhetoric, as she transcribes her heroine's mental historiography in the *style indirect libre* characteristic of this novel, invokes a gendered language of ruin that recalls her earlier refashioning of the gothic. Painfully aware of the eye of her returned former lover Wentworth, and continually reminded of encroaching age, Anne represents herself as an artefact, the dusty relic of an inexorable history that has brought more pain than progress. Although only eight years have passed since Anne's failed romance, her sister Mary reports that " 'Captain Wentworth is not very gallant by you, Anne . . . [H]e said, 'You were so altered he should not have known you again' " (60). Consuming her own history as the narrative in Wentworth's eyes, Anne compulsively watches him, watches his "observing her altered features . . . trying to trace in them the ruins of the face which had once charmed him" (72). Wentworth enjoys the same history, pleased to find Anne "wretchedly altered" in his eight-year absence, though he takes no personal pride in her decay. Gender assures, at least in Anne's mind, that what is maturity in him is ruination in her. Her masochistic comparisons reveal that "the years which had destroyed her youth and bloom had only given him a more glowing, manly, open look" (61).

Like Catherine Morland, in what Austen now makes an explicitly female as well as a psychological difficulty, Anne must repeatedly encounter and engage with gothic ruins. But Anne's ruins, unlike Catherine's, are the product of a history she herself has lived. Her encounters with the gothic past, though informed by her own and Austen's reading in national history and the history of national aesthetics, are deeply personalized: gothic ruins comprise not only Anne's own ravaged family estate but her own ageing body. Her "ruined" face, obsessively read and re-read by herself, Wentworth, and others, approximates her role in the novel to that of the gothic fictions and decaying abbeys Catherine loves, as well as to the role played by Catherine herself. Thus history, in *Persuasion*, becomes a problem of interiors. Although Austen's heroine brings down the weight of history on herself, she can also overcome its damage by perfecting her ways of reading.

For *Persuasion*, like *Northanger Abbey*, is a romance in which gender and aesthetics intertwine with right and wrong ways of reading history, and it, too, opens with the wrong ways. As the novel begins, Sir Walter Elliot is reading the *Baronetage* as the most titillating of fictions, and he pores over his own face and figure in the many "large looking-glasses" in his dressing-room with self-deluding admiration. His reading responds to his despair in the face of national history and "domestic affairs." Even "if every other leaf were powerless," the accounts he finds there of the creation and ruin of other baronets bringing no relief from his own estate's decay, "he could read his own history with an interest which never failed" (3). His self-interest in history is shared by the other men in the novel. The widowed Captain Benwick, in particular, is Elliot's mirror image. Emotionally rather than genealogically self-indulgent, he is as over-warm as Elliot is cold. Anne and Austen meditate ironically on Benwick's excessive sensibility as he reads aloud "with tremulous feeling" from Scott's poems, dwelling on the "lines which imaged a broken heart, or a mind destroyed by wretchedness . . . entirely as if he meant to be understood" (100). Reading, to Benwick as to Elliot, reflects nothing beyond his own face. But Wentworth, too, replaces real history with self-centred autobiography. When he considers his role in his country's defeat of Napoleon, he thinks only of the woman he has lost; more often, like Benwick, he considers nothing beyond his own circumstances. Of his first battle, he remarks only that " 'It was a great object with me, at that time, to be at sea,' " and he compromises himself with the Musgrove sisters, too singleminded in anger with Anne to be "in the least aware of the pain he was occasioning."[74]

In contrast, although Austen designates Anne a bad reader as the novel begins, Anne finds not too much, but too little of herself in texts. Her obsessive reflection on personal history marks her failure to apply the texts of philosophy and history to her reading of her own situation. She prescribes "our best moralists . . . collections of the finest letters" and "memoirs of characters of worth and suffering" to counter Benwick's self-indulgent consumption of books, but she also recognizes that she is "eloquent on a point in which her own conduct would ill bear examination": she reads the past, that is, as Benwick reads Scott's poetry (101). In recognizing the flaws in her reading, incorporating moral and historical analysis with her autobiographical reflections, Anne gradually improves her responses to her own history. Her newly gendered and personalized reading of the " 'examples' " of " 'woman's inconstancy' " in " 'histories,' " and her analysis of the dominance in letters that gives men " 'every advantage of us in telling their own story,' " re-establish her engagement to Wentworth at novel's end. Not least, Wentworth says, Anne's account of her reading to his friend Captain Harville teaches him to " 'read your feelings, as I think you must have penetrated mine' " (234, 237).

Self-absorption and mistaking representation for the real have been stereotypical failings of female romance reading since Charlotte Lennox's *Female Quixote* (1752). As Adela Pinch points out, they dominate Austen's *Persuasion* as they do *Northanger Abbey*.[75] Only the gendering of bad reading has changed. By marking her male characters as self-indulgently insular readers – the effeminate Sir Walter Elliot; the "little man" Benwick (97); Charles Musgrove, whose days are "trifled away, without benefit from books" (43) – Austen shows how Britain's socioeconomic institutions have decayed in male, English, presumably New Whig hands. She reveals the role of gothic and other romantic ideologies of inheritance and sentiment, Burkean in character, in institutional decay. At the same time, by equating bad reading with a more widespread crossing of gender conventions, which touches her heroine as much as her hero, Austen proposes a re-establishment of gendered character. As Anne's final reading of gendered " 'histories' " suggests, gender is promoted in the field of letters and inflected by the self-consciousness of writers and readers. At the end of *Persuasion*, the interplay of gender with the reading of history acts as a temporary, makeshift brake to a careening, out-of-control national history that seems beyond lasting or fundamental repair.

Austen places, or acknowledges, strict limits on the remediation of this history. The novel's conclusion is often read as an idealized reconciliation between upper- and middle-class characters and ethics.[76] Yet if the weaknesses of the aristocratic Elliots reveal the faultlines in a Burkean ideology of inheritance and tradition, the novel's extant models of *embourgeoisement* offer equally little to the Kellynch neighbourhood. In Austen's portrait of the Musgrove family, into which Mary Elliot marries, and into whose "social commonwealth" Anne moves on leaving Kellynch, "improvement" supersedes the Elliot ruin. In the economic polemics and cultural pretensions of the time, such rhetorics of "improvement" palliate capitalization and abandonment of feudal responsibilities. Austen is as ironic in using it as many Scottish and English landlords are defensive or self-deluding.[77] She describes the Musgroves' "old-fashioned square parlour,"

which the present daughters of the house were gradually giving the proper air of confusion by a grand piano forte and a harp, flower-stands and little tables placed in every direction. Oh! could the originals of the portraits against the wainscot . . . have been conscious of such an overthrow of all order and neatness! The portraits themselves seemed to be staring in astonishment. (40)

That "The Musgroves, like their houses, were in a state of alteration, perhaps of improvement" (40) ironically answers Burke's complaint that the French revolutionaries should "have built on those old foundations" (*Reflections* 31). "Perhaps" bears a weighty irony: there is little to choose between the gothic ruin and the Burkean economic remedies that "overthrow" convention, betraying Britain's spoliation at New Whig hands. That Henrietta and Louisa are merely the "present" daughters pessimistically acknowledges the unstoppable contemporary shifts in Britain's ongoing history. Taken together, Austen's Musgrove and Elliot family portraits answer Burke's call for the moneyed and titled classes – the "illustrious in rank, in descent, in hereditary and in acquired opulence" – to unite in ruling what he, too, calls the "commonwealth" (*Reflections* 38–9, 41). The response is a considered negative.

But Burke's British blended family is not simply exposed by Austen's irony as a self-interested alliance. In *Persuasion* – and it is here that Austen moves her responses to Burke beyond Burney's or Wollstonecraft's – Austen renders it ideologically irrelevant as well. In a sense, Austen's conclusion does unite virtuous representatives of Burke's moneyed and landed interests by marrying a prosperous landless hero to her bankrupt baronet's daughter: in neither *Persuasion* nor *Northanger Abbey* are differences in birth fantastically recanted, as in Radcliffe's *Italian* or Burney's *Wanderer*. In *Persuasion*, however, the aristocracy and middling sort have answered Burke's call, and already resemble each other: the remaining differences between them are particular, not general. Sir Walter Elliot's attachment to titles, for example, hides a deeper, more pathological interest in appearances. His rhetorics of history and inheritance disguise a modern, bourgeois attachment to the surface. His complaint that Wentworth has "nothing to do with the Strafford family" exemplifies the emptiness of his genealogical investments, for the last earl of Strafford, Frederick-Thomas Wentworth, had died in 1799, and the title with him (23). The earldom had long since become a purely nominal patent, separated from its hereditary lands, which had passed by entail into the Fitzwilliam family, more financially provident and more productive of heirs-male, as Austen's portrait of the Fitzwilliams in *Pride and Prejudice* suggests.[78] Elliot's respect for the profligate, barren Straffords over the landed lesser branch marks his respect for empty forms over living families – a feeling that the Musgroves visibly share. Thus Elliot accepts Wentworth as Anne's husband because his "superiority of appearance" and "well-sounding name," backed by neither land nor lineage, make a gentleman of him – just as buying "a grand piano forte and a harp, flower-stands and little tables" and "the usual stock of accomplishments" for their daughters transforms the comfortably landed Musgroves into moneyed people of fashion (40, 248). Burke's landed and moneyed principles, the class-marked traits of Musgroves and Elliots, are revealed as effects of the surface. Sir Walter and General Tilney, Captain Benwick and Catherine Morland, the Musgrove sisters and Isabella Thorpe resemble each other in their lack of ideological substance as well as in their enthusiasm for gothic ruins, whether architectural, legal, political, or literary.

Thus Austen's historical remedy in *Persuasion*, as in *Northanger Abbey*, supplements representation with reproduction, but it also pulls back from the public histories of British inheritance and aesthetics. In *Persuasion*, history begins at home, and Britain's future is salvageable only in the private sphere, in the spaces it opens as correctives to Britain's broader economic and social decay. In rejecting both Musgroves and Elliots, *Persuasion* enacts the exchange of a generation at once obsessed with and wholly uninterested in economic and political history for a new one whose virtuous historical engagement, embodied and taught by Anne, plays out in domesticity and moral discussion. The replacement unfolds geographically and temporally in the romance-history of its heroine, and its reproduction depends on the novel's circulation through other reading households. Austen moves Anne from her father's house into marriage with Wentworth, while Elliot gives up Kellynch to Wentworth's sister and her husband, whose small practical "improvements" – repairing the "laundry-door" and "sending away some of the large looking-glasses" from the master's dressing-room – restore the fashionable estate to use (127). The resulting metaphoric ties between woman and estate not only bind romance to national history, but suggest that what is good for the one is good for the other: that romance acts, in some limited and contingent sense, as national history's private, circumscribed, but locally powerful antidote and anchor.

The first of the new generation, as Austen portrays it, the Crofts are superior to Sir Walter because they are his perfect inverse. Their "weather-beaten" looks testify to their national service and "very handsome fortune" in the same way that the impoverished Sir Walter's handsome looks reveal his preservation of appearances at the expense of real property, and the baronet dismisses the "mahogany, rough and rugged" sailors as he might dismiss old furniture from his fashionable drawing-room (20–1, 48). Yet although it is Elliot who cries up aristocratic tradition, it is the Crofts who preserve Kellynch's feudal character, motivated by a reflective conservatism and an active approach to their own and Britain's history.[79] Their very name associates them with that geographically broad-based and historically ancient British landholding tradition of which the Scottish crofts, already beginning to be capitalized, and their crofters, already being "cleared" by cattle-boat to North America, were among the last surviving exemplars. Like the Jacobite sympathies of the Hanoverian Prince Regent to whom Austen dedicated *Emma*, the Crofts' landlordism offers an ethically and economically traditional, broadly British, and thus ideologically radical alternative to the Elliots, the lineal inheritors of the estate. Their sympathizer Anne believes "the parish to be so sure of a good example, and the poor of the best attention and relief" from the Crofts that "she could not but in conscience feel that they were gone who deserved not to stay,

and that Kellynch-hall had passed into better hands than its owners'"
(125). The Crofts perform not improvements of the estate, but a utopian,
though very temporary, restoration. Yet, as Regency precursors of the
National Trust, they hold Britain's ideological future in their hands.

The Crofts are Austen's first economic and ethical model, a pattern for
the genteel landholder. Her second, middle-class model is Frederick
Wentworth, who has, like his brother-in-law, won a "handsome fortune"
(30). That the Crofts spend their fortune in restoring Kellynch, granting
new life to old customs and domains, heralds Wentworth's near-magical
ability to restore "the bloom and freshness of youth" to Anne's ruined
face (29–30, 104). As in the equation of the Musgrove sisters with the
"improvements" to their parents' estate, the homology ties domestic
romance to the economic and cultural state of the nation. The final words
of *Persuasion* underline the parallels. Austen notes that Anne

gloried in being a sailor's wife, but she must pay the tax of quick alarm for
belonging to that profession which is, if possible, more distinguished in its
domestic virtues than in its national importance. (252)

Anne's "belonging" to her "profession" must be read in at least two
ways. Austen's ambiguous phrase indicates not only her heroine's attachment to a "sailor," but her own role as a "wife" as well. Together, in
their double profession, each in a safely separate sphere but each with a
share of national importance and domestic virtue, they produce a
dialectic between public and private histories and events that embodies
Britain's best hope for its future history.[80] Even so, the double restorations of Austen's idyllic conclusion are as fragile and circumscribed as
the Prince Regent's sentimental Jacobitism. Anne's two "professions"
are equally alarmed by impending war – and so, perhaps, is a third,
Anne's "belonging," as Austen's creation, to Austen's own "profession"
as a writer of national romance, which leads to the yoking of fiction and
the state of the nation in the uncertain months before Waterloo.

It is only in reading, in the machinery of textual distribution and the
remembered ghosts of history, Austen seems to suggest, setting her novel
amid the fragile peace of 1814, that Britain can follow Wentworth and
Anne in their "re-union" and "return into the past" (240). No reader
can ignore the real present of the British Union, which remains fraught,
agitated by questions of political Reform, Catholic emancipation, and
cultural nationalist pamphleteering in Scotland and Ireland, or its
recent past in the novel's setting, caught between unresolved Napoleonic wars. And none can forget that the corrupt and violent Elliot heir

is the estate's real-historical inheritor. It is William Walter Elliot who will guide Kellynch – and, if he wishes, Britain's judiciary, Church, and Parliament, all still attached to the landed estate and its hereditary proprietor – into the nineteenth century.

The contingency of *Persuasion*'s historiographic conclusion is striking, and yet it may well be from contingency – or historiographical flexibility – that Austen's novel derives its greatest ideological strength. The ending replaces Britain's history of competing classes with the British heroine's domestic life: Austen writes her own privatized version of history over the formal genealogical account Sir Walter reads in the *Baronetage*. As firmly as Samuel Richardson, Austen in *Persuasion* roots good order in the "domestic" sphere, but the sphere itself is in Austen's novel unambivalent about its own artifice and assimilation to letters (252). In insisting on charity as the first criterion for landlords, in particular, Anne Elliot resembles an equally utopian, but on Austen's part admittedly ideological, rewriting of Richardson's Clarissa Harlowe.

Engaged for the second time, Anne and Wentworth join self-consciously in Austen's historical reflection, a process that both name " 'thinking over the past' " (246–7):

> soon words enough had passed between them to decide their direction towards the comparatively quiet and retired gravel-walk, where the power of conversation would make the present hour a blessing indeed; and prepare it for all the immortality which the happiest recollections of their own future lives could bestow . . . There they returned again into the past, more exquisitely happy, perhaps, in their re-union, than when it had been first projected . . . And there . . . they could indulge in those retrospections and acknowledgments . . . which were so poignant and so ceaseless in interest. (240–1)

Anne and Wentworth, like Sir Walter, read their own history, but in a moralized, reflective, and consciously unstable version. As Austen originally planned it, the *éclaircissement* is even more explicit about Anne's reflexive approach to a history still in process, describing a "mind deeply busy in revolving what she had heard, feeling, thinking, *recalling, and foreseeing* everything" (253, emphasis added). Wentworth and Anne relive their own narratives and take pleasure in their own ways of making sense of the past, and of the present that will become part of it. At the same time, they re-read and re-interpret the past as a way of understanding the present and of shaping the future that will in time become part of their history, with "all the immortality" the happiness shaped by the past will "bestow." Austen's reader watches the *dynamics* of personal and national history.

In becoming Austen's ideal readers, Anne and Wentworth also become ideal histories, read and re-read by one another within the plot as well as by the reader from without. Austen calls to the reader for moral assessment in a way that recalls the tongue-in-cheek reflexiveness of *Northanger Abbey*'s ending. Her conclusion reinforces the symbolic, exemplary status of "a" Wentworth and "an Anne":

> Who can be in doubt of what followed? When any two young people take it into their heads to marry, they are pretty sure by perseverance to carry their point, be they ever so poor, or ever so imprudent, or ever so little likely to be necessary to each other's ultimate comfort. This may be bad morality to conclude with, but I believe it to be truth; and if such parties succeed, how should a Captain Wentworth and an Anne Elliot, with the advantage of maturity of mind, consciousness of right, and one independent fortune between them, fail of bearing down every opposition? (248)

Wentworth's and Anne's assessment of their own history is national romance and gendered domestic rule book both at once. Sir Walter's masturbatory reading of "his own history" through his inflated sense of his own national importance opens the frame that the conclusion closes with the real "national importance" of Anne's and Wentworth's re-reading of the past (252). By framing *Persuasion* as at once a popular and instructive work, complete with generalized but personal directions for its use, Austen produces not one but two generative moral tales. For, read well and guided by the wide circulation of Austen's novel, Anne's history *and* each reader's particular history provide a form of restoration – for the Burkean "commonwealth" of each reader's family and the commonwealth as a whole.

In *Persuasion* and *Northanger Abbey*, Austen countered lending-library and radical gothic with a romance that hailed its reader as what Armstrong calls a "domestic woman": the bearer of a subjectivity that Austen's and other national romances produce and teach.[81] Yet in doing so, Austen established a vital dialectic between home and state, with men and women playing distinctive roles in both. At the same time, she embraced the radical view that the role of women in families is indeed a conservative political fiction – for Austen, a desirable, nationally vital fiction, generated and supported by writing, selling, and reading moral romance. In 1815, Scott praised Austen for creating "such characters as occupy the ordinary walks of life," contrasting her skilled illustrations of domestic life with Maria Edgeworth's "power of embodying and illustrating national character."[82] He overlooked Austen's prescriptions for British national character, for it is precisely domestic privacy, with its power to absorb and redeploy ideological contradictions, that gives her romance its force in Britain's future national history. It was only after genre had emerged, in retrospect, as genealogy that Scott fully acknowledged Austen's national myth, and his own: that legitimate social order can be produced by romance-reading in a chain of homes across Great Britain.

CHAPTER 5

Bastard romance: Scott, Hazlitt, and the ends of legitimacy

Walter Scott's 1825 *Tales of the Crusaders* opens with the minutes of the "joint-stock company . . . for the purpose of writing and publishing the class of works called the Waverley Novels." Elected to the chair by the "editors" of Scott's earlier works, "the Author of Waverley" proposes that "the labor of composing these novels might be saved by the use of steam," adapting a "mechanical process like that by which weavers of damask alter their patterns" to recombine *ad infinitum* those "parts of the narrative . . . composed out of commonplaces." When the company react as weavers had a decade earlier (" 'Blown up . . . Bread taken out of our mouths' "), the chair accuses them of ingratitude:

> you are like the young birds, who are impatient to leave their mother's nest – take care your own pen-feathers are strong enough to support you . . . I am tired of supporting on my wing such a set of ungrateful gulls . . . I will no longer avail myself of such weak ministers as you – I will discard you – I will unbeget you . . . I will leave you and your whole hacked stock in trade – your caverns and your castles – your modern antiques, and your antiquated moderns . . . I will vindicate my own fame with my own right hand . . . I will lay my foundations better than on quicksands – I will rear my structure of better materials than painted cards; in a word, I will write HISTORY![1]

Most readers of the preface emphasize its blend of capitalist and communitarian sentiment, equating romance-writing with commerce in the social and economic senses of the word.[2] Those who point out the speaker's concluding turn away from community tend to interpret the diversion as a promotion of historiography over romance, evidence for Scott's developing remasculinization of his markedly feminine genre.[3] Yet as "the Author of Waverley" represents it, the generic turn is not an end, but a byproduct of his search for subjects appropriate to his newly entrepreneurial approach to letters.[4] His quest is impelled not by desire for literary innovation, but by that sense of generic and socioeconomic crisis represented by the shareholders' resistance. At the same time,

Scott's "eidolon" speaks with the voice of an outraged father "unbegetting" – illegitimating – his sons. His speech unites rhetorics of familial and literary legitimacy on the ground of commercial individualism. The unity is brought about as a literary father – who is also, simultaneously, a "mother" – transforms himself into a heroic son, the independent firstborn of romance. This chapter argues that Scott's late romances provisionally remedy an ideological problem, a legitimation crisis, publicly debated and unresolved since the 1790s. His new model of legitimacy brings conservative historical ideologies of nation and family together with a liberal end to political history, uniting them in an endless economic and political modernity made possible by romance.

In redefining legitimacy in 1825, Scott reinvented his own career, offering it as a model of literary production for the nineteenth century. The model was quickly accepted by the mainstream press. The Tory *Quarterly Review*, for example, had left Scott's work unreviewed for several years, accumulating an unprecedented backlog of six novels. The essay that broke the silence explained the long neglect, and reviving interest, in terms that echo Scott's introduction to *Tales of the Crusaders*, but remove it from its political economic context:

It has been with him as with fiction itself, in the several stages of its history. In the earlier stages, there was an exuberance of action and of manners . . . In time, a principle of selection obtains; and the feelings are touched, and interest sufficiently excited, by the skilful developement of a few well-chosen incidents and characters. In the subsequent stages of its progress, their number is still further diminished, and the intervals are filled up with speculation on motive, and description of scenery; with sentiment and eloquence, and philosophical solution. This course is advantageous with regard to fiction in general; yet . . . not so conducive to the interest of an individual author's latest productions.[5]

Contrary to Scott's portrait of the socioeconomic crisis that conditions his generic change, neither random variation nor historical contingency is permitted to disrupt the developmental history this reviewer offers.[6] The progressive ontogeny of Scott's career recapitulates the phylogeny of romance, and the tedium of the recent novels is a necessary byproduct of the evolutionary "principle of selection" that has refined the genre. According to the *Quarterly*, Scott's late novels, with their "dramatic" narration, are the "legitimate progeny of his own creative genius" and the genre of romance.[7] The legitimacy of these novels, and of *St. Ronan's Well* (1824) in particular, places romance newly alongside tragedy atop the classical hierarchy of genres, and Scott at the teleological end of literary history.

What makes the *Quarterly*'s essay especially striking is the redefinition of legitimacy it implies – a rethinking that is consistent with Scott's own. Five years earlier, the *Quarterly* had upheld the radical critic William Hazlitt's view of Scott as a would-be retailer of "charms and philtres to our love of Legitimacy," by whose "bastard philosophy," "restoring the claims of the Stuarts by the courtesy of romance, the House of Brunswick are more firmly seated . . . and the Bourbons become legitimate" – although the *Quarterly* valued Scott's narrative absolutism very differently, celebrating his "absolute, almost . . . tyrannical" solutions to traps of historical plotting apparently beyond hope of "legitimate extrication."[8] But in lauding Scott in the terms of the 1825 essay, the *Quarterly* turned away from Hazlitt's Scott while moving closer, with Scott's aid, to Hazlitt's progressive view of history. In responding in literary terms to Hazlitt's political attack, the *Quarterly* foreshadowed Scott's claim, in his 1832 preface to *St. Ronan's Well*, that his late works were "the most legitimate" of English fictions.[9] In coming to view Scott as the most legitimate of novelists, they refocused their attention on the romance form instead of the content of his novels. They shifted priority from the first to the second of Hazlitt's implicit, conflicting definitions of legitimacy: from an ideology justifying aristocratic and monarchical government toward a broadly accepted cultural authority. This second definition underwrites the *Quarterly*'s 1825 comments on Scott: the latest novels, the *Quarterly* suggests, are not *about* legitimacy, but embody it.[10]

Scott's late romances offered a means of bringing together British Protestants, whose tenuous ideological unity, forged in defensive response to the Jacobite Rebellion of 1745 and shattered in the Revolution debates of the 1790s, had been renewed only, and unpleasantly, by Mary Wollstonecraft's radical insistence that Whig and Tory meant much the same thing. Earlier Tories had contended that the Stuarts derived their right to rule from God, while Whigs had argued that kings' rights derived solely from their effectiveness in reigning, a skill they denied the Stuarts. After 1745, however, Whig polemicists declared *de jure* that the consent of a free people alone could legitimate a monarchy, while anti-Jacobite Tories argued that the Hanoverian succession had a *de facto* right to loyalty because they now occupied the throne.[11] Both parties envisioned the Hanoverian monarchy as an epitome of Britishness, and Gerald Newman and Linda Colley contend that their efforts to legitimate the Hanoverian succession played an unparalleled part in creating a sense of British homogeneity and community.[12] But both arguments were based on interpretations of British history rather than on any inherent validity of kingship or the Act of Succession. Thus when political events exploded at the end of the 1780s, history itself – besieged by the 1688 centenary, the French Revolution, and the incapacity of George III – lost its reliability as a source of legitimation.

Conservative Whigs and Tories sought to replace history with some quality intrinsic to the monarchy: to revive the *de jure* absolutism of the Stuarts by finding some liberal, Protestant, but nevertheless unanswerable alternative to it. Led by Edmund Burke, they discovered legitimacy. In *Reflections on the Revolution in France* (1790), Burke literalized and dehistoricized the word, creating that delicate, highly literary balance of primogeniture, feminine chastity, true sensibility, "virtuous" domestic life, and Protestantism that Wollstonecraft attacked as a product of romance and that Jane Austen, in her self-conscious romances, ironically embraced. Liberal Whigs, Dissenters, and radicals, including Hazlitt, responded by highlighting the public side of legitimacy, which Burke had founded on privacy and sexuality: they located legitimation in the will of the people, with monarchy only its most contingent product. Legitimacy is a word that many readers associate with Scott, often without defining it. They tacitly associate Scott's legitimacy with its discrepant modern meanings: literary worth and reputation, *or* primogeniture and the birth of heirs within Hardwicke's Marriage Act and Scotland's separate law.[13] But it was in the specific and still-unresolved debate on Burkean ideology that Scott's own specific styling of legitimacy intervened, in his earliest novels and throughout his career.

To analyze Scott's intervention requires plotting his novels, early and late, on a generic graph shaped by intersecting axes of history and romance. What the *Quarterly Review* called Scott's "historical romances" – in particular, *Guy Mannering* and *The Antiquary* – collectively form a zone where the mingled traces of older, oral, magical genres are recovered and dedicated to his writing of the present. These works are romances of restoration, plotting the return of legitimate minor-aristocratic heirs to lands and positions they have lost. They are defended against accusations of Jacobitism by the individual and domestic character of their heroes' restoration and the explicit banishment of political history from their endings. Reading these romances, critics of Scott have often viewed him in Hazlitt's terms: as an ideologue who puts historiography to work in the service of legitimacy or, in other words, a Burkean. Even Georg Lukács, while arguing that Scott's approach to writing history abandoned the dogmas of party and class, emphasized his smooth development of past into present.[14]

More recent readers have seen Scott's novels as teleological narratives whose goal is a legitimate, domesticated British "present" towards
which public national history, including Scotland's separate history, is
shown to have been progressing. As Ian Duncan puts it, these works
promote an ideology for which "history's limit or end" becomes a
cultural goal.[15] Despite the resemblance between this view and the
remarks with which Scott began *Tales of the Crusaders*, these readers
have tended to take Scott's historiography either separately from his
own literary history or to see it as the key thematic content giving his
novels the canonical status the *Quarterly* and other reviews assigned
them. Yet Scott's *portraits* of history's end in his early novels exist in
clear contrast to his late works' reflexive *embodiment* of it, and the novels
themselves comment on this contrast. In his novels of the 1820s –
especially *St. Ronan's Well*, as we will see – Scott replaces archaic oral
culture with a commercial present that lacks a definite origin and,
avowedly, an end. Just as Duncan notes of Scott that all romance is
"modern" romance, producing its own archaizing history, so to Scott
the only cultural history was a literary-historical construction.[16] And so
Scott rereads and rewrites his earlier works: moving his interest in
history from the content to the genre of the text, he replaces the
romances of legitimacy with legitimate romance. Not the aristocrat,
but the Author, through his virtuoso command of literary history,
becomes Britain's representative of legitimacy.

I read the shift in the *Quarterly*'s response to Scott as the official mark
of a broad-based rapprochement between conservative intellectuals
and progressive ideologies of political and literary authority. The
change in evaluating Scott's form depends, in turn, on a change that
took place in the ideological content of his novels. Scott turned away
from the romances of restoration that shaped his early works, turning
first to a new subgenre I will call "bastard romance" as a base from
which to begin remaking his novelistic career. He would finally give up
illustrating the end of political history to embody, instead, the endpoint
of literary progress, trading political for literary legitimacy. The source
of British Protestant unity that resulted, as Scott shifted the fount of
legitimacy from aristocratic primogeniture and royal succession to letters and the literary canon, provided a new set of national symbols for
Britain – and an ideological basis for consolidating economic and social
power in liberal middle-class hands.

THE ROMANCE OF LEGITIMACY: THE HEIR COMES
HOME TO ELLANGOWAN

At the conclusion of Scott's second novel *Guy Mannering; or, The Astrologer* (1815), the heir of the Bertrams returns to claim his father's estate on Scotland's border. Having been kidnapped in infancy and deprived of his name and fortune, Harry Bertram is nevertheless easily recognized at the age of twenty-one, because he is " 'the very image of his father.' "[17] He needs neither documentation nor legal confirmation, for the tenantry of his usurped estate hail him as laird of Ellangowan, trusting the evidence of legitimate resemblance:

"Look at him . . . all that ever saw his father or his grandfather, and bear witness if he is not their living image?" A murmur went through the crowd – the resemblance was too striking to be denied. (IV: 336)

As the heir's formulaic resemblance to his father makes clear, there is something slightly magical about Harry's reappearance and his easy acceptance by the tenantry and local gentry. That Harry – raised in India and Holland – should have found his way to Britain at all, let alone back to Ellangowan, is a chain of coincidences that Scott's self-conscious romance framework can alone make believable. His homecoming marks the quasi-mystical bond that links an heir to his hereditary estate in Scott's early novels: like the divine right of kings, though with fewer public consequences, it is a bond disrupted at the disrupter's peril.

Everything about this novel unites to emphasize the magical symbiosis of laird and land. Like Sir Walter Elliot in Austen's *Persuasion*, Godfrey Bertram, Harry's father, loses the family estate because he allows fashion, consumption, and commerce to distract him from his feudal obligations. Displeased by the untidiness of his tenants' cottages and vain of his bureaucratic power as a peace officer, he conducts a series of clearances, setting in motion the events that lead to his wife's death, the disappearance of his son, and his family's forfeiture of property and position. Among those banished are the gypsy clan led by Meg Merrilies, whose response invokes a poetic justice based on feudal symmetry:

There's thirty hearts there, that wad hae wanted bread ere ye had wanted sunkets [delicacies], and spent their life-blood ere ye had scratched your finger . . . that ye have turned out o' their bits o' bields, to sleep with the tod and the blackcock in the muirs! – Ride your ways, Ellangowan. – Our bairns are hinging at our weary backs – look that your braw cradle at hame be the fairer spread up. (III: 80)

In disrupting Meg's family, Godfrey completes the carving out of a
private sphere from the public realm of his feudal authority, a process
that a long series of increasingly bourgeois ancestors have begun. He
breaks ancient chains of responsibility and duty that tie the two families
together, and ends by destroying his own. A mixture of curse and
blessing, invocation and prediction, Meg's words wield the novelist's
authority. Scott's text is driven by her prophecy and the feudal magic
that powers it – here and in concluding the novel, where it is Meg's
prediction that brings Harry home, and her determination to "set him
in his father's seat, if every step was on a dead man," that reveals his
Bertram face before the tenantry (IV: 337). To Meg, loyally versed in
Bertram genealogies, Harry is the worthiest heir since his family
changed its name from MacDingawaie during the Crusades. His restoration cancels the long process of anglicization and commercialization
of which Godfrey is the last scion, returning family and fiefdom into the
distant, romantic past.

For Scott's recent critics, the self-conscious idealism of romance
solves problems of ideology and history in this novel and in Scott's other
novels of restoration. Duncan, Ina Ferris, and Judith Wilt all contend
that Scott presses romance, in Austen's sense of a restorative fiction
expressing full consciousness of itself, into history's service, as a means of
mediating conflicts between private desire and public history, and
between historical change and national identity.[18] The idealistic "romance" plot of reconciliation, that is, here applied to reconcile competing discourses, is aptly suited to the intertextual capaciousness of romance in its more generalized eighteenth-century understanding as a
"species" or genre. Harry's homecoming, in particular, is a scene from
romance in both senses: Duncan argues that the romance that allows
Harry's return forges a new balance between a "lost archaic world" of
"ancient right" and the "new historical economy" that has apparently
superseded it. Yet part of romance's function here, according to Duncan, is to indicate, aided by the novel's narrative self-consciousness, its
own fragility and impossibility: "We raise the dead to learn – that they
are dead; that we must die too."[19] Not least among the fragilities of *Guy
Mannering's* romance is the exceptionality, the extreme localism, of its
conclusion. Scott emphasizes this localism by consigning his hero, a
military veteran and world traveller, to private life on the isolated
Ellangowan estate at novel's end.

I propose that it is not so much the generic category of romance as
Scott's particular romance, at this moment, that is fragile, contingent,

and limited – and that the fragility of Scott's romance exists less because
of any inherent delicacy and fictionality of the genre than because of the
specific ideological content in Scott's narrative. The domestic inheritance plot of this romance is composed of borrowed slogans (blood is
thicker than water, what's bred in the bone, and so forth), and it should
be read in its intertextual ties to an existing discourse and to more than
one existing genre. I am arguing that, for Scott, romance as the idealistic
fiction of a national tradition is linked inextricably with the contemporary discourse of legitimacy – not as the triumphant solution to legitimacy's weakness that Wilt and Ferris propose, but as an emblem of its
failure.[20] It is in reaction to legitimacy's limitations, and not as a means
of transforming them, that inheritance and romance coincide in Scott's
early novels. Genre and ideology alike are outmoded, unsatisfying, but
the only sources of order available as yet to a Protestant traditionalist.

In *Reflections*, Burke described his organic conception of British social
structure, bringing public and private authority together in "just correspondence and symmetry with the order of the world" through which
"power" was to become "legitimate."[21] Burke insisted that legitimacy
would always unite the families and government of Britain, replacing
the divine right of kings with a holistic, and therefore secure, domestic
relation. "The princes of the House of Brunswick," he argued, "came to
the inheritance of the crown, not by election, but by the law as it stood at
their several accessions of Protestant descent and inheritance," just as
"We" – British gentlemen – "now wish to derive all we possess *as an
inheritance from our forefathers*" (27). Thus Burke brought the British succession in line with "the natural order of things" (43). Scott's use of
legitimist ideology in his early historical romances suggests that he did
not, as Hazlitt would in 1817, condemn Burke's "fiction of Legitimacy"
for producing "the history of literary patriotism and prostitution for the
last twenty years."[22] Nevertheless, his reading of Burkean discourse in
Guy Mannering and the other early novels uneasily approaches Hazlitt's
conclusions about the fictionality of legitimacy. Harry Bertram is hailed
with joy by the Ellangowan tenants, yet Harry lacks jurisdiction beyond
his estate. His father's feudal authority has been transferred to the
modern, nonlanded administrative power that is gaining ground in
late-eighteenth-century Britain; Godfrey Bertram's magistracy is not
included in Harry's inheritance, but passes by state apparatuses out of
Bertram hands (IV: 368–9). Ellangowan Castle, seat of the MacDin-
gawaies' feudal power but destroyed by their fashionable Bertram
successors, remains a ruin. Harry's restoration is unique, brought about

as much by magic as by inheritance. Unlike Hazlitt, Scott suggests not that a politics founded on legitimate fictions is unjust, but that the fiction of legitimacy is too narrow, and too rare, to provide a reliable basis for real political order.

Designated as legitimacy's literary counterpart, romance is fragile and limited, yet legitimacy's failings, according to Scott, are as much literary as practical. In 1815, as he began writing *Guy Mannering*, Scott had already explicitly and publicly named his frustration with the limits of romance. In the *Quarterly Review*, he remarked that the rigid conventions of romance, as inherited from late-eighteenth-century writers such as Radcliffe, made it a uniquely private genre, and that the genre's privacy was the source both of popularity and of mediocrity: "fettered by many peculiarities derived from the original style of romantic fiction," writers produced " 'bread eaten in secret' " – morally high-flown but unliterary domestic novels. "Hence it has happened, that in no branch of composition . . . have so many writers, and of such varied talents, exerted their powers."[23] The recent emphasis of readers such as Ferris and Duncan on Scott's "remasculinization" – his publicizing and canonizing – of this traditionally private, popular, feminized sentimental romance genre understates the degree to which Scott himself continued to view romance as feminine and private even after writing *Waverley*, *Guy Mannering*, and *The Antiquary*, the related work that followed.[24] His use of romance to convey confinement and public impotence reconfirmed the privacy of the genre – and the femininity of privacy – as well as underscoring the limits of legitimacy.[25]

Scott's novel is remarkable, therefore, not only for its reconsideration of romance, but for the way that critique also comments on the ideology of legitimacy. In *Guy Mannering*, legitimacy and romance go inseparably together. In addition to Scott's romancing about Harry, Harry reads romances, and his restoration depends in several ways on this reading. Returning to Ellangowan twenty years after his disappearance, Harry does not recall his real name or birthplace, but memory lurks in the Scottish landscape. He writes to a friend about his instinctive sympathy for his native country in terms that, in his mid-eighteenth-century context, can only have come from romance: "Despite my Dutch education, a blue hill to me is as a friend, and a roaring torrent like the sound of a domestic song that hath soothed my infancy" (III: 213). He is instinctively aware of the fiction within which he places himself, remarking that the ruined castle of Ellangowan seems to inspire "dreams of early and shadowy recollection, such as my old Bramin Moonshie would have ascribed to a state of previous existence" (IV: 153). What Harry dismisses as romance is in fact his reality: no past life but recent memory shapes his impression of the castle. Even as Scott, like Harry himself, equates these feelings with "moonshi[n]e," Harry's response to Ellangowan reflects on Scott's plotting of inheritance in the novel rather than on the "wonderful effects which . . . the romances of the East produce upon their hearers," with which Harry associates his feelings (III: 170–1, 209). As Scott aligns legitimacy with fairytale in *Guy Mannering*'s magical conclusion, Harry links genetic inheritance with romance reading. The idea of a natural race-memory that governs inherited traditions in Burke's *Reflections* reappears in Scott's novels in the form of a well-constructed plot.

I am suggesting that romance, as Scott conceived and defined it, was the only possible genre for his nineteenth-century narratives of restoration – not because aristocracy has become an impossible dream, but because an aristocracy founded on legitimacy, and serving as the bulwark of Scott's society, is philosophically shaky and in need of being replaced. Romance is not a symptom of antiquated and tenaciously held ideals, or even of self-consciously renovated ones, but an admission of ideological frustration that is rooted in explicitly literary concern with political economic authority. As late as 1825, Scott conceded that there was a place for this kind of formulaic genre-writing. In his comic-allegorical introduction to *Tales of the Crusaders*, romance defines its writers as father and sons, bringing them together in mutual support and the production of legitimacy. As Scott practises and theorizes the genre, romance serves the same function as the discourse of legitimacy, one more reason why he considers the issue of legitimacy in romance form. Yet the labour of writing and reading romance, in theory as in practice, is confined within the sphere of family life. The genre cannot, in Scott's model, be pushed into the public realm of commercial production and political influence and, by extension, the discourse of legitimacy remains equally private. Like Harry Bertram's restoration, Scott's writing of romance exists solely within the private sphere. Scott himself inherited neither landed property nor political power. The solutions of *Guy Mannering* are as limited as Duncan suggests, because the ideology of legitimacy is limited as well.

THE PROBLEM OF FEMININE SENSIBILITY IN ROMANCE AND HISTORY

The limits on legitimacy received their strongest nineteenth-century exposition in the criticism of Hazlitt, who began *Political Essays* by exposing the internal contradictions of Burkean conservatism. Taking Scott as a case study, he drew the Waverley novels, though not Scott himself, into the liberal fold:

An Elector of Hanover . . . made king of England, in contempt and to the exclusion of the claims of the old, hereditary possessors and pretenders to the throne, on any other plea except that of his being the chosen representative and appointed guardian of the rights and liberties of other nations, would indeed be a solecism more absurd and contemptible than any to be found in history. What! Send for a petty Elector of a petty foreign state to reign over us from respect to *his* right to the throne of these realms, in defiance of the legitimate heir to the crown, and "in contempt of the choice of the people!" Oh monstrous fiction! Miss Flora MacIvor would not have heard of such a thing: the author of Waverley has well answered Mr. Burke.[26]

Hazlitt contrasts Burke's modern argument for legitimacy with the unwavering inheritance desired by the Jacobite Flora MacIvor in Scott's first novel, *Waverley* (1814). He accuses Scott of being "besotted as to the moral of his own story": although Scott writes to strengthen the existing lines of authority in Britain, Hazlitt asserts, his plots and characters are wiser than he, and the novels produce an unintended critique of the New Whig legitimacy he promotes. Hazlitt's reading of Scott's ideological entrapment is based on the ill fit between the restorations that end historical turmoil in Scott's novels and the plotted "horrors" that these domestic conclusions cannot quite exorcise. It is also shaped by gender ideology. Hazlitt's view of *Waverley* extends to other early novels – including *Guy Mannering*, for Meg Merrilies instinctively recognizes and loves the legitimate heir as easily as Flora MacIvor does Charles Edward Stuart. Like Scott, Hazlitt aligns women with "the beauty of Legitimacy," but he redefines legitimate beauty as "lawless power and savage bigotry," the embodiment of misgivings that Scott will not acknowledge.[27] The "light, agreeable, effeminate" closures Scott enforces on plots "rugged" with "traditional barbarism" fail in part, Hazlitt argues, because they are blind to the disruptive possibility of feminine sensibility, violence, and desire.[28] Either a darker, more gothic dream than Burke's domestic ideal motivates Scott's closures, or Scott writes liberal-progressive fables in spite of himself.

What Hazlitt pinpoints is the ideological impossibility of Scott's conclusions. For even as Scott's romance of legitimacy resolves political history in his early novels, his enclosure of legitimacy in the domestic sphere already raises questions about his relative placement of romance and history. Whereas Hazlitt argues that history subverts romance, however, recent readers view the problem of Scott's historiography more complexly. What Duncan calls "history" appears in the struggle between modern problems (in *Guy Mannering*, the dispossession and dislocation that the heir's return resolves) and archaic solutions and genre fragments (the magical texts and feudal loyalty of Meg Merrilies, which enable Harry Bertram's restoration). These opposing forces finally cancel each other, cancelling history in the process, yet although the generic capaciousness of romance defeats history, Scott's enclosure of the legitimist ending suggests a temporary and unstable victory. Duncan argues that the contingency of the conclusion privileges the imagination of the novelist-as-proprietor – transmuting the hero's fictional, magical success against history into a celebration of Scott's creative power.[29] But the Author of *Waverley* had not yet appeared as a character in Scott's novels, and Scott himself remained officially anonymous: no one proprietary mind comes forward to be privileged. I have suggested that the unease of Harry Bertram's restoration results from the too-evident marks of artifice on legitimacy, a reading that approaches Hazlitt's. But alternatives to Hazlitt's interpretation exist, if Scott acknowledges and registers in his novels (as Duncan suggests) the fictions his ideology requires. What might it mean, for example, if Scott's limitation of legitimacy to the space of romance – domestic and visibly fictional – is neither subverted by "real" history nor simply critical of legitimate ideology, but intensely defensive of legitimacy?

In their work on early-nineteenth-century fiction, Duncan, Ferris, and Trumpener identify an intertwining of history and romance in the works of Scott and other novelists, a "dialectic" or "dialectical relation between the spheres of male and female authorship" represented by Scott on one hand and writers, such as Sydney Owenson, who promoted sensibility in sentimental marriage plots, on the other.[30] Like Hazlitt, and like Wollstonecraft before him, these readers see an exchange between genders and genres where most of Scott's contemporaries wished to see only opposition. They supplement Scott's masculinization of romance by redrawing the lines of dialogue and resemblance between Scott and his female contemporaries. Yet Scott's early conclusions neither privatize history nor make sentimental romance openly public and political, but rather feminize and enclose the plot they type as romance, highlighting the contingency of its solution-narratives and insulating it from the political history it resolves. As Hazlitt pointed out, the uneasy domestic closures of Scott's early novels protect against the dangers *of* as well as *to* legitimacy, introducing the internal contradictions of domestic space into Scott's already unsettled conclusions.

These contradictions derive in part from the ambiguous gendering of romance: like romance itself, the contradictions have both a textual and a sexual component. Scott wrote his national romances in the context of an imperial discourse of legitimacy that turned the opposing arguments of Whigs and Tories into fruitless contradiction or mutual accusation. Twenty-five years earlier, in his influential *Reflections*, Burke had inaugurated the distinctive form of public–private split that characterized legitimist ideology. The "family affections" were British, sentimental, and legitimate, characterized by natural love of mother-queen and hereditary respect for father-king, and productive of social order (30). Britain's private peace existed far removed from the illegitimate public turmoil of France, where abuse of the queen by mobs of men and "the vilest of women" signalled Revolutionary disrespect for the father-king Louis XVI (62–3).[31] But Burke's insistence on the heritability of social order moved opponents to point out the violence primogeniture had occasioned in British homes as well as in British society. After Wollstonecraft, in particular, few could read Burke's sentimental romance of social order without being reminded of its gothic underside, as Hazlitt's remarks on Scott's "monstrous fiction" suggest. Because both sides in the Revolution debate claimed to have cornered the market on familial virtue, either side – or the opponents of both – could marshal sexual or domestic dissent to shake the theoretical foundations of British society. As Claudia Johnson shows, each side easily accused the other of "unnaturally" blurring the line between genders, and thus, because reformer and reactionary shared an ideology of domestic sentiment and natural law, of political impropriety.[32] What surfaces even in Scott's earliest novels is a recognition that some radically new way of discussing social order was necessary if Burke's conservative ideals for family and nation were to be preserved. Legitimacy and sentimental romance needed replacement.

Legitimacy's weakness lay not in the family *per se*, but in its partisans' assertion of the naturalness of gender and domesticity. To claim status for *Reflections* as a natural rather than a political history, Burke describes Britain's political economic order in genealogical terms as "a relation in blood," and, in sentimental language dating back to Richardson's *Clarissa*, as a bond of "hearts" and "hearths." From the Act of Succession onwards, Burke argues, the Protestantism and chastity of Sophia of Hanover, inherited by British women as British men inherit lands and titles, have been a "root" holding succession, social order, and family enduringly in place (21). All Britons "bind . . . up the constitution of our country with our dearest domestic ties . . . keeping . . . and cherishing within the warmth of all their combined and mutually reflected charities" the institutions that will be inherited unchanged by Britain's and Burke's legitimate heroes – the king and the aristocrat (30). Burke's language is suggestive, revealing that natural history cannot proceed without a rigid patrolling of the "natural." "Binding" and "keeping" are the shadowy doubles of "cherishing": beneath the sentimental surface of British domesticity lies unmistakable evidence of imprisonment.

Burke calls further attention to this ambivalence in the home by insulating Britain and domestic life from the gothic counter-history of French radicals, in which "the natural order of things," founded on the domestic and economic "principle of property," has been "systematically subverted" (34, 43). In France, "The gallery is in the place of the house": Burke's metaphor brings together theatre, government, and home as mobs intrude into and mix up what in Britain are the discrete spaces of aristocratic leisure, legislation, and family life (9). But his banishment of disorder from Britain and his enclosure of order within the *domus* cannot undo the similar blurring of publicity and privacy in his idealized England – for what is the virtue of Sophia of Hanover if not a bridge between private and public life? His unhistorical domestication of British women looks in the end less like nature than like ideological sleight-of-hand. Arguing that France "has abandoned her interest, that she might prostitute her virtue," becoming illegitimate on principle, Burke reveals Britain as the ideological inverse, whose "virtue" is "her" defining feature (33). The danger, as Scott first hints and then explicitly concedes, is that the opposition might reverse.

Scott's ideological problems were gendered; consequently, Scott controlled ideological damage by means of gender. When he discusses his romances explicitly, he represents them not as attempts at respectable masculinization of a dangerously feminized kind of narrative, but as a literally feminine genre. In his introduction to *Tales of the Crusaders*, he establishes romance as the medium that transforms writers into fathers and sons – a maternal apparatus for reproducing tradition, but also the ground of intergenerational conflict.[33] Scott emphasizes that the genre becomes a mediator because it is the characteristic literary form of legitimacy, the "mother's nest" and "foundation" of Scott's literary dynasty. Like the women who uphold legitimacy in Scott's early novels, however, the genre is unpredictable as well as private, in need of simultaneous protection and control. Romance looks very much like the domestic sphere on which legitimacy rests, and to which both genre and ideology belong. For Scott, the domestic sphere, its ideologies, and their literary means alike invoke a femininity from which rebellion, desire, and political ambition have been forcibly kept apart. But as Wollstonecraft revealed and Frances Burney feared, the use of romance to buttress a family-based social order promotes, as legitimacy does, a gendering that poses an internal danger to Burkean social order and the efficacy of romance.[34] In Scott's novels in particular, praise for the natural domesticity and fidelity of women coexists increasingly uneasily with desire for their regulation. The resurfacing of rigidly masculine traits – publicity, rebellion – in female characters and feminized genres is another way to read the dialectic of genres and genders Trumpener describes. Scott is not, as Hazlitt suggested, blind to the potential for gender inversion and the mingling of publicity and privacy that romance and legitimacy harbour. Rather, he is profoundly troubled by it.

To view Scott's conclusions as simple failures is to miss the self-consciousness he brings to their ambivalence. Certainly Scott's critics have noted that his acute sense of Scottishness and of political history – the traits that Hazlitt identifies with Scott's liberalizing unconscious or the political unconscious of his texts – clashes noticeably in his novels with the sentimentalized political philosophy and nationalistic Britishness he inherited from Burke.[35] As a Scottish member of the Church of England, Scott lamented the sporadic disruptions that peasant radicalism, female and male, had caused for Britain and British Protestantism: the Presbyterian zealot Mause Headrigg in *Old Mortality*, at once a comical and terrifying figure, manifests the suppressed radical side of a Meg Merrilies.[36] As a Scottish Tory, however, Scott was equally suspicious of upper-class Englishwomen's influence on the succession and social order. His account of Queen Caroline's political maneuverings in *The Heart of Midlothian* hints at the dangers female domestic dissent poses to public order, in the peasant society Meg Merrilies represents, among the landowning Bertrams, and beyond.[37] Within and between these marks of his suspicion of history, Scott repeatedly registers the slipperiness of gender. The cross-dressing of powerful women such as Madge Wildfire in *The Heart of Midlothian* and Die Vernon and Helen MacGregor in *Rob Roy* is a potently gendered symbol for their illicit sexuality or – equally troublesome – their illegitimate political intrusion.[38]

Above all, illegitimacy intrudes into the domestic closures of Scott's early novels, where the circumscription of the domestic in the face of illegitimate threats signals the real impossibility of legitimacy. History permeates the romance of legitimacy that seems to supersede it, partly because Scott is seeking public as well as private solutions to the troubles of history, but also because there is nothing inherently quiescent about the feminized British domesticity his conclusions idealize. In *Guy Mannering*, for example, although the heir's return "restores" the organic links between tenant and lord, the preservation of these links during the estate's usurpation depends on Meg Merrilies, whose memory is the last repository of Ellangowan's "ancient" history. Meg's loyalty to Harry Bertram remains unshaken even in banishment, because it is as instinctive as it is deferential: "this woman's ancient attachment to the family, repelled and checked in every other direction, seemed to rejoice in having some object on which it could yet repose and expand itself" (III: 73). Smuggled into Ellangowan by Harry's mother, Meg works her magic in such domestic tasks as midwifery, healing, and, above all, spinning. During her first appearance in the novel, she sings charms over the infant Harry's cradle while spinning "thread, drawn from wool of three different colours, black, white, and grey" with "those ancient implements of housewifery, now almost banished from the land, the distaff and spindle":

> Twist ye, twine ye! even so
> Mingle shades of joy and woe. (III: 41–2)

Meg's distaff is triply symbolic of legitimate authority and community. Its twining threads symbolize the divisions of labour binding women to men in the household and tenants to laird on the estate – relationships, according to Scott, now under threat – and Meg's traditional place within them. It is a heraldic emblem of the feminine diligence and chastity that guarantee legitimacy: the strength and fidelity of Ellangowan rest, literally, on the distaff side. Finally, Meg's spinning and the imperative mood of her charms imply a more maternal relation to Harry's fate than the mere ability to predict it. As the representative of romance reconciliation, ancient tradition, and domesticity, she herself confers legitimacy. Yet the conservative power she wields is also a threat to Scott's conclusion.

Although Harry's adult authority over wife and family counterbalances Meg's dominance, Scott violently circumscribes Meg's power to confer legitimacy. Meg encloses her second and final charm in a letter to

Harry's solicitor as the novel draws to a close. It raises as many questions as it answers:

> *Dark shall be light,*
> *And wrong done to right,*
> *When Bertram's right and Bertram's might*
> *Shall meet on Ellangowan's height.*   (IV: 258)

Does Meg prophesy or conjure history? Who or what is the rightful efficient agent of the "to be" verbs in the charm? Does the exchange of "wrong" and "right" reverse historic wrongs, or does it invert the moral order? What happens when magical prophecy takes on legal weight? These uncertainties of feminine authority, exaggerated versions of ideological threats posed by all the women on whom legitimist doctrine and romance rely, make an ideological necessity of Meg's death at the apex of her power, the moment of Harry's restoration. As a legal and economic matter whose settlement demands unambiguous fidelity of women, Harry's return is a test case for legitimacy. Legitimacy fails the test by producing as many new tensions as it resolves. Having defined the conduits of legitimacy as essentially private and sentimental, Scott is unable to bring his legitimate endings into the public sphere without risking destructive contradiction. Either a public, ambitious side to femininity emerges to override the masculine authority his conclusion supports, or public exposure contaminates the feminized privacy of the household with political and sexual unrest. History infects romance, that is, because women intrude on history. Even within Scott's novel, then, the gendered instability inherent in the constitution of legitimacy accounts for its weakness as a political economic discourse of social order.

Reviewing Scott's "romances of resolution," Wilt wonders "how much . . . national, social, religious, personal, and sexual conflict is reconciled and how much is simply abandoned" in Scott's conclusions. She points to Scott's "ritual en-witching," his scapegoating or convenient killing, of women in his novels who enter the public field of history.[39] Certainly Scott's early novels offer only the most protected and covertly violent kinds of reconciliation. Yet by responding protectively to legitimacy's ideological fragility, Scott both highlights the weakness of legitimist romance and supplements its inadequacy. Accusing him of narrative effeminacy, closet liberalism, or ideological retreat, as readers from Hazlitt to Wilt have done, repeats a charge that his narratives anticipate and confront – and openly admit their inability to resolve.

FROM ROMANCE TO TRAGEDY: PURGING THE FAMILY IN
THE BRIDE OF LAMMERMOOR

Nevertheless, identifying hypocrisy or capitulation in Scott's conclusions pinpoints the source of the narrative tension that marks his early fiction: the split Lukács noted between Scott's conception of historical process and his stated social ideals, and the generic conflict Gary Kelly remarks between the "protagonist's plot" of "return" and the "progressive plot of history" Scott shares with Scots Enlightenment historians.[40] Scott's most politically conservative novels, that is – the romances of restoration – are also his most historiographically liberal. I have been arguing that the ambivalence visible in these unexpected contrasts point to weaknesses in the modern ideology of legitimacy, and not to Scott's backtracking or, as Kelly more kindly puts it, "ambivalence" toward legitimist ends.[41] Scott offers his most Whiggish illustration of history's movement by translating the liberal doctrine of the end of history into the high-Tory terms of elegy. For Whig historiography's "progress" toward history's end, as most recent readers have noted, Scott substitutes retrogression, an ideology of return brought about by an eruption of energies linked with ancient magic, pre-commercial domesticity, and organic feudal tradition.[42] But his goal is arguably the same: a model for the United Kingdom in which lasting peace and social cohesion lock in the best of all possible improvements.

In *The Bride of Lammermoor* (1819), however, Scott's first tragic novel and his first returned-heir plot since 1816's *The Antiquary*, the modernizing march of history is unstoppable. As Scott portrays it in the year of Peterloo and the Six Acts, history rolls on with a "relentless" determinacy, a logic no more progressive than legitimacy itself.[43] It is because of this sense of inevitability that the novel, as Graham McMaster puts it, is "very little concerned with process."[44] The movement of history toward a commercial and bureaucratic ascendancy is shown to be tyrannical, illegitimate, and immutable: a modern counterpart of those Catholic, aristocratic, *de jure* social assumptions that history and legitimacy, in their earlier turn, replaced. This triumph of progress is not simply a turn toward "Tory pessimism," as Robert Gordon argues, but neither is it solely a conservative attack on the "individual subjectivism" of romance, as Duncan contends.[45] I root the problem in the very specific conservative politics of post-Revolutionary legitimacy. In Scott's plotting of *The Bride*, the restorative romance that once conquered an illegitimate and usurping history empowers it instead.

The Jacobite hero of *The Bride of Lammermoor*, like Harry Bertram in *Guy Mannering* or Glenallan in *The Antiquary*, has lost his lands and title to what English liberals and Dissenters called progress, and what High Church conservatives such as Burke and even Scott saw as the fulfillment of the British crown's legitimacy. As punishment for his fidelity to James II during the 1689 rising against William of Orange, Lord Ravenswood has been attainted, his title made extinct, and his estate forfeited to the "politic, wary, and worldly" Sir William Ashton, a Presbyterian Whig of commercial origin, rather than inherited by Edgar, Master of Ravenswood, a member of the outlawed Church of England and Ravenswood's only son.[46] Presbyterianism, diplomacy, and commerce outweigh legitimacy, organicism, and tradition in *The Bride*'s conclusion, and unlike Scott's earlier heroes, Edgar fails in his quest for restoration, thwarted by a historical momentum that legitimacy alone cannot overcome. In *The Bride*, Scott for the first time allows the instability of legitimacy to become legitimacy's failure. The half-spoken contradictions of his legitimist plotting progress toward a turning point beyond which legitimate ideology leads only to greater chaos and violence, with no possible resolution but the purging of untenable oppositions in a concluding bloodbath.

Following this crisis in Scott's romance of restoration, critical acknowledgement of the internal problems plaguing legitimacy and its romances spreads from Hazlitt's radical essays to the liberal and conservative press. When the *New Monthly Magazine* synopsized *The Bride*, it highlighted the crisis with undesigned, and therefore revealing, precision:

Alice Grey is a venerable old woman, who shews a deep and unintelligible interest in the fate of Ravenswood and Lucy. She is blind; but the loss of vision is remunerated by an extraordinary sagacity and penetration bordering on a prophetic spirit. Three frightful hags, half allied to the spirits of darkness, are occasionally seen flitting in the back ground, and give consistence and probability to events which occur in the course of the story.[47]

The *New Monthly* reviewer offers an equalized, symmetrical, and thus explicit opposition between the disruptive and loyal sides of Scott's peasant women, as embodied in the "hags" and Alice Grey. This new separation of affiliations that formerly competed uneasily within a single character illustrates not only Scott's division of "gothic" danger from the "romantic" fidelity wielded by female peasants, but also the symmetry between characters seemingly drawn from different genres. In *The Bride of Lammermoor*, the loyal seer confers legitimacy on the heir's quest for restoration, and her authority has lost the potential for disruption with which the power of Meg Merrilies troubled *Guy Mannering*'s conclusion. Instead, the romantic power of Alice Grey, a naturalized English tenant, is opposed by a second tenant, the ambitious Ailsie Gourlay, leader of the "three hags." Ailsie is Alice's Scots double in name and position. But unlike Alice, who directs "the sight" in Ravenswood's interest, she uses her corrupt magic to benefit the Ashtons. Alice, like Meg Merrilies, instinctively trusts the heir's virtue and the legitimacy of his right. Her impotence against Ailsie's ascendancy microcosmically reworks the larger historical claim Scott's narrative illustrates: however much the English wish to represent the Hanoverian present as the culmination of legitimacy and order, they will always confront Scotland's Dissenting Whigs, who read the same history as an invitation to further "progress."[48] Juxtaposing his two peasant women, Scott rewrites Burke's "English" sentimental romance and foreign gothic history as two halves of a single British tale. The *New Monthly* marks Scott's replacement of his own established romance with the extravagant binaries of gothic: *Guy Mannering*'s ambivalence about genre gives way to generic self-subversion.

At the same time, contemporary reviews of *The Bride* emphasized Scott's vexed politics of gender, pointing to the stresses on sexuality and domesticity that, having threatened to undo the conclusions of *Guy Mannering* and *The Antiquary*, in *The Bride* explode in violence. The *New Monthly* lists the problems caused by the "masculine temperament" of Lady Ashton, who as the *éminence grise* behind Sir William signals the supersession of the faithful aristocratic mothers of Scott's earlier romances by a *parvenu*'s wife totally dedicated to "enhancement of her [own] family's power. To her," the *New Monthly* notes, "the name of Ravenswood was particularly odious."[49] The *Quarterly Review* points out that Lady Ashton embodies the risks of the "firm and decisive" character she shares with Edgar: her masculinity is dangerous where his is admirable, and its dangers are "strengthened by the subservience of him who fills the station of her superior" – her husband Sir William, whose "flexible and timid" character the *Quarterly* contemptuously compares with that of his daughter Lucy.[50] This separation of gendered character from biological sex discredits the putatively natural post-Lockean division of authority along gendered lines.

This second split in the legitimacy plot produces a division within the aristocratic household, which parallels the fracturing of Meg Merrilies into Alice Grey and Ailsie Gourlay. The opposition between Lady

Ashton and her daughter Lucy emphasizes their equal inadequacy to legitimist notions of gender and disrupts the bonds that, in legitimist ideology as in sentimental romance from its post-Richardsonian roots through its self-conscious renovation by Austen, hold families together. Firmly anchored to genders that are severed, in *The Bride*, from natural character, the irreparable breakdown of romance and legitimacy transects socioeconomic classes and generations. Lucy is the classic Scott heroine stretched to an improbable extent. She keeps close to home because she is "soft and yielding" to the point of imbecility, and her mother despises her "softness of temper . . . allied to feebleness of mind" (XIII: 299, 301). Lucy, though idealized, is wholly without power: domestically constrained and driven into madness, she can neither support Edgar's claim nor submit to his domestic authority. In contrast, the ambitious, politically intrusive Lady Ashton, with her "strong powers and violent passions," brings to its fullest fruition Scott's suspicion of the virtuous mothers who assure the rights of earlier heroes by guaranteeing their legitimacy (III: 284). Like Lucy, Lady Ashton represents a classic Scott preoccupation extended into untenable excess.

Excess is the defining quality of *The Bride of Lammermoor*. Above all, it marks Scott's discussions of gender and romance, which meet in his paired portraits of Ailsie and Alice. In Alice, Scott forecloses all possibility of ambition, desire, or Jacobinical fervor, concentrating exclusively on her Englishness, loyalty, and lack of worldly appetites. Alice improbably rejects Sir William Ashton's offered " 'friendship,' " stating that " 'Those of my age . . . make no new friends . . . I have all I want, and I cannot accept more at your lordship's hands.' " When he raises the stakes by offering rent-free tenancy, she reminds him that this was " 'an article in the sale of Ravenswood to your lordship' " (XIII: 315). As her loyalty to the Ravenswoods suggests, Alice's only passion is her intense feudal allegiance: her Jacobite railing against " 'the usurer, and the oppressor, and the grinder of the poor man's face, and the remover of ancient land-marks, and the subverter of ancient houses' " transmutes and makes safe all threats of (proto-)Jacobin violence that might otherwise lurk in her labouring-class hostility (XIV: 151). Alice expresses her loyalty in physical symptom and Burkean metaphor, going blind that her " 'eyes might not witness the downfall of the tree which overshadows my dwelling' " (XIII: 351). The Ravenswoods themselves she continues to "see," for she is "permitted . . . to touch [Edgar's] features with her trembling hand," whereupon her face "kindle[s]" as "an ancient feudal vassal might have done" (XIV: 149). This interplay of quasi-maternal love and magically self-willed blindness aids the prophecies with which she attempts to protect the Ravenswood heir, and insulates her from the pain her foresight causes: " 'if my mortal sight is closed,' " she tells Edgar, " 'I can look with more steadiness into future events' " (XIV: 152).

Alice is an excessive rewriting of Meg Merrilies: the village outsider, devoting loyal magic to the heir's preservation. In predicting the future, Alice draws, like Meg, on the past. She repeats from ancient romances two stories that shape Edgar's future just as Meg's charm guides Harry Bertram's disappearance and return. One is of impossible love between a naiad and a Ravenswood knight, ending in tragedy at a sacred well now "fatal to the Ravenswood family." The story is symbolic: of the blood spilled when legitimate and illegitimate bloods combine; of an estate and lands that themselves seem to betray the Ravenswoods, colluding in their tragedy. Yet Alice foresees without aiding the reanimation of the story, lacking either the hostile desire to bring it about or the power to prevent it as loyalty demands (XIV: 152). At this site Edgar falls in love with Lucy, who, "Beautiful and pale as the fabulous Naiad," is "dripping with the water" of the fatal well (XIII: 327–8; XIV: 160).

The second strand in Alice's prediction, confirming the first, is a verse-prophecy of the medieval visionary Thomas the Rhymer:

> When the last Laird of Ravenswood to Ravenswood shall ride,
> And woo a dead maiden to be his bride,
> He shall stable his steed in the Kelpie's flow,
> And his name shall be lost for evermoe!   (XIV: 128)

Invaded by the forces of history, the Ravenswood lands literally set upon their master. Forced by her mother to marry the Whig squire Bucklaw instead of Edgar, Lucy suffers a "wild paroxysm of insanity," stabbing Bucklaw and dying in convulsions on her wedding night (XIV: 354). When Lucy's brother challenges Edgar, Edgar rides to Ravenswood, vanishing into quicksand at this second "fatal spot" of prophecy (XIV: 367). Contemporary reviewers objected to Scott's magical narrative, but it is crucial to his playing out of the crisis of romance. He presents the end of progress ironically in this novel: Edgar is not the best, but only "the *last* Laird of Ravenswood"; aided by Scott's critical reading of earlier romances of reconciliation and her own ancient magic, Alice sees accurately. She places her visions at the service of her feudal lord, yet even when her ghost appears to warn Edgar one last time of his danger, Alice is powerless to restore the heir she loves (XIV: 219–20). She admits that Edgar is "predestined" as much as "infatuated" with Lucy – fated, if only by Scott's romance, which transports rather than holding back the violent and disruptive momentum of history (XIV: 155).

Because she is loyal and powerless, Alice is free from the potentially disruptive force that taints Scott's earlier peasant-seers. But one could also argue that her powerlessness results from her lacking the taints of ambiguous desire and authority. For female power and disruption go inevitably together in Scott, a consequence of legitimist ideology. In *The Bride*, Scott confers the dangerous authority of romance on Ailsie Gourlay, who has placed herself firmly on the side of "progress." A puritan and diplomat, Ashton is a quintessentially modern laird. His rule is impersonal and bureaucratic, administrative emphases that bring down Godfrey Bertram in *Guy Mannering*. Ashton, "more frequently heard of than seen by his tenants and dependants," is unaware until Lucy tells him that Alice lives on his estate (XIII: 307, 313). But his detachment from land and people suits Ailsie, Alice's malignant double, just as intimacy with Edgar's "features" suits Alice. Ailsie's magic requires isolation and secrecy. Not "fool enough to acknowledge a compact with the Evil One," she proceeds "as successfully as if . . . she had been aided in those arts by Beelzebub himself" (XIV: 315). Her secretive, disruptive magic casts a retrospective shadow over the collusion Meg Merrilies shares with Mrs. Bertram in *Guy Mannering*. Working with Lady Ashton, Ailsie nurses and seduces the grieving, half-mad Lucy: like Alice, she holds "her attention captive by the legends in which she was well skilled, and to which Lucy's habits of reading and reflection induced her to 'lend an attentive ear' " (XIV: 317). Having "narrowed her magic circle around the devoted victim," she retells Alice's prophecies: "the fatal fountain was narrated at full length" and "The prophecy . . . concerning the dead bride, who was to be won by the last of the Ravenswoods, had its own mysterious commentary" (XIV: 317). Ailsie is, as Merrilies threatens to be but never becomes, a "diabolical agent . . . in secret domestic crimes" uniting subversion of the laird and patriarch's domestic authority and a suspect, sexualized intimacy with his wife and daughter (XIV: 315). It is Ailsie's sexual ambiguity and her intrusion into family affairs and thus into legitimacy that condemn her in Scott's narrative as a "female agent of hell" (XIV: 321).

As an *agent provocateur* for domestic and social rebellion, Ailsie enacts the worst actions Burke attributed to his revolutionary hags, bringing about the bloody bedroom stabbing that recasts Burke's vignette of the march on Versailles with a more troubling, because transgendered, perpetrator and victim. She shares the "unsexed" passions of the Burkean radical woman.[51] Yet if disruptive Ailsie is too undistinguished from loyal Alice for ideological comfort, Lucy, too, as her willing ear for Ailsie suggests, contributes to the failure of romance by her insufficient domestic fidelity. She contributes to Edgar's tragedy because her "taste and feelings" are "peculiarly accessible to . . . a romantic cast." Like *Guy Mannering*'s romance-consuming Mrs. Mannering and secretive Mrs. Bertram, Lucy keeps her romance involvements secret. Her self-indulgent reading hints, like Ailsie's magic, at illicit desires, extending the privacy of romance to excess.

Her secret delight was in the old legendary tales of ardent devotion and unalterable affection, chequered . . . with strange adventures and supernatural horrors. This was her favoured fairy realm, and here she erected her aerial palaces. But it was only in secret that she laboured at this delusive, though delightful architecture . . . In her retired chamber, or in the woodland bower which she had chosen for her own. (XIII: 299)

Reading romance, Lucy is outside the reach of paternal authority and the confines of family life. Scott emphasizes the isolation in which she feeds her fantasies about Edgar: "It is, perhaps, at all times dangerous for a young person to suffer recollection to dwell repeatedly, and with too much complacency, on the same individual." Lucy, whose "residence remained solitary, and her mind without . . . means of dissipating her pleasing visions," continues "weaving her enchanted web of fairy tissue" uninterrupted (XIII: 334–5, 337). The problem is that more is endangered by Lucy's romance in this novel than Lucy's peace of mind: no less is at stake than the future of legitimacy itself. As Scott's earlier romances of restoration show, women's passions are safe only when channelled into heterosexual and feudal loyalty. When the heir and the lover are distinct from one another, or, as in *The Bride*, when the heir cannot be restored, romance unleashes the waywardness of feminine desire. Scott notes that no "fiend can suggest more desperate counsels, than those adopted under the guidance of our own violent and unresisted passions" (XIII: 292). His claim applies equally to Lucy and to Edgar, but, as in the battles for the British succession, it is on feminine fidelity that the domestic resolution of romance depends. And it is Lucy's fidelity that wavers.

Easily coopted into rebellion and tainted by female passion, romance interferes with rather than forwards Scott's legitimate ends. Romance and legitimacy are untrustworthy, their ambivalence registered in the violent contests between chivalric legend and gothic magic, Alice's bardic poetry and Lucy's excessive reading. It is in this novel that Scott's history looks most like the necessity Lukács ascribed to it, its unstoppable momentum sweeping even opposition to its aid.[52] History triumphs in the feminized privacy of the bridal chamber. "Flooded with blood," overseen by a Lucy unable to speak except in "gibbers," this grotesque and violent conclusion realizes all the welling fears of Scott's earlier novels, and proves to Hazlitt that Scott envisions the worst of legitimacy as well as he can himself (XIV: 353–4). As Hazlitt notes sarcastically, "We want a Burke" to give monarchy and aristocracy "a legitimate turn at present," for Scott cannot do it. "Poor Sir Walter!," Hazlitt adds, "the times are changed indeed."[53]

Everything takes place in *The Bride of Lammermoor* as if, on his returning to familiar plots and themes, Scott's former unease about gender and nature, his ambivalence toward the domestic sphere, and his sense of the fragility within romance have become, even in his brief absence from the genre, points of irretrievable and violent fragmentation. Scott revisits the site of the earlier impasse between history and progress, romance and legitimacy, only to find legitimacy, romance, and history alike disappearing into violence and excess. John Farrell remarks that *The Bride*'s tragedy is less a departure from Scott's earlier romance plots than the fulfillment of them.[54] But what Farrell views as a pessimistic allegory of "the dilemma of the moderate" in times of revolution can also be seen as despair about the still-seductive romance of restoration and legitimacy. The novel demonstrates legitimacy's inadequacy to provide an ideological basis for social order, and the inability of inheritance to do other than contribute to the usurpation, chaos, and violence the legitimate heir deplores. The novel is tragic precisely because Scott for the first time allows the battle of legitimacy and romance with modernity and history to follow out the logic established in *Guy Mannering*, and permits the historicity of his characters to assert itself. Scott's novel marks out no political middle. Rather, it fully and painfully delineates the impossible tasks of Burkean conservatism confronted by a history dominated by liberalism and "the moneyed interest."

ILLEGITIMATE TRANSFORMATIONS: DISGUISE, POLITICS, GENERIC CHANGE

Despair, however, is not pessimism. Pessimism gazes down the gentle slope of an ever-more imperfect future. In contrast, despair – like *The Bride of Lammermoor* itself – is extreme, absolute, and therefore potentially dialectical. James Chandler argues that the novel never "abandons the picture of a world where agents engage in a struggle for representation," including the powers of speech and written and printed political comment.[55] Demonstration of Scott's enduring commitment comes even as the novel registers the inescapable "issue of class disharmony in Britain," which Ravenswood fails to remedy in his debates with Ashton.[56] Ravenswood's speeches recapitulate the novel's framing assertion that merit will triumph in the field of aesthetic production – that is, Scott's self-referential performance of literary superiority. If Scott holds onto literary legitimacy once all hope of political legitimacy is gone, his tenacity at the end of his reading of political history makes the romance-legitimacy pairing useful once again. I date Scott's harnessing of the legitimist potential of literary production later than Chandler does: five years after publication of *The Bride*, *St. Ronan's Well* enacts this new legitimacy's emergence from the coffin of the romance of restoration. However one dates its fruition, however, it is clear that, in pronouncing the death of legitimacy and the triumph of modernity, and in allowing his genre of national mythmaking to explode in cathartic violence, Scott dynamically restarts his search for a theoretical ground on which to unite the Protestant "nation" of Great Britain. *The Bride of Lammermoor*, with its eruptions of fire, water, blood, and feminine desire, brings about a crisis in literary history, in the literary politics of gender, and in the ideology of legitimacy.

As Hazlitt's half-serious sympathy for Scott demonstrates, Scott's turn from the triumphant romance of 1816 to the romance-gone-tragedy of 1819, and finally to a renovated, supply-side romance after *The Bride*, does not take place in a vacuum. It responds to and helps shape a shift in the ongoing legitimation debate, and is responded to in turn. The terms of the debate had long been set by neoconservatives of essentially Whiggish political economic views, whose sentimental version of legitimate authority, proposed by Burke and variously promoted by Ann Radcliffe, Hannah More, the *Quarterly* and *Anti-Jacobin Reviews*, and Scott, among others, had supplied the debate with its preferred genres (sentimental and gothic romance) and favourite locations (the landed estate, the law courts – with all actions taking place off-stage – and, most popular of all, the home). The debate's radical participants, including Paine, Hazlitt, and Wollstonecraft, had attacked legitimacy primarily by denying the naturalness and justice of what conservatives naturalized. But the gendered terms and generic forms of the debate most often remained in place.

Hazlitt, for example, represented Hanoverian rule and the wars with America and France as effects of a legitimist political romance inaugurated by George III, who

has been constantly mounted on a great War-horse [as the] . . . eyes of all his faithful subjects have been fixed on the career of the Sovereign . . . all hearts anxious for the safety of his person and government. Our pens and our swords have been drawn alike in their defence . . . His Majesty has indeed contrived to keep alive the greatest public interest ever known, by his determined manner of riding his hobby for half a century together, with the aristocracy – the democracy – the clergy – the landed and monied interest – and the rabble, in full cry after him! and at the end of his career, most happily and unexpectedly succeeded – amidst empires lost and won – kingdoms overturned and created – and the destruction of an incredible number of lives – in restoring the divine right of Kings, – and thus preventing any further abuse of the example which seated his family on the throne![57]

Hostilely reviewing Burney's *The Wanderer* as a tame court fiction, Hazlitt argues that the king's master-fiction has engrossed all the national energy once expended on comedy and romance. Thus romance, whether appearing in hobbyhorsical metrical form in Robert Southey's "hobbling illegitimate verse" or in Burney's anxiously traditionalist romances, drew off all disruptive energies.[58] But Hazlitt's criticism indicts not only the writers of Britain, but also all classes and political parties: "the rabble" and "democracy," those who see a mob and those who see a people, have alike paid their subscriptions to the royal romance. Most of all, in Hazlitt's view, women pay – by fulfilling its demands too well, submitting, like Burney, to be confined by an artificial and foolish agglomeration of beliefs.

It may be that the king's madness and impending death, or that Peterloo blood, inescapably made manifest the corruption, violence, and self-interest lurking in British government. Whatever the reason, a major shift in the discourse on legitimacy becomes apparent in 1819 and 1820, in the writings of Hazlitt and Scott. Hazlitt's urbane irony at the expense of national fictions turns to bitter satire. Heralding *The Bride of Lammermoor*'s portrait of Ailsie Gourlay, he grotesquely exaggerates the affective and familial arguments of the Burkean camp to expose an underside of corruption and coercion; as Hazlitt puts it, to take "a pretty peep behind 'the dark blanket' of Legitimacy."[59] By working within the established genres of legitimacy – the sentimental romance of Burke, the restoration romances of Scott – Hazlitt radicalizes the debate, revealing "monstrous" corruption inside private families and the public life of

Britain. This corruption, as in Scott and Burke, centres on failures of femininity. Hazlitt begins to personify "Legitimacy," discussing "her" in ironic versions of domestic vignettes whose originals look very much like the conclusions to Scott's early prose romances, or Burke's domestic interiors:

> We thank Mr. Macirone for having introduced us once more to the old lady of that name ["Legitimacy"] in her dressing-room. What a tissue of patches and of paint! What a quantity of wrinkles and of proud flesh! What a collection of sickly perfumes and slow poisons, with her love-powders and the assassin's knife placed side by side! . . . What an old hypocritical hag it is! What a vile, canting, mumbling, mischievous witch! "Pah! and smells so." The very wind that kisses all it meets, stops the nose at her . . . Yet this is the heroine of all heroines.[60]

Hazlitt levels the anti-chivalric, anti-sentimental "lady's dressing-room" tradition at Burke's "heroine of heroines," the "Legitimacy" embodied in such figures as Sophia of Hanover and Marie Antoinette. Burke had rigorously separated these "virtuous" women from bad ones, dividing English from French women, and prostitutes from the starry French queen and dependable German princess. Scott had pressed even the ancient desires of peasant women into legitimacy's service, denying the sentimental and gothic doubleness of Burke's political romance. But Hazlitt, pressing the weakness within Burke's rigidly dualistic account of gender convention, tears down the walls separating romance from gothic history. He re-employs Burke's bugbear, the revolutionary witch, hag, or prostitute, to symbolize Burke's own legitimist ideology.

Noticeable in Hazlitt's anti-legitimist tracts is a misogyny that is intense beyond its instrumental purpose. For Hazlitt's "Legitimacy," unlike Burke's revolutionary women, does not act alone. Legitimacy can exist only when celebrated as a "heroine" by poets and novelists: Hazlitt's target is not the chimera "herself," but her powerful literary promoters. Absolutism, an "old bawd masked," seduces writers to "shew . . . their gallantry," becoming harmful only in reproduction. Once absolutism has "pulled off her mask of Legitimacy,"

> and shewed herself "the same, that is, that was, and is to be," . . . the poets, either charmed with the paint and patches of the hag, or with her gold and trinkets, put a grave face upon the matter, make it . . . a match for life – *for better or worse*, stick to their filthy bargain, go to bed, and by lying quiet and keeping close, would fain persuade the people out of doors that all is well, while they are fumbling at the regeneration of mankind out of an old rotten carcase.[61]

The defenders of legitimacy, including Scott, become pimps of corrupt power, and legitimist romance a gilded shelter for their pandering. Yet Hazlitt directs his satire at women and legitimacy more than at the men who reproduce their connection. He endows his personified "Legit-imacy" with all the appetites of Burke's *citoyenne*-hags and all the desires that Scott half-denies and half-acknowledges in Meg Merrilies, and concedes to Ailsie Gourlay. In this way Hazlitt identifies an incongruous lust for domination at the heart of legitimate domesticity. The hag-heroine Absolutism, by means of her "love-powders," and Scott, with his "charms and philtres," reproduce a "brood of hornbooks and catechisms" and texts of "bastard philosophy."[62] But in a gender-inversion that heralds Scott's role-reversals in *The Bride*, it is Scott himself who gives birth to "the most barefaced of all impostures, this ideot sophism, this poor, pettifogging pretext of arbitary power, this bastard interpretation of divine right – Legitimacy," with romance as his midwife.[63] The legitimists "ingraft . . . the principles of the house of Stuart on the illustrious stock of the House of Brunswick": the Hanover-ian bastard reinvents himself as a legitimate heir, but legitimacy itself, after 1688, is already thoroughly discredited.[64] Hazlitt's protest is founded on his desire to reorder political history. Thus he insists that gender convention be strictly patrolled.

Like Wollstonecraft, who argued that feminine attempts to exercise covert, manipulative power over economic and political events stem from the disenfranchisement of women, Hazlitt feminizes illegitimate power. But to Hazlitt, as to Scott, female political activity is *intrinsically* illegitimate. It points to the impossibility of neoconservative Whig attempts to base social order on government within families.[65] Scott's unease at this impasse received a boost from an added element in the legitimacy debates of 1819 and 1820: the return of Caroline, Princess of Wales, from years of European exile. The attempts of the Prince of Wales, and then of the newly succeeded George IV, to divorce his wife brought Caroline's chastity and her daughter's paternity under open scrutiny. Although Caroline's behaviour had been investigated before, the press reports of 1819 and 1820 introduced a grotesque literalness into the ongoing legitimacy debates.[66] In the Commons and the press, with tactics similar to those Burke's opponents had used to discredit Marie Antoinette thirty years before, Caroline was accused of "unnatural" sexuality and motherhood. Scott recalled in 1821 that the London mob followed Caroline through the streets with cries of "*Shame, Shame, Home, Home.*"[67] He privately wrote at length of Caroline's "abandoned and beastly" conduct. Though Scott limited his public comment to the general discussions of legitimacy in the novels, Hazlitt publicly connected Scott's turn to gender-inverting tragedy, his shaken respect for legitimacy, and the Caroline affair.[68] The affair disturbed Scott from the start, and he believed that "the sound well judging and well principled body of the people" were "much shocked" as well.[69] Above all, however, Scott lamented that "there are so many disaffected persons who will take advantage of these shameful investigations to throw dirt on the King and royal family." His conclusion to his thinking about Caroline is revealingly, and despairingly, Burkean: the "general Honour and welfare of the country," he decided, "cannot consistently admit of her holding in her hands its public & national honour by bearing the character of Q[ueen]."[70]

Scott was troubled by the implications of the Caroline affair for the Hanoverian royal family – whose history of ideological reliance on the chastity of German princesses left the monarchy in a particularly shaky position. More crucially, he feared for a social order broadly based on legitimacy and domestic life. Caroline's acts reflected badly on Britain, Scott argued, largely because they were mirrored in the generally passionate and ambitious conduct of British women. He ironically observed that Caroline's battles with her husband had catalyzed the domestic revolt of Whig wives:

> while so much factious interest in the Queens innocence is expressd no lady in London seems to have expressd the usual confidence in it by paying her the usual civilities of a visit – Are Whig husbands so void of influence over their ladies.[71]

Scott's censure of Whig women twists curiously from asserting their care for propriety to condemning their domestic rebellion and personal ambition. It audibly echoes his portrait of the Whig Lady Ashton, that domestic plotter, rebel, and rigid subscriber to forms, whose public appearance of propriety included insistence on her husband's authority and her own submission. In recasting Lady Ashton as a representative of all Whig women, Scott casts suspicion on the sincerity of Whig loyalty to the Hanoverian royal family and on the domestic order of a Whig-dominated England. Legitimacy topples under the combined weight of a Whiggish, and therefore illegitimate, domestic history.

The grotesque turn in the legitimacy debates took place as the gender-assumptions and gender-unease of legitimism exploded to the charge of Caroline's disgrace. Together with Hazlitt's misogynous personifications of legitimacy, the turn called Scott's own half-suppressed misogyny into the open, as his unguarded reference to "the Bedlam Bitch of a Queen" makes clear.[72] Even more than his portraits of aristocratic women, his female peasants, bearers of the heir's legitimacy, began to wear an overtly double face. What was in Scott's treatment of Meg Merrilies only an instability carefully controlled becomes in Alice Grey and Ailsie Gourlay an explicit doubling, and perhaps an inter-changeability, of romantic loyalty with gothic disruption. Ailsie looks and behaves like Hazlitt's personified Legitimacy, but whereas Hazlitt insists that Scott composes "philtres to our love of legitimacy," Ailsie herself has long "composed philtres" meant to disrupt it (Scott, *Bride* xiv: 315). In allowing desire to subvert fidelity in *The Bride of Lammermoor*, Scott follows Hazlitt in acknowledging the power of real history, and especially undomestic desire and gender ambiguity, to disrupt his ro-mance conclusions and ideology of order. In *The Bride*, as in Hazlitt's satire of Scott's earlier legitimist romances, romance is self-subverting, perpetually producing the historical illegitimacy Scott tries to shut out. The genre's inclusions intensify rather than end the novel's history of violence and corruption.

Crisis as purgation: Scott does away with his old story, legitimate romance, in a welter of blood and storm. A tragic bravado is apparent in the excess of its effacement. After *The Bride of Lammermoor*, it seems, legitimacy is not merely unachievable: its path can no longer be marked at all. As the shared myth of a nation's aristocracy, the romance of restoration has vanished into history's sands to be smothered with Edgar Ravenswood. As the animus and reflection of domestic life, romance has gone violently mad with Lucy Ashton, disrupted forever by the passions Scott, like other legitimists, had earlier sought to banish. The devastating explosion of the legitimate family, in the "real history" of George IV's household and the symbolic household of Lammermoor Castle, jolts Scott's attachment to legitimacy clear of the symbolically intertwining fields of politics and domesticity. As Chandler puts it, the novel simultaneously enacts a "gruesome materialist critique of subjec-tivity *and* . . . acknowledgment of the material power of representation in the construction of the contexts of action: something like Marx's notion about making one's history but not just as one pleases."[73] Scott has already begun his soft landing in the field of cultural production, even before the explosion is complete. It is there, though only there, that history – and legitimacy – can be made.[74]

BASTARD ROMANCE: *ST. RONAN'S WELL*

In 1829, Scott began revisiting his career in a series of prefaces to the "Magnum Opus" edition of his novels. Despite the tragedy and sterility of *The Bride of Lammermoor*'s conclusion, he looked back on the 1820s to remember, and celebrate, a series of rebirths. Laying the groundwork for the canonizing moves of the 1827 *Quarterly Review* essay with which I began – writing in identical terms to those used in that essay – Scott re-introduced *St. Ronan's Well* (1824) as a new generic beginning for the "Author of Waverley":

> The novel . . . is upon a plan different from any other that the Author has ever written, although it is perhaps the most legitimate which relates to this kind of light literature.
>
> It is intended, in a word – *celebrare domestica facta* – to give an imitation of the shifting manners of our own time, and paint scenes, the originals of which are daily passing round us, so that a minute's observation may compare the copies with the originals. It must be confessed that this style of composition was adopted by the author . . . from the tempting circumstance of its offering some novelty in his compositions, and avoiding worn-out characters and positions.[75]

Scott revisits his earlier construction of his works, in his 1815 *Quarterly* essay on Austen's *Emma*, as the legitimate romance heirs and successors to Austen, whom he casts as his outgrown and superseded mother.[76] As a description of the novel's plotting, however, Scott's use of "legitimate" and his claim to have "domestic events" to "celebrate" can only be ironic, for once again, in *St. Ronan's Well* as in *The Bride*, domestic restoration ends in violence. Although the deaths of characters are treated less graphically in the later work, the death of an ideology is represented more explicitly. Illegitimacy runs deeper than in *The Bride*: it is more pervasive and more literal. The illegitimacy that impels tragedy in *St. Ronan's Well* is not merely the subversion of what Scott represents as natural laws of primogeniture and inheritance, as in the Ashton assumption of the Ravenswood estate. Instead it appears as an ever-widening circle of domestic crime and an endless reduplication of literal bastardy. On the level of form, however, there is no irony in Scott's self-legitimating claim for the novel. The metaphor of naturalistic painting he evokes in the Magnum Opus introduction grounds the "celebration" of domestic life not on the virtue of the subject, but on the exactness of Scott's own delineation of his "originals," a word by which his audience should also understand grotesques.[77] Scott's rhetoric of novelty celebrates domestic events for marking "the Author's" turn away from an old and "worn-out" genre. In *St. Ronan's Well*, for the first time, Scott defamiliarizes legitimacy, re-employing it not as a familial and historical trait, but as a literary-evaluative criterion.

Although it is in prefacing *St. Ronan's Well* that Scott first declares himself canonical in broadly accepted terms, no critic writing later than 1827 has offered an extended reading of the novel. Fiona Robertson, whose discussion is the most detailed to date, notes that Scott's "travesties" of sentimental and gothic romance plots in *St. Ronan's Well* mark Scott not as an authoritative transformer of feminine romance tradition, but rather as a borrower from the maternal tradition he names – listing writers from Charlotte Smith to Susan Ferrier – and claims to supersede. In reading Scott as the agent of a historicized, masculine renovation of romance, Robertson remarks, literary history is "remarkably responsive" to Scott's own self-consciously masculine and canon-forming approach to his own novels.[78] Robertson's opposition of romance to history is more accurate to the early works, her emphasis, than to later novels such as *St. Ronan's Well*, and she leaves Scott's turn from restoration to despair undiscussed. Yet even in these later works, in concluding by rejecting his romances of legitimist restoration in a way that banishes their continuity and sympathy with history, Scott casts off his earlier form of romance not in favour of public national history, but rather of a personal literary history that is, as the *Quarterly Review* would point out, a synecdoche for a broadly national literary progress. What is most important in this revisioning of romance is Scott's self-placement at the pinnacle of progress: his embodiment of the end of history for progressives dissatisfied with political affairs; and his simultaneous and continuing commitment to tradition-centred notions of authority embodied in an inheritance-based literary canon. Scott is committed, that is, both to an evolutionary notion of history and to legitimacy. Arguing that Scott re-masculinizes a feminized genre, Ferris and Duncan provide the necessary counterpoint to Robertson's account of Scott and literary history. Whereas Robertson would have readers reject Scott's own literary-historical myth, Duncan in particular argues that Scott's self-mythologizing is at the heart of his career's significance. When Scott replaced his romances of legitimacy with a romance of Authorship, he masculinized his genre by making himself a "public man," offering a challenge to romanticized national history and its domestic ends.

If Scott is to supersede Austen's and Burke's versions of romance successfully, the national romances of the recent literary past, including his own, must be seen to fail. Yet I have been arguing throughout this chapter that what fails, in Scott's terms, is legitimacy first, romance second and in consequence. I have also suggested that romance fails less as a feminized genre, gender-identified in its production, as Duncan suggests, than as a *feminine* one, homologically defined by its gendered ideological content. Scott's early reading of political historiography bound romance to an ideology placing women in symbolically crucial roles, so that the genre remained stubbornly dependent on an impossibly naturalized and generalized version of femininity and feminine desire throughout Scott's earliest, best attempts at its renewal. What he finally masculinized was not romance *per se*, but his own self-conscious version of it. And he rewrote the genre not by revising its content, but by transforming his own place in relation to it – his unique version of Clifford Siskin's Romantic individualist "lyric turn."[79] The failure of romance in Scott's late novels is not, therefore, the consequence of "Tory pessimism." Rather, it is a failure with a purpose, a controlled collapse of romance engineered in order to build the new genre that will supersede it. Scott's new romance is a liberal genre, reconciling High Church Tories with progressive Whigs in his tradition-centred but markedly progressive reading of history.

Despite celebrating his new beginnings in the Preface to *St. Ronan's Well*, Scott nevertheless revisits the range of intertexts, "worn out characters and positions" threaded through the romance of legitimacy. *St. Ronan's Well* constitutes his final rewriting of the plot of *Guy Mannering*, with its recursive movements of return, rediscovery, and domestic renewal. From the outset, however, Scott's pun on the Latin *domestica* frames his recycling by collapsing the homeland (the meaning of the Horatian passage Scott quotes) with the home (where Scott locates the "domestic" novelists on the list of literary ancestors he enumerates in the Preface). Scott's critical folding of national history into home life in the Preface reproduces a similar reduction in the plot of the novel: unlike Edgar Ravenswood, who loses his lands to his father's Whig-Presbyterian enemy in time of rebellion, or Harry Bertram, who struggles to prove the relevance of his land claim in a fast-commercializing world, Francis Tyrrel, the hero of *St. Ronan's*, fights his legitimist battles within the privacy of the family. The domestic conclusion that resolved the earlier novels is in place at the start, but it contributes to rather than remedies the heir's dispossession.

Just as Scott limits history to family life, the family, in turn, is trapped in an ongoing history of illegitimacy that is inextricable, and almost indistinguishable, from legitimate descent. Francis Martigny Tyrrel, the legitimate heir of the earl of Etherington, has a younger half-brother who has been given the same first name despite his illegitimacy. A rake in youth and a politician in maturity, the father of the two Francises, Lord Etherington, has married twice to suit his two characters, but without waiting for his first wife to die before finding a second. His dilemma is this: to conceal his bigamy, he must illegitimate one of his sons, either of whom might successfully sue for the right to inherit the Etherington title, publicly disgracing his father in the process. As the heir's namesake, Francis Valentine Bulmer Tyrrel, called Valentine, easily usurps the family lands and title, while his physical resemblance to the real heir allows him to intrude chaotically into his elder brother's romantic and financial affairs. Valentine points out the slipperiness of legitimacy as he quotes a dispute in which, on his mother's " 'borrowing from the vulgar two emphatic words' " with which to accuse her husband, his father responds " 'that if there *was* a whore and bastard connected with his house, it was herself and her brat' " (xxxiv: 98). Whichever son Etherington chooses, the title will be tainted. From having once worked, however unstably, to resolve the problems history posed to natural law, family affections in *St. Ronan's Well* only proliferate illegitimacy.

There is something very arbitrary about legitimacy in *St. Ronan's Well*. In this late novel, Scott interprets primogeniture, earlier represented as a natural and irresistible right of the firstborn son, as a set of corrupt choices that face an "unnatural" aristocratic father. Valentine explains that his father's first marriage, to " 'a certain beautiful orphan, Marie de Martigny,' " was performed in France by a Catholic priest, and therefore debarred from legal status in England. Its illegality was confirmed by Etherington's subsequent marriage, " 'in the face of the church,' " to the English aristocrat "Ann Bulmer of Bulmer-hall" (xxxiv: 97). Yet Francis produces documents signed by the Church of England chaplain in Paris, proving that his own mother was herself a Huguenot countess and that her marriage to Etherington was Protestant and therefore legally binding (xxxiv: 166). Two identical heirs make two equivalent claims – one apparently Catholic and illegitimate, yet legal; one evidently legal and Protestant, yet the product of bigamy. Etherington, unable to choose, banishes both sons to Scotland. He cautions Valentine, as his apparently legitimate heir, against " 'the folly and iniquity of private marriages,' " warning that in Scotland " 'the matrimonial noose often lies hid under flowers, and that folks find it twitched round their neck when they least expect such a cravat' " (xxxiv: 101). Yet it is the father's sound if coarse advice, aimed at preserving his title's legitimacy, that begins the reproduction of bigamy – and the production of the new illegitimacy of incest – in his sons' generation.

Valentine puts his information to unintended and illegal use. Hoping to benefit from a warning he alone has received and to profit by his father's anger, he urges Francis to imitate the paternal example and marry Clara Mowbray, daughter of a decrepit Scottish landlord, in a secret ceremony. Although Francis and Clara become engaged, the tragic logic of the family intervenes. When Etherington learns that a family will leaves "a large and fair estate . . . to the eldest son and heir of the Earl of Etherington" on condition of marriage to a Mowbray, he orders Valentine to court Clara himself (xxxiv: 112). By activating the will, marriage to Clara will mark her husband as the eldest son and legitimate heir of Etherington. From having been the source of illegitimation through the father's displeasure, Clara becomes the fountain of legitimacy. The Etherington heir's position now depends not only on the validity of the marriage that produced him, but also on the legality of the marriage he himself will make. Ironically, illegitimacy and bigamy repeat themselves in the second generation precisely because of Clara's changed, legitimated position, and precisely under the direction, as Etherington puts it, of "the hand of nature" (xxxiv: 212). Pretending to be Francis and working under the covers of darkness, a mask, and the name of "Francis Tyrrel," Valentine marries Clara, although " 'full confidence and intimacy' " have long since been " 'established' " between Clara and Francis (xxxiv: 105). Like Etherington himself, the origin of the Tyrrels' legitimacy, the new fount of Tyrrel legitimacy is polluted by bigamy, now underscored by incest: Clara becomes the shared bride of twin sons of a bigamous father. The ease with which she is deceived enhances the reader's sense – already the father's guiding theory – that there is little to choose between the heir and his bastard brother.

But illegitimacy, as *St. Ronan's Well* presents it, does not originate only with patriarchs. The problem lies in the institution of legitimacy itself. This ideology presumes that only an impossibly wise child knows who his father is, so that the sole proof of birth rests on the mother and necessitates either indisputable "virtue" or (too frequently, where sensibility is an inadequate or ambiguous sign) confinement. Taken together, Scott's portraits of Marie Martigny, Ann Bulmer, and especially Clara Mowbray highlight what Scott earlier, in deploring the rebellious and falsely modest conduct of British women during the Caroline affair, and in illustrating the intrusions of history into the private natures of his earlier female characters, declares a serious threat to legitimacy. Martigny's willingness to marry clandestinely, Bulmer's disregard for bigamy, and in particular Clara's equal ease with Valentine and Francis, disrupt the "natural" chastity and virtue of the feminine character on which legitimist ideology rests.

Scott invariably linked the question of legitimacy with romance. Clara's problems, and the problems she poses to orderly primogeniture, result from her firm association with the genre. Educated entirely "at her own hand," she, like Lucy Ashton, reads nothing beyond "a library full of old romances," which shape her "wild," "lively," and "natural" character (XXXIII: 127; XXXIV: 103). She meets Francis when, imitating a long line of romance heroines and female quixotes, she "dresse[s] . . . herself and her companion like country wenches" to roam freely in the woods. In Scott's novel, tellingly, the masquerade only creates a dangerous class mistake, which damages the legitimist romance ideals of visible birthright and peasant loyalty: a "'country fellow . . . saw not the nobility of blood through her disguise, and accosted the daughter of a hundred sires as he would have done a ewe-milker'" (XXXIV: 104). Rescued by Francis, Clara trades an ancient romance plot for the newer, sentimental genre. Valentine remarks ironically that she thereafter finds it "'safer to roam in the woods with an escort than alone,'" making Francis "'her constant companion'"(XXXIV: 104–5). As the novel begins, eight years after Valentine's masked marriage, Clara has developed a "shade of insanity, which deranged, though it had not destroyed, her powers of judgment" (XXXIII: 162). Her condition recalls the beginnings of Lucy's, and it similarly enacts what late-eighteenth-century critics supposed to be the "unspeakably perverting and inflammatory" effects of popular sentimental romance on female minds and sensibility.[80]

There is a great deal that remains "unspeakable" about Clara, and especially about her sexuality. Near the end of the novel, when Clara's brother asks if her engagement to Francis was consummated before her marriage to Valentine, he cannot name "bigamy" or "incest":

There are strange reports going below. By Heaven! they are enough to disturb the ashes of the dead! Were I to mention them, I should expect our poor mother to enter the room. Clara Mowbray, can you guess what I mean? . . . By Heaven! I am ashamed – I am even *afraid* to express my own meaning!

Clara herself can barely answer: "with the utmost exertion, yet in a faltering voice . . . she was able to utter the monosyllable, '*No!*'" (XXXIV:

286). Her "no" simultaneously denies the sexual involvement with Francis that makes her marriage to Valentine legal incest, and marks her inability to discuss it. Gordon notes that Scott excised a more explicit account of Clara's affair with Francis on the plea of his printer James Ballantyne, while leaving its psychological consequences intact: in Gordon's view, Scott yielded to an ill-timed persuasion. Yet contemporary works, such as Byron's *Manfred* (1817), suggest links between suspense-creating genres, wayward sexuality, and horrors too great for speech.[81] Scott brings these together as the effects of romance on Clara's feminine character and therefore on legitimist ideology.

Such a triangle as Clara's cannot provide the romance of Francis's dispossession with an orderly conclusion, and indeed no such domestic conclusion results. An acquaintance's chance remark about the Tyrrels, that " 'The family seem addicted to irregular matrimony,' " generalizes the impossibility of establishing domestic order beyond the tangles of the Etherington estate (xxxiv: 131). The Tyrrel family and the institution of the family itself, at least as it is represented in romance and the romantic ideology of Burkean primogeniture, are equally "addicted" to illegitimacy. The "unseemly conjunction of the legitimate and illegitimate" in the Tyrrel succession symbolizes the unattainability of a legitimate British succession – and perhaps of legitimate inheritance in Britain (xxxiv: 98). It is because of this gendered impossibility that Scott allows romance to fail in the prehistory of his plot. Yet even romance's failure, an ideological tool that undoes the ends Scott's earlier versions of the genre uphold, is an indication of generic power. In *St. Ronan's Well*, Scott writes not failed romance, but bastard romance: his self-conscious rendering of that failure, that gothic inversion of legitimacy most feared by Burke and most invoked by Wollstonecraft. In this new genre, the romance of restoration collapses, as in *The Bride of Lammermoor*, because of its untrustworthy associations with women, passion, and the household. At the same time, however, because it produces and proliferates bastardy, romance demands new things of the novelist and radically transforms his role. As a response to national political history, *St. Ronan's* insists, the romance of legitimacy and its domestic conclusion must be done away with altogether. In their place Scott tells a story with a new conclusion that confirms "the Author's" power and native worth. Scott never rejects legitimacy, that is, but reinvents it. He abandons his romance of legitimacy to write legitimate romance.

LEGITIMATE ROMANCE IN THE LIBERAL ECONOMY:
ST. RONAN'S WELL, ROMANTICISM, AND AFTER

Histories of bigamy, incest, usurpation, and madness form the secrets that Clara cannot and Francis will not speak, and make unrealizable the heir's restoration at the end of *St. Ronan's Well*. These hidden tales, the gothic romance narratives that Robertson highlights, form its emotional centre and impel the acts of its major characters: the novel begins, soon after the death of Lord Etherington, as the mature Francis returns to St. Ronan's to seek meetings with Valentine and Clara. The engrossing centrality to the novel of the Etherington family's tangled gothic narratives makes it easy to forget that, in *St. Ronan's*, Scott places history, and the failure of romance that accompanies it, firmly in the past. He detaches both from the present, which they have produced but can no longer continue to shape. The historical disruptions of primogeniture that have shaped Francis's present, as well as the romance plotting of restoration they disrupt, take place in the far-off prehistory of the novel's present events. History and romance appear in Scott's "little drama of modern life" only as they are remembered and recounted in letters from Valentine and in Francis's conversation (XXXIII: iv). Although the end of the novel sees Francis's legitimacy confirmed, his assumption of his place as earl of Etherington has long since been rendered ideologically impossible by history's gothic disruption of the romance of legitimacy, and by Francis's consequent detachment from both.

As if to emphasize the impossibility of returning into any revered order or legitimate past, the confirmation of Francis's inheritance at the end of *St. Ronan's* is neither legal nor magical, but, like the end of *The Bride of Lammermoor*, jarringly violent. Francis's legitimation is contingent on Clara's death, the end of her convulsive struggle with the emotional horror of incest in scenes that recall the death of Lucy Ashton. Soon after, reprising the challenge issued by Sholto Ashton at the end of *The Bride*, John Mowbray shoots Valentine Bulmer in revenge for his sister's seduction and madness. When news of the duel reaches Francis as he sits by Clara's deathbed, he speaks the last words spoken in the novel: "'You bring tidings of death to the house of death . . . and there is nothing in this world left that I should live for!'" (XXXIV: 349). The "house of death" literally designates the inn at St. Ronan's, where Clara's body lies after her struggle. But Francis's speech is symbolic as well as literal, for the House of Etherington, with the family it stands for, is equally a "house of death." Its tangled relations produce the deaths of

Valentine, its titular head, and of Clara, wife of the titular earl and lover of the earl in law.

On such symbolic rejections of the family Scott's new ideological structure is founded, for Francis embraces a new relation to the family precisely in rejecting it. Although his last words are bitter, they are also self-consciously wise: echoing biblical proscription of the "house of mirth," Francis enters the "house of mourning," declaring his self-reliant independence of the worldly ties the wisdom books call "vanity."[82] The double valence of Francis's conversion shades even the grammar of his speech, which at once embodies despair and stoical morality. In a complex play on the ambiguous resemblance between present subjunctive and future indicative verb forms, Francis allows his "should" to be read in the subjunctive mood, as a statement of contingency, with the unlikely prospect of his choosing to live as the posited condition on which the contingency depends. Alternatively, and with equal justice, the verb may be read indicatively, as a moral pronouncement on Francis's requirements for his future life. Although neither Francis nor Scott promotes one interpretation over the other – the chapter ends with Francis's speech – the subsequent, concluding chapter of the novel suggests that despair and loss within families are necessary conditions for a new kind of legitimacy made possible by the failure of the family and the sentimental romances and romances of legitimacy that celebrate domestic cohesion. Having lost both his love and his desire for revenge, Francis is a man without ties: a free agent rather than a family man. When Valentine's death frees his title and the right to his lands, Francis occupies neither. Instead he goes into the world as an itinerant poet and painter, dependent for a living on cultural production. Few readers of *The Bride of Lammermoor* can be surprised by the collapse of primogeniture in this conclusion, but the hero's artistic profession and his self-sufficient survival are new. They mark the beginning of an explicitly modern kind of romance, in which history is over, primogeniture irrelevant, and legitimacy relocated in aesthetic production and consumption.

For Scott to proceed with his self-reflexive renovation of the romance genre, turning Francis's despair and the family's collapse into sources of a new legitimacy, modernity must first lose the exclusive ties to "trade" and the end of aristocracy that Scott established in his early novels and *The Bride of Lammermoor*. At first, Scott's modernity in *St. Ronan's Well* seems to resemble the bureaucratic and legalized world he portrays in earlier works, at least outside the space of his own magical conclusions: if history fails to conclude with the heir's restoration at the end of the novel, so too does modernity refuse Francis his property. Scott's chief representative of commerce and the commercialized present in the novel is Meg Dods, in her own words " 'baith land*lord* and land*leddy*' " of the inn at St. Ronan's (xxxiii: 41). Her inn occupies the "deserted mansion" of the Mowbrays, who, in search of "a more pleasant and commodious" as well as a cheaper house, have auctioned their lands to Dods's prosperous publican father (xxxiii: 11). The Dods family's business success literally displaces the authority of ancient landed wealth: Dods is, in Scott's terms, a "considerable heiress" to aristocratic privilege bought and assumed by her parents, and as such a representative of history's bastardizing force (xxxiii: 12). Yet despite her family position at the height of commercial progress, Meg Dods, like the earlier Meg Merrilies, is also the novel's keeper of feudal loyalty. Even as she occupies the Mowbrays' lost estate, she resembles Merrilies in knowing everything about her old landlord's lineage and in lamenting its increasing weakness, which culminates in the present generation and deprives the family of power. " 'It's a shame o' the young Laird, to let his auld patrimony gang the gate it's like to gang, and my heart is sair to see't,' " Dods remarks, adding that John Mowbray's father has " 'No other son . . . and there's e'en eneugh, unless he could have left a better ane' " (xxxiii: 42–3).

In short, Dods's loyalties, like those of Lucy Ashton, are divided, but unlike Lucy she feels no conflict in their division. Legitimacy and feudal ties are easily reconciled with commerce and its displacement of aristocracy, in Dods's mind and in the novel as well. Scott brings the ancient and modern together in a new kind of "ancient" lore and "family honour," a species of wisdom newly made antique, of which Dods is the repository. Precisely because of Dods's paradoxical blend of commercial acumen and nostalgia for the landlord class, the female retainer's part in *St. Ronan's* marks Scott's modernized retelling of the cooperation of female peasant wisdom with legitimacy, and his rewriting of the threat posed to aristocracy by commercial activity – both classic narratives now ironically and comically deprived of power. Like Meg Merrilies, Dods frightens her neighbours with nostalgic rants, but her speeches, emptied of magic and the accumulated weight of oral history, represent nothing more occult than nostalgia for an earlier stage of the trade in drink and lodgings and a wish to revert from contemporary commerce to an older economic history.

Dods sees herself as "a landlady of the olden world, even after the nineteenth century had commenced" (XXXIII: 14). She is elegiac over Mowbray honour in part because of its connection to her own present standing as a businesswoman. When John Mowbray himself enters the lodgings trade, investing in a large new resort hotel nearby, Dods remarks, " 'I might shut up house . . . if it was the thing I lived by – me, that has seen a' our gentlefolk bairns, and gien them snaps and sugar-biscuit maist of them wi' my ain hand!' " Yet Scott's footnote to Dods's complaint adds commercial skill to her feudal indignation, for "although her inn had decayed in custom, her land" – the land bought from the improvident Mowbrays – "had risen in value in a degree which more than compensated the balance on the wrong side of her books" precisely because of the hotel and the town's growing reputation as a resort (XXXIII: 18). Land speculation, Dods's most modern source of profit, increases its gains in inverse proportion to her feudal landlords' decay. It is for this complex combination of reasons that she retains her loyalty even as she bitterly remarks that the Mowbrays " 'wad hae seen my father's roof-tree fa' down and smoor me before they wad hae gien a boddle a-piece to have propped it up – but they could a' link out their fifty pounds ower head to bigg a hottle at the Well yonder' " (XXXIII: 38). Dods's feudal loyalty is closely related – but only in part reducible – to her interest in the commercial present.

In *St. Ronan's Well*, as in *The Bride of Lammermoor*, Scott recasts the romance that surfaces to aid the returning heir in his early novels, and the female peasant figures who wield its power. What separates Meg Dods from *The Bride*'s Ailsie Gourlay and Alice Grey is that Dods is a comic rather than a tragic figure or a sign of Scott's despair. This change in narrative mood is closely related to a transformation of the female peasant's power. Whereas Meg Merrilies shares an ancient, land-based historical tie with the Bertram family, Meg Dods first meets Francis when he and Valentine stay for several months at her inn during their late-adolescent Scottish exile. And when Dods encounters the adult Francis on his return to St. Ronan's, she recognizes neither him nor his rank, thinking him a "bagman" or "Nabob" (XXXIII: 29, 31). Even once she knows his name, she views him not as the rightful but dispossessed earl of Etherington, an heir in need of her loyalty and assistance, but as a profitable returning guest and a figure from the recent commercial past. Dods's unmagically faulty memory symbolically divides her from Meg Merrilies, and she is powerless, unlike the female peasants in the early novels but like the defeated Alice Grey in *The Bride*, either to restore the Etherington heir to his position as firstborn son or to assist the declining fortunes of the local landed family. Yet unlike Ailsie Gourlay, Grey's forceful opponent, Dods equally lacks the power or desire to harm Francis Tyrrel or John Mowbray, despite her detestation of Mowbray's hotel investment and her admiring preference for Valentine, Francis's half-brother and rival, as a " 'bonny laddie . . . wi' een like diamonds, cheeks like roses . . . and . . . a laugh that wad hae raised the dead' " (XXXIII: 36).

What is most important in the ties between working-class women and legitimacy in the 1824 novel, however, is that the dispossessed heir and hero neither expects nor desires feudal allegiance or counsel: addressed by Dods simply as " 'Francie Tirl, the wild callant that was fishing and bird-nesting here seven or eight years syne,' " and then as " 'Maister Francie,' " Francis responds that " 'a name that sounded like former kindness . . . is more agreeable to me than a lord's title would be' " (XXXIII: 31). Scott's portrait of Dods unites folk wisdom with commercial shrewdness. Because Dods represents both the romance of legitimacy and the modernizing forces that oppose it, her lack of power complements Francis's lack of ambition. By disempowering Dods, Scott plots economic modernity as a safe field for legitimist endeavour, one requiring no further progress while visibly registering the substantial progress that has already been made. Rewriting commerce makes space for Francis's specific, and specifically legitimate, brand of economic individualism. Throughout the novel's present plot, Francis is engaged in what Dods calls " 'the painting trade' " (XXXIII: 32). In a series of staged encounters between the hero and other characters, within the novel and in intertextual comparisons with his earlier works, Scott establishes the legitimacy of Francis's art in the marketplace and the domain of critical comment in ways that reflect the legitimacy of his own literary enterprise. Dods is a key figure in this canon-forming move. That Dods finds Francis's painting unimpressive is the first stage in his establishment as a high-cultural figure. The terms of her evaluation, at once aesthetic and financial, distinguish a purely popular criticism from Francis's economic and artistic expertise. The contrast also highlights the resemblance between Francis's art and Scott's.

Dods confronts Francis directly, and in overtly popular commercial terms, about his artistic shortcomings:

"What signified," she said, "a wheen bits of paper, wi' black and white scarts upon them, that he ca'd bushes, and trees, and craigs? – Couldna he paint them wi' green, and blue, and yellow, like the other folk? Ye will never mak your bread that way, Maister Francie. Ye suld munt up a muckle square of canvass, like Dick Tinto, and paint folks ainsells, that they like muckle better to see than ony craig in the haill water." (XXXIII: 48–9)

Dods refers intertextually to Dick Tinto, the painter of her inn's sign, whose biography is first recounted by Scott's frame-narrator Peter Pattieson in the first chapter of *The Bride* (Scott, *St. Ronan's* XXXIII: 18; *Bride* XIII: 257–78). Tinto's story is a cautionary tale. His rapid rise, from village tailor to journeyman sign-painter to peasant portraitist, ends as ambition lures him to London and ruin. "There is scarce an alternative betwixt distinguished success and absolute failure," Pattieson notes: "in the fine arts mediocrity is not permitted, and . . . he who cannot ascend to the very top of the ladder, will do well not to put his foot upon it at all" (Scott, *Bride* XIII: 269–70). Despite the "Author of *Waverley*'s" eventual rejection of his fictional frame-narrators in prefacing *Tales of the Crusaders*, Scott's narrative sympathies here remain with Pattieson. Once again, Scott deprives Dods of power in order to help his hero develop new sources of legitimacy. The disenfranchisement of the "popular" critic helps to link, to elevate, and at length to legitimate the commercial and cultural spheres.

Scott's distinction between Francis and Tinto in *St. Ronan's* re-emphasizes the contrast *The Bride* establishes between Tinto's highly coloured productions and Pattieson's own narrative, to which Tinto in his turn objects. Pattieson's account of Tinto's critique, which inserts ironic evaluation into quotations from Tinto, aligns this narrator's taste with Francis's and Scott's:

Your characters . . . make too much use of the *gob box*; they *patter* too much – (an elegant phraseology, which Dick had learned while painting the scenes of an itinerant company of players) – there is nothing in whole pages but mere chat and dialogue. (Scott, *Bride* XIII: 271)

Tinto's vulgar phrasing, and Pattieson's ironic reproduction of it, pinpoints the source of Dods's error in agreeing with Tinto's aesthetic biases and in preferring Tinto's work to Francis's. The vulgarity of Tinto's speech, and of Dods's taste for his work, establishes a hierarchy of gentility and legitimacy within the commercial cultural sphere. Meg Dods can hope to be prosperous, but never to be legitimate. This judgment is replayed, and confirmed by Scott *in propria persona*, in the 1832 Magnum Opus notes to *St. Ronan's Well*, which praise Dods for having "produced herself of late from obscurity as authoress of a work on Cookery," which has made her "a distinguished . . . figure" (XXXIV: 358).

In contrast, Pattieson is assigned some share of Scott's own self-conscious gentility. Though Pattieson's cautionary biography records Tinto's insistence that " 'Description . . . was to the author of a romance exactly what drawing and tinting were to a painter; words were his colours,' " Pattieson's ironic perspective on Tinto, and on Tinto's prosperous but illegitimate success, prevents him from following his advice (Scott, *Bride* XIII: 272). Pattieson's own preference for outlining characters by the spare means of their speeches prefigures the "black and white scarts" with which Francis outlines figures and landscapes in *St. Ronan's Well*. Pattieson's method also necessarily resembles Scott's, as the tale he tells is, of course, Scott's own. In the parallels he establishes between *The Bride*'s narrative method and the drawings that earn Francis an income in *St. Ronan's Well*, Scott tightens the symbolic links between Francis's art and the *Waverley* novels. In neither case does commercial production – even commercial purpose – lessen aesthetic legitimacy.

But Scott's ekphrasis – his representation of his own work in Francis's art – extends well beyond the contrast between his own and Francis's black and white outlines and Tinto's florid signs. His publication of "Pattieson's" narratives gives the lie to Pattieson's claim in *The Bride* that Tinto's ignominious death in debtor's prison is " 'sufficient to warn' " anyone " 'against seeking happiness, in the celebrity which attaches itself to a successful cultivator of the fine arts' " (XIII: 259). Scott publishes the *Waverley* novels as Pattieson wishes – in tongue-in-cheek anonymity – although it is Scott and not the fictive Pattieson who "remain[s] behind the curtain unseen" to enjoy "the astonishment and conjectures of my audience," overhearing

the productions of the obscure Peter Pattieson praised by the judicious, and admired by the feeling, engrossing the young, and attracting even the old; while the critic traced their fame up to some name of literary celebrity, and the question when, and by whom, these tales were written, filled up the pause of conversation in a hundred circles and coteries. (Scott, *Bride* XIII: 257–8)

Pattieson's self-concealment is based partly on financial caution, driven by fear that in "the universal mart of talent . . . as is usual in general marts of most descriptions, much more of each commodity is exposed to sale than can ever find purchasers" (XIII: 269). But his fears for the *Waverley* novels are unfounded and his best hopes realized, as an 1818 review in the Edinburgh literary journal *The Portfolio* suggests:

That any man, who has the least thirst for the everlasting remembrance of his country, or the present admiration of a polished age, should, after having produced what gives him a just title to both of these enviable stations, still keep himself behind the curtain, is a circumstance fitted to excite the wonder of all who have caught the spirit or unravelled the tendency of the author's writings . . . Upon whom the honours due ought to be bestowed has long been a question, agitated in the private circle alone. Should my feeble efforts have any effect in calling the attention of writers to such a subject, I shall consider my attempt to unmask this *first of Scotchmen* to be amply rewarded.[83]

The reviewer points a preliminary finger toward "the House of Scott."

Scott, unlike Pattieson, as Jane Millgate and others have shown, saw publication as a solution to rather than source of debt. Consequently, Pattieson's "identity" can be publicly exposed, while Scott's own anonymity is an open secret. The "ornamented and illustrated edition" Tinto proposes for his "romances" finds fruition not in illustration and ornament, but in the newly introduced, fully annotated, and openly acknowledged Magnum Opus edition with which Scott finally legitimates the body of his *Waverley* novels.

When Meg Dods invokes Tinto's talent in *St. Ronan's Well,* she unwittingly participates in Scott's self-canonizing intertext, so that her comparison of Francis's work to Tinto's helps legitimate not only Francis's art, but Scott's as well. Like Pattieson and Scott, Francis finds, and tells Dods, that his

sketches . . . were held of such considerable value, that very often an artist in that line received much higher remuneration for these than for portraits or coloured drawings. He added, that they were often taken for the purpose of illustrating popular poems, and hinted as if he himself were engaged in some labour of that nature. (XXXIII: 49)

Francis transforms painting from a "mere" commercial act into participation in a commercial sphere of culture that has expanded to include textual as well as visual production. In explaining the literary and cultural canonicity of his paintings, he legitimates commerce and the commercial exchange of cultural products as well.

Scott unites economics with criticism through the metaphor of "speculation." Having gained a reputation as "an illustrious poet," despite his anonymity, Francis assures his own entry into the aristocratic circle at St. Ronan's, for his secrecy plays on their thirst for cultural capital: "A mighty poet . . . who could it possibly be? – All names were recited – all Britain scrutinized, from Highland hills to the Lakes of Cumberland – from Sydenham Common to St. James's Place" (XXXIII: 68). Their words echo the buzz in the Edinburgh and

London literary press as critics and journalists speculated on the identity of the "Author of *Waverley*," raising Francis's social standing without reference to his contested title. At the same time, however, their speculation proves the value of Francis's artistic ventures, gaining him the income independent of patronage he requires: they are gratified to hear Francis admit to abandoning several sketches " 'at the foot of the tree I have been sketching,' " which have been found, according to Lady Penelope Penfeather, who sets the St. Ronan's fashions, " 'as Orlando left his verses in the Forest of Ardennes' " (XXXIII: 105). Once again, the link between visuality and textuality is clear, its legitimacy crowned by the allusion to Shakespeare and the foreshadowing ("penfeather") of the canon-forming Preface to *Tales of the Crusaders*. Like Scott, Francis establishes his new form of legitimacy by first concealing and then unveiling his identity. Cultural gossip adds to the market value of his works and legitimates his bids for literary and aesthetic recognition.

Scott's writing of family and political history in *St. Ronan's Well* is a self-reflexive rewriting of romance: as an intertextual narrative enacting political economic order in the explicit terms of literary production and ideological reproduction. Francis carries the burden of Scott's commentary on his own work. His new idiom is a curious blend of Wordsworthian rhetorics of imagination, Byronic individualism, and Burkean national ideals, placing Scott's "most legitimate" novel in a thoroughly modern and canonical literary context. Francis reads his world through Romantic metaphors for pastness and progress. Comparing "the faded hues of the glimmering landscape" at sunset with "those of human life, when early youth and hope have ceased to gild them" (XXXIII: 46), he echoes William Wordsworth's "Ode: Intimations of Immortality from Recollections of Early Childhood" (1807), published exactly contemporaneously with Scott's novel's setting:

> Our birth is but a sleep and a forgetting:
> The Soul that rises with us, our life's Star,
> Hath had elsewhere its setting.[84]

" 'Time changes all around us,' " Francis thinks as the novel begins; " 'wherefore should loves and friendships have a longer date than our dwellings and our monuments?' " (XXXIII: 34). His words are Wordsworthian in their monument-metaphor for the passage of time; they gesture in particular toward "Hart-Leap Well," which is also echoed in the tragic romance and magic well of *The Bride of Lammermoor*. They are also anti-Burkean, for it is with the metaphor of monuments' and dwellings' survival in Britain that Burke defends the British constitution.

Yet as Scott frames Francis's words, they carry a Burkean force. As a "course of natural though trite reflection," his sentiments unite him with his peers precisely because they are the natural, inevitable, and therefore slightly banal, product of his analysis of the visible marks of historical progress, and most likely of contemporary reading as well (XXXIII: 34). Francis envisions himself as part of a contemplative "we" – a series of men, each considering, in a private reverie that he knows to be duplicated in other lives, a history that is at once his country's and his own. The chain of imagining minds, according to Wordsworth and then to Percy Shelley, has an explicitly national significance: a consequence of shared language and cultural sympathy, it is headed by poets, whose wisdom trickles down to other men.[85] It is worth recalling that Francis's views had become "trite" only recently, with the cultural visibility of canonical Romantic poetry, which in rendering such views legitimate had begun the process of making them banal.[86]

Francis's new legitimacy is constructed on a double base – both on independence of his forebears and absorption of their authority. At novel's end, the St. Ronan's aristocrats misread his disappearance: because he leaves Britain to elude his patrimony, they whisper that he has "entered . . . a Moravian mission" and donated all his money (XXXIV: 354). But the joke is on them and their stalemated aristocracy for equating Francis's escape from primogeniture with the radical egalitarianism of an anabaptist sect. When at last Francis separates himself from the rights of primogeniture, refusing to succeed his father and unable to marry Clara, he retains his membership in a different kind of lineal tradition, operating at the endpoint of generic progress in the arts and commerce. In a precociously Eliotic assimilative moment, a precursor of the "Author of Waverley's" self-presentation before his "joint-stock company" partners, the poet-painter becomes at once the sum of his forefathers' work and the father of his own aesthetic fame.[87] The failure of his romance of legitimacy lays the groundwork for his own and Britain's future and the future of narrative genre.

What is a hyperbolic statement of the emotional importance of Francis's "trade" at the start of *St. Ronan's Well* (" 'I cannot live without it' ") becomes literally true by its end (XXXIII: 33). Having begun the novel as an itinerant artist with an aristocratic, landed future, Francis becomes a true cultural entrepreneur, making his own way in the world with his title and family behind rather than before him. Yet although

Francis escapes the romance of legitimacy, his escape makes his role as a Romantic hero possible. His participation in a British aristocracy of letters – and its replacement of aristocracies founded on birth and inherited fortune – sets *St. Ronan's Well* apart, according to Scott and to the *Quarterly Review*, as the most legitimate of the *Waverley* series. At the same time, Scott's self-canonization, legible from the demand side as a contingent terminus in an ongoing process of generic evolution, helps to redefine, to modernize, to nationalize, and therefore to relegitimate the genre of romance as well.[88]

EPILOGUE

Sensibility, genre, and the cultural marketplace

In Walter Scott's late novels, economic agency became nakedly literary and strictly masculine, and participation in the cultural marketplace had become both the defining quality of the self-authorizing British subject and the unabashed matter of romance. But the "family economy" on which writers from Samuel Richardson to Scott's contemporary Jane Austen had focused their attention to social and national order, and toward which they had directed the force of their ideological production or critique, did not simply disappear from the fields of finance and letters, even after Scott's explicit banishment of feminine sensibility and genealogical authority and his radical generic transformation of the *domus* itself. This epilogue reflects on the closure of Scott's legitimate romances: turning away from Scott's conclusions and toward the conditions they foreclose, it seeks to identify what falls out as the nineteenth century looks in new ways at its own fictional and political economic narratives, as well as to examine the lasting consequences of that reframing. I direct my attention, therefore, to two distinct but historically continuous cultural arenas: nineteenth-century mass-market literature and its production and circulation; and the twentieth-century culture industries that are its most recent descendants. Both arenas respond remedially, however indistinctly or even unknowingly, to the irreconcilable discomfiture with feminine sensibility, that mirror image and descendant of the naturally gendered and ideologically stable ethical and economic standard sought by Richardson, articulated in Scott's late novels. In what follows, I discuss two of these responses: the proliferation of masochistic models of feminine sensibility in nineteenth-century British literature, and the recent embrace in British and North American popular culture of female-dominant images and fetishistic practices, which has displaced this pervasive feminine masochism.

In December 1997, the Canadian *Saturday Night Magazine* – a journal resembling in form and purview the American *Atlantic Monthly*, *Harper's*, and the *New Yorker*, or the British *New Statesman and Society* – concluded with a photograph, the latest in a series featuring images of "Saturday Nights" in diverse places. Taken at "11:30 P.M., Fetish Night, The Docks, Toronto" – Canada's economic, though not its political, capital – the photograph shows two headless, bodiless, seemingly female trunks, outfitted in patent leather from waist to toe (Figure 1).[1] The "fetish" character of the image is emphasized in its centring and truncation. Thus the "fetish" designates the leather clothing and high-heeled boots of the two figures while excluding, by means of the foreshortened bodies and the pervasiveness of clothing within the image's small frame, the possibility of reference to the body itself. As a cultural practice, the fetishists' performance is reassuring. The photograph simultaneously documents the absolute centrality, even the dominance, of their passion, gendered feminine, and illustrates their withholding of the fulness of the feminized body and, in particular, of those influences that Richardson's *Clarissa* trusted most, that Austen sought to reconcile, and that Scott pessimistically abandoned: the guidance of "head" and "heart." The image is "a body without a subject," as Diana Fuss has argued elsewhere of such images. As readers from John Berger to Fuss suggest, such conflicted performances of feminized desire reach out to their subject and reader, coding and teaching complicity in the scene they enact.[2] Coalescing instruction in how to desire with a lesson in how to exhibit desirability, the fetishists undo the separation between these kinds of instruction that were the business of eighteenth-century romance, and that it was also the business of eighteenth-century romance to hold apart.

Karl Marx reflected on the commodification of persons in ways that bear directly on Sigmund Freud's account of the "fetish" as the displaced embodiment of its viewer's desire. It would be a cliché to insist at length on the shared rhetorics that unite Marx's reading of the "commodity fetish," with its mysterious secrets and magical properties, and Freud's account of the substitution of consumer goods for persons as the objects of sexual want.[3] Yet the circumstances in which the *Saturday Night* photograph was selected and published illustrate such a nexus in an insistently literal way. The "fetish" photograph I am discussing appeared in a periodical whose recent cover stories, concerning, among other things, the flight of disillusioned working women from the workplace to the avowedly de-economized sanctuary of the home, had gained it a controversial reputation for upholding a mode of socioeconomic organization said to reinforce, gender, and naturalize a

Figure 1 Anne Bayin, "11:30 P.M., Fetish Night, The Docks, Toronto."
permission of Anne Bayin

split between public and private spheres.[4] The resulting debate on *Saturday Night*'s recommendations for a changed role for women in relation to economic *production* deflect attention from a continuing investment – in this sense the decision to publish this edgy photograph only *seems* to conflict with the domestic ideology underlying the magazine's recently published editorials – to a view of gender relations that is centred on and defined by economic *exchange*. Irrespective of their configuration, families consume; desire unites the fields of sex and commerce, and women, regardless of their relations to the gross national product or to biological reproduction, are envisioned primarily in relation to goods to be consumed. Among the photographed fetishists, in a way that is perfectly continuous with this economic focus, a feminized sexuality reveals itself in, indeed is embodied by, consumer goods, bought by the wearers to replace bodies as the focus of desire – for their implied viewers as for the subjects themselves.

As Frances Burney complained and as David Hume and Richardson insisted, the character of feminine consumption – both desire and taste – is the ethical, representational, and polemical heart of the image of the marketplace and its practices. What Scott found it necessary to purge from the nineteenth-century public sphere reappears in our time safely identified with and constrained by fetish-clothing, a set of fashionable consumer goods that are paradoxically but quite unironically paraded as signs of sexual power and freedom. Nor is this simultaneous ubiquity, simulated freedom, and real displacement unique to Canada or periodicals: the same process has emerged in quasi-fetishist American comic films such as *East of Eden*, based on a pseudonymous novel by the best-selling novelist Anne Rice; in erotica published by Rice under the name "A. N. Roquelaure" and in other recent popular novels; in filmed fantasies of masculine identification from *The Rocky Horror Picture Show* to *To Wong Foo, Thanks for Everything, Julie Newmar* and *Priscilla, Queen of the Desert*; and in British and American advertising campaigns that feature humorous or seductive portraits of "dominatrixes." Whether eroticized, comic, or both, these images present a feminized desire whose assertiveness overlays consumer practices that are encouraged within and by the cultural form, and which is also intimately connected with consumption of the cultural form itself. Late capitalism provides women and men with a fantasy of untrammelled and controlling feminine want, which serves not to disrupt but to normalize, and so to justify, a social order that is perfectly consistent with consumption without borders or restraints.

Janice Radway and Nancy Friday have argued, in the very different contexts of a scholarly study of mass-market romance readers and a popular psychological survey of female sexual response, that female passions themselves have recently begun an ongoing process of change. In the fields of consumer demand and psychological orientation, these writers argue, a willful, powerful desire is replacing, in a broad-based and economically significant way, the imputed wish to experience being desired and overpowered, and to name that experience, that was central to nineteenth- and early-twentieth-century mass cultural items produced for female consumers.[5] In late-capitalist Anglo-American culture, however, the wayward feminized "sensibility" that Scott feared and banished for its disruptive effects on lineage and domestic peace has been renamed "desire" and brought home once more. Under this name it enacts within the twentieth-century culture industry a reassuring and consoling role, providing a foundation and limits for a world given over to commodity objects and consumer choice. The fetishized dominant woman of late capitalism is a renovation of Scott's feminine economic scapegoat: his Clara Mowbray, maddened by loss and banished by death from his revisioned liberal economy, is reborn as a woman existing only to want, valued for wanting, and guaranteeing the worth of goods and their buyers through the means of all-powerful and unstoppable longings that are none the less restrained by the singlemindedness of their socially sanctioned direction toward commodities. Late-capitalist sexual radicalisms, with their commodification of sexuality and their absolute symbolic induction of female desire into the sphere of cultural power, are the perhaps unknowing descendants of Richardson's romantic ideology of economic liberalism.[6]

Despite the fully realized success of liberal ideology in late-twentieth-century mass culture, then, the autonomous masculine subject by whose means Scott defended his conception of social order has not carried all before him. Even in the nineteenth and early twentieth centuries, visible traces survive of the feminized gold standard of sensibility promoted in late-eighteenth-century romance. One such survival took the paradoxical form (paradoxical, if one accepts that sexual desire is always natural and free) of masochistic representations of female desire, which in part recapitulated earlier narratives of the type recently discussed in Andrea Henderson's and Claudia Johnson's readings of Burney's *Camilla*: a representation of "sensibility" in the experience of suffering and self-abasement at the hands of Britain's economy and its agents.[7] Charlotte M. Yonge's extraordinarily popular *The Dove in the Eagle's Nest* (1866), for example, defines the character of its heroine, the titular "dove," against the "eagle's nest" of the society into which she is first unwillingly carried, then confined, and into which she finally marries. Yonge's "eagles" are, in terms that resonate with nineteenth-century socioeconomic developments, "robber barons."[8] The "dove" is a merchant's adopted daughter, raised in a household that respects and demands formal regulation of production and trade. The novel itself is set in fifteenth-century Germany, amid a feudalism that is visibly declining, making way for mercantile regulation, entrepreneurism, and the individualistic reformation of religion. Like Richardson's Clarissa, Yonge's Christina is a conservative whose traditionalist sentiments include a fondness not for aristocracy, but for a declining form of commercial society. Like Scott's Clara, Christina ranges among the sublime crags of a mountain pass: unlike Clara, however, who roams at will before her wayward character is banished from Scott's conclusion, Christina does not wander by choice. Fifty years after Burney's *Wanderer* failed to sell, but in a now wholly naturalized cultural marketplace, Yonge's popular heroine, like Burney's Juliet, travels in consequence of her banishment – which is, in turn, the immediate condition allowing her captivity.

Mary Poovey has argued that feminine desire, at once disruptive and economically crucial, was simultaneously invoked and controlled by nineteenth-century British popular fictions.[9] Yet the absolute centrality of female desire and will to socioeconomic events in such works as Yonge's is undercut by the violence that shapes desire to economic necessity: these narratives recapitulate the cautionary tales of Eliza Haywood, which insisted in the early eighteenth century that the inevitable wages of sexualized political and economic longings are confinement and death. Yonge's characterization of Christina's desires centres on, and never moves away from, the unwillingness with which her heroine finds herself banished from one economy and imported into another, and the suffering she experiences before capitulating to each new economy she encounters. Whether mercantile and regulated or lawless and entrepreneurial, the spheres in which Christina is forced to exist demand considerable feats of reconciliation, of a kind unseen so explicitly since Richardson's *Clarissa*, among desire, conscience, and necessity or, as Yonge puts it, Clarissa-like, among Christina's "heart" and "will" and the "matters" that surround her (71–2). Yonge regales her readers with descriptions of Christina's "helpless, meek, and timid" character, her "drooping," "roseate" figure, and the humility with which she kneels to remove her father's "long, steel-guarded" boots with "quivering" hands hardly up to the job. These fragmented, iconic descriptions are the nineteenth-century inverse, but also the counterpart, of the late-twentieth-century consumer goods that are the trappings of the most avowedly liberated feminized desire, for, as Gilles Deleuze states, "there can be no masochism without fetishism in the primary sense."[10] Christina is transported, emotionally and geographically, only unwillingly (16, 21–2, 71). She resists her absorption into the "robber baron" economy and then, once settled, rebels against returning to the mercantile world. In each case, her resistance is at once sexual, domestic, and economic, and her situation is always confined: she is her father's "chattel" and then her husband's, whether or not she is banished from the household; whether or not she remains in the eagle's nest (24).

The Dove in the Eagle's Nest is usually assigned to the didactic category of mid-Victorian children's fiction, a shelfmate, for example, of Charles Kingsley's exactly contemporary exhortations to cleanliness and godliness in *The Water-Babies* (1863). The pleasure Yonge offers her apparently impressionable and developing readers is specifically political and economic, and sentimental in its didacticism: the enjoyment lies in recognizing and sympathizing with the economic and sexual resistance of Christina's sensibility, and in acknowledging her confinement. This pleasure is readable as masochism, certainly. It is also just possible to argue that the novel presents a critique, carried out in an ideologically and culturally fruitful context, of an economic ideology that seeks to objectify, consume, or banish the desires of its female agents. Yet it is not that Christina herself is masochistic that lends the novel its distinctively painful pleasures, but rather that Yonge's readers are expected to take pleasure not only in Christina's detachment from and resistance to the competing entrepreneurial and mercantile economies whose violence Yonge's narrative reveals, but also in her repeated capitulation to them, so that her earlier resistance is reducible to the knowing pleasures of suspense. Thus although *Saturday Night*'s celebratory fetishists seem wholly divergent from Yonge's illustrations of her heroine's resistance to the economic appropriation of desires, both insist on the force of a feminine desire that economies and their ideologies are established to create and shape.

In a normative embrace of the extra-domestic feminine sensibility Scott ritually destroyed at the end of *St. Ronan's Well*, *Saturday Night*'s publication of the fetish image celebrates but also controls the theatrical enactment of desire in culture. In contrast, Yonge explicates the economic violence latent in marriage, which is defined in her novel as a chain of banishments and losses that are the culmination of female economic and sexual maturity. Both portraits, however, address the problem of feminine desire, which, once produced to answer an economic need, frequently resists reduction to the terms of the need it serves. And both *The Dove* and *Saturday Night*, in their different ways, further the naturalization of desire, or sensibility, itself – Yonge by abstracting it from the economy, to which it is demonstrably led only reluctantly, though absolutely; *Saturday Night* by celebrating its economic immersion.

The cultural legacy of eighteenth-century liberal romance and political economy, therefore, appears to be riven, caught between masochism and a ritualized but empty freedom and sway. The pleasures of reading the line of modern sentimental romances I have traced in this book lie largely and historically in identification with powerless sensibility, and currently in a fallacious fantasy of liberty and power – both oriented to, even subdued by, the marketplace. There is, however, a third possible avenue leading from this generic legacy, toward which the unfinished narratives of Wollstonecraft's *Wrongs of Woman* gesture. Wollstonecraft's text caps a career dedicated to exposing the economic substrates of sensibility in narratives not of desire but of its inadequacy and constraints. The novel holds out the possibility of a satisfaction that lies (for its characters) beyond the text and (for readers) in the encounter with it. In *Wrongs*, Wollstonecraft exchanges her critique of desire – and the pleasures of seeking fulfillment – for the proffered pleasure of fulfillment itself. The "unfinished parts" of *The Wrongs of Woman*, as Tilottama Rajan has argued, call on Wollstonecraft's readers to complete them: the drive to complete, and not to be completed or satisfied, holds her readers' longings forever in abeyance. They are also famously unreadable within a society steeped in liberalism and its culture of desire, its borders marked out by the romance of human nature and feminine sensibility.

Notes

INTRODUCTION: ROMANTIC ECONOMIES

1 Samuel Richardson, *Pamela; or Virtue Rewarded*, ed. T. C. Duncan Eaves and Ben Kimpel (Boston: Houghton, 1971), 8.

2 Anna Barbauld, "On the Origin and Progress of Novel-Writing," in *British Novelists* (London: Rivington, 1820), 1: 59.

3 Michel Foucault, *The Order of Things: An Archaeology of the Human Sciences* (New York: Vintage, 1973), 125–6. See also Alan Bewell, " 'Jacobin Plants': Botany as Social Theory in the 1790s," in *Wordsworth Circle* 20 (1989): 137–8; review of Walker's *Elements of Geography* in *Anti-Jacobin Review* 3 (1799): 323–33.

4 Barbauld, "Origin and Progress," makes "romance" and "Novel" "species" within the "species" of fiction (34). Subsequently cited in the text.

5 Ian Watt, *The Rise of the Novel: Studies in Defoe, Richardson and Fielding* (London: Hogarth, reprint 1987), 290; J. Paul Hunter, *Before Novels: The Cultural Contexts of English Fiction* (New York: Norton, 1990), 7, 355; Michael McKeon, *Origins of the English Novel, 1600–1740* (Baltimore: Johns Hopkins University Press, 1987), 20.

6 Deborah Ross, *The Excellence of Falsehood: Romance, Realism, and Women's Contribution to the Novel* (Lexington: University Press of Kentucky, 1991), 3–4.

7 Nancy Armstrong, *Desire and Domestic Fiction: A Political History of the Novel* (New York: Oxford University Press, 1987); Lennard J. Davis, *Factual Fictions: The Origins of the English Novel* (New York: Columbia University Press, 1983), 25.

8 Northrop Frye, *Anatomy of Criticism* (New York: Atheneum, 1965), 186–206; Richard Hurd, *Letters on Chivalry and Romance* (London: Millar, 1762); Clara Reeve, *Progress of Romance* (Colchester: Keymer, 1785).

9 Tobias Smollett, *Adventures of Roderick Random*, ed. Paul-Gabriel Boucé (Oxford: Oxford University Press, 1979), xxxiii.

10 For Ian Duncan, in *Modern Romance and Transformations of the Novel: The Gothic, Scott, Dickens* (Cambridge: Cambridge University Press, 1992), 58–60, romance is always modern, inventing pasts with power to shape the present. See also James Chandler, *England in 1819: The Politics of Literary Culture and the Case of Romantic Historicism* (Chicago: University of Chicago Press, 1998), 339–47; Ina Ferris, *The Achievement of Literary Authority: Gender, History, and the*

Waverley Novels (Ithaca: Cornell University Press, 1991), 79–104; Katie Trumpener, *Bardic Nationalism: The Romantic Novel and the British Empire* (Princeton: Princeton University Press, 1997), 128–57; Nicola Watson, *Revolution and the Form of the British Novel, 1790–1825* (Oxford: Clarendon, 1994), 156–7.

11 See Ralph Cohen, "History and Genre," in *NLH* 17 (1986): 203–18, rebutting Jacques Derrida's "The Law of Genre," in *Glyph* 7 (1980): 202–29, and Hans Robert Jauss's *Toward an Aesthetic of Reception*, trans. Timothy Bahti (Minneapolis: University of Minnesota Press, 1982).

12 Clifford Siskin, *The Work of Writing* (Baltimore: Johns Hopkins University Press, 1998), 17–23; *The Historicity of Romantic Discourse* (New York: Oxford University Press, 1988), 15–36.

13 Laurie Langbauer, *Women and Romance: The Consolations of Gender in the English Novel* (Ithaca: Cornell University Press, 1990), 2.

14 Ioan Williams, *Novel and Romance, 1700–1800* (New York: Barnes, 1970).

15 William Godwin, "Of History and Romance," Appendix, *Caleb Williams*, ed. Maurice Hindle (London: Penguin, 1988), 359, 361–2.

16 Maria Edgeworth, *Castle Rackrent*, ed. George Watson (Oxford: Oxford University Press, 1980), 1–2.

17 Reeve, *Progress of Romance*, 1: 9. Subsequently cited in the text.

18 McKeon, 52–5.

19 Review of Mary Wollstonecraft, *Rights of Woman*, in *Monthly Review* n.s. 8 (1792): 209; Hannah More, *Strictures on the Modern System of Female Education*, in *Works* (New York: Harper, 1840), 1: 320. See also review of Godwin, *Memoirs*, in *Anti-Jacobin Review* 1 (1798): 93–100 and *European Magazine* 33 (1798): 247–8.

20 For "reading market," see review of Whitelaw's *History of the City of Dublin*, in *Edinburgh Review* 68 (1820): 320. For "republic of letters," see Thomas Paine, *Rights of Man*, in *Political Writings*, ed. Bruce Kuklick (Cambridge: Cambridge University Press, 1989), 166; Elizabeth Heckendorn Cook, *Epistolary Bodies: Gender and Genre in the Eighteenth-Century Republic of Letters* (Stanford: Stanford University Press, 1996), 8–13.

21 Carol Kay, *Political Constructions: Defoe, Richardson, and Sterne in Relation to Hobbes, Hume, and Burke* (Ithaca: Cornell University Press, 1988); Catherine Gallagher, *Nobody's Story: The Vanishing Acts of Women Writers in the Marketplace, 1670–1820* (Berkeley: University of California Press, 1994); Claudia Johnson, *Equivocal Beings: Politics, Gender, and Sentimentality in the 1790s* (Chicago: University of Chicago Press, 1995); James Thompson, *Models of Value: Eighteenth-Century Political Economy and the Novel* (Durham: Duke University Press, 1996).

22 David Kaufmann, *The Business of Common Life: Novels and Classical Economics between Revolution and Reform* (Baltimore: Johns Hopkins University Press, 1995), 15–16.

23 Kaufmann, *Business of Common Life*, 12, 17–18; Theodor Adorno, "Cultural Criticism and Society," in *Prisms*, trans. Samuel and Shierry Weber (Cambridge: MIT Press, 1981), 32–4.

24 See Pierre Bourdieu's superimposed maps of capital systems, in *Distinction: A Social Critique of the Judgement of Taste*, trans. Richard Nice (Cambridge: Harvard University Press, 1984), 128–9.

25 Kaufmann, *Business of Common Life*, 23–9.

26 Alexander Pope, *Essay on Man*, in *Poetical Works*, ed. Herbert Davis (Oxford: Oxford University Press, 1966), I: 24–5, 57–60.

27 Edmund Burke, *Reflections on the Revolution in France*, ed. J. G. A. Pocock (Indianapolis: Hackett, 1987), 68; Samuel Taylor Coleridge, *Statesman's Manual*, in *Collected Works*, ed. R. J. White (London: Routledge, 1972), VI: 34.

28 Seamus Deane, *Strange Country: Modernity and Nationhood in Irish Writing since 1790* (Oxford: Clarendon, 1997), 1–48.

29 See also Zillah Eisenstein, *The Radical Future of Liberal Feminism* (New York: Longman, 1981), 33–44; Carole Pateman, *The Sexual Contract* (Stanford: Stanford University Press, 1988) and *The Disorder of Women: Democracy, Feminism and Political Theory* (Stanford: Stanford University Press, 1989), 39. J. C. D. Clark, in *English Society, 1688–1832: Ideology, Social Structure and Political Practice During the Ancien Regime* (Cambridge: Cambridge University Press, 1985), asserts that Locke "accepted a large part of the patriarchalist case" (76).

30 Hume's 1741 "Of the Study of History," in *Essays Moral, Political, and Literary*, ed. Eugene F. Miller (Indianapolis: Liberty, 1987), 563–8, promoting "history" over "secret history," or "romance," appeared before Richardson's *Clarissa*, which upheld the order Hume theorized. The essay is rebutted by Godwin's and Edgeworth's preference for romance over political history, by Barbauld's replacement of political economy with romance, and by Jane Austen's claim in *Northanger Abbey* that national histories are romantic in character. Hume repudiated the essay after 1760.

31 See Adam Smith, in *Wealth of Nations*, ed. R. H. Campbell and A. S. Skinner (Oxford: Clarendon, 1976), II, 428: "theories" or "systems of political œconomy" are accounts, simultaneously descriptive and prescriptive, of the distribution of economic resources, and consequently of the social order, of "nations"; political economy is social order itself. See also Samuel Johnson's *Dictionary of the English Language* (London: Knapton, 1755): definitions of "ECONOMY" include "System of motions; distribution of every thing to its proper place," "Disposition of things; regulation," and "management of a family."

32 E.g. C. B. Macpherson, *The Political Theory of Possessive Individualism* (Oxford: Clarendon, 1962); Christopher Hill, *The World Turned Upside Down: Radical Ideas During the English Revolution* (Harmondsworth: Penguin, 1975), 361–86; Lawrence Stone, *The Family, Sex and Marriage in England, 1500–1800* (London: Penguin, 1979), 149–80.

33 Clark, *English Society*, 119–98, and "Reconceptualizing Eighteenth-Century England," in *British Journal for Eighteenth-Century Studies* 15 (1992): 135–9.

34 See Theresa M. Kelley, *Reinventing Allegory* (Cambridge: Cambridge University Press, 1997), 2, on allegory's "border raids" on "history," such that the

story of representation and art inserts itself into the apparently empirical evidence of the real historians like to present.

35 On Scott, James Buzard, "Translation and Tourism: Scott's *Waverley* and the Rendering of Culture," in *Yale Journal of Criticism* 8 (1995): 31–59; Katie Trumpener, "National Character, Nationalist Plots: National Tale and Historical Novel in the Age of *Waverley*, 1806–1830," in *ELH* 60 (1993): 685–731; Duncan, *Modern Romance*, 146–73; Robert Crawford, *Devolving English Literature* (Oxford: Clarendon, 1992), 11–51; and chapter 5. On Austen, Maaja Stewart, *Domestic Realities and Imperial Fictions: Jane Austen's Novels in Eighteenth-Century Contexts* (Athens: University of Georgia Press, 1993); Edward Said, *Culture and Imperialism* (New York: Vintage, 1994), 80–97.

36 See Gerald Newman, *The Rise of English Nationalism: A Cultural History, 1740–1830* (New York: St. Martin's, 1987); Linda Colley, *Britons: Forging the Nation, 1707–1837* (London: Vintage, 1996); Benedict Anderson, *Imagined Communities: Reflections on the Origin and Spread of Nationalism*, rev. ed. (London: Verso, 1991).

37 Adam Anderson, *Historical and Chronological Deduction of the Origin of Commerce* (Dublin: Byrne, 1790), 111.

38 J. G. A. Pocock, *Virtue, Commerce, and History: Essays on Political Thought and History, Chiefly in the Eighteenth Century* (Cambridge: Cambridge University Press, 1985), 215–53; Newman, 63–84.

39 Clark, *English Society*, 89.

40 Clark, *Revolution and Rebellion: State and Society in England in the Seventeenth and Eighteenth Centuries* (Cambridge: Cambridge University Press, 1986), 92.

41 Paul Monod, *Jacobitism and the English People, 1688–1788* (Cambridge: Cambridge University Press, 1989); Murray Pittock, *Poetry and Jacobite Politics in Eighteenth-Century Britain and Ireland* (Cambridge: Cambridge University Press, 1994); Howard Erskine-Hill, "Literature and the Jacobite Cause: Was There a Rhetoric of Jacobitism?," in Eveline Cruickshanks, ed., *Ideology and Conspiracy: Aspects of Jacobitism, 1689–1759* (Edinburgh: Donald, 1982), 49–69; Clark, "On Moving the Middle Ground: The Significance of Jacobitism in Historical Studies," in Cruickshanks and Jeremy Black, eds., *The Jacobite Challenge* (Edinburgh: Donald, 1988), 177–88.

42 Pittock, *Poetry and Jacobite Politics*, 238–9. See also Newman, *Rise of English Nationalism*, 223–5.

43 Clark, *English Society*, 50.

44 Max Horkheimer and Adorno, *Dialectic of Enlightenment*, trans. John Cumming (New York: Continuum, 1972), 120–67; Jürgen Habermas, *Structural Transformation of the Public Sphere: An Inquiry into a Category of Bourgeois Society*, trans. Thomas Burger (Cambridge: MIT Press, 1989), 160–2.

45 Pittock's epigraph to *Poetry and Jacobite Politics*.

46 See Richard Sharp, *The Engraved Record of the Jacobite Movement* (Aldershot: Scolar, 1996).

47 Wollstonecraft, *Vindication of the Rights of Woman*, in *Works*, ed. Janet Todd and Marilyn Butler (New York: New York University Press, 1989), v: 88.

48 Margaret Anne Doody, *Frances Burney: The Life in the Works* (New Brunswick: Rutgers University Press, 1988), 147.
49 Wollstonecraft, *Vindication of the Rights of Men*, in *Works*, v: 8.
50 James Raven, *Judging New Wealth: Popular Publishing and Responses to Commerce in England, 1750–1800* (Oxford: Clarendon, 1992), 54–5.

I MARKETING AGREEMENT: RICHARDSON'S ROMANCE OF CONSENSUS

1 Richardson, *Pamela*, 5. Subsequently cited in the text, abbreviated *P*1.
2 Franco Moretti, *Signs Taken for Wonders: Essays in the Sociology of Literary Forms*, rev. ed., trans. Susan Fischer, David Forgacs, and David Miller (London: Verso, 1988), 255; Cohen, "History and Genre," 207.
3 See Siskin, *Work of Writing*, 19.
4 Habermas, *Public Sphere*, 57–66. See Nancy Fraser, "Rethinking the Public Sphere: A Contribution to the Critique of Actually Existing Democracy," in Craig Calhoun, ed., *Habermas and the Public Sphere* (Cambridge: MIT Press, 1992), 113–18; Joan B. Landes, *Women and the Public Sphere in the Age of the French Revolution* (Ithaca: Cornell University Press, 1988), 38–65.
5 Watt, *Rise of the Novel*, 174–207; R. F. Brissenden, *Virtue in Distress: Studies in the Novel of Sentiment from Richardson to Sade* (New York: Harper, 1974), 159–86; John Mullan, *Sentiment and Sociability: The Language of Feeling in the Eighteenth Century* (Oxford: Clarendon, 1988), 63–77; McKeon, *English Novel*, 371–4.
6 Kay, *Political Constructions*, 170–1; Watt, *Rise of the Novel*, 140–4. On "affective families," see Stone, *Family, Sex and Marriage*; Susan Moller Okin, "Patriarchy and Married Women's Property in England," *Eighteenth-Century Studies* 17 (1983–4): 122–5. Historians who contest the primacy of middle-class individualism in eighteenth-century Britain also question Stone; see Clark, *English Society*.
7 See Cook, *Epistolary Bodies*; Madeleine Kahn, *Narrative Transvestism: Rhetoric and Gender in the Eighteenth-Century English Novel* (Ithaca: Cornell University Press, 1991); Linda Kauffman, *Discourses of Desire: Gender, Genre, and Epistolary Fictions* (Ithaca: Cornell University Press, 1986); Terry Castle, *Clarissa's Ciphers: Meaning and Disruption in Richardson's Clarissa* (Ithaca: Cornell University Press, 1982); Terry Eagleton, *The Rape of Clarissa: Writing, Sexuality, and Class Struggle in Samuel Richardson* (Oxford: Blackwell, 1982); William Beatty Warner, *Reading Clarissa: The Struggles of Interpretation* (New Haven: Yale University Press, 1979).
8 Cook, *Epistolary Bodies*, 7, 9, 15.
9 Richardson helped establish conditions in which the "systems" of the 1790s, discussed in Kaufmann's *Business of Common Life*, 28–9, were produced.
10 Eagleton, *Rape of Clarissa*, 14; Thompson, *Models of Value*, 152–5.
11 For recent debates, see Monod, *Jacobitism*; Clark, "Middle Ground," 177–88 and "Reconceptualizing Eighteenth-Century England," 135–9; Roy Porter, "Georgian Britain: An Ancien Regime?," in *British Journal for*

Eighteenth-Century Studies 15 (1992): 141–4; special issue of *ELH* on Samuel Johnson and Jacobitism (64 [1997]).

12 Newman, in *English Nationalism*, 21–47, 58. Typical of cultural historians before the late 1980s, Newman does not discuss Jacobitism.

13 Colley, *Britons*, 43–9.

14 Clark, in *English Society*, 58, points out that most contemporary political philosophers were ordained Church of England ministers. On dynasty, see 119–98.

15 For feminist critique of *Two Treatises* emphasizing Locke's continuity with patriarchalism, see Eisenstein, *Radical Future*, 33, and Pateman, *Sexual Contract*, 21–5. See also Christopher Durston, *The Family in the English Revolution* (Oxford: Blackwell, 1989), 171–4.

16 Clark, *English Society*, 50.

17 "Speech of Thomas Freeman, Made at a Late Meeting of the Principal Inhabitants of *Edinburgh*" (1745), 2; "Serious Address to the Gentlemen SOLDIERS under the Command of M------L W------E," 2. On the diversity of Jacobite rhetorics, see Pittock, *Poetry and Jacobite Politics*, 134, 188–9, 207–22.

18 Terry Eagleton, *Ideology of the Aesthetic* (Oxford: Blackwell, 1990), 42–3. See also Mullan, *Sentiment and Sociability*, 23, 30.

19 Joyce Appleby argues, in *Liberalism and Republicanism in the Historical Imagination* (Cambridge: Harvard University Press, 1992), 66–7, 89, that the transformation began as Locke presented coin as a "natural" fetish-object; Locke remained the only exponent of natural law in economics until Adam Smith. I argue that Hume may be seen as Locke's first economic successor.

20 E.g. in Smollett's *Roderick Random*, xxxiii. Hume, however, in "Of the Study of History," *Essays Moral, Political, and Literary*, 563–8, saw the two categories as interchangeable.

21 McKeon, *English Novel*, 48.

22 McKeon, *English Novel*, 21, 131.

23 Doody, *A Natural Passion: A Study of the Novels of Samuel Richardson* (Oxford: Clarendon, 1974), 14–34, details *Pamela*'s sources in contemporary fiction.

24 Ros Ballaster, *Seductive Forms: Women's Amatory Fiction from 1684–1740* (Oxford: Clarendon, 1992), 79.

25 Sarah Fielding, Letter to Richardson, in Richardson, *Correspondence*, ed. Barbauld (London: Phillips, 1804), II: 60–1.

26 Mullan, *Sentiment and Sociability*, 61. See also Markman Ellis, *Politics of Sensibility* (Cambridge: Cambridge University Press, 1996), 15–48; Ann Jessie Van Sant, *Eighteenth-Century Sensibility and the Novel: The Senses in Social Context* (Cambridge: Cambridge University Press, 1993), 2–15; Janet Todd, *Sensibility: An Introduction* (London: Methuen, 1986); Brissenden, *Virtue in Distress*, 11–55. On late-century suspicions, see Ellis, *Politics of Sensibility*, 207–8.

27 [Richardson,] *Pamela: Or, Virtue Rewarded. The Third and Fourth Volumes* (London: Rivington, 1742), III: 378. Subsequently cited in the text, abbreviated *P2*.

28 See for example Richardson, *Correspondence*, I: 100.

29 Richardson, *Correspondence*, V: 132.

30 Richardson, *Clarissa; or the History of a Young Lady*, ed. Angus Ross (Harmondsworth: Penguin, 1985), 71, 72, 79. Subsequently cited in the text, abbreviated *C*.

31 For Johnson's possible Jacobitism, see Erskine-Hill, "Literature and the Jacobite Cause," 49–69, and "The Political Character of Samuel Johnson: *The Lives of the Poets* and a Further Report on *The Vanity of Human Wishes*," in Cruickshanks and Black, *Jacobite Challenge*, 161–76.

32 Johnson, *Rambler* 60 (13 October 1750), in *The Rambler* (London: Payne, 1752), II: 207–8, 211. See also *Rambler* 4 (31 March 1750), I: 27, 31.

33 Johnson qtd. in James Boswell, *Life of Samuel Johnson*, ed. George Birkbeck Hill and L. F. Powell (Oxford: Clarendon, 1934), II: 175.

34 The *OED* cites Bradshaigh's as the first use of "sentimental" to imply elevated feeling. See Richardson, *Correspondence*, IV: 282–3; IV: 305; Cook, *Epistolary Bodies*, 1–3, 6.

35 Appleby, *Liberalism*, 89.

36 Fiction writers had a more diverse readership than Caroline Robbins's "commonwealthmen," in *The Eighteenth-Century Commonwealthman* (Cambridge: Harvard University Press, 1959), or Pocock's neo-Harringtonian political writers, in *Virtue, Commerce, and History*.

37 John Locke, *Essay Concerning the True Original, Extent, and End of Civil Government*, in *Two Treatises of Government*, ed. Peter Laslett (Cambridge: Cambridge University Press, 1988), 268. Subsequently cited in the text, abbreviated *T2*.

38 See Pateman, *Sexual Contract*, 19–38.

39 Locke, *First Treatise*, in *Two Treatises*, 173–4. Subsequently cited in the text, abbreviated *T1*.

40 Eliza Haywood, *The Mercenary Lover: or, the Unfortunate Heiresses. Being a True, Secret History of a City Amour* (London: Dobb, 1726), 9–10, 16. Subsequently cited in the text.

41 Aphra Behn's *Love-Letters between a Nobleman and his Sister*, 3rd ed. (London: Brown, 1708) places legal incest at the heart of a thinly disguised contemporary historical family. Ellen Pollak's "Beyond Incest: Gender and the Politics of Transgression in Aphra Behn's *Love-Letters between a Nobleman and His Sister*," in Heidi Hutner, ed., *Rereading Aphra Behn: History, Theory, and Criticism* (Charlottesville: University Press of Virginia, 1993), 157–8, suggests that Behn represents incest as the type of endogamy on which inheritance-based social systems depend. See also Janet Todd, "Who is Silvia? What is She? Feminine Identity in Aphra Behn's *Love-Letters between a Nobleman and his Sister*," in *Aphra Behn Studies* (Cambridge: Cambridge University Press, 1996), 202.

42 Adam Smith, *Theory of the Moral Sentiments*, ed. D. D. Raphael and A. L. Macfie, in *Works* (Oxford: Clarendon, 1976), I: 54.

43 Habermas, *Public Sphere*, 7–9.

44 Robert Filmer, *Patriarcha; or the Natural Power of Kings* (London: Davis, 1680).

45 Richardson's portrait of B's neighbours diverges from Pocock's view of contemporary politics, *Virtue, Commerce, and History*, 239.

46 Clark, *English Society*, 125, 131; *Revolution and Rebellion*, 45–67.

47 John Locke, *Essay Concerning Human Understanding*, ed. Peter Nidditch (Oxford: Clarendon, 1975), 64–5. Subsequently cited in the text.

48 See R. J. Smith, *The Gothic Bequest: Medieval Institutions in British Thought, 1688–1863* (Cambridge: Cambridge University Press, 1987), 29; Samuel Kliger, *The Goths in England: A Study in Seventeenth and Eighteenth Century Thought* (Cambridge: Harvard University Press, 1952), 118. Charles Stuart's French asylum was much emphasized. See, for example, Henry Fielding's representation of French duplicity and gallantry in *Tom Jones*, ed. R. P. C. Mutter (London: Penguin, 1966), 247–8, 258–9. On the "Frenchness" of absolutism, see Landes, *Women and the Public Sphere*, 17–28.

49 Richardson's treatment of B's neighbours raises questions for Toni Bowers's argument for Richardson's Toryism, in *The Politics of Motherhood: British Writing and Culture, 1680–1760* (Cambridge: Cambridge University Press, 1996), 201–5.

50 Armstrong, *Desire and Domestic Fiction*, 5–6; McKeon, 360. Thus Pamela's struggle for interpretive power is not, as Warner argues, an end in itself.

51 For Marie-Paule Laden, in *Self-Imitation in the Eighteenth-Century Novel* (Princeton: Princeton University Press, 1987), 78, B's costuming of Pamela reproduces "aristocratic" theatricality. It seems to me, rather, to underline his absolute reform.

52 Armstrong, *Desire and Domestic Fiction*, 5–6, 30. See also Davis, *Factual Fictions*, 175–87.

53 Laura Brown, *Ends of Empire: Women and Ideology in Early Eighteenth-Century Literature* (Ithaca: Cornell University Press, 1993), 103–35.

54 Pocock, *Virtue, Commerce, and History*, 240–2.

55 [Richard Allestree,] *The Ladies Calling* (Oxford, 1673), n.p.

56 Pope, *The Dunciad*, II: 157–166, in *Poetical Works*, 507; Reeve, *Progress of Romance*, I: 119–20. Recent discussions include Jane Spencer, *The Rise of the Woman Novelist: From Aphra Behn to Jane Austen* (Oxford: Blackwell, 1986), 15, 75–6; Todd, *The Sign of Angellica: Women, Writing, and Fiction, 1600–1800* (New York: Columbia University Press, 1989), 14–19, 104.

57 See Todd's Introduction to *Love-Letters* (London: Penguin, 1996), xi–xiv.

58 Behn, *Love-Letters*, 43. Subsequently cited in the text.

59 Pateman, *Disorder of Women*.

60 Fielding, *Apology for the Life of Mrs. Shamela Andrews*, ed. Sheridan W. Baker, Jr. (Berkeley: University of California Press, 1953), 43, 47, 49.

61 Appleby, *Liberalism*, 133.

62 David Hume, *Treatise of Human Nature*, ed. L. A. Selby-Bigge, 2nd ed. (Oxford: Clarendon, 1978), 281. Subsequently cited in the text, abbreviated *T*.

63 Hume, "Polygamy and Divorces," 182–4, 189; "Of Love and Marriage," 560–2, in *Essays*; Hume, *Treatise*, 491–2, 499.

64 So persistent that Mary Poovey, in *Uneven Developments: The Ideological Work of Gender in Mid-Victorian England* (Chicago: University of Chicago Press, 1988), traces a similar recuperation of feminine "sexuality" (a nineteenth-century version of "sensibility"?) for the British "nation" in Victorian fiction – and the inevitable failures of such containment. Poovey's discussion of governesses, in particular, 126–63, suggests continuities with *Pamela*'s ambiguities.

65 See Tassie Gwilliam, *Samuel Richardson's Fictions of Gender* (Stanford: Stanford University Press, 1993), 15–49; Terri Nickel, "*Pamela* as Fetish: Masculine Anxiety in Henry Fielding's *Shamela* and James Parry's *The True Anti-Pamela*," *Studies in Eighteenth-Century Culture* 22 (1992): 37–49; Ruth Bernard Yeazell, *Fictions of Modesty: Women and Courtship in the English Novel* (Chicago: University of Chicago Press, 1991), 83–4.

66 Kaufmann, *Business of Common Life*, theorizes the ongoing mutual supplementation and correction of parallel systems. Such moments of rapid change or ideological crisis make the mutually corrective role of these discourses more explicit.

67 See Clark, *English Society*; Colley, *Britons*.

68 Newman, *English Nationalism*, 58.

69 Jill Campbell, *Natural Masques: Gender and Identity in Fielding's Plays and Novels* (Stanford: Stanford University Press, 1995), 142, 158–9.

70 "Lady Kilmarnock and Lady Balmerino's Sorrowful Lamentation for the Death of their Lords, who were beheaded for High-Treason on Tower-Hill, on Monday, August 18th, 1746," 17–20. Such connections highlight Davers's Toryism as well as the power of Richardson's gendered representations.

71 As, e.g., in Fielding's *Tom Jones*, 515–17.

72 *Brief Account of the Life and Family of Miss Jenny Cameron, the Reputed Mistress of the Pretender's Eldest Son* (London: Gardner, 1746), 51. Trews portraits conclude two printings of *Life of Dr. Archibald Cameron, Brother to Donald Cameron of Lochiel, Chief of that Clan* (London: Cooper, 1753); the pamphleteer concedes that their purpose is "to gratify the Reader's Curiosity" with a "militant Lady" (30). The very hostile *Life of Miss Jenny Cameron, the Reputed Mistress of the Deputy Pretender* (London: Whitefield, 1746) portrays her in a tartan frock; from the neck up she resembles portraits of Charles Edward Stuart.

73 "A List of the Goods and Effects taken after the Battle of Culloden, belonging to the Young Pretender, and brought from Scotland, to be sold To-morrow, under Prime Cost, at the Ax on Tower-Hill."

74 Andrew Henderson, *History of the Rebellion, MDCCXLV and MDCCXLVI*, 5th ed. (London: Millar, 1753), 120.

75 "Poem by a Lady on Seeing his Highness the Prince Regent." See also "Copy of a Letter from a Lady to the Lady G--dd-s, at K-l-v-ick, to the Care of Mr. James R---- Merchant in Inverness," which remarks of Charles Edward, "O would God I had been a Man, that I might have shared his Fate . . . never to be removed from him!" This was an element of homoeroticism that anti-Jacobites quickly seized.

76 Hume, "Of the Parties of Great Britain," in *Essays*, 64–5; "Of the Original Contract," in *Essays*, 465–6.
77 See R. J. Smith, *Gothic Bequest*.
78 Richardson, *Clarissa*, 1495; subsequently cited in the text.
79 Arguing that *Clarissa*'s morality is more sentimental than committed to Locke's Providence is not necessarily to concur with Kay's *Political Constructions*, 136, that *Clarissa* is a sceptical novel from which natural morality and divine influence have disappeared.
80 Cook, *Epistolary Bodies*, 7.
81 Newman, *English Nationalism*, 21–47.
82 McKeon, *Origins of the English Novel*, 174–5.
83 A possible source is George Cheyne's *English Malady: or, a Treatise of Nervous Diseases of All Kinds* (London: Strahan, 1733), blaming national weakness on deformities in particular bodies within the body politic – caused by excessive consumption of imported foods.
84 On the ethical ambiguities of the elopement, see Bowers, 209–13.
85 Even within the novel Lovelace's rape is unequivocally a rape. Clarissa dies, according to the converted Belford, in "unblemished virtue" (1363).
86 For the naturalness of virtue, see *Clarissa*, 657 and 878–9. For the Harlowes' unnatural passions, see 518, 987.
87 Eaves and Kimpel, *Samuel Richardson*, 41.
88 Richardson, *Correspondence*, v: 109.
89 Jerome Christensen, *Practicing Enlightenment: Hume and the Formation of a Literary Career* (Madison: University of Wisconsin Press, 1987), 4, 11, 84–7.
90 See Descartes, *Meditations on the First Philosophy*, trans. John Veitch, in *The Rationalists* (New York: Doubleday, 1974), 137, 141–2: "it is absolutely necessary to conclude . . . that God exists: for . . . I should not . . . have the idea of an infinite substance, seeing I am a finite being, unless it were given me by some substance in reality infinite."
91 Eagleton, *Ideology of the Aesthetic*, 51.
92 See David Miller, *Philosophy and Ideology in Hume's Political Thought* (Oxford: Clarendon, 1981), 102–3.
93 On this reasoning Hume grudgingly gestures toward God in later essays. His remark in "Original Contract," 466 – "That the DEITY is the ultimate author of all government, will never be denied by any, who . . . allow, that all events in the universe are conducted by an uniform plan, and directed to wise purposes" – retains all his earlier scepticism, but the essay unfolds as if Hume places himself among those who allow precisely that.
94 See Hume, "Polygamy and Divorces," 183, 189. Hume's recent commentators point out the force his sentimental social contract requires; see Eagleton, *Ideology of the Aesthetic*, 42–3.
95 [William Kenrick,] *The Whole Duty of Woman* (Newbury: Mentorian, n.d.), 78; John Gregory, *A Father's Legacy to his Daughters* (London: Strahan, 1774), 10.
96 Nicholas Hudson, "Arts of Seduction and the Rhetoric of *Clarissa*," in *Modern Language Quarterly* 51 (1990): 31.

97 Richard Cumberland, *Observer* 46, in *The Observer: Being a Collection of Moral, Literary and Familiar Essays*, 2nd ed. (London: Dilly, 1788), II: 156.

98 John P. Zomchick, *Family and the Law in Eighteenth-Century Fiction: The Public Conscience in the Private Sphere* (Cambridge: Cambridge University Press, 1993), 58–80.

99 Caroline Gonda, *Reading Daughters' Fictions, 1709–1834: Novels and Society from Manley to Edgeworth* (Cambridge: Cambridge University Press, 1996), 80–2.

100 Zomchick's *Family and the Law* argues that Clarissa's faith is the last repository of Tory resistance. But her investment in families as the original source of a social contract marks her as a Lockean holdover. For Locke's practical theology of social order, see John Dunn, "From Applied Theology to Social Analysis: The Break Between John Locke and the Scottish Enlightenment," in Istvan Hont and Michael Ignatieff, eds., *Wealth and Virtue: The Shaping of Political Economy in the Scottish Enlightenment* (Cambridge: Cambridge University Press, 1983), 119–35.

101 Richardson, *Correspondence*, II: 215–16. See also Gonda, *Reading Daughters' Fictions*, 66–104.

102 From Clarissa's second letter to Anna, 41–2, it appears she has held the estates for at least two years, since the summer of 1745 at latest.

103 On the "*feme sole*" and marital property, see Susan Staves, *Married Women's Separate Property in England, 1660–1833* (Cambridge: Harvard University Press, 1990); see also Okin, "Patriarchy and Married Women's Property".

104 Walter Scott, *Waverley* (Edinburgh: Cadell, 1829). Like Robert C. Gordon, in *Under Which King? A Study of the Scottish Waverley Novels* (Edinburgh: Oliver, 1969), 17, Scott quotes Shakespeare, *Henry IV Part II*, V. iii. For Jacobitism's threat, see the work of Clark, Cruickshanks, Erskine-Hill, and Monod.

105 On the allegorical preoccupations of Jacobitism, see Monod, *passim*. On allegory as a byproduct of thinking history in the eighteenth century, see Kelley, *Reinventing Allegory*, 70.

106 Warner, *Reading* Clarissa, 64.

2 "SUMMONED INTO THE MACHINE": BURNEY'S GENRES,
SHERIDAN'S SENTIMENT, AND CONSERVATIVE CRITIQUE

1 Gwyn Walters, "The Booksellers in 1759 and 1774: The Battle for Literary Property," *Library*, 5th series, 29 (1974): 287–311; Terry Belanger, "Publishers and Writers in Eighteenth-Century England," in Isabel Rivers, ed., *Books and their Readers in Eighteenth-Century England* (Leicester: Leicester University Press, 1982), 5–25.

2 Frances Burney, *Early Diary 1768–1778*, ed. Annie Raine Ellis (London: Bell, 1971), I: 285–9. Subsequently cited in the text, abbreviated *ED*.

3 On response to the Marriage Act, see Paul Langford, *A Polite and Commercial People: England, 1727–1783* (Oxford: Clarendon, 1989), 114–15. The Act's

costly controls, aimed at dowried women, often prevented labouring-class women from marrying. See Stone, *Family, Sex and Marriage*, 397–404.

4 For example, Lydia's seduction in Austen's *Pride and Prejudice*; the fatal pursuit of Lochiel and his English bride in Thomas Campbell's "Lord Ullin's Daughter."

5 Boswell, *Life of Johnson*, 1: 437–9; 2: 259, 272.

6 Before reluctantly contracting for *Wanderer*, Burney declared, "I wish ardently to superintend the press." See *Journals and Letters*, ed. Joyce Hemlow *et al.* (Oxford: Oxford University Press, 1972–84), VII: 104, 165. On subscription, see Jan Fergus and Janice Farrar Thaddeus, "Women, Publishers, and Money, 1790–1820," *Studies in Eighteenth-Century Culture* 17 (1987): 193, 201.

7 Burney, *Evelina, or, The History of a Young Lady's Entrance into the World*, ed. Edward A. Bloom (Oxford: Oxford University Press, 1968), 1.

8 For a contrasting argument, for fiction's agency in dividing domestic from political economy, see Thompson, *Models of Value*, 174–84.

9 Leonore Davidoff and Catherine Hall, *Family Fortunes: Men and Women of the English Middle Class, 1780–1850* (Chicago: University of Chicago Press, 1987), 30–4. See also the few domestic studies in John Brewer and Roy Porter, eds., *Consumption and the World of Goods* (London: Routledge, 1993) and the supply-side emphasis of Neil McKendrick, Brewer, and J. H. Plumb, *Birth of a Consumer Society: The Commercialization of Eighteenth-Century England* (Bloomington: Indiana University Press, 1982).

10 See Poovey, *The Proper Lady and the Woman Writer* (Chicago: University of Chicago Press, 1984); Claudia L. Johnson, *Equivocal Beings: Politics, Gender, and Sentimentality in the 1790s* (Chicago: University of Chicago Press, 1995), 144–6; Katherine Sobba Green, *The Courtship Novel, 1740–1820: A Feminized Genre* (Lexington: University Press of Kentucky, 1991); Yeazell, *Fictions of Modesty*.

11 For example, Gaye Tuchman, *Edging Women Out: Victorian Novelists, Publishers, and Social Change* (New Haven: Yale University Press, 1989); Raven, *Judging New Wealth*; Terry Lovell, *Consuming Fiction* (London: Verso, 1987), 47–72; Spencer, *Woman Novelist*.

12 The teleology is realized in Fielding's *Amelia* (1751) and Charlotte Lennox's *Henrietta* (1758), but not in Frances Sheridan's *The Memoirs of Miss Sidney Bidulph* or Jean-Jacques Rousseau's *Julie, or the New Eloise* (both 1761).

13 Sheridan's son Richard Brinsley was subsequently elected to Parliament. Her husband Thomas was targeted by pamphleteers for promoting the Irish "Patriot Party" (*Case of the Stage in Ireland* [Dublin: Coote, n.d.]). On their politics, see R. B. McDowell, *Ireland in the Age of Imperialism and Revolution, 1760–1801* (Oxford: Clarendon, 1979), 317; Joep Leerssen, *Mere Irish and Fíor-Ghael: Studies in the Idea of Irish Nationality* (Amsterdam: Benjamins, 1986), 130–2.

14 See Doody, "Frances Sheridan: Morality and Annihilated Time," in Mary Anne Schofield and Cecilia Macheski, eds., *Fetter'd or Free? British Women Novelists, 1670–1815* (Athens: Ohio University Press, 1986), 324–58.

15 Sidney, in Sheridan's *Sidney Bidulph* (London: Virago, 1987), 80, highlights the abbreviation: "I could hear with pleasure, that Mr Faulkland was married to that Miss B. I wish I knew the other letters that compose her name." Subsequently cited in the text.

16 Her name, Burchell, is revealed in closing vol. I.

17 Celia's postscript has Sidney living on for a decade, her "retirement" disrupted by the "exquisite distress" of her daughters, which recapitulates her own. In 1767 Sheridan added two volumes about "the Misses Arnold."

18 Review of Sheridan, in *London Magazine* 30 (March 1761): 168. The *Monthly Review* 24 (1761): 260 similarly feared moral corruption: Sheridan has "no other design, than to draw tears from the reader by distressing innocence and virtue . . . [S]uch representations are by no means calculated to encourage and promote Virtue." For related Anglican critiques of predestination, see Christopher Hill, *The World Turned Upside Down: Radical Ideas During the English Revolution* (Harmondsworth: Penguin, 1975), 173, 328–31.

19 Review of Frances Sheridan, in *Critical Review* 11 (1761): 186, 187; Boswell, *Life of Johnson*, 1: 390.

20 Quoted in Colin Campbell, *The Romantic Ethic and the Spirit of Modern Consumerism* (Oxford: Blackwell, 1987), 141.

21 See Ellis, *Politics of Sensibility*, 5–6, for the contemporary distinction – though Ellis's analysis collapses the two.

22 See Toby's encounter with Le Fever and Tristram's with Maria, in Laurence Sterne's *The Life and Opinions of Tristram Shandy, Gentleman*, ed. Ian Watt (Boston: Houghton, 1965), 321–8, 484; or Henry Mackenzie's *Man of Feeling* (London: Scholartis, 1928), 80, in which Harley rewards a beautiful "maniac" with "a couple of guineas" and a "burst into tears." Robert Markley, "Sentimentality as Performance: Shaftesbury, Sterne, and the Theatrics of Virtue," in Felicity Nussbaum and Brown, eds., *The New Eighteenth Century: Theory, Politics, English Literature* (New York: Methuen, 1987), 220–2, notes Sterne's and Mackenzie's uncertainty about the value of Richardsonian sentiment. See also Andrea Henderson, *Romantic Identities: Varieties of Subjectivity, 1774–1830* (Cambridge: Cambridge University Press, 1996), 144–5; Patricia Meyer Spacks, "Oscillations of Sensibility," in *NLH* 25 (1994): 505–20.

23 Reviews acknowledged the generic connection. The *Monthly* noted, 260, that despite claims "that *Romance* is the last physic that can be administered to a corrupt people," "Two of our countrymen . . . have succeeded in this design" – in Richardson's *Clarissa* and Sheridan's "Romance now before us."

24 Ann Ellsworth, in "Resisting Richardson: Sarah Fielding, Frances Sheridan, Charlotte Lennox, and the Didactic Novel" (unpublished diss., University of Washington, 1997), 122–5, opposes Sheridan's "realism" to contemporary "didacticism."

25 Richardson, *Clarissa*, 1495.

26 See Ellsworth, "Resisting Richardson," for the assertion that Cecilia and "the Editor" voice Sheridan's personal views.

27 Descartes, *Meditations on the First Philosophy*, trans. John Veitch, in *The Rationalists*, 116. Recall that Hume represents his *Treatise* as a rejection of Cartesian theology as well as a supplement to Locke's political history. Spacks, in "Oscillations," 509, reads the gendered damage wrought by Richardsonian sentiment as a target of Sheridan's "interrogation."

28 Spacks, in *Desire and Truth: Functions of Plot in Eighteenth-Century English Novels* (Chicago: University of Chicago Press, 1990), 115, places this work amid a sceptical trend in plotting culminating in *Tristram Shandy*.

29 Todd, *Sign of Angellica*, 166.

30 Hume, *Treatise*, 498–500.

31 Adam Smith, *Theory of the Moral Sentiments*, 1: 184–5. Subsequently cited in the text, abbreviated *TMS*. Kaufmann, in *Business of Common Life*, 47–50, glosses this passage as a bridge to the political economy of system in *Wealth of Nations*: Smith here defends self-regulating economies on naturalized theological grounds.

32 Todd, *Sign of Angellica*, 173.

33 Sheridan's *History of Nourjahad* (Dublin: Wilson, 1767) ends with the sultan's comment, 221, that "gratification of our passions" cannot "satisfy the human heart . . . in a world . . . never meant for our final place of abode." Nussbaum, in *Torrid Zones: Maternity, Sexuality, and Empire in Eighteenth-Century English Narratives* (Baltimore: Johns Hopkins University Press, 1995), 132–3, argues that Sheridan defends romance ethically but finally rejects it through the sultan's revelation of his theatrical deceit – another reading of Sheridan's generic ambivalence.

34 Burney's heroine's anonymity and social adventures recall earlier romances in which Behn's and Haywood's heroines temporarily trade fixed identities for illicit liaisons. But Evelina, immersed in the market, has no identity, and illicit encounters are forced on her in consequence.

35 The Branghtons are a "city" silversmith, nephew to Evelina's grandmother, and his children. Toward Macartney, they reiterate contempt, and they dun him for the rent despite his risk of suicide (Burney, *Evelina*, 176, 185; subsequently cited in the text).

36 Gonda, in *Reading Daughters' Fictions*, 130, interprets Burney's emotional focus on fathers psychologically. But kinship in *Evelina* cannot fully be interpreted apart from questions of socioeconomic value.

37 Newman's *Rise of English Nationalism*, 136, importantly names *Evelina* as a nationalist novel. See also the frequent attacks on Evelina's grandmother for wishing "to take[Evelina] . . . to Paris, that she may . . . improve herself" (166); Caroline Evelyn marries Belmont in Paris, under Duval's guardianship. Burney redirects English bigotry from Scotland toward France.

38 Gallagher, *Nobody's Story*, 215–27.

39 For a fuller account, in Burney's *Memoir* of Charles Burney, see *Evelina*, ed. Stewart J. Cooke (New York: Norton, 1998), 345–52.

40 See Raven, *Judging New Wealth*; on literary production and nationalism, see Newman, 87–120.

41 Thurlow qtd. in Walters, "Booksellers," 304.

42 Cumberland, *Observer*, I: 163–5, 267, 272–3.

43 That Burney protests credit need not imply that a "consumer revolution" was taking place, as McKendrick, Brewer, and Plumb, *Birth of a Consumer Society*, 13, suggest; nor need one agree with Raven that the rich became a new scapegoat as publishers defended their own ongoing desire for profit. A variety of dates and processes have been proposed for the "consumer revolution" and its "development" or "acceptance." Reading these in "Consumer Culture in Historical Perspective," in Brewer and Porter, *Consumption and the World of Goods*, 19–39, Jean-Christophe Agnew argues that studying consumerism from the supply-side masks the ideologies that lend "things" value.

44 Letter from "Mr. Edwards," in *Correspondence of Samuel Richardson*, ed. Barbauld, III: 2–3.

45 Richardson, *Clarissa*, 1495–8; Richardson, *Pamela*, 5.

46 Agnew's *Worlds Apart: The Market and the Theater in Anglo-American Thought, 1550–1750* (Cambridge: Cambridge University Press, 1987), 187, embeds this question or threat of spectacle in contemporary theories of the marketplace.

47 Streatfield occupies a week's letters. Her fame preceded her: Burney was warned "she had tears at command." See *Diary and Letters of Frances Burney, Madame d'Arblay*, ed. Sarah Chauncey Woolsey (Boston: Roberts, 1880), II: 71–7. Subsequently cited in the text, abbreviated *DL*.

48 Joyce Hemlow, "Fanny Burney and the Courtesy Books," in *PMLA* 65 (1950): 732–61.

49 Gregory, *Father's Legacy*, vi. Subsequently cited in the text.

50 She would marry Archibald Alison, whose *Essays on the Nature and Principles of Taste* (Edinburgh: Robinson, 1790), 131, equate "Modesty" with appearances.

51 Kenrick, *Whole Duty*, 24, 45.

52 The subtitle echoes Sheridan.

53 Burney, *Cecilia*, ed. Peter Sabor and Doody (Oxford: Oxford University Press, 1988), 291. Subsequently cited in the text.

54 For a contrasting account of Burney and conduct books, see Hemlow, "Fanny Burney," 733; Gina Campbell, "How to Read like a Gentleman: Fanny Burney's Instructions to her Critics in *Evelina*," *ELH* 57 (1990): 557–84.

55 Fordyce, *Sermons*. Fordyce's "generous sensibility" equates charitable spending with virtue. Women must also "spread. . . grace and embellishment over human life" (I: 164) by beauty, dress, and "ELEGANT ACCOMPLISHMENTS" (I: 184) – or "disappoint the design of their creation" (I: 15–16).

56 Burney, *Camilla*, ed. Bloom and Lillian Bloom (Oxford: Oxford University Press, 1983), 159–60. Subsequently cited in the text.

57 For Clarissa's posthumous letters, see Richardson, *Clarissa*, 1367–8, 1370–7.
58 Richardson, *Clarissa*, 1361.
59 See Eagleton, *Ideology of the Aesthetic*.
60 See McKendrick, Brewer and Plumb, *Birth of a Consumer Society*, 204–10.
61 Austen, *Pride and Prejudice*, ed. James Kinsley (Oxford: Oxford University Press, 1970), 260.
62 Edward Copeland, in "Jane Austen and the Consumer Revolution," in J. David Grey, ed., *The Jane Austen Companion* (New York: Macmillan, 1986), 79, distinguishes Burney's terms from Austen's. See also Julia Epstein, *The Iron Pen: Frances Burney and the Politics of Women's Writing* (Madison: University of Wisconsin Press, 1989), 152, 159.
63 Anderson, *Origin of Commerce*, v, subsequently cited in the text; letter on Anderson, *Gentleman's Magazine* 53 (1783): 41–2.
64 Burke discussed Anderson in 1796; see *Correspondence*, ed. R. B. McDowell (Cambridge: Cambridge University Press, 1969), VIII: 413–14, 421, 447. On *Camilla*, see *Correspondence*, VIII: 423.
65 *The Laws Respecting the Ordinary Practice of Impositions in Money Lending, and the Buying and Selling of Public Offices* (London: Clarke, n.d.), 408.
66 Robert Harley, *An Essay Upon Public Credit* (London: Baynes, 1797), 8–9, 12–13.
67 See also *Facts and Observations Relative to the Coinage and Circulation of Counterfeit or Base Money; with Suggestions for Remedying the Evil* (London: Fry, 1795), 1; *The Iniquity of Banking: Or, Bank Notes Proved to be Injurious to the Public, and the Real Cause of the Exorbitant Price of Provisions* (London: Jordan, 1797), 10.
68 Burney, *Camilla*, 892–3.
69 As conservative pamphleteers lament. See McKendrick, Brewer, and Plumb, *Birth of a Consumer Society*, 214.
70 See Christopher Kent, " 'Real Solemn History' and Social History," in David Monaghan, ed., *Jane Austen in a Social Context* (Totowa: Barnes, 1981), 86–104. Hester Chapone's *Letters on the Improvement of the Mind*, in *Works* (London: Murray, 1807), I: 209, 217, recommend Hume's "most entertaining" account of Britain's economic and political ascendancy. See also Fordyce, *Sermons*, I: 214.
71 Hume, "Of the Standard of Taste," in *Essays*, 230. Subsequently cited in the text, abbreviated *ST*.
72 Hume, "Of the Dignity or Meanness of Human Nature," in *Essays*, 84. Eagleton, *Ideology of the Aesthetic*, 31–69, details the social implications of "the beautiful." See also Christensen, *Practicing Enlightenment*, 99–100.
73 Hume, *Treatise*, 316–17. Subsequently cited in the text, abbreviated *T*.
74 Hume, "Of Commerce," in *Essays*, 261.
75 On women in "social contracts" see Pateman, *Sexual Contract*, 1–18 and *Disorder of Women*, 17–32. For Hume, in "Of the Delicacy of Taste and Passion," *Essays*, 3–8, taste cements masculine communities.
76 For example, Mirvan in *Evelina*, 109; ridiculed by Elinor in *Wanderer*, 399.

77 See Pocock, *Virtue, Commerce, and History*, 106–115. On translations of classical republicanism into politically diverse economic nationalism, see Newman, 21–47.

78 Hume, "Of Refinement in the Arts," in *Essays*, 272, 277, 280.

79 See John Barrell, *The Political Theory of Painting from Reynolds to Hazlitt* (New Haven: Yale University Press, 1986), 1–68; for Hume, see John Robertson, in "The Scottish Enlightenment at the Limits of the Civic Tradition," in Hont and Ignatieff, eds., *Wealth and Virtue*, 137–78.

80 Pocock, *Virtue, Commerce, and History*, 194–5, 199.

81 Armstrong, *Desire and Domestic Fiction*.

82 See Gary Kelly, "Revolutionary and Romantic Feminism," in *Revolution and English Romanticism*, ed. Keith Hanley and Raman Selden (New York: St. Martin's, 1991), 115–17. For Burney's ambivalence as feminist protest, see Judith Lowder Newton, *Women, Power, and Subversion: Social Strategies in British Fiction, 1778–1860* (Athens: University of Georgia Press, 1981), 11; Terry Castle, *Masquerade and Civilization: The Carnivalesque in Eighteenth-Century English Culture and Fiction* (Stanford: Stanford University Press, 1986), 276, 285. In Kristina Straub's historical-formalist reading, *Divided Fictions: Fanny Burney and Feminine Strategy* (Lexington: University Press of Kentucky, 1987), Burney parodies her own political uncertainty.

83 Doody calls *Cecilia* "the first of the 'Jacobin' novels," in *Frances Burney: The Life in the Works* (New Brunswick: Rutgers University Press, 1988), 147; see also D. Grant Campbell, "Fashionable Suicide: Conspicuous Consumption and the Collapse of Credit in Frances Burney's *Cecilia*," in *Studies in Eighteenth-Century Culture* 20 (1990): 122. While Burney's novels lament that "Wealth governs . . . society" and "the highest sin . . . is running out of money," a mercenary world is not an aristocracy. Burney assails modern social and ethical fluidity, tracing them to liberal finance and trade – not the aristocratic values that *The Wanderer* restores.

84 See Mary Douglas and Baron Isherwood, *The World of Goods* (New York: Basic, 1979), 12, 67.

85 Green, *Courtship Novel*, 80–1.

86 *Diary and Letters of Madame d'Arblay* (London: Colburn, 1842), v: 306, 311–13.

87 See Grant McCracken, *Culture and Consumption: New Approaches to the Symbolic Character of Consumer Goods and Activities* (Bloomington: Indiana University Press, 1988), 31; Roland Barthes, *The Fashion System*, trans. Matthew Ward and Richard Howard (New York: Hill, 1983).

88 Burney, *The Wanderer; or, Female Difficulties*, ed. Doody, Robert L. Mack, and Peter Sabor (Oxford: Oxford University Press, 1991), 229. Subsequently cited in the text.

89 Van Sant's *Sensibility*, 5, links sensibility to "immediate moral and aesthetic responsiveness."

90 Sheridan, *Sidney Bidulph*, 330–1.

91 See Bourdieu, *Distinction*, 99–168.

92 See Bourdieu, *Distinction*, 164: "competitive struggle" between social groups "makes everlasting . . . not different conditions but the difference between conditions."
93 McCracken, *Culture and Consumption*, 34.
94 See *Cecilia*, 119–23.
95 Doody, *Frances Burney*, 147.
96 Burney, *Journals and Letters*, VII: 166; see also VII: 103–4, 153; VII: 564–6, XII: 639–40.

3 WOLLSTONECRAFT AND THE REVOLUTION OF ECONOMIC HISTORY

1 Mary Favret, *Romantic Correspondence: Women, Politics, and the Fiction of Letters* (Cambridge: Cambridge University Press, 1993), 110.
2 Review of William Godwin, *Memoirs of the Author of the Vindication of the Rights of Woman*, in *Anti-Jacobin Review* 1 (1798): 97; Wollstonecraft, *Letters Written during a Short Residence in Sweden, Norway, and Denmark*, in *Works*, VI: 339, subsequently cited in the text.
3 See Staves, *Married Women's Property*.
4 Fredric Jameson, *Postmodernism: or, the Cultural Logic of Late Capitalism* (Durham: Duke University Press, 1994), 16–18. Compare Charlotte Lennox's 1752 *Female Quixote* (London: Oxford University Press, 1970), whose heroine chooses between distinct worlds of romance or reality. Wollstonecraft's pastiche, sentimental as well as bottomlessly textual, marries Burney's economic romances with Sterne's *Tristram Shandy*.
5 Judith Butler's *Gender Trouble: Feminism and the Subversion of Identity* (New York: Routledge, 1990), 32, 146. See also Slavoj Žižek, *For They Know Not What They Do: Enjoyment as a Political Factor* (London: Verso, 1991), 13, for the "double inversion" that "calls into question the very standard of 'normality'" by which it "measure[s] the invertedness" of what it negates.
6 See Siskin, *Historicity of Romantic Discourse*, 67–93; Alan Liu, *Wordsworth: The Sense of History* (Stanford: Stanford University Press, 1989), 138–63; Duncan, *Modern Romance*; Jon Klancher, *The Making of English Reading Audiences, 1790–1832* (Madison: University of Wisconsin Press, 1987) and "Godwin and the Republican Romance: Genre, Politics, and Contingency in Cultural History," in *MLQ* 56 (1995): 146–8. See also chapter 5.
7 Horkheimer and Adorno, *Dialectic of Enlightenment*.
8 See Georg Lukács, *The Historical Novel*, trans. Hannah and Stanley Mitchell (Lincoln: University of Nebraska Press, 1983); Watt, *Rise of the Novel*. Recent critiques include McKeon's argument that genres rhetorically produce their own genealogy, in *Origins of the English Novel*, 45–7; Moretti, *Signs Taken for Wonders*; Siskin, *Work of Writing*; Cohen, "History and Genre."
9 Wollstonecraft's account of this competition is a combative precursor of Kaufmann's description, in *Business of Common Life*, of novels and political economy as competing but mutually supplemental discourses.
10 On more traditional gothics and their role in denaturing sensibility and

romance, see Duncan, *Modern Romance*, 35–50; Andrea Henderson, *Romantic Identities* (Cambridge: Cambridge University Press, 1996), 38–58.

11 François Furet, *Interpreting the French Revolution*, trans. Elborg Forster (Cambridge: Cambridge University Press, 1978), 23.

12 On the Revolution's phases, see Albert Soboul, *Short History of the French Revolution 1789–1799*, trans. Geoffrey Symcox (Berkeley: University of California Press, 1965), 86–111.

13 Genre historians and critics of Wollstonecraft rarely address her genres; Favret, *Romantic Correspondence*, and Tilottama Rajan, *The Supplement of Reading: Figures of Understanding in Romantic Theory and Practice* (Ithaca: Cornell University Press, 1990) are important exceptions.

14 I am mindful of questions asked in Liu's "Local Transcendence: Cultural Criticism, Postmodernism, and the Romanticism of Detail," in *Representations* 32 (1990): 75–113, about the neo-Romantic consequences of placing "texts" synecdochically against "real history"; and in Marjorie Levinson's "Romantic Criticism: The State of the Art," in Favret and Watson, eds., *At the Limits of Romanticism: Essays in Cultural, Feminist, and Materialist Criticism* (Bloomington: Indiana UP, 1994), 269–81, about reading Romantic texts as negating "real history." But no apologies are necessary for reading the genres of the 1790s as historical interventions: such interventions were already implicit as these genres were used in debating Revolutionary history. Reading the debates need not recapitulate Romantic historiography – treating history as a discursive event or quailing before the new sublime of unrepresentable history.

15 Review of Godwin, *Memoirs*, *European Magazine* 33 (1798): 251; Margaret Kirkham, *Jane Austen: Feminism and Fiction* (Brighton: Harvester, 1983), 48–50.

16 Favret, *Romantic Correspondence*, 129–30; Daniel O'Quinn, "Trembling: Wollstonecraft, Godwin and the Resistance to Literature," in *ELH* 64 (1997): 761–88.

17 Review of Wollstonecraft, *Rights of Men*, in *Monthly Review* n.s. 4 (1791): 96.

18 The *Anti-Jacobin* review of Godwin's *Memoirs* damns Wollstonecraft's "ardent sensibility" for promoting "theories" of "JACOBIN MORALITY" (95, 98).

19 Review of Elizabeth Inchbald's *Simple Story*, in *European Magazine* 19 (1791): 197.

20 Inchbald, *A Simple Story*, ed. J. M. S. Tompkins (Oxford: Oxford University Press, 1988), 50. Subsequently cited in the text.

21 Review of Inchbald, *Simple Story*, in *Monthly Review*, n.s. 4 (1791): 436, 437–8.

22 Doody, "Frances Sheridan," 350–5; Spacks, *Desire and Truth*, 202. For the opposing view, see Jo Alyson Parker, "Complicating *A Simple Story*: Inchbald's Two Versions of Female Power," in *Eighteenth-Century Studies* 30 (1997): 255–70.

23 Castle, *Masquerade and Civilization*, 323.

24 The *Anti-Jacobin*'s review of Godwin's *Memoirs* ironically notes that Wollstonecraft – fancying herself "a phænomenon of nature" – "*undertook* to answer that wonderful production" (95).

25 For Burke's family romance, see Ronald Paulson, *Representations of Revolution (1789–1820)* (New Haven: Yale University Press, 1983), 59–62. See also Duncan's discussion of Burkean gothic in *Modern Romance*, 23–5.

26 See Liu, *Wordsworth*, 138–63.

27 See Duncan, *Modern Romance*, 23, 53.

28 Edmund Burke, *Reflections on the Revolution in France*, ed. Pocock (Indianapolis: Hackett, 1987), 30. Subsequently cited in the text.

29 See chapter 1.

30 Duncan, *Modern Romance*, 53.

31 See R. J. Smith, *Gothic Bequest*.

32 Horace Walpole, *The Castle of Otranto*, ed. W. S. Lewis (London: Oxford University Press, 1964), 7.

33 Paulson, *Representations of Revolution*, 60–1.

34 Linda M. G. Zerilli, "Text/ Woman as Spectacle: Edmund Burke's 'French Revolution,'" in *The Eighteenth Century: Theory and Interpretation* 33 (1992): 59.

35 See Lynn Hunt, *The Family Romance of the French Revolution* (Berkeley: University of California Press, 1992), 103–23; Castle, *The Apparitional Lesbian: Female Homosexuality and Modern Culture* (New York: Columbia University Press, 1993), 127–40.

36 Wollstonecraft's review of *Simple Story*, in *Contributions to the* Analytical Review *1788–1797*, *Works*, VII: 369–370.

37 See Johnson, Preface to *The Plays of Shakespeare*, in *Samuel Johnson*, ed. Donald Greene (Oxford: Oxford University Press, 1984), 420–1.

38 See Tom Furniss, *Edmund Burke's Aesthetic Ideology: Language, Gender, and Political Economy in Revolution* (Cambridge: Cambridge University Press, 1993), 221. Paulson's work is an exception.

39 R. J. Smith, *Gothic Bequest*, 35; rhetorical bar-trading between Whigs and Tories is also discussed in Monod, *Jacobitism and the English People*, 15–27.

40 Kelly, *Revolutionary Feminism: The Mind and Career of Mary Wollstonecraft* (New York: St. Martin's, 1992), 88; Furniss, *Edmund Burke's Aesthetic Ideology*, 223.

41 See Pocock, *Virtue, Commerce, and History*, 194–9.

42 See Pocock, *Virtue, Commerce, and History*, 194–9.

43 Thomas Paine, *Rights of Man*, in *Political Writings*, ed. Bruce Kuklick (Cambridge: Cambridge University Press, 1989), I: 54–5.

44 Paine, *Rights of Man*, I: 133–4; II: 198, 200. Subsequently cited in the text.

45 See Klancher, *Making of English Reading Audiences*.

46 Quoted in *Speeches of the Hon. Thomas Erskine (Now Lord Erskine), When at the Bar, on Subjects Connected with the Liberty of the Press, and Against Constructive Treasons*, ed. James Ridgway (London: Ridgway, 1810), II: 48.

47 Habermas describes this short-lived ideal in *Structural Transformation of the Public Sphere*, xviii. See also Klancher, *Making of English Reading Audiences*, 110; Marilyn Butler, *Burke, Paine, Godwin, and the French Revolution Controversy* (Cambridge: Cambridge University Press, 1984), 14, 16.

48 See Paine, *Rights of Man*, ed. Eric Foner (London: Penguin, 1984), 80, which unlike Kuklick's text, 89, reproduces the first edition.

49 Gerald P. Tyson, *Joseph Johnson: A Liberal Publisher* (Iowa: University of Iowa Press, 1979), 155. The LCS admitted all those "perswaded that the welfare of these kingdoms requires that every person of *Adult* years . . . should have a vote for a Member of Parliament [*sic*]." But member rolls in Mary Thale's *Selections from the Papers of the London Corresponding Society 1792–1799* (Cambridge: Cambridge University Press, 1983) include no women. A delegate to the 1793 Edinburgh Convention sheds light on LCS definitions of majority in its temporal and electoral senses: conventions should " 'represent six or seven hundred thousand males . . . a majority of all the adults in the kingdom' " (quoted in Erskine, *Speeches*, II: 262).

50 In *Friends of Liberty: The English Democratic Movement in the Age of the French Revolution* (Cambridge: Harvard University Press, 1979), 319, Albert Goodwin notes that John Thelwall praised France for "throwing open the nunneries" to "emancipate . . . many potential wives and mothers."

51 Thelwall, *Rights of Nature, Against the Usurpations of Establishments*, in *Politics of English Jacobinism: Writings*, ed. Gregory Claeys (University Park: Pennsylvania State University Press, 1995), 396–7; see also Thale, *Papers of the London Corresponding Society*; Erskine, *Speeches*.

52 David Worrall, in *Radical Culture: Discourse, Resistance and Surveillance, 1790–1820* (New York: Harvester, 1992), 107, notes that Spa Fields Rising organizers planned "a parade of young women" " 'to take off the attention of soldiers, so that they should not ride over us, and to give us time to address them.' " See also J. Ann Hone, *For the Cause of Truth: Radicalism in London, 1796–1821* (Oxford: Clarendon, 1982), 308.

53 Goodwin, *Friends of Liberty*, 383; E. P. Thompson, *Making of the English Working Class* (London: Penguin, 1980), 67–72. See also John Bohstedt, "The Myth of the Feminine Food Riot: Women as Proto-Citizens in English Community Politics, 1790–1810," in *Women and Politics in the Age of the Democratic Revolution*, ed. Harriet B. Applewhite and Darline G. Levy (Ann Arbor: University of Michigan Press, 1990), 38–9.

54 Helen Maria Williams, *Letters Written in France* (London: Cadell, 1790), 63.

55 Review of Burke, *Reflections*, in *Monthly Review* n.s. 3 (1790): 315.

56 Review of *Reflections*, 313.

57 Review of *Reflections*, 465.

58 Cora Kaplan, "Wild Nights: Pleasure/Sexuality/Feminism," in Armstrong and Leonard Tennenhouse, eds., *The Ideology of Conduct: Essays on Literature and the History of Sexuality* (New York: Methuen, 1987), 181; Moira Ferguson, *Colonialism and Gender Relations from Mary Wollstonecraft to Jamaica Kincaid* (New York: Columbia University Press, 1993), 19. See also Poovey, *Proper Lady*, 96.

59 Wollstonecraft, *Vindication of the Rights of Men*, in *Works*, V: 29. Subsequently cited in the text, abbreviated *RM*.

60 Anne K. Mellor, "English Women Writers and the French Revolution," in *Rebel Daughters: Women and the French Revolution*, ed. Sara E. Melzer and Leslie W. Rabine (New York: Oxford University Press, 1991), 256.

61 Zillah Eisenstein, *Radical Future of Liberal Feminism*, 101.
62 See Orrin C. Wang, "The Other Reasons: Female Alterity and Enlighten-
    ment Discourse in Mary Wollstonecraft's *A Vindication of the Rights of Woman*,"
    Yale Journal of Criticism 5 (1991): 129–49; Johnson, *Equivocal Beings*, 31.
63 Wollstonecraft, *Vindication of the Rights of Woman*, in *Works*, v: 128. Subse-
    quently cited in the text, abbreviated *RW*.
64 Adam Smith, *Theory of the Moral Sentiments*, 52–6.
65 See Paine, *Rights of Man*, II: 196–200.
66 For example, sales of *A Tale of Two Cities*, by Britain's first "mass" novelist.
    See N. N. Feltes, *Modes of Production of Victorian Novels* (Chicago: University of
    Chicago Press, 1986), 1–17. Scott's sales of "The Field of Waterloo" and
    Paul's Letters to his Kinsfolk are also relevant – see John Sutherland, *Life of
    Walter Scott* (Oxford: Blackwell, 1995), 186–7; Duncan, *Modern Romance*, 77–8.
67 Kaufmann, in *Business of Common Life*, 39, begins uncovering these.
68 Mona Ozouf's *Festivals and the French Revolution*, trans. Alan Sheridan (Cam-
    bridge: Harvard University Press, 1988) discusses "the Revolution as Festi-
    val"; Furet, *Interpreting the French Revolution*; Hunt, *Politics, Culture, and Class in
    the French Revolution* (Berkeley: University of California Press, 1984) and
    Family Romance.
69 See Klancher, *Making of English Reading Audiences*, 111, 116.
70 Louis Montrose, *The Purpose of Playing: Shakespeare and the Cultural Politics of the
    Elizabethan Theatre* (Chicago: University of Chicago Press, 1996), 6.
71 Pocock's account of influences on Burke and Paine, in *Virtue, Commerce, and
    History*, provides a significant nonliterary link (288).
72 On Wollstonecraft's relation to More and others, see Kelly, *English Fiction of
    the Romantic Period 1789–1830* (London: Longman, 1989), 40; Lucinda Cole
    and Richard G. Swartz, "Why Should I Wish for Words? Literacy, Articu-
    lation, and the Borders of Literary Culture," in Favret and Watson, *At the
    Limits of Romanticism*, 146. On Wollstonecraft and economic ideology, see
    Johnson, *Equivocal Beings*, 59–61.
73 See Regina M. Janes, "On the Reception of Mary Wollstonecraft's *A
    Vindication of the Rights of Woman*," in *Journal of the History of Ideas* 39 (1978):
    293–302; Anna Wilson, "Mary Wollstonecraft and the Search for the
    Radical Woman," in *Genders* 6 (1989): 88–101.
74 Review of Wollstonecraft, *Rights of Woman*, in *Monthly Review* n.s. 8 (1792):
    205; first emphasis added.
75 Review of *Rights of Woman*, 209.
76 See Eve Kosofsky Sedgwick, *The Coherence of Gothic Conventions* (New York:
    Arno, 1980), 12.
77 Ferguson, *Colonialism and Gender Relations*, 16; see also Ferguson, "Mary
    Wollstonecraft and the Problematic of Slavery," in Maria J. Falco, ed.,
    Feminist Interpretations of Mary Wollstonecraft (University Park: Pennsylvania
    State University Press, 1996), 145.
78 See Hazel V. Carby, *Reconstructing Womanhood: The Emergence of the Afro-
    American Woman Novelist* (Oxford: Oxford University Press, 1987), 34–8.

79 See also Wollstonecraft's *Rights of Men*, 45: little "sensibility" appears "in the fair ladies, whom . . . captive negroes curse in all the agony of bodily pain, for the unheard of tortures they invent." Compare Olaudah Equiano, *Interesting Narrative of the Life of Olaudah Equiano, or Gustavus Vassa, the African*, ed. Vincent Carretta (London: Penguin, 1995), 78, 104–7, 165; Aphra Behn, *Oroonoko, or, the Royal Slave*, ed. Joanna Lipking (New York: Norton, 1997), 40, 61–3.

80 Burke, *Correspondence*, VIII: 303–4.

81 Review of Godwin, *Memoirs*, *European Magazine* 33 (1798): 246, 251; Hannah More, *Strictures on the Modern System of Female Education*, in *Works* (New York: Harper, 1840), I: 320. A letter to the editor in *Anti-Jacobin Review* 3 (1799): 209 (concerning Kotzebue's play *Pizarro*) blamed "principle" for Wollstonecraft's licence.

82 Vivien Jones, "Women Writing Revolution: Narratives of History and Sexuality in Wollstonecraft and Williams," in Stephen Copley and John Whale, eds., *Beyond Romanticism: New Approaches to Texts and Contexts 1780–1832* (London: Routledge, 1992), 180.

83 Review of Godwin's *Memoirs*, *Anti-Jacobin Review*, 98; O'Quinn, "Trembling," 778; Favret, *Romantic Correspondence*, 132.

84 Wollstonecraft, *The Wrongs of Woman: or, Maria. A Fragment*, ed. Gary Kelly (Oxford: Oxford University Press, 1976), 73. Subsequently cited in the text.

85 Rajan, *Supplement of Reading*, 174–6.

86 Godwin, Preface, *Wrongs of Woman*, 72.

87 Rajan, *Supplement of Reading*, 183.

88 Nancy K. Miller, "Emphasis Added: Plots and Plausibilities in Women's Fiction," *PMLA* 96 (1981): 46.

89 For example, Cole, "(Anti)Feminist Sentiments: The Politics of Relationship in Smith, Wollstonecraft, and More," in *ELH* 58 (1991): 107–40.

90 The classic argument for feminotopia is Todd's *Women's Friendship in Literature* (New York: Columbia University Press, 1980), 207–26.

91 Jane Austen, *Northanger Abbey*, ed. John Davie (Oxford: Oxford University Press, 1980), 112.

92 Mary Jacobus, "Genre, Gender, and Autobiography," in *Romanticism and Sexual Difference* (Oxford: Oxford University Press, 1989), 203–5; see also Derrida, "Law of Genre," 202–29.

4 ROMANCE AT HOME: AUSTEN, RADCLIFFE, AND THE CIRCULATION OF BRITISHNESS

1 Austen, *Northanger Abbey*, 85. Subsequently cited in the text.

2 See Kent, "Learning History with, and from, Jane Austen," in J. David Grey, ed., *Jane Austen's Beginnings: The Juvenilia and Lady Susan* (Ann Arbor: UMI Research, 1989), 64.

3 Austen, *History of England from the reign of Henry the 4th to the death of Charles the 1st*, in *Catharine and Other Writings*, ed. Doody and Douglas Murray (Oxford: Oxford University Press, 1993), 142–4. Subsequently cited in the text.

4 Austen uses "England" where Scotland's inclusion suggests "Britain." To Austen, the kingdoms of the United Kingdom, in a national equivalent of marital *couverture*, become one, and that one is England.

5 See Kent, "Learning History," for Austen's Jacobitism; Lionel Trilling, *The Opposing Self* (New York: Viking, 1955), and Marvin Mudrick, *Jane Austen: Irony as Defense and Discovery* (Berkeley: University of California Press, 1968) for her irony.

6 Review of James Hogg, *Jacobite Relics of Scotland*, in *Edinburgh Review* 34 (1820): 149.

7 Siskin, *Work of Writing*, 69–99. On the unifying role of Scottishness in "British culture," and the changing position of Jacobitism within it, see Crawford, *Devolving English Literature*, 44–110.

8 Scott, review of Austen, *Emma*, *Quarterly Review* 14 (1815): 189.

9 Scott, *St. Ronan's Well* (Edinburgh: Cadell, 1832), xxxiii: iii–iv.

10 [Hurd], *Letters on Chivalry and Romance*, subsequently cited in the text. See also Reeve, *Progress of Romance*.

11 See William Hazlitt, "The Times Newspaper," in *Examiner*, 1 December 1816, in *Literary and Political Criticism, Complete Works*, ed. P. P. Howe (New York: AMS, 1967), xix: 20. Hazlitt had directed similar rhetorics of bastardy against Burke since 1814; see chapter 5.

12 See Armstrong, *Desire and Domestic Fiction*; for related arguments, see Gonda, *Reading Daughters' Fictions*; Cook, *Epistolary Bodies*.

13 Klancher, "Godwin and the Republican Romance," 146–7. See also Siskin, *Work of Writing*; Kaufmann, *Business of Common Life*, 23–9.

14 That home is usually taken to be more British than Scottish, though with misgivings; see Duncan, *Modern Romance*, 146–73; Crawford, *Devolving English Literature*, 11–51; Buzard, "Translation and Tourism," 31–59.

15 James Stuart, quoted in John Sutherland, *Life of Scott*, 258; John Prebble, *The King's Jaunt: George IV in Scotland, August 1822* (London: Collins, 1988), 269. See Scott's anonymous *Hints Addressed to the Inhabitants of Edinburgh and Others, in Prospect of his Majesty's Visit* (Edinburgh: Bell, 1822).

16 See Claudia Johnson's reading of *Emma*, in *Equivocal Beings*, 191–203.

17 The genre label is Armstrong's, in *Desire and Domestic Fiction*.

18 Ferris, *Achievement of Literary Authority*, 35; Trumpener, "National Character," 697.

19 Sydney Owenson, *The Wild Irish Girl* (London: Routledge, 1986), 112, 253. Subsequently cited in the text.

20 Owenson changed her mind in *Absenteeism* (London: Colburn, 1825), 150, remarking that "Corruption and injustice" characterize Union: "from that epoch every evil which can afflict humanity and degrade a nation has gathered to a foul and purulent head; every sad succeeding year has been marked by some new step towards social disorganization and national extinction."

21 Ferris, *Achievement of Literary Authority*, 105–33.

22 Trumpener, "National Character," 689. In Trumpener, *Bardic Nationalism*,

18–19, 174–84, although *Mansfield Park* is said to protest British colonial policy and appropriation of Celtic cultures, Austen remains "localist" rather than nationalist.

23 Johnson, *Equivocal Beings*, 191–2; Stewart, *Domestic Realities*; Said, *Culture and Imperialism*, 80–97. For Siskin, in *Work of Writing*, 193–209, Austen's de-polemicizing of concepts such as national culture narrows the category "literature" she was instrumental in inventing.

24 Austen, *Letters*, ed. Deirdre Le Faye, 3rd ed. (Oxford: Oxford University Press, 1997), 166.

25 Cohen, "History and Genre"; Moretti, *Signs Taken for Wonders*, 255. See also Siskin, *Work of Writing*; McKeon, *Origins of the English Novel*, 20–1; Mikhail Bakhtin, *The Dialogic Imagination*, ed. Michael Holquist, trans. Caryl Emerson and Holquist (Austin: University of Texas Press, 1981), 259–422.

26 Trumpener, "National Character," 693. See also Eagleton, *Heathcliff and the Great Hunger: Studies in Irish Culture* (London: Verso, 1995), 147.

27 McKendrick, Brewer, and Plumb, *Birth of a Consumer Society*, 13; Philip Corrigan and Derek Sayer, *The Great Arch: English State Formation as Cultural Revolution* (London: Blackwell, 1985), 4.

28 Respectively, by Mary Evans, *Jane Austen and the State* (London: Tavistock, 1987); Butler, *Jane Austen and the War of Ideas* (Oxford: Clarendon, 1987); Kirkham, *Jane Austen*; Kent, "Learning History."

29 In *Jane Austen*, xxiii, Butler rejects "a single feminism of the day that embraced Wollstonecraft along with Austen" for "*different* ideologies in which perceptions of the nature and role of women played an important part."

30 Johnson, *Equivocal Beings*, 18.

31 See Newman, *English Nationalism*, 21–47, 87–120.

32 Walters, "Booksellers."

33 See Raven, *Judging New Wealth*, 42–5.

34 Thus George Croly's *Beauties of the British Poets*, 2nd ed. (London: Whittaker, 1831): "the writings of the great poets of England cannot be put into the popular hand too often, in too pleasing a form, or under too accessible circumstances" (xiv). He includes Irish and Scottish works.

35 See chapter 1. I will not rehearse here the historiographic turns of English liberalism, which emerged as a clear (and to Burke and Scott, clearly conservative) category only at the end of the eighteenth century. I am arguing, with Appleby, in *Liberalism and Republicanism*, 133, that the category "virtue," domesticated and feminized, was assimilable to liberal, individual-ist, and commercial political economy – and that such philosophies are traceable *to* Locke *through* the work of figures as diverse as Paine and Burke. See also Richard K. Matthews, *Virtue, Corruption, and Self-Interest: Political Values in the Eighteenth Century* (Bethlehem: Lehigh University Press, 1994), 13–26.

36 Burke, *Reflections*, 27. Subsequently cited in the text. See Paulson, *Representations of Revolution*, 60–5; see also chapter 3.

37 Paulson, *Representations of Revolution*, 37–9.
38 On "the gothic" in Whig politics, see R. J. Smith, *Gothic Bequest*.
39 Wollstonecraft, *Rights of Woman*, 88. Subsequently cited in the text.
40 Compare Burke, *Reflections*, 62, 66–7 with Wollstonecraft, *Rights of Men*, 10, 48.
41 See review of [John Hurford Stone and Williams,] *Copies of Original Letters recently written by Persons in Paris to Dr. Priestley in America*; and review of Charlotte Smith, *The Young Philosopher*, in *Anti-Jacobin Review* 1 (1798): 146–7, 190; [Richard Polwhele], *The Unsex'd Females* (London: Cadell, 1798); Laetitia Matilda Hawkins, *Letters on the Female Mind, Its Powers and Pursuits. Addressed to Miss H. M. Williams* (London: Hookham, 1793).
42 Newman, *English Nationalism*, 97.
43 Scott, *Biographical Memoirs*, in *Miscellaneous Prose Works* (Boston: Wells, 1829), III: 223, 226–7, 235; Walpole, *Castle of Otranto*, 7.
44 William Gilpin, *Observations Relative Chiefly to Picturesque Beauty*, 2nd ed. (London: Blamire, 1788), I: 16. Subsequently cited in the text.
45 See Newman, *English Nationalism*; R. J. Smith, *Gothic Bequest*; Duncan, *Modern Romance*, 25. Duncan separates the "radical nationalist" character of English gothicism from conservative distaste for foreign aesthetic invasion, arguing that these meet in Burke's *Reflections*. I suggest they are in conflict within New Whig conservatism from the start.
46 Levinson, *Wordsworth's Great Period Poems* (Cambridge: Cambridge University Press, 1986), 26–9.
47 Newman, *English Nationalism*, 115–16.
48 Burke, *Reflections*, 31, 53. Subsequently cited in the text.
49 R. J. Smith, *Gothic Bequest*, 35.
50 See Frank W. Bradbrook, *Jane Austen and her Predecessors* (Cambridge: Cambridge University Press, 1967), 62.
51 Gilpin, *Observations Relative Chiefly to Picturesque Beauty*, II: 122–3.
52 For Kaufmann, in *Business of Common Life*, 82, the process begins with Radcliffe, who fails.
53 See Daniel Cottom, *The Civilized Imagination* (Cambridge: Cambridge University Press, 1985), 42–6; Henderson, *Romantic Identities*, 55–8.
54 Ann Radcliffe, *The Italian, or the Confessional of the Black Penitents: A Romance*, ed. Frederick Garber (Oxford: Oxford University Press, 1968), 158–9. Subsequently cited in the text.
55 Burke's sublime, in *Philosophical Enquiry into the Origin of our Ideas of the Sublime and Beautiful*, 2nd ed. (London: Dodsley, 1759), 116, results from "strength, which is *natural* power," or "institution in kings and commanders," or "grandeur" (140), especially of "a tower" or "rock or mountain" (127). Beauty is a function of "grace" (102), "delicacy" (218), "smoothness . . . softness; the easy and insensible swell" of "gradual variation" (214–17). He associates sublimity with fathers and beauty with mothers. Women are "guided by nature" to "learn to lisp, to totter in their walk, to counterfeit weakness" (204).

I do not suggest that women, in Radcliffe's or Burke's formulation, cannot perceive the sublime, but that their pleasure in it is not aesthetic. Ellena views such landscapes only from *inside* her convent prison, and her "soul," not her heart or taste, is "refreshed." Thus Ellena finds no pleasure in sublimity, but "the awful veil which obscures the features of the Deity" (90). See also Kaufmann, *Business of Common Life*, 84.

56 I quote Jean Bethke Elshtain's *Public Man, Private Woman: Women in Social and Political Thought* (Princeton: Princeton University Press, 1981) to underline the consonance between Radcliffe's Burkean aesthetics and the political economy of Locke and Hume.

57 For Bourdieu, in *The Field of Cultural Production: Essays on Art and Literature*, ed. Randal Johnson (New York: Columbia University Press, 1993), 112–41, this form and field of capital represents itself as money's opposite and strongest competitor.

58 Radcliffe, in contrast, was famed for her huge circulation. See Judith Stanton, "Charlotte Smith's 'Literary Business': Income, Patronage, and Indigence," *Age of Johnson* 1 (1987): 388.

59 See Barrell, "Sportive Labour: The Farm Worker in Eighteenth-Century Poetry and Painting," in Brian Short, ed., *The English Rural Community: Image and Analysis* (Cambridge: Cambridge University Press, 1992), 105–31.

60 See Hume, "Standard of Taste," 232: the "finer emotions of the mind . . . require the concurrence of many favourable circumstances to make them play with facility and exactness, according to their general and established principles. The least exterior hindrance . . . confounds the operation of the whole machine." In *Treatise*, 402, Hume contends that "The skin, pores, muscles, and nerves of a day-labourer are different from those of a man of quality: So are his sentiments, actions and manners. The different stations of life influence the whole fabric, external and internal." For Burke, the sublime exercises the mind as some "exercise is essential to . . . the constitution." But "great bodily labour . . . weakens . . . the mental faculties" (*Sublime and Beautiful*, 256).

61 Johnson finds Radcliffe's conclusion so "absurd" that she concludes it is ironic (*Equivocal Beings*, 136–7). But consistency with earlier set-pieces suggests not irony but ideological desperation.

62 For an opposing view, see Kelly, *English Fiction*, 122.

63 See Burke, *Reflections*, 53–4.

64 Johnson, *Jane Austen: Women, Politics, and the Novel* (Chicago: University of Chicago Press, 1988), 37.

65 For Julia Prewitt Brown, in *Jane Austen's Novels: Social Change and Literary Form* (Cambridge: Harvard University Press, 1979), 51, however, this conclusion attacks Austen's readers.

66 John Aikin, in *Description of the Country from thirty to forty Miles round Manchester* (London: Stockdale, 1795), 136, comments that "prodigious additions made within a few years to the system of inland navigation" "now extend . . . to almost every corner of the kingdom." Gothic revivalists also remarked the

progress of transportation systems. See Thomas Gray, *Journal in the Lakes*, *Works in Prose and Verse*, ed. Edmund Gosse (New York: AMS, 1968), I: 262. That, like Gilpin, *Observations Relative to Picturesque Beauty*, I: ix–x, they lamented the destruction of picturesque scenes makes Austen's praise the more significant. See Raven, *Judging New Wealth*, 35, 54–5, on canals and roads in provincial book distribution.

67 See Johnson, *Jane Austen*, 43; Brown, *Jane Austen's Novels*, 53–4. But for Butler, in *Jane Austen*, 179, "an act of rudeness is not villainy."

68 See Johnson, *Equivocal Beings*, 203.

69 Austen, *Persuasion*, in *Novels*, ed. R. W. Chapman, 3rd ed. (London: Oxford University Press, 1932), V: 111. Subsequently cited in the text.

70 Horkheimer and Adorno, *Dialectic of Enlightenment*, 120–67; Habermas, *Structural Transformation of the Public Sphere*, 160–2; Jameson, *Postmodernism*, 17.

71 Kelly's "Jane Austen's Real Business: The Novel, Literature and Cultural Capital," in *Jane Austen's Business: Her World and Her Profession*, ed. Juliet McMaster and Bruce Stovel (Basingstoke: Macmillan, 1996), 161, makes a related argument about Austen's creation of "cultural capital" in "Literature."

72 She produces a female partner to the self- and class-conscious English reader that Klancher, in *Making of English Reading Audiences*, 49–50, sees produced in the up-market literary periodical.

73 Judith Wilt, *Ghosts of the Gothic: Austen, Eliot, and Lawrence* (Princeton: Princeton University Press, 1980), 123, 129–30.

74 Austen, *Persuasion*, 65, 82. See also his praise of Louisa's obduracy, 87–8.

75 Adela Pinch, "Lost in a Book: Jane Austen's *Persuasion*," in *Studies in Romanticism* 32 (1993): 97–8.

76 John Vernon, *Money and Fiction: Literary Realism in the Nineteenth and Early Twentieth Centuries* (Ithaca: Cornell University Press, 1984), 44, 59–60; see also Mudrick, *Jane Austen*, 232; Johnson, *Jane Austen*, 144–66; and Alistair Duckworth, *The Improvement of the Estate: A Study of Jane Austen's Novels* (Baltimore: Johns Hopkins University Press, 1971), 179–208.

77 See Duckworth, *Improvement of the Estate*. For Highland landlords' defences of improvements, see *Prize Essays and Transactions of the Highland Society of Scotland*, ed. Henry Mackenzie *et al.* (Edinburgh: Constable, 1799–1824), treating as "proper and legitimate" what "prejudice . . . is very apt to mistake or to misrepresent" (III: xxiv), and aligning Scotland's "animated spirit for improvement" with "the Moral Virtues" (VI: lvii).

78 The earls of Fitzwilliam underlie Fitzwilliam Darcy in *Pride and Prejudice*. Darcy is grandson to an earl whose name must have been Fitzwilliam (his cousin, the earl's son's younger son, is Colonel Fitzwilliam; his maternal aunt is Lady Catherine Fitzwilliam DeBurgh, and his mother must have been Lady Anne Fitzwilliam). A "distaff" descendant, he has all the money the heirs-male lack, saving the Bennet family from ruin by heirless entail. Wentworths figure similarly in *Emma*: intermarrying with Watsons (Emma's name in early drafts) and Woodhouses, they inherited the lands of these decaying families before themselves dying out. Austen insists that

legitimacy and inheritance be coupled with vitality – supplied by Went-worth in *Persuasion*. But her successive lines of inheritors, each differently legitimating itself, marks the risky contingency of legitimist ideology. See *Burke's Genealogical History of the Dormant, Abeyant, Forfeited, and Extinct Peerages of the British Empire* (London: Harrison, 1883), 570–1, 575–7; see also *Complete Peerage of England, Scotland, Ireland, Great Britain and the United Kingdom, Extant, Extinct, or Dormant* (London: Bell, 1890), III: 381–2. Stewart's *Domestic Realities* notes a Woodhouse connection, 72.

79 See Croft's sympathy for Benwick, "'only a commander'" in the present "'bad times for getting on'" (171), and the Crofts' thoughtful commentary on their rapid wartime courtship (92).

80 Kaufmann, *Business of Common Life*, 41, discusses Anne's "profession."

81 Armstrong, *Desire and Domestic Fiction*, 3.

82 Scott, review of Austen, *Emma*, 193.

5 BASTARD ROMANCE: SCOTT, HAZLITT, AND THE ENDS OF LEGITIMACY

1 Walter Scott, *The Betrothed* (Edinburgh: Cadell, 1832), XXXVII: xxvii–xxviii, xxxix. Subsequently cited in the text.

2 Patricia S. Gaston, *Prefacing the Waverley Prefaces* (New York: Lang, 1991), 103; Kathryn Sutherland, "Fictional Economies: Adam Smith, Walter Scott and the Nineteenth-Century Novel," *ELH* 54 (1987): 104.

3 Duncan, *Modern Romance*, 63–73; Ferris, *Achievement of Literary Authority*, 79–104; Judith Wilt, *Secret Leaves: The Novels of Walter Scott* (Chicago: University of Chicago Press, 1985), 8.

4 Siskin comments, in *Historicity of Romantic Discourse*, 94, that this "lyric turn" in Romantic letters results from a desire to valorize individualist forms of labour and subjectivity.

5 Review of Scott, *Peveril of the Peak* and others, *Quarterly Review* 35 (1827): 521.

6 Scott is closer to Moretti's Darwinian *Signs Taken for Wonders*, 262–78.

7 Review of *Peveril*, 529.

8 William Hazlitt, "Sir Walter Scott," in *The Spirit of the Age, Complete Works*, XI: 65–6. Compare review of Scott, *Rob Roy* and others, in *Quarterly Review* 26 (1822): 110.

9 Hazlitt, "What is the People? (Concluded)," from *Examiner*, 14 March 1818, in *Political Essays, with Sketches of Public Characters, Complete Works*, VII: 269. Scott, *St. Ronan's Well* (Edinburgh: Cadell, 1832), XXXIII: iii.

10 Loren Kruger's discussion of popular demand for "legitimation" through (theatrical) representation, in revolutionary France and Reform Britain, in *The National Stage: Theater and Cultural Legitimation in England, France, and America* (Chicago: University of Chicago Press, 1992), 3–29, helps differentiate Scott's patrilineal "legitimacy" from Bruce Beiderwell's liberal definition in *Power and Punishment in Scott's Novels* (Athens: University of Georgia Press, 1992), 29.

11 Thus Hanoverian rule brought Protestants ideologically together. See R. J. Smith, *Gothic Bequest*, 35; see also Clark, *English Society*, 82–5, on mid-eighteenth-century religious agreement and political "consensus."

12 Newman shows in *Rise of English Nationalism*, 171, that George III actively legitimated Britishness. See also Colley, *Britons*, 43–9.

13 For literary worth, see Fiona Robertson, *Legitimate Histories: Scott, Gothic, and the Authorities of Fiction* (Oxford: Clarendon, 1994), 1–30. For primogeniture, see Wilt, *Secret Leaves*, 18–48.

14 Lukács, *Historical Novel*, 53–5.

15 Duncan, *Modern Romance*, 53.

16 Duncan, *Modern Romance*, 8–9.

17 Walter Scott, *Guy Mannering; or, The Astrologer* (Edinburgh: Cadell, 1829), IV: 272. Subsequently cited in the text.

18 Duncan, *Modern Romance*, 108–11; Ferris, *Achievement of Literary Authority*, 79–88; Wilt, *Secret Leaves*, 19.

19 Duncan, *Modern Romance*, 116–17, 134–5.

20 Wilt, *Secret Leaves*, 24; Ferris, *Achievement of Literary Authority*, 104, 122.

21 Burke, *Reflections*, 30, 83. Subsequently cited in the text.

22 Hazlitt, "The Times Newspaper: On the Connexion Between Toad-Eaters and Tyrants," in *Political Essays*, 147.

23 Walter Scott, review of *Emma*, *Quarterly Review* 14 (1815): 188.

24 See Robertson, *Legitimate Histories*, 23–30.

25 See Alexander Welsh's *Hero of the Waverley Novels* (New Haven: Yale University Press, 1963) for the confinement of Scott's heroes.

26 Hazlitt, *Political Essays* (1819), *Complete Works*, VII: 8.

27 Hazlitt, "Scott," 65.

28 Hazlitt, "Scott," 60, 62.

29 Duncan, *Modern Romance*, 116. For a related reading of *Waverley*, see James Kerr, *Fiction Against History: Scott as Storyteller* (Cambridge: Cambridge University Press, 1989), 33–8.

30 Ferris, *Achievement of Literary Authority*, 35; Trumpener, "National Character," 689.

31 In *Family Romance*, 1–16, Hunt shows that Revolutionary discourse supports readings of the Revolution as family romance. See also Paulson, *Representations of Revolution*, 60–4.

32 Johnson, *Equivocal Beings*, 8–10. Landes, *Women and the Public Sphere*, 45–65, traces a similar process in Republican France, emphasizing the part played by fiction.

33 See Watson, *Revolution and the Form of the British Novel*, 137–8.

34 On Wollstonecraft, see Johnson, *Equivocal Beings*, 47–69, 186–8, and Wang, "Other Reasons," 129–49.

35 On Scott's conflict between Jacobite Toryism and British progress, see Gordon, *Under Which King*, 30–4. See also David Daiches, "Scott and Scotland," in Alan Bell, ed., *Scott Bicentenary Essays: Selected Papers Read at the Sir Walter Scott Bicentenary Conference* (Edinburgh: University of Edinburgh,

1973), 38–60. For recent discussions, see Duncan, *Modern Romance*; Buzard, "Translation and Tourism," 31–59; Crawford, *Devolving English Literature.*

36 See Scott, *Old Mortality* (Edinburgh: Cadell, 1830), especially Cuddie Headrigg's fear that his mother will be burnt for witchcraft (x: 103).

37 Scott, *The Heart of Midlothian* (Edinburgh: Cadell, 1830), xii: 379.

38 Scott, *Heart of Midlothian*, xii: 31. In *Rob Roy* (Edinburgh: Cadell, 1829), Die Vernon is a "fair Amazon" in men's riding clothes (vii: 64).

39 Wilt, *Secret Leaves*, 24, 48.

40 Lukács, *Historical Novel*, 54; Kelly, *English Fiction*, 144–5.

41 Kelly, *English Fiction*, 160.

42 Duncan, *Modern Romance*, 119; Sutherland, "Fictional Economies," 121–4; Jane Millgate, *Walter Scott: The Making of the Novelist* (Toronto: University of Toronto Press, 1984), 72–4.

43 Duncan, *Modern Romance*, 135.

44 Graham McMaster, *Scott and Society* (Cambridge: Cambridge University Press, 1981), 167.

45 Gordon, *Under Which King?*, 100; Duncan, *Modern Romance*, 141.

46 Scott, *The Bride of Lammermoor* (Edinburgh: Cadell, 1830), xiii: 300. Additional references in the text.

47 Review of Scott, *Tales of My Landlord*, Third Series, in *New Monthly Magazine* 12 (1819): 70.

48 Kerr's contrary argument in *Fiction Against History* – that the hero represents Scott's ambivalence toward historical progress in failing to take "the opportunity" "history" offers "to escape the fatality with which history threatens him" (91) – dismisses too easily the authority of peasant women, and the context Scott's earlier novels establish for it.

49 Review of Scott, *Tales of My Landlord*, in *New Monthly Magazine* 12 (1819): 69.

50 Review of *Rob Roy* and others, 121.

51 That is, violent desire and dissent from heterosexuality-on-demand; see Johnson, *Equivocal Beings*, 11–12.

52 Lukács, *Historical Novel*, 27.

53 Hazlitt, "Arguing in a Circle," *The Liberal*, July 1823, in *Literary and Political Criticism, Complete Works*, xix: 267, 271.

54 John Farrell, *Revolution as Tragedy: The Dilemma of the Moderate from Scott to Arnold* (Ithaca: Cornell University Press, 1980), 73.

55 Chandler, *England in 1819*, 346.

56 Chandler, *England in 1819*, 334, 346.

57 Hazlitt, "Standard Novels and Romances," from *Edinburgh Review* 24 (February 1815), in *Contributions to the Edinburgh Review, Complete Works*, xvi: 20.

58 Hazlitt's assault on legitimist poetry, "Mr. Macirone's Interesting Facts," in *Political Essays*, 153, is aimed at Robert Southey. "Standard Novels and Romances," 20, 22, attacks Burney's recent *Wanderer*.

59 Hazlitt, "Macirone," 153.

60 Hazlitt, "Macirone," 153.

61 Hazlitt, "The Press – Coleridge, Southey, Wordsworth, and Bentham,"

from *Yellow Dwarf*, 3 January 1818, in *Literary and Political Criticism*, 204–5; Hazlitt, "The Times Newspaper," from *The Examiner*, 1 December 1816, in *Literary and Political Criticism*, 178.

62 Hazlitt, "The Press," 205; "What is the People? (Concluded)," 269.

63 Hazlitt, "The Times," 178.

64 Hazlitt, "What is the People?," from *The Examiner*, 7 March 1818, in *Political Essays*, 261; Colley, *Britons*, 46.

65 In "Whether the Friends of Freedom can Entertain any Sanguine Hopes of the Favourable Results of the Ensuing Congress?," in *Political Essays*, 85, Hazlitt remarks that the defeated French, "who boast of their submission as a fine thing, are not a nation of men, but of women . . . [A]n effeminate public is a nonentity."

66 Pornographers and journalists had targeted Caroline since the "delicate investigation" of 1806; see Iain McCalman, *Radical Underworld: Prophets, Revolutionaries and Pornographers in London, 1795–1840* (Cambridge: Cambridge University Press, 1988), 162–77. Printed accounts equated her sexual rebellion with political revolt. [Thomas Ashe's] pro-Caroline *Spirit of 'The Book': or, Memoirs of Caroline, Princess of Hasburgh, A Political and Amatory Romance*, 3rd ed. (London: Allen, 1811), I: 12 gives her a Wollstonecraftian defence: "English wives [cannot be] . . . immured by worse than eastern barbarity . . . their passions sublimated; every finer motive of action extinguished by the inevitable consequences of treating them like slaves." Raped on her wedding night, a situation foreshadowing Lucy Ashton's, Caroline condemns her husband's "dominion over my person" as "in no degree over my mind" (III: 43). For the French pamphlet war, see Hunt, *Family Romance*, 89–123.

67 Scott, Letter to James Ballantyne, 21 July 1821, in *Letters*, ed. H. J. C. Grierson (London: Constable, 1932–5), VI: 503.

68 In 1820, in *Conversations of James Northcote, Esq., R.A.*, *Complete Works*, XI: 240, Hazlitt notes that the two "somehow got from Sir Walter to the Queen's trial."

69 Scott, Letter to Lord Montagu, 22 February 1820, in *Letters*, VI: 138.

70 Scott, Letter to Cornet Walter Scott, 27 June 1820, in *Letters*, VI: 215; Scott, Letter to Ballantyne, circa 27 June 1820, in *Letters*, VI: 197.

71 Scott, Letter to Ballantyne, 24 July 1820, in *Letters*, VI: 237.

72 Scott, Letter to Ballantyne, 21 July 1821, in *Letters*, VI: 503.

73 Chandler, *England in 1819*, 346. For the geographical metaphor, see Bourdieu, *Field of Cultural Production*.

74 Scott's conclusion attempts to end the parallelism of economic and cultural production as Kaufmann outlines it. Scott's culture industry will not merely remark political history's inadequacies; it will seek to supersede them. See Kaufmann, *Business of Common Life*, 113, 137.

75 Scott, *St. Ronan's Well*, XXXIII: iii. Additional references in the text.

76 Scott, review of Austen, *Emma*, *Quarterly Review* 14 (1815): 189.

77 The eccentric innkeeper Meg Dods is famed for "originality" (XXXIII: 16).

78 Robertson, *Legitimate Histories*, 22, 30.
79 Siskin, *Historicity of Romantic Discourse*, 12.
80 Fordyce, *Sermons*, 1: 126.
81 See Manuel's description of Manfred's incestuous love for Astarte: "her, whom of all earthly things/ That lived, the only thing he seemed to love,/ As he indeed by blood was bound to do,/ The lady Astarte, his – Hush! Who comes here?" Byron, *Manfred*, in *Poetical Works* (Oxford: Oxford University Press, 1945), III: iii. 44–7.
82 Ecclesiastes 7: 2.
83 *Portfolio* 1 (1818): 7–8, emphasis added.
84 William Wordsworth, "Ode: Intimations of Immortality," in *Poetical Works*, ed. Thomas Hutchinson (London: Oxford University Press, 1911), 58–60.
85 Wordsworth, Preface to *Lyrical Ballads*, in *Selected Poems and Prefaces*, ed. Jack Stillinger (Boston: Riverside-Houghton, 1965), 455–6; Percy Bysshe Shelley, "A Defence of Poetry," in *Shelley's Poetry and Prose*, ed. Donald H. Reiman and Sharon B. Powers (New York: Norton, 1977), 482.
86 By the early 1820s, the working-class readers of the chapbook *Odds and Ends, Or, a Groat's-Worth of Fun For a Penny*, 3, were expected to appreciate these "exquisite lines, the result of a true appreciation of the sublime and beautiful in nature . . . copied from the Album kept at a small inn on the Banks of the Windermere . . .

> I never eats no meat,
> Nor drinks no beer,
> But sighs and ruminates
> On Windermere."

87 See T. S. Eliot, "Tradition and the Individual Talent," in *The Sacred Wood: Essays on Poetry and Criticism* (London: Methuen, 1960), 49–51.
88 As Cohen remarks in "History and Genre," 210, especially germane to the return-and-rejection plot, genre "Groupings arise at particular historical moments . . . subject to repeated redefinitions or abandonment" by their readers.

EPILOGUE: SENSIBILITY, GENRE AND THE
CULTURAL MARKETPLACE

1 The trunks are those of cross-dressed men, and if the viewer interprets them in this way, the image appears still more readily as a fantastic rapprochement between desire, femininity, and cultural authority. See also *Saturday Night* (December 1997–January 1998): 106.
2 John Berger, *Ways of Seeing* (London: Penguin, 1972), 51; Diana Fuss, "Fashion and the Homospectatorial Look," in *Critical Inquiry* 18 (1992): 715–16, 730.
3 Karl Marx, "The Fetishism of Commodities and the Secret Thereof," in *Capital, Marx-Engels Reader*, 321; Sigmund Freud, "The Sexual Aberrations,"

in *Freud Reader*, ed. Peter Gay (New York: Norton, 1989), 250.

4 For example, Paula Brook, "Superwoman Goes Home," in *Saturday Night* (June 1996): 30–8.

5 Janice Radway, *Reading the Romance*, rev. ed. (Chapel Hill: University of North Carolina Press, 1991), 15–16, 159–60; Nancy Friday, *Women on Top: How Real Life has Changed Women's Sexual Fantasies* (New York: Pocket, 1991).

6 See the "liberatory" claims of Lorraine Gamman and Merja Makinen for "recognition of female sexual activity" in "fetishism," in *Female Fetishism: A New Look* (London: Lawrence, 1994), 80. For critical reflections on relations between radical sexualities and late-capitalist economic conditions, see Donald Morton, "Birth of the Cyberqueer," in *PMLA* 110 (1995): 369–81; Ebert, *Ludic Feminism and After*, 45–126, especially 89.

7 Henderson, "Commerce and Masochistic Desire in the 1790s: Frances Burney's *Camilla*," in *Eighteenth-Century Studies* 31 (1997): 69–86; Johnson, *Equivocal Beings*, 141–64.

8 Charlotte M. Yonge, *The Dove in the Eagle's Nest* (London: Collins, 1866), 57. Subsequently cited in the text.

9 See Poovey, *Uneven Developments*, 127.

10 Gilles Deleuze, *Masochism: An Interpretation of Coldness and Cruelty*, trans. Jean McNeil (New York: Braziller, 1971), 30.

Bibliography

Adorno, Theodor, "Cultural Criticism and Society," in *Prisms*, trans. Samuel and Shierry Weber, Cambridge: Massachusetts Institute of Technology Press, 1981.

Agnew, Jean-Christophe, "Consumer Culture in Historical Perspective," in Brewer and Porter, 19–39.

Worlds Apart: The Market and the Theater in Anglo-American Thought, 1550–1750, Cambridge: Cambridge University Press, 1987.

Aikin, John, *A Description of the Country from thirty to forty Miles round Manchester*, London: Stockdale, 1795.

Alison, Archibald, *Essays on the Nature and Principles of Taste*, Edinburgh: Robinson, 1790.

Allestree, Richard, *The Ladies Calling*, Oxford, 1673.

Anderson, Adam, *Historical and Chronological Deduction of the Origin of Commerce, from the Earliest Accounts, Containing An History of the Great Commercial Interests of the British Empire*, Dublin: P. Byrne, 1790.

Anderson, Benedict, *Imagined Communities: Reflections on the Origin and Spread of Nationalism*, rev. ed., London: Verso, 1991.

Appleby, Joyce, *Liberalism and Republicanism in the Historical Imagination*, Cambridge: Harvard University Press, 1992.

Armstrong, Nancy, *Desire and Domestic Fiction: A Political History of the Novel*, New York: Oxford University Press, 1987.

Ashe, Thomas, attrib., *The Spirit of 'The Book': or, Memoirs of Caroline, Princess of Hasburgh, A Political and Amatory Romance*, 3rd ed., 3 vols., London: Allen, 1811.

Austen, Jane, *The History of England from the reign of Henry the 4th to the death of Charles the 1st*, in *Catharine and Other Writings*, ed. Margaret Anne Doody and Douglas Murray, Oxford: Oxford University Press, 1993, 134–44.

Letters, ed. Deirdre Le Faye, 3rd ed., Oxford: Oxford University Press, 1997.

Northanger Abbey, ed. John Davie, Oxford: Oxford University Press, 1980.

Persuasion, in vol. v of *Novels*, ed. R. W. Chapman, 3rd ed., 5 vols., London: Oxford University Press, 1932.

Pride and Prejudice, ed. James Kinsley, Oxford: Oxford University Press, 1970.

"The Author of *Guy Mannering* etc. Unmasked," *The Portfolio* 1 (1818): 5–6.

Bakhtin, Mikhail, *The Dialogic Imagination: Four Essays*, ed. Michael Holquist, trans. Caryl Emerson and Holquist, Austin: University of Texas Press, 1981.

Ballaster, Ros, *Seductive Forms: Women's Amatory Fiction from 1684–1740*, Oxford: Clarendon, 1992.

Barbauld, Anna Laetitia Aikin, "On the Origin and Progress of Novel-Writing," in vol. 1 of *The British Novelists; with an Essay and Prefaces Biographical and Critical*, ed. Barbauld, 50 vols., London: Rivington, 1820, 1–59.

Barrell, John, *The Political Theory of Painting from Reynolds to Hazlitt*, New Haven: Yale University Press, 1986.

"Sportive Labour: The Farm Worker in Eighteenth-Century Poetry and Painting," in Brian Short, ed., *The English Rural Community: Image and Analysis*, Cambridge: Cambridge University Press, 1992, 105–31.

Barthes, Roland, *The Fashion System*, trans. Matthew Ward and Richard Howard, New York: Hill, 1983.

Behn, Aphra, *Love-Letters between a Nobleman and his Sister: With the History of their Adventures*, 3d ed., London: Brown, 1708.

Love-Letters between a Nobleman and his Sister, ed. Janet Todd, London: Penguin, 1996.

Oroonoko, or, the Royal Slave: A True History, ed. Joanna Lipking, New York: Norton, 1997.

Beiderwell, Bruce, *Power and Punishment in Scott's Novels*, Athens: University of Georgia Press, 1992.

Belanger, Terry, "Publishers and Writers in Eighteenth-Century England," in Isabel Rivers, ed., *Books and their Readers in Eighteenth-Century England*, Leicester: Leicester University Press, 1982, 5–25.

Berger, John, *Ways of Seeing*, London: BBC-Penguin, 1972.

Bewell, Alan, " 'Jacobin Plants': Botany as Social Theory in the 1790s," *Wordsworth Circle* 20 (1989): 132–9.

Bohstedt, John, "The Myth of the Feminine Food Riot: Women as Proto-Citizens in English Community Politics, 1790–1810," in Harriet B. Applewhite and Darline G. Levy, eds., *Women and Politics in the Age of the Democratic Revolution*, Ann Arbor: University of Michigan Press, 1990, 21–60.

Boswell, James, *Life of Samuel Johnson*, ed. George Birkbeck Hill and L. F. Powell, 6 vols., Oxford: Clarendon, 1934.

Bourdieu, Pierre, *Distinction: A Social Critique of the Judgement of Taste*, trans. Richard Nice, Cambridge: Harvard University Press, 1984.

The Field of Cultural Production: Essays on Art and Literature, ed. Randal Johnson, New York: Columbia University Press, 1993.

Bowers, Toni, *The Politics of Motherhood: British Writing and Culture, 1680–1760*, Cambridge: Cambridge University Press, 1996.

Bradbrook, Frank W., *Jane Austen and her Predecessors*, Cambridge: Cambridge University Press, 1967.

Brewer, John, and Roy Porter, eds., *Consumption and the World of Goods*, London: Routledge, 1993.

A Brief Account of the Life and Family of Miss Jenny Cameron, the Reputed Mistress of the Pretender's Eldest Son, London: Gardner, 1746.

Brissenden, R. F., *Virtue in Distress: Studies in the Novel of Sentiment from Richardson to Sade*, New York: Harper, 1974.

Brook, Paula, "Superwoman Goes Home," *Saturday Night* (June 1996): 30–8.

Brown, Julia Prewitt, *Jane Austen's Novels: Social Change and Literary Form*, Cambridge: Harvard University Press, 1979.

Brown, Laura, *Ends of Empire: Women and Ideology in Early Eighteenth-Century Literature*, Ithaca: Cornell University Press, 1993.

Burke, Edmund, *Correspondence*, ed. R. B. McDowell, 10 vols., Cambridge: Cambridge University Press, 1969.

  Philosophical Enquiry into the Origin of our Ideas of the Sublime and Beautiful, 2nd ed., London: Dodsley, 1759.

  Reflections on the Revolution in France, ed. J. G. A. Pocock, Indianapolis: Hackett, 1987.

Burke, John Bernard, Sir, *Burke's Genealogical History of the Dormant, Abeyant, Forfeited, and Extinct Peerages of the British Empire*, London: Harrison, 1883.

Burney, Frances, *Camilla; or, A Picture of Youth*, ed. Edward A. Bloom and Lillian D. Bloom, Oxford: Oxford University Press, 1972.

  Cecilia, or Memoirs of an Heiress, ed. Peter Sabor and Margaret Doody, Oxford: Oxford University Press, 1988.

  Diary and Letters of Frances Burney, Madame d'Arblay, ed. Sarah Chauncey Woolsey, 2 vols., Boston: Roberts, 1880.

  Diary and Letters of Madame d'Arblay. Edited by her niece, 7 vols., London: Colburn, 1842.

  Early Diary 1768–1778, ed. Annie Raine Ellis, 2 vols., London: Bell, 1971.

  Evelina, or, The History of a Young Lady's Entrance into the World, ed. Edward A. Bloom, Oxford: Oxford University Press, 1968.

  Evelina, or, The History of a Young Lady's Entrance into the World, ed. Stewart J. Cooke, New York: Norton, 1998.

  Journals and Letters, ed. Joyce Hemlow *et al.*, 12 vols., Oxford: Oxford University Press, 1972–84.

  The Wanderer; or, Female Difficulties, ed. Margaret Anne Doody, Robert L. Mack, and Peter Sabor, Oxford: Oxford University Press, 1991.

Butler, Judith, *Gender Trouble: Feminism and the Subversion of Identity*, New York: Routledge, 1990.

Butler, Marilyn, *Burke, Paine, Godwin, and the French Revolution Controversy*, Cambridge: Cambridge University Press, 1984.

  Jane Austen and the War of Ideas, rev. ed., Oxford: Clarendon, 1987.

Buzard, James, "Translation and Tourism: Scott's *Waverley* and the Rendering of Culture," *The Yale Journal of Criticism* 8 (1995): 31–59.

Byron, George Gordon, Lord, *Poetical Works*, Oxford: Oxford University Press, 1945.

Campbell, Colin, *The Romantic Ethic and the Spirit of Modern Consumerism*, Oxford: Blackwell, 1987.

Campbell, D. Grant, "Fashionable Suicide: Conspicuous Consumption and the Collapse of Credit in Frances Burney's *Cecilia*," in *Studies in Eighteenth-Century Culture* 20 (1990): 131–45.

Campbell, Gina, "How to Read like a Gentleman: Fanny Burney's Instructions to her Critics in *Evelina*," *ELH* 57 (1990): 557–84.

Campbell, Jill, *Natural Masques: Gender and Identity in Fielding's Plays and Novels*, Stanford: Stanford University Press, 1995.

Campbell, Thomas, "Lord Ullin's Daughter," *Poetical Works of Thomas Campbell*, Edinburgh: Gall, 1880, 172–4.

Carby, Hazel V., *Reconstructing Womanhood: The Emergence of the Afro-American Woman Novelist*, Oxford: Oxford University Press, 1987.

The Case of the Stage in Ireland, Dublin: Coote, n.d.

Castle, Terry, *The Apparitional Lesbian: Female Homosexuality and Modern Culture*, New York: Columbia University Press, 1993.

   Clarissa's Ciphers: Meaning and Disruption in Richardson's Clarissa, Ithaca: Cornell University Press, 1982.

   Masquerade and Civilization: The Carnivalesque in Eighteenth-Century English Culture and Fiction, Stanford: Stanford University Press, 1986.

Chandler, James, *England in 1819: The Politics of Literary Culture and the Case of Romantic Historicism*, Chicago: University of Chicago Press, 1998.

Chapone, Hester, *Letters on the Improvement of the Mind*, vol. 1 of *Works*, 4 vols., London: Murray, 1807.

Cheyne, George, *The English Malady: or, a Treatise of Nervous Diseases of All Kinds*, London: Strahan, 1733.

Christensen, Jerome, *Practicing Enlightenment: Hume and the Formation of a Literary Career*, Madison: University of Wisconsin Press, 1987.

Clark, J. C. D., *English Society, 1688–1832: Ideology, Social Structure and Political Practice During the Ancien Regime*, Cambridge: Cambridge University Press, 1985.

   "On Moving the Middle Ground: The Significance of Jacobitism in Historical Studies," in Cruickshanks and Black, 177–88.

   "Reconceptualizing Eighteenth-Century England," in Speck, 135–9.

   Revolution and Rebellion: State and Society in England in the Seventeenth and Eighteenth Centuries, Cambridge: Cambridge University Press, 1986.

Cohen, Ralph, "History and Genre," *New Literary History* 17 (1986): 203–18.

Cole, Lucinda, "(Anti)Feminist Sentiments: The Politics of Relationship in Smith, Wollstonecraft, and More," *ELH* 58 (1991): 107–40.

Cole, Lucinda, and Richard G. Swartz, "Why Should I Wish for Words? Literacy, Articulation, and the Borders of Literary Culture," in Favret and Watson, 143–69.

Coleridge, Samuel Taylor, *The Statesman's Manual*, in *Lay Sermons*, vol. VI of *Collected Works*, ed. R. J. White, London: Routledge, 1972, 3–52.

Colley, Linda, *Britons: Forging the Nation, 1707–1837*, London: Vintage, 1996.

Complete Peerage of England, Scotland, Ireland, Great Britain and the United Kingdom, Extant, Extinct, or Dormant, London: Bell, 1890.

Cook, Elizabeth Heckendorn, *Epistolary Bodies: Gender and Genre in the Eighteenth-Century Republic of Letters*, Stanford: Stanford University Press, 1996.

Copeland, Edward, "Jane Austen and the Consumer Revolution," in J. David Grey, ed., *The Jane Austen Companion*, New York: Macmillan, 1986, 77–92.

"Copy of a Letter from a Lady to the Lady G--dd-s, at K-l-v-ick, to the Care of Mr James R---- Merchant in Inverness."

Corrigan, Philip, and Derek Sayer, *The Great Arch: English State Formation as Cultural Revolution*, London: Blackwell, 1985.

Cottom, Daniel, *The Civilized Imagination*, Cambridge: Cambridge University Press, 1985.

Crawford, Robert, *Devolving English Literature*, Oxford: Clarendon, 1992.

Croly, George, *Beauties of the British Poets*, 2nd ed., London: Whittaker, 1831.

Cruickshanks, Eveline, and Jeremy Black, eds., *The Jacobite Challenge*, Edinburgh: Donald, 1988.

Cumberland, Richard, *The Observer: Being a Collection of Moral, Literary and Familiar Essays*, 2nd ed., 5 vols., London: Dilly, 1788.

Daiches, David, "Scott and Scotland," in Alan Bell, ed., *Scott Bicentenary Essays: Selected Papers Read at the Sir Walter Scott Bicentenary Conference*, Edinburgh: University of Edinburgh, 1973, 38–60.

Davidoff, Leonore, and Catherine Hall, *Family Fortunes: Men and Women of the English Middle Class, 1780–1850*, Chicago: University of Chicago Press, 1987.

Davis, Lennard J., *Factual Fictions: The Origins of the English Novel*, New York: Columbia University Press, 1983.

Deane, Seamus, *Strange Country: Modernity and Nationhood in Irish Writing since 1790*, Oxford: Clarendon, 1997.

Deleuze, Gilles, *Masochism: An Interpretation of Coldness and Cruelty*, trans. Jean McNeil, New York: Braziller, 1971.

Derrida, Jacques, "Le loi du genre/ The Law of Genre," *Glyph* 7 (1980): 202–29.

Descartes, René, *Meditations on the First Philosophy*, trans. John Veitch, in *The Rationalists*, New York: Doubleday, 1974, 97–175.

Doody, Margaret Anne, *Frances Burney: The Life in the Works*, New Brunswick: Rutgers University Press, 1988.

"Frances Sheridan: Morality and Annihilated Time," in Mary Anne Schofield and Cecilia Macheski, eds., *Fetter'd or Free: British Women Novelists 1670–1815*, Athens: Ohio University Press, 1986, 324–58.

A Natural Passion: A Study of the Novels of Samuel Richardson, Oxford: Clarendon, 1974.

Douglas, Mary, and Baron Isherwood, *The World of Goods*, New York: Basic, 1979.

Duckworth, Alistair, *The Improvement of the Estate: A Study of Jane Austen's Novels*, Baltimore: Johns Hopkins University Press, 1971.

Duncan, Ian, *Modern Romance and Transformations of the Novel: The Gothic, Scott, Dickens*, Cambridge: Cambridge University Press, 1992.

Dunn, John, "From Applied Theology to Social Analysis: The Break Between John Locke and the Scottish Enlightenment," in Hont and Ignatieff, 119–35.

Durston, Christopher, *The Family in the English Revolution*, Oxford: Blackwell, 1989.

Eagleton, Terry, *Heathcliff and the Great Hunger: Studies in Irish Culture*, London: Verso, 1995.

The Ideology of the Aesthetic, Oxford: Blackwell, 1990.

The Rape of Clarissa: Writing, Sexuality, and Class Struggle in Samuel Richardson, Oxford: Blackwell, 1982.

Eaves, T.C. Duncan, and Ben D. Kimpel, *Samuel Richardson: A Biography*, Oxford: Clarendon, 1971.

Ebert, Teresa L., *Ludic Feminism and After: Postmodernism, Desire, and Labor in Late Capitalism*, Ann Arbor: University of Michigan Press, 1996.

Edgeworth, Maria, *Castle Rackrent*, ed. George Watson, Oxford: Oxford University Press, 1980.

Eisenstein, Zillah, *The Radical Future of Liberal Feminism*, New York: Longman, 1981.

Eliot, T. S., "Tradition and the Individual Talent," *The Sacred Wood: Essays on Poetry and Criticism*, London: Methuen, 1960, 47–59.

Ellis, Markman, *The Politics of Sensibility*, Cambridge: Cambridge University Press, 1996.

Ellsworth, Ann, "Resisting Richardson: Sarah Fielding, Frances Sheridan, Charlotte Lennox, and the Didactic Novel," unpublished Ph.D. diss., University of Washington, 1997.

Elshtain, Jean Bethke, *Public Man, Private Woman: Women in Social and Political Thought*, Princeton: Princeton University Press, 1981.

English Literary History 64 (1997), special issue on Samuel Johnson and Jacobitism.

Epstein, Julia, *The Iron Pen: Frances Burney and the Politics of Women's Writing*, Madison: University of Wisconsin Press, 1989.

Equiano, Olaudah, *The Interesting Narrative of the Life of Olaudah Equiano, or Gustavus Vassa, the African*, ed. Vincent Carretta, London: Penguin, 1995.

Erskine, Thomas, *The Speeches of the Hon. Thomas Erskine (Now Lord Erskine), When at the Bar, on Subjects Connected with the Liberty of the Press, and Against Constructive Treasons*, ed. James Ridgway, 4 vols., London: Ridgway, 1810.

Erskine-Hill, Howard, "Literature and the Jacobite Cause: Was There a Rhetoric of Jacobitism?," in Eveline Cruickshanks, ed., *Ideology and Conspiracy: Aspects of Jacobitism, 1689–1759*, Edinburgh: Donald, 1982, 49–69.

"The Political Character of Samuel Johnson," in Cruickshanks and Black, 161–76.

Evans, Mary, *Jane Austen and the State*, London: Tavistock, 1987.

Facts and Observations relative to the Coinage and Circulation of Counterfeit or Base Money; with Suggestions for Remedying the Evil, London: Fry, 1795.

Farrell, John, *Revolution as Tragedy: The Dilemma of the Moderate from Scott to Arnold*, Ithaca: Cornell University Press, 1980.

Favret, Mary, *Romantic Correspondence: Women, Politics, and the Fiction of Letters*, Cambridge: Cambridge University Press, 1993.

Favret, Mary, and Nicola J. Watson, eds., *At the Limits of Romanticism: Essays in Cultural, Feminist, and Materialist Criticism*, Bloomington: Indiana University Press, 1994.

Feltes, N. N., *Modes of Production of Victorian Novels*, Chicago: University of Chicago Press, 1986.

Fergus, Jan, and Janice Farrar Thaddeus, "Women, Publishers, and Money, 1790–1820," *Studies in Eighteenth-Century Culture 17* (1987): 191–207.

Ferguson, Moira, *Colonialism and Gender Relations from Mary Wollstonecraft to Jamaica Kincaid: East Caribbean Connections*, New York: Columbia University Press, 1993.

"Mary Wollstonecraft and the Problematic of Slavery," in Maria J. Falco, ed., *Feminist Interpretations of Mary Wollstonecraft*, University Park: Pennsylvania State University Press, 1996.

Ferris, Ina, *The Achievement of Literary Authority: Gender, History, and the Waverley Novels*, Ithaca: Cornell University Press, 1991.

Fielding, Henry, *Amelia*, ed. David Blewett, Harmondsworth: Penguin, 1987.

An Apology for the Life of Mrs. Shamela Andrews, ed. Sheridan W. Baker, Jr., Berkeley: University of California Press, 1953.

The History of Tom Jones, a Foundling, ed. R. P. C. Mutter, London: Penguin, 1966.

Filmer, Robert, Sir, *Patriarcha; or the Natural Power of Kings*, London: Davis, 1680.

Fordyce, James, *Sermons to Young Women*, 2 vols., London: Millar, 1794.

Foucault, Michel, *The Order of Things: An Archaeology of the Human Sciences*, New York: Vintage, 1973.

Fraser, Nancy, "Rethinking the Public Sphere: A Contribution to the Critique of Actually Existing Democracy," in Craig Calhoun, ed., *Habermas and the Public Sphere*, Cambridge: Massachusetts Institute of Technology Press, 1992, 109–42.

Freud, Sigmund, "The Sexual Aberrations," 1: 240–58, "Three Essays on the Theory of Sexuality," in *The Freud Reader*, ed. Peter Gay, New York: Norton, 1989, 239–93.

Friday, Nancy, *Women on Top: How Real Life has Changed Women's Sexual Fantasies*, New York: Pocket, 1991.

Frye, Northrop, *The Anatomy of Criticism: Four Essays*, New York: Atheneum, 1965.

Furet, François, *Interpreting the French Revolution*, trans. Elborg Forster, Cambridge: Cambridge University Press, 1978.

Furniss, Tom, *Edmund Burke's Aesthetic Ideology: Language, Gender, and Political Economy in Revolution*, Cambridge: Cambridge University Press, 1993.

Fuss, Diana, "Fashion and the Homospectatorial Look," *Critical Inquiry 18* (1992): 713–37.

Gallagher, Catherine, *Nobody's Story: The Vanishing Acts of Women Writers in the Marketplace, 1670–1820*, Berkeley: University of California Press, 1994.

Gamman, Lorraine, and Merja Makinen, *Female Fetishism: A New Look*, London: Lawrence, 1994.

Gaston, Patricia S., *Prefacing the Waverley Prefaces: A Reading of Sir Walter Scott's Prefaces to the Waverley Novels*, New York: Lang, 1991.

Gilpin, William, *Observations Relative Chiefly to Picturesque Beauty, Made in the Year 1772, on Several Parts of England; Particularly the Mountains, and Lakes of Cumberland, and Westmoreland*, 2 vols., London: Blamire, 1788.

Godwin, William, "Of History and Romance," Appendix, *Things as they Are; or the Adventures of Caleb Williams*, ed. Maurice Hindle, London: Penguin, 1988.

Gonda, Caroline, *Reading Daughters' Fictions, 1709–1834: Novels and Society from Manley to Edgeworth*, Cambridge: Cambridge University Press, 1996.

Goodwin, Albert, *The Friends of Liberty: The English Democratic Movement in the Age of the French Revolution*, Cambridge: Harvard University Press, 1979.

Gordon, Robert C., *Under Which King? A Study of the Scottish Waverley Novels*, Edinburgh: Oliver, 1969.

Gray, Thomas, *Journal in the Lakes*, vol. 1 of *Works in Prose and Verse*, ed. Edmund Gosse, 4 vols., New York: AMS, 1968.

Green, Katherine Sobba, *The Courtship Novel, 1740–1820: A Feminized Genre*, Lexington: University Press of Kentucky, 1991.

Gregory, John, *A Father's Legacy to his Daughters*, London: Strahan, 1774.

Gwilliam, Tassie, *Samuel Richardson's Fictions of Gender*, Stanford: Stanford University Press, 1993.

Habermas, Jürgen, *The Structural Transformation of the Public Sphere: An Inquiry into a Category of Bourgeois Society*, trans. Thomas Burger, Cambridge: Massachusetts Institute of Technology Press, 1989.

Harley, Robert, *An Essay Upon Public Credit*, London: Baynes, 1797.

Hawkins, Laetitia Matilda, *Letters on the Female Mind, Its Powers and Pursuits. Addressed to Miss H. M. Williams, with particular reference to Her Letters from France*, 2 vols., London: Hookham, 1793.

Haywood, Eliza, *The Mercenary Lover: or, the Unfortunate Heiresses. Being a True, Secret History of a City Amour, in a Certain Island Adjacent to the Kingdom of Utopia*, London: Dobb, 1726.

Hazlitt, William, *Complete Works*, ed. P. P. Howe, 21 vols., New York: AMS, 1967.
  Contributions to the Edinburgh Review, vol. xvi of *Complete Works*.
  Conversations of James Northcote, Esq., R.A., vol. xi of *Complete Works*.
  Literary and Political Criticism, vol. xix of *Complete Works*.
  Political Essays, with Sketches of Public Characters, vol. vii of *Complete Works*.
  The Spirit of the Age, vol. xi of *Complete Works*.

Hemlow, Joyce, "Fanny Burney and the Courtesy Books," *PMLA* 65 (1950): 732–61.

Henderson, Andrea, "Commerce and Masochistic Desire in the 1790s: Frances Burney's *Camilla*," *Eighteenth-Century Studies* 31 (1997): 69–86.

Romantic Identities: Varieties of Subjectivity, 1774–1830, Cambridge: Cambridge University Press, 1996.

Henderson, Andrew, *The History of the Rebellion, MDCCXLV and MDCCXLVI*, 5th ed., London: Millar, 1753.

Hill, Christopher, *The World Turned Upside Down: Radical Ideas During the English Revolution*, Harmondsworth: Penguin, 1975.

Hone, J. Ann, *For the Cause of Truth: Radicalism in London, 1796–1821*, Oxford: Clarendon, 1982.

Hont, Istvan, and Michael Ignatieff, eds., *Wealth and Virtue: The Shaping of Political Economy in the Scottish Enlightenment*, Cambridge: Cambridge University Press, 1983.

Horkheimer, Max, and Theodor Adorno, *The Dialectic of Enlightenment*, trans. John Cumming, New York: Continuum, 1972.

Hudson, Nicholas, "Arts of Seduction and the Rhetoric of *Clarissa*," *Modern Language Quarterly* 51 (1990): 25–43.

Hume, David, *Essays, Moral, Political, and Literary*, ed. Eugene F. Miller, rev. ed., Indianapolis: Liberty, 1987.

　Treatise of Human Nature, ed. L. A. Selby-Bigge, 2nd ed., Oxford: Clarendon, 1978.

Hunt, Lynn, *The Family Romance of the French Revolution*, Berkeley: University of California Press, 1992.

　Politics, Culture, and Class in the French Revolution, Berkeley: University of California Press, 1984.

Hunter, J. Paul, *Before Novels: The Cultural Contexts of English Fiction*, New York: Norton, 1990.

Hurd, Richard, *Letters on Chivalry and Romance*, London: A. Millar, 1762.

Inchbald, Elizabeth, *A Simple Story*, ed. J. M. S. Tompkins, Oxford: Oxford University Press, 1988.

The Iniquity of Banking: Or, Bank Notes Proved to be Injurious to the Public, and the Real Cause of the Exorbitant Price of Provisions, London: Jordan, 1797.

Jacobus, Mary, *Romanticism and Sexual Difference: Essays on* The Prelude, Oxford: Oxford University Press, 1989.

Jameson, Fredric, *Postmodernism: or, the Cultural Logic of Late Capitalism*, Durham: Duke University Press, 1994.

Janes, Regina M., "On the Reception of Mary Wollstonecraft's *A Vindication of the Rights of Woman*," *Journal of the History of Ideas* 39 (1978): 293–302.

Jauss, Hans Robert, *Toward an Aesthetic of Reception*, trans. Timothy Bahti, Minneapolis: University of Minnesota Press, 1982.

Johnson, Claudia, *Equivocal Beings: Politics, Gender, and Sentimentality in the 1790s*, Chicago: University of Chicago Press, 1995.

　Jane Austen: Women, Politics, and the Novel, Chicago: University of Chicago Press, 1988.

Johnson, Samuel, *Dictionary of the English Language*, London: Knapton, 1755.

　Preface to *The Plays of William Shakespeare*, in *Samuel Johnson*, ed. Donald Greene, Oxford: Oxford University Press, 1984, 419–56.

The Rambler, 6 vols, London: Payne, 1752.

Jones, Vivien, "Women Writing Revolution: Narratives of History and Sexuality in Wollstonecraft and Williams," in Stephen Copley and John Whale, eds., *Beyond Romanticism: New Approaches to Texts and Contexts 1780–1832*, London: Routledge, 1992, 178–99.

Kahn, Madeleine, *Narrative Transvestism: Rhetoric and Gender in the Eighteenth-Century English Novel*, Ithaca: Cornell University Press, 1991.

Kaplan, Cora, "Wild Nights: Pleasure/Sexuality/Feminism," in Nancy Armstrong and Leonard Tennenhouse, eds., *The Ideology of Conduct: Essays on Literature and the History of Sexuality*, New York: Methuen, 1987, 160–84.

Kauffman, Linda, *Discourses of Desire: Gender, Genre, and Epistolary Fictions*, Ithaca: Cornell University Press, 1986.

Kaufmann, David, *The Business of Common Life: Novels and Classical Economics between Revolution and Reform*, Baltimore: Johns Hopkins University Press, 1995.

Kay, Carol, *Political Constructions: Defoe, Richardson, and Sterne in Relation to Hobbes, Hume, and Burke*, Ithaca: Cornell University Press, 1988.

Kelley, Theresa M., *Reinventing Allegory*, Cambridge: Cambridge University Press, 1997.

Kelly, Gary, *English Fiction of the Romantic Period 1789–1830*, London: Longman, 1989.

"Jane Austen's Real Business: The Novel, Literature and Cultural Capital," in Juliet McMaster and Bruce Stovel, eds., *Jane Austen's Business: Her World and Her Profession*, Basingstoke: Macmillan, 1996, 154–67.

"Revolutionary and Romantic Feminism: Women, Writing, and Cultural Revolution," in Keith Hanley and Raman Selden, eds., *Revolution and English Romanticism*, New York: St. Martin's, 1991, 107–30.

Revolutionary Feminism: The Mind and Career of Mary Wollstonecraft, New York: St. Martin's, 1992.

Kenrick, William, attrib., *The Whole Duty of Woman. By a Lady. Revised, Corrected, and Improved by Original Additions*, Newbury: Mentorian, n.d.

Kent, Christopher, "Learning History with, and from, Jane Austen," in J. David Grey, ed., *Jane Austen's Beginnings: The Juvenilia and Lady Susan*, Ann Arbor: UMI Research, 1989, 59–72.

" 'Real Solemn History' and Social History," in David Monaghan, ed., *Jane Austen in a Social Context*, Totowa: Barnes, 1981, 86–104.

Kerr, James, *Fiction Against History: Scott as Storyteller*, Cambridge: Cambridge University Press, 1989.

Kirkham, Margaret, *Jane Austen: Feminism and Fiction*, Brighton: Harvester, 1983.

Klancher, Jon, "Godwin and the Republican Romance: Genre, Politics, and Contingency in Cultural History," *MLQ* 56 (1995): 145–65.

The Making of English Reading Audiences, 1790–1832, Madison: University of Wisconsin Press, 1987.

Kliger, Samuel, *The Goths in England: A Study in Seventeenth and Eighteenth Century Thought*, Cambridge: Harvard University Press, 1952.

Kruger, Loren, *The National Stage: Theater and Cultural Legitimation in England, France, and America*, Chicago: University of Chicago Press, 1992.

Laden, Marie-Paule, *Self-Imitation in the Eighteenth-Century Novel*, Princeton: Princeton University Press, 1987.

"The Lady Kilmarnock and Lady Balmerino's Sorrowful Lamentation for the Death of their Lords, who were beheaded for High-Treason on Tower-Hill, on Monday, August 18th, 1746."

Landes, Joan B., *Women and the Public Sphere in the Age of the French Revolution*, Ithaca: Cornell University Press, 1988.

Langbauer, Laurie, *Women and Romance: The Consolations of Gender in the English Novel*, Ithaca: Cornell University Press, 1990.

Langford, Paul, *A Polite and Commercial People: England, 1727–1783*, Oxford: Clarendon, 1989.

The Laws Respecting the Ordinary Practice of Impositions in Money Lending, and the Buying and Selling of Public Offices, London: Clarke, n.d.

Leerssen, Joep, *Mere Irish and Fíor-Ghael: Studies in the Idea of Irish Nationality*, Amsterdam: Benjamins, 1986.

Lennox, Charlotte, *The Female Quixote*, London: Oxford University Press, 1970.
Henrietta, London: Millar, 1758.

Letter on Adam Anderson, *Gentleman's Magazine* 53 (1783): 41–2.

Letter to the editor, *Anti-Jacobin Review* 3 (1799): 209.

Levinson, Marjorie, "Romantic Criticism: The State of the Art," in Favret and Watson, 269–81.
Wordsworth's Great Period Poems, Cambridge: Cambridge University Press, 1986.

Life of Dr. Archibald Cameron, Brother to Donald Cameron of Lochiel, Chief of that Clan . . . With a Curious Print of Dr. Cameron, and another of Miss Jenny Cameron, in her Military Habit, London: M. Cooper, 1753.

Life of Miss Jenny Cameron, the Reputed Mistress of the Deputy Pretender, London: Whitefield, 1746.

"A List of the Goods and Effects taken after the Battle of Culloden, belonging to the Young Pretender, and brought from Scotland, to be sold To-morrow, under Prime Cost, at the Ax on Tower-Hill."

Liu, Alan, "Local Transcendence: Cultural Criticism, Postmodernism, and the Romanticism of Detail," *Representations* 32 (1990): 75–113.
Wordsworth: The Sense of History, Stanford: Stanford University Press, 1989.

Locke, John, *An Essay Concerning Human Understanding*, ed. Peter Nidditch, Oxford: Clarendon, 1975.
Two Treatises of Government, ed. Peter Laslett, Cambridge: Cambridge University Press, 1988.

Lovell, Terry, *Consuming Fiction*, London: Verso, 1987.

Lukács, Georg, *The Historical Novel*, trans. Hannah and Stanley Mitchell, Lincoln: University of Nebraska Press, 1983.

Mackenzie, Henry, *The Man of Feeling*, 2nd ed., 1772; London: Scholartis, 1928.

Mackenzie, Henry, *et al.*, eds., *Prize Essays and Transactions of the Highland Society of Scotland*, 6 vols., Edinburgh: Constable, 1799–1824.

Macpherson, C. B., *The Political Theory of Possessive Individualism*, Oxford: Clarendon, 1962.

Markley, Robert, "Sentimentality as Performance: Shaftesbury, Sterne, and the Theatrics of Virtue," in Felicity Nussbaum and Laura Brown, eds., *The New Eighteenth Century: Theory, Politics, English Literature*, New York: Methuen, 1987, 210–30.

Marx, Karl, "The Fetishism of Commodities and the Secret Thereof," in *Capital*, trans. Samuel Moore and Edward Aveling, *The Marx-Engels Reader*, ed. Robert C. Tucker, New York: Norton, 1978, 319–29.

Matthews, Richard K., ed., *Virtue, Corruption, and Self-Interest: Political Values in the Eighteenth Century*, Bethlehem, Penn.: Lehigh University Press, 1994.

McCalman, Iain, *Radical Underworld: Prophets, Revolutionaries and Pornographers in London, 1795–1840*, Cambridge: Cambridge University Press, 1988.

McCracken, Grant, *Culture and Consumption: New Approaches to the Symbolic Character of Consumer Goods and Activities*, Bloomington: Indiana University Press, 1988.

McDowell, R. B., *Ireland in the Age of Imperialism and Revolution, 1760–1801*, Oxford: Clarendon, 1979.

McKendrick, Neil, John Brewer, and J. H. Plumb, *The Birth of a Consumer Society: The Commercialization of Eighteenth-Century England*, Bloomington: Indiana University Press, 1982.

McKeon, Michael, *The Origins of the English Novel, 1600–1740*, Baltimore: Johns Hopkins University Press, 1987.

McMaster, Graham, *Scott and Society*, Cambridge: Cambridge University Press, 1981.

Mellor, Anne K., "English Women Writers and the French Revolution," in Sara E. Melzer and Leslie W. Rabine, eds., *Rebel Daughters: Women and the French Revolution*, New York: Oxford University Press, 1991.

Miller, David, *Philosophy and Ideology in Hume's Political Thought*, Oxford: Clarendon, 1981.

Miller, Nancy K., "Emphasis Added: Plots and Plausibilities in Women's Fiction," *PMLA* 96 (1981): 36–48.

Millgate, Jane, *Walter Scott: The Making of the Novelist*, Toronto: University of Toronto Press, 1984.

Monod, Paul Kléber, *Jacobitism and the English People, 1688–1788*, Cambridge: Cambridge University Press, 1989.

Montrose, Louis, *The Purpose of Playing: Shakespeare and the Cultural Politics of the Elizabethan Theatre*, Chicago: University of Chicago Press, 1996.

More, Hannah, *Strictures on the Modern System of Female Education*, in vol. 1 of *Works*, 2 vols., New York: Harper, 1840, 313–415.

Moretti, Franco, *Signs Taken for Wonders: Essays in the Sociology of Literary Forms*, rev. ed., trans. Susan Fischer, David Forgacs, and David Miller, London: Verso, 1988.

Morton, Donald, "Birth of the Cyberqueer," *PMLA* 110 (1995): 369–81.

Mudrick, Marvin, *Jane Austen: Irony as Defense and Discovery*, Berkeley: University of California Press, 1968.

Mullan, John, *Sentiment and Sociability: The Language of Feeling in the Eighteenth Century*, Oxford: Clarendon, 1988.

Newman, Gerald, *The Rise of English Nationalism: A Cultural History, 1740–1830*, New York: St. Martin's, 1987.

Newton, Judith Lowder, *Women, Power, and Subversion: Social Strategies in British Fiction, 1778–1860*, Athens: University of Georgia Press, 1981.

Nickel, Terri, "*Pamela* as Fetish: Masculine Anxiety in Henry Fielding's *Shamela* and James Parry's *The True Anti-Pamela*," *Studies in Eighteenth-Century Culture* 22 (1992): 37–49.

Nussbaum, Felicity, *Torrid Zones: Maternity, Sexuality, and Empire in Eighteenth-Century English Narratives*, Baltimore: Johns Hopkins University Press, 1995.

Odds and Ends, Or, a Groat's-Worth of Fun For a Penny. Being a Collection of the best Jokes, Comic Stories, Anecdotes, Bon Mots, &c., N.pp.: n.p., n.d.

Okin, Susan Moller, "Patriarchy and Married Women's Property in England: Questions on Some Current Views," *Eighteenth-Century Studies* 17 (1983–4): 121–38.

O'Quinn, Daniel, "Trembling: Wollstonecraft, Godwin and the Resistance to Literature," *ELH* 64 (1997): 761–88.

Owenson, Sydney, Lady Morgan, *Absenteeism*, London: Colburn, 1825.

The Wild Irish Girl, London: Routledge, 1986.

Ozouf, Mona, *Festivals and the French Revolution*, trans. Alan Sheridan, Cambridge: Harvard University Press, 1988.

Paine, Thomas, *The Rights of Man*, ed. Eric Foner, London: Penguin, 1984.

The Rights of Man, Parts 1 and 2, in *Political Writings*, ed. Bruce Kuklick, Cambridge: Cambridge University Press, 1989, 49–203.

Parker, Jo Alyson, "Complicating *A Simple Story*: Inchbald's Two Versions of Female Power," *Eighteenth-Century Studies* 30 (1997): 255–70.

Pateman, Carole, *The Disorder of Women: Democracy, Feminism and Political Theory*, Stanford: Stanford University Press, 1989.

The Sexual Contract, Stanford: Stanford University Press, 1988.

Paulson, Ronald, *Representations of Revolution (1789–1820)*, New Haven: Yale University Press, 1983.

Pinch, Adela, "Lost in a Book: Jane Austen's *Persuasion*," *Studies in Romanticism* 32 (1993): 97–117.

Pittock, Murray, *Poetry and Jacobite Politics in Eighteenth-Century Britain and Ireland*, Cambridge: Cambridge University Press, 1994.

Pocock, J. G. A., *Virtue, Commerce, and History: Essays on Political Thought and History, Chiefly in the Eighteenth Century*, Cambridge: Cambridge University Press, 1985.

"Poem by a Lady on Seeing his Highness the Prince Regent [Charles Edward Stuart.]"

Pollak, Ellen, "Beyond Incest: Gender and the Politics of Transgression in Aphra Behn's *Love-Letters between a Nobleman and His Sister*," in Heidi Hutner, ed., *Rereading Aphra Behn: History, Theory, and Criticism*, Charlottesville: University Press of Virginia, 1993, 151–86.

Polwhele, Richard, attrib., *The Unsex'd Females: A Poem, addressed to the author of the Pursuits of Literature*, London: Cadell, 1798.

Poovey, Mary, *The Proper Lady and the Woman Writer*, Chicago: University of Chicago Press, 1984.

   Uneven Developments: The Ideological Work of Gender in Mid-Victorian England, Chicago: University of Chicago Press, 1988.

Pope, Alexander, *Poetical Works*, ed. Herbert Davis, Oxford: Oxford University Press, 1966.

Porter, Roy, "Georgian Britain: An Ancien Regime?," in Speck, 141–4.

Prebble, John, *The King's Jaunt: George IV in Scotland, August 1822*, London: Collins, 1988.

Radcliffe, Ann, *The Italian, or the Confessional of the Black Penitents: A Romance*, ed. Frederick Garber, Oxford: Oxford University Press, 1968.

Radway, Janice, *Reading the Romance*, rev. ed., Chapel Hill: University of North Carolina Press, 1991.

Rajan, Tilottama, *The Supplement of Reading: Figures of Understanding in Romantic Theory and Practice*, Ithaca: Cornell University Press, 1990.

Raven, James, *Judging New Wealth: Popular Publishing and Responses to Commerce in England, 1750–1800*, Oxford: Clarendon, 1992.

Reeve, Clara, *The Progress of Romance and the History of Charoba, Queen of Egypt*, 2 vols., Colchester: Keymer, 1785.

Review of Edmund Burke, *Reflections on the Revolution in France*, *Monthly Review* n.s. 3 (1790): 313–26, 438–65.

Review of William Godwin, *Memoirs of the Author of the Vindication of the Rights of Woman*, *Anti-Jacobin Review* 1 (1798): 93–100.

Review of Godwin, *Memoirs of the Author of the Vindication of the Rights of Woman*, *European Magazine* 33 (1798): 246–51.

Review of James Hogg, *The Jacobite Relics of Scotland*, *Edinburgh Review* 34 (1820): 148–60.

Review of Elizabeth Inchbald, *A Simple Story*, *European Magazine* 19 (1791): 196–7.

Review of Inchbald, *A Simple Story*, *Monthly Review* n.s. 4 (1791): 436–8.

Review of Ann Radcliffe, *The Italian*, *European Magazine* 31 (1797): 35.

Review of Walter Scott, *Peveril of the Peak, Quentin Durward, St. Ronan's Well, Redgauntlet, Tales of the Crusaders, Woodstock*; Anonymous, *Brambletye House*; Friedrich Schiller, *Wallenstein*, trans. S. T. Coleridge, *Quarterly Review* 35 (1827): 518–66.

Review of Scott, *Rob Roy, The Heart of Midlothian, The Bride of Lammermoor, A Tale of Montrose, Ivanhoe, Monastery, The Abbot*, and *Kenilworth*, *Quarterly Review* 26 (1822): 109–48.

Review of Scott, *Tales of My Landlord*, Third Series [*The Bride of Lammermoor* and *A Legend of Montrose*], *New Monthly Magazine* 12 (1819): 6–72.

Review of Frances Sheridan, *Memoirs of Miss Sidney Bidulph, Critical Review* 11 (1761): 186–98.

Review of Sheridan, *Memoirs of Miss Sidney Bidulph, London Magazine* 30 (1761): 168.

Review of Sheridan, *Memoirs of Miss Sidney Bidulph, Monthly Review* 24 (1761): 260–6.

Review of Charlotte Smith, *The Young Philosopher, Anti-Jacobin Review* 1 (1798): 187–90.

Review of John Hurford Stone and Helen Maria Williams, *Copies of Original Letters recently written by Persons in Paris to Dr. Priestley in America, Anti-Jacobin Review* 1 (1798): 146–50.

Review of Walker, *Elements of Geography, Anti-Jacobin Review* 3 (1799): 323–33.

Review of Whitelaw, *History of the City of Dublin, Edinburgh Review* 68 (1820): 320–38.

Review of Mary Wollstonecraft, *Maria, or the Wrongs of Woman, Anti-Jacobin Review* 1 (1798): 91–3.

Review of Wollstonecraft, *A Vindication of the Rights of Men, Monthly Review* n.s. 4 (1791): 95–7.

Review of Wollstonecraft, *Vindication of the Rights of Woman, Monthly Review* n.s 8 (1792): 198–209.

Richardson, Samuel, *Clarissa; or the History of a Young Lady*, ed. Angus Ross, Harmondsworth: Penguin, 1985.

Correspondence of Samuel Richardson, ed. Anna Barbauld, 6 vols., London: Richard Phillips, 1804.

Pamela; or Virtue Rewarded, eds. T. C. Duncan Eaves and Ben D. Kimpel, Boston: Houghton, 1971.

Pamela: Or, Virtue Rewarded. In a Series of Familiar Letters from a Beautiful Young Damsel to her Parents: And afterwards, In her Exalted Condition, Between Her, and Persons of Figure and Quality, Upon the Most Important and Entertaining Subjects in Genteel Life. The Third and Fourth Volumes, Publish'd in order to cultivate the Principles of Virtue and Religion in the Minds of the Youth of Both Sexes, London: Rivington, 1742.

Robbins, Caroline, *The Eighteenth-Century Commonwealthman: Studies in the Transmission, Development, and Circumstance of English Liberal Thought from the Restoration of Charles II until the War with the Thirteen Colonies*, Cambridge: Harvard University Press, 1959.

Robertson, Fiona, *Legitimate Histories: Scott, Gothic, and the Authorities of Fiction*, Oxford: Clarendon, 1994.

Robertson, John, "The Scottish Enlightenment at the Limits of the Civic Tradition," in Hont and Ignatieff, 137–78.

Ross, Deborah, *The Excellence of Falsehood: Romance, Realism, and Women's Contribution to the Novel*, Lexington: University Press of Kentucky, 1991.

Rousseau, Jean-Jacques, *La nouvelle Héloïse: Julie, or the New Eloise. Letters of Two Lovers, Inhabitants of a Small Town at the Foot of the Alps*, trans. Judith H. McDowell, University Park: Pennsylvania State University Press, 1968.

Said, Edward, *Culture and Imperialism*, New York: Vintage, 1994.

Saturday Night (December 1997–January 1998): 106.

Scott, Walter, Sir, anonymous review of Jane Austen, *Emma*, *Quarterly Review* 14 (1815): 188–201.

    The Betrothed, vol. XXXVII of *The Waverley Novels*.

    Biographical Memoirs, vol. III of *Miscellaneous Prose Works*, 6 vols., Boston: Wells, 1829.

    The Bride of Lammermoor, vols. XIII and XIV of *The Waverley Novels*.

    Guy Mannering; or, The Astrologer, vols. III and IV of *The Waverley Novels*.

    The Heart of Midlothian, vols. XIII and XIV of *The Waverley Novels*.

    Hints Addressed to the Inhabitants of Edinburgh and Others, in Prospect of his Majesty's Visit. By an Old Citizen, Edinburgh: Bell, 1822.

    Letters, ed. H. J. C. Grierson, 12 vols., London: Constable, 1932–5.

    Old Mortality, vols. X and XI of *The Waverley Novels*.

    Rob Roy, vols. VII and VIII of *The Waverley Novels*.

    St. Ronan's Well, vols. XXXIII and XXXIV of *The Waverley Novels*.

    The Waverley Novels, 48 vols., Edinburgh: Cadell, 1829–32.

    Waverley; or, 'Tis Sixty Years Since, vols. I and II of *The Waverley Novels*.

Sedgwick, Eve Kosofsky, *The Coherence of Gothic Conventions*, New York: Arno, 1980.

"A Serious Address to the Gentlemen SOLDIERS under the Command of M------L W-----E."

Shakespeare, William, *Henry IV, Part II*, *The Riverside Shakespeare*, Boston: Houghton, 1997.

Sharp, Richard, *The Engraved Record of the Jacobite Movement*, Aldershot: Scolar, 1996.

Shelley, Percy Bysshe, "A Defence of Poetry," in *Shelley's Poetry and Prose*, ed. Donald H. Reiman and Sharon B. Powers, New York: Norton, 1977, 478–508.

Sheridan, Frances, *The History of Nourjahad*, Dublin: Wilson, 1767.

    The Memoirs of Miss Sidney Bidulph, London: Pandora, 1987.

Siskin, Clifford, *The Historicity of Romantic Discourse*, New York: Oxford University Press, 1988.

    The Work of Writing: Literature and Social Change in Britain, 1700–1830, Baltimore: Johns Hopkins University Press, 1998.

Smith, Adam, *An Inquiry into the Nature and Causes of the Wealth of Nations*, ed R. H. Campbell and A. S. Skinner, vol. II of *The Glasgow Edition of the Works and Correspondence*.

    The Theory of the Moral Sentiments, ed. D. D. Raphael and A. L. Macfie, vol. I of *The Glasgow Edition of the Works and Correspondence*.

    The Glasgow Edition of the Works and Correspondence, D. D. Raphael and A. S. Skinner, gen. eds., 6 vols., Oxford: Clarendon, 1976.

Smith, R. J., *The Gothic Bequest: Medieval Institutions in British Thought, 1688–1863*, Cambridge: Cambridge University Press, 1987.

Smollett, Tobias, *The Adventures of Roderick Random*, ed. Paul-Gabriel Boucé,

Oxford: Oxford University Press, 1979.

Soboul, Albert, *Short History of the French Revolution 1789–1799*, trans. Geoffrey Symcox, Berkeley: University of California Press, 1965.

Spacks, Patricia Meyer, *Desire and Truth: Functions of Plot in Eighteenth-Century English Novels*, Chicago: University of Chicago Press, 1990.

"Oscillations of Sensibility," *New Literary History* 25 (1994): 505–20.

Speck, W. A., ed., *1688 and All That, British Journal for Eighteenth-Century Studies* 15 (1992): 131–49.

"The Speech of Thomas Freeman, Made at a Late Meeting of the Principal Inhabitants of Edinburgh," 1745.

Spencer, Jane, *The Rise of the Woman Novelist: From Aphra Behn to Jane Austen*, London: Blackwell, 1986.

Stanton, Judith, "Charlotte Smith's 'Literary Business': Income, Patronage, and Indigence," *The Age of Johnson* 1 (1987): 375–401.

Staves, Susan, *Married Women's Separate Property in England, 1660–1833*, Cambridge: Harvard University Press, 1990.

Sterne, Laurence, *Life and Opinions of Tristram Shandy*, ed. Ian Watt, Boston: Houghton, 1965.

Stewart, Maaja, *Domestic Realities and Imperial Fictions: Jane Austen's Novels in Eighteenth-Century Contexts*, Athens: University of Georgia Press, 1993.

Stone, Lawrence, *The Family, Sex and Marriage in England, 1500–1800*, London: Penguin, 1979.

Straub, Kristina, *Divided Fictions: Fanny Burney and Feminine Strategy*, Lexington: University Press of Kentucky, 1987.

Sutherland, John, *The Life of Walter Scott*, Oxford: Blackwell, 1995.

Sutherland, Kathryn, "Fictional Economies: Adam Smith, Walter Scott and the Nineteenth-Century Novel," *ELH* 54 (1987): 97–127.

Thale, Mary, *Selections from the Papers of the London Corresponding Society 1792–1799*, Cambridge: Cambridge University Press, 1983.

Thelwall, John, *The Rights of Nature, Against the Usurpations of Establishments. A Series of Letters to the People, In Reply to the False Principles of Burke*, in *The Politics of English Jacobinism: Writings of John Thelwall*, ed. Gregory Claeys, University Park: Pennsylvania State University Press, 1995, 389–500.

Thompson, E. P., *The Making of the English Working Class*, London: Penguin, 1980.

Thompson, James, *Models of Value: Eighteenth-Century Political Economy and the Novel*, Durham: Duke University Press, 1996.

Todd, Janet, *Sensibility: An Introduction*, New York: Methuen, 1986.

The Sign of Angellica: Women, Writing, and Fiction, 1660–1800, New York: Columbia University Press, 1989.

"Who is Silvia? What is She? Feminine Identity in Aphra Behn's *Love Letters between an English Nobleman and his Sister*," in Todd, ed., *Aphra Behn Studies*, Cambridge: Cambridge University Press, 1996.

Women's Friendship in Literature, New York: Columbia University Press, 1980.

Trilling, Lionel, *The Opposing Self*, New York: Viking, 1955.

Trumpener, Katie, *Bardic Nationalism: The Romantic Novel and the British Empire*, Princeton: Princeton University Press, 1997.

"National Character, Nationalist Plots: National Tale and Historical Novel in the Age of Waverley, 1806–1830," *ELH* 60 (1993): 685–731.

Tuchman, Gaye, *Edging Women Out: Victorian Novelists, Publishers, and Social Change*, New Haven: Yale University Press, 1989.

Tyson, Gerald P., *Joseph Johnson: A Liberal Publisher*, Iowa City: University of Iowa Press, 1979.

Van Sant, Ann Jessie, *Eighteenth-Century Sensibility and the Novel: The Senses in Social Context*, Cambridge: Cambridge University Press, 1993.

Vernon, John, *Money and Fiction: Literary Realism in the Nineteenth and Early Twentieth Centuries*, Ithaca: Cornell University Press, 1984.

Walpole, Horace, *The Castle of Otranto: A Gothic Story*, ed. W. S. Lewis, London: Oxford University Press, 1964.

Walters, Gwyn, "The Booksellers in 1759 and 1774: The Battle for Literary Property," *Library* 5th series 29 (1974): 287–311.

Wang, Orrin C., "The Other Reasons: Female Alterity and Enlightenment Discourse in Mary Wollstonecraft's *A Vindication of the Rights of Woman*," *Yale Journal of Criticism* 5 (1991): 129–49.

Warner, William Beatty, *Reading* Clarissa: *The Struggles of Interpretation*, New Haven: Yale University Press, 1979.

Watson, Nicola, *Revolution and the Form of the British Novel, 1790–1825: Intercepted Letters, Interrupted Seductions*, Oxford: Oxford University Press, 1994.

Watt, Ian, *The Rise of the Novel: Studies in Defoe, Richardson, and Fielding*, London: Hogarth, 1957.

Welsh, Alexander, *The Hero of the Waverley Novels*, New Haven: Yale University Press, 1963.

Williams, Helen Maria, *Letters Written in France*, London: Cadell, 1790.

Williams, Ioan, *Novel and Romance, 1700–1800: A Documentary Record*, New York: Barnes, 1970.

Wilson, Anna, "Mary Wollstonecraft and the Search for the Radical Woman," *Genders* 6 (1989): 88–101.

Wilt, Judith, *Ghosts of the Gothic: Austen, Eliot, and Lawrence*, Princeton: Princeton University Press, 1980.

Secret Leaves: The Novels of Walter Scott, Chicago: University of Chicago Press, 1985.

Wollstonecraft, Mary, *Contributions to the* Analytical Review, *1788–1797*, vol. VII of *Works*.

Letters Written during a Short Residence in Sweden, Norway, and Denmark, in vol. VI of *Works*.

Vindication of the Rights of Men, in vol. V of *Works*, 1–60.

Vindication of the Rights of Woman, in vol. V of *Works*, 61–266.

Works, eds. Janet Todd and Marilyn Butler, New York: New York University Press, 1989.

The Wrongs of Woman: or, Maria. A Fragment, ed. Gary Kelly, Oxford: Oxford University Press, 1976.

Wordsworth, William, *Poetical Works*, ed. Thomas Hutchinson, London: Oxford University Press, 1911.

Preface to *Lyrical Ballads*, in *Selected Poems and Prefaces*, ed. Jack Stillinger, Boston: Houghton, 1965, 445–68.

Worrall, David, *Radical Culture: Discourse, Resistance and Surveillance, 1790–1820*, New York: Harvester, 1992.

Yeazell, Ruth Bernard, *Fictions of Modesty: Women and Courtship in the English Novel*, Chicago: University of Chicago Press, 1991.

Yonge, Charlotte M., *The Dove in the Eagle's Nest*, London: Collins, 1866.

Zerilli, Linda, "Text/Woman as Spectacle: Edmund Burke's 'French Revolution,'" *The Eighteenth Century: Theory and Interpretation* 33 (1992): 47–74.

Žižek, Slavoj, *For They Know Not What They Do: Enjoyment as a Political Factor*, London: Verso, 1991.

Zomchick, John P., *Family and the Law in Eighteenth-Century Fiction: The Public Conscience in the Private Sphere*, Cambridge: Cambridge University Press, 1993.

Index

CAMBRIDGE STUDIES IN ROMANTICISM

General editors
MARILYN BUTLER
University of Oxford
JAMES CHANDLER
University of Chicago